CHILDREN'S FOLKLORE

GARLAND REFERENCE LIBRARY OF SOCIAL SCIENCE
VOLUME 647

CHILDREN'S FOLKLORE
A SOURCE BOOK

EDITED BY
BRIAN SUTTON-SMITH
JAY MECHLING
THOMAS W. JOHNSON
FELICIA R. McMAHON

GARLAND PUBLISHING, INC.
NEW YORK AND LONDON
1995

Copyright © 1995 by Brian Sutton-Smith, Jay Mechling, Thomas W. Johnson, and Felicia R. McMahon

Library of Congress Cataloging-in-Publication Data

Children's folklore : a source book / edited by Brian Sutton-Smith . . .
[et al.].
      p.   cm. — (Garland reference library of social science ; vol. 647)
      Includes bibliographical references (p.   ) and index.
      ISBN 0-8240-5418-0 (acid-free paper)
      1. Folklore and children—Research.   2. Folklore and children—History
and criticism.   3. Children—Folklore.   I. Sutton-Smith, Brian.   II. Series:
Garland reference library of social science ; v. 647.
GR43.C4C45   1995
398'.083—dc20   95-5152
                                              CIP

Cover illustration: Children outside tenements in Lynn, Massachusetts, in 1895. Photograph by Frances B. Johnston. Courtesy of the Library of Congress.

Printed on acid-free, 250-year-life paper
Manufactured in the United States of America

Contents

Contributors

SIMON J. BRONNER
American Studies and
Humanities
Pennsylvania State University,
Capitol Campus
Middletown

GARY ALAN FINE
Department of Sociology
University of Georgia
Athens

SYLVIA ANN GRIDER
Graduate College
Texas A & M University
College Station

LINDA A. HUGHES
Cochranville, PA

THOMAS W. JOHNSON
Liberal Studies
California State University
Chico

MARILYN JORGENSEN
Sacramento, CA

JOHN H. MCDOWELL
Folklore Institute
Indiana University
Bloomington

FELICIA R. MCMAHON
Anthropology
Syracuse University
Syracuse, NY

JAY MECHLING
American Studies Program
University of California
Davis

BERNARD MERGEN
American Studies
George Washington
University
Washington, DC

ANN RICHMAN BERESIN
Philadelphia, PA

DANIELLE M. ROEMER
Department of Language and
Literature
Northern Kentucky University
Highland Heights

C.W. SULLIVAN III
Department of English
East Carolina University
Greenville, NC

BRIAN SUTTON-SMITH
Sarasota, Florida

ELIZABETH TUCKER
Department of English
State University of New York
Binghamton

ROSEMARY LÉVY ZUMWALT
Department of Anthropology
and Sociology
Davidson College
Davidson, NC

PREFACE

This book began when the late Sue Samuelson, my first teaching assistant in 1977 for the children's folklore course at the University of Pennsylvania, told me that it would not be possible to do a thesis in children's folklore because there was absolutely no interest in children either at the American Folklore Society (AFS) or in the Folklore Department at the university. Whatever the truth of her indictment, it led me to approach Barbara Kirshenblatt-Gimblett and Tom Burns (also of that department) with the proposal that we begin a Children's Folklore Society within AFS. And we did just that. The society continues with admirable autonomy, now issuing its own journal, *Children's Folklore Review,* under the editorship of C.W. Sullivan III.

The idea for the second phase, which became the present work, emerged one evening in 1980 at the annual Folklore Meeting. Jay Mechling, Tom Johnson, and I decided that the next step in assisting children's folklore to academic credibility would be the development of a handbook for course use. It took about five years to find the authors and get the first outlines of the present work on the table. For the next five years I used the outline as a text in my children's folklore course and benefited immeasurably from the student critiques of it. During those ten years the manuscript wandered in and out of the University of Pennsylvania Press and the Smithsonian Press, finally coming to rest at Garland Publishing, owing to the zest of Garland editor Marie Ellen Larcada. From 1990 to the present, we all suffered the vicissitudes of trying to get all this material into the computer.

Ultimately we were saved by Felicia R. McMahon of Syracuse University, who undertook the prodigious work of scholarly editorship to bring the work to fruition—as well as to add materials from her own research. Along the way it was decided that our work was not comprehensive enough to be a handbook, but that it was a step in that direction and a useful first sourcebook. Her efforts were aided greatly by the assistance of Dr. Nancy

Shawcross of the University of Pennsylvania and Professor Susan Wadley of Syracuse University.

For my part, all of this was originally made possible because Barbara Kirshenblatt-Gimblett had once suggested that a course I had taught for ten years at Teachers College, Columbia University, which I entitled "The Psychology of Childlore," be called "Children's Folklore" and brought to the University of Pennsylvania. I did that for a year and then joined the University of Pennsylvania with appointments in both education and folklore, a move made possible by the support of Kenneth Goldstein and Henry Glassie of the Folklore Department and Dell Hymes and Erling Boe of the Education School. I owe to all these people—and particularly to Barbara—a distinct debt of gratitude for the good life I've found and the interdisciplinary flavor that became possible in my scholarship after that career change.

Brian Sutton-Smith

CHILDREN'S FOLKLORE

INTRODUCTION

WHAT IS CHILDREN'S FOLKLORE?

Brian Sutton-Smith

Children's folklore is not easy to define. Folklore itself as a scholarly discipline is in a process of transition. In earlier definitions, attention was given predominantly to traditional stories, dances, proverbs, riddles, poetry, material culture, and customs, passed on orally from generation to generation. The emphasis was upon recording the "survivals" of an earlier way of life, believed to be fading away. Attention, therefore, was on the antique, the anonymous in origin, the collective in composition, and the simple in character (Ben-Amos 1971).

Today's definitions, by contrast, place more emphasis on the living character of these customs in peoples, whether tribal, ancient, ethnic, or modern. Folklorists today are more concerned with the actual living performance of these traditional materials (dance, song, tale) in their particular settings, with their functional or aesthetic character in particular contexts. Unfortunately, such "live" studies are more difficult to carry out than studies of collected records or reports—and so we have very few of them. In the chapters that follow, contributions range from attempts to catch contemporary children's play and games (Zumwalt, McDowell, Beresin and Hughes) to surveys of collected children's folklore (Sullivan, Roemer, Tucker, and Jorgensen). Most chapters share some of both, the "contextual" and the "textual."

THE RHETORICS OF CHILDREN'S FOLKLORE

What these changes in the definition of folklore make clear is the relativity of definitions of folklore to the scholarly rhetorics of a particular time and place. Apparently, there is never going to be any final definition of children's folklore (or of any other human subject matter). At any given time folklore will be a cumulative subject, young scholars contending that their new perspectives are more valid than those of their predecessors. If we are lucky we will have, as a result, an increasing number of excellent records to argue about. What all children's folklorists seem to have in common, however, is their interest in expressive rather than instrumental culture; in celebration rather than work; and perhaps in humor rather than sobriety. There is also the recurrent note of empathy that these folklorists appear to share with those folk who are not in the mainstream of modern culture but who find themselves on its edge. Folklore is a "romantic" undertaking, still not divorced from its antiquarian origins in the early 1800s. Whether or not current folklorists are any more faithful to the "folk" than were the Brothers Grimm, the identification lives on (Ellis 1983; Tatar 1992). For some of us childhood itself is such an edge, and within its sometimes sullen joys we find also solace for our idiosyncratic selves.

But children's folklore is primarily about children, and is therefore heir to all the difficulties the concept of "childhood" has encountered in this century. What seems remarkable about the chapters that follow is that the children who appear in these pages are so different from the children who appear almost everywhere else in twentieth-century social-science literature. We can seek therefore to discover how the rhetoric of childhood in folklore differs from that, for example, in psychology, where child development has been a major subject. We must hurriedly add that there are many rhetorics of childhood—a subject in the context of psychology we have dealt with elsewhere (Sutton-Smith 1994). In the psychological literature, there is a rhetoric of children as relatively passive experimental subjects who become attached to their parents, who begin to gain understanding of the world around them, who progress through various steps in language development, in social development, and in moral development. They learn to relate to their peers and to their teachers, and in due course they go through their physical, emotional, and intellectual growth and become adolescents. We hear either of the extent to which their behavior is determined by patterns of child rearing or sex-role stereotyping, or we hear about the inevitability of the growth crises and growth sequences through which they pass.

What we do not hear about are the many ways in which they react to or do not fit into these apparently normative schemes of socialization. It is true that in this sober psychological literature the function of peer interaction and peer groups is said to be to socialize children into sex and aggression. But we are not given any real sense of the antithetical character of the events that such "socialization" might well and often does imply. It is not that we are not given indications of extreme behavior such as child abuse, infantile autism, and anorexia nervosa; it is just that these extremes are used, if anything, to mark the regularity of normal and predictable patterns. By emphasizing atypical extremes, the ordinary "extremities" of everyday life are overlooked in this psychological rhetoric. Given what Foucault has written, even if perhaps exaggeratedly, about psychology and its use of clinical and developmental information to empower its experts in the control of other people's lives, it is hard to treat their doings as purely the science that they think it is (Foucault 1973, 1987). It is hard not to agree that much of developmental and child psychology includes a set of political rhetorics about childhood.

What the contents of this present *Source Book* seem to say, to the contrary of that psychological rhetoric of childhood, is that ordinary life is much more marked by disruptive interest and reaction than the conventional psychological or sociological story of child development usually brings to our attention. Thus, the chapters that follow discuss the literature on ghosts, verbal dueling, obscenity, graffiti, parties, levitation, slang, pranks, automobile lore, autograph and yearbook verses, puns and parodies, special argots, initiation rituals, folk speech, institutional legends, urine and excrement play, toilet lore, panty raids, riots, fire play, food fights, recreational drug use, jokes, insults, sex play, folk beliefs, skits, camp songs and verses, scoff lore, hazing, rituals of separation and incorporation, school lore, types of playgrounds, oral transmission, gaming rhetoric, forts, go-carts, toys, playthings, empty lots, play equipment, oral legislation, wit and repartee, guile, riddles, impropriety, nicknames, epithets, jeers and torments, half beliefs, calendrical customs, fortune, partisanship, ambushes, telephone jokes, shockers, prejudice and scapegoating, fartlore, kissing games, superstitions, scaries, divination, mean play, Halloween and April Fool's Day, among many others. While this miscellaneous list of items hardly adds up to an alternative rhetoric of childhood, it does imply the need for a rhetoric that unites such Dionysian or irrational elements with the Apollonian conventionalities of "normal" childhood socialization theory (Spariosu 1989).

It is true that there are some modern psychologists who consider the antithesis of the child and the aleatoric quality of life as important as the predictability of growth and development, but they are by and large exceptional (Gergen 1982). Most social scientists of growth are caught into prediction as the measure of their science, and therefore are not particularly interested in, or tolerant of, the unpredictable waywardness of everyday child behavior and the surreptitious antitheticality of child-instigated traditions that are often the concern of the folklorist. What appears to have happened is that the scientists of human development have taken an adult-centered view of development within which they privilege the adult stages over the childhood ones. It is implicit in their writings that it is better to be at the moral stage of conscience than at the earlier stage of fear of consequences; better to have arrived at ego integrity than to be still concerned with ego autonomy; better to be capable of adult genitality than of childhood latency. The "hero" story they tell, however, is a story on behalf of adults. In its "scientific" character it does not acknowledge that this version of the classic Western "hero" tale is a "vestige" of the theory of cultural evolution long rejected within anthropology (see, for example, the chapter by Zumwalt in this volume).

It can be argued that the linear directionality in these theories of development does disservice to our understanding of the gestaltlike character and intrinsic qualities of each phase of child life. We constantly subsume present activities to their utility for sober and sensible (hence conservative) adult outcomes. By contrast, the present work pronounces so strongly that what children find most enjoyable is often ecstatic or subversive: It is a revelry of their own youthful actions that no longer seem profound or moving to adults or it is an antithetical reaction to the institutional and everyday hegemonies of the life about them.

RHETORICS OF PLAY

This brings us to the point where we acknowledge that children's folklore is not only influenced by our underlying concepts of childhood, it is also influenced by our underlying concepts of play, or some synthesis of the concepts of childhood and those of play. More important, we must repeat that we are not just dealing here with scientific concepts of two different kinds, but rather with two rhetorics about how we should think about our scholarship. At this point it is useful to think of the possibility that large-scale, historically derived attitudes and values can be seen as determiners of what we think it is worthwhile to study and how we think we should go about it. The rhetoric of developmental psychology, for example, seems to be the familiar "rhetoric of progress" in the service of a conservative view of child growth. It is a rhetoric highly influenced by the historical intellectual inheritance from the Enlightenment of the eighteenth century and from the theory of evolution in the nineteenth century.

The rhetoric of much of the chapters that follow with their celebration of childish culture, including childish protest, is as we have said, by contrast, a rhetoric deriving from historical romanticism. We might call it a rhetoric of play, as the imagination or as fancy. The faculty of the imagination, as Kant called it, however, has been tied too strongly to rationalistic enterprises for explaining mental functions to be useful as a governing term. We need some term that implies not only the creativity of the imagination but also its irrational capacities. We are dealing not just with Shirley Temple here, we are also dealing with *Mad Magazine* (Sutton-Smith 1988). Presumably some rhetorics of fancy underly not only folklore but are also influential throughout the arts and humanities in thought about play.

Elsewhere we have dealt with the two other rhetorics that seem to share with these first two the larger part of the intellectual grasp of the world of play; they have their impact in this volume also. These are the rhetoric of power and the rhetoric of optimal experience. The first is a rhetoric of play as power, contest, conflict, war, competition, hierarchy, hidden transcripts, and so forth. It is a rhetoric that dominates the thinking about play to be found in sport sociology, in mathematical game theory, and in anthropology; in the present volume it is particularly apparent in the gaming analyses of girls by Hughes. The second rhetoric is about the quality of optimal experience (fun, flow, etc.) in play; it is found in phenomenological writings and in the leisure sciences. It has also become a popular way of thinking in modern consumer culture where good experiences are said to be those that allow for a choice, freedom, and fun, all of which are said to occur in play (Sutton-Smith 1993).

The children in children's folklore as seen through the spectacles of fancy or power are very different from children seen through the progress rhetoric of psychology. In bringing them into view as we do in this work, our own implicit rhetorical purpose is to ask our readers not to deny or repress this socially creative childhood that we have described. We ask them to take fully the measure of the fact that if play is what is most important to children, why is it we do so much to ignore that fact? Why is it we continue to combat in childhood that play that has become so central to the childhood we have unwittingly created these past several hundred years?

This is not to say that the children's societies are not themselves often remarkably conservative, ritualistic, and governed by routine, as well as manifesting moments of high fantasy and silly innovation (see McDowell, below). Within their groups, children appear to be governed by a dialectical representation of the society of which they are a part (Zumwalt). They capture its conservative organization and attitudes in their mimicry of mothers and monsters, but at the same time they willfully caricature what they thus represent. Both mimicry and mockery are the substance of child play and children's folklore, at least as viewed through spectacles of a rhetoric of fancy. Our rhetoric of children's folklore, then, is that it is a branch of folklore characterized by that dialectical mimicry and mockery, performance and parody, of which children seem to be especially capable, given their adaptively neotonous and sociologically marginal characteristics.

Our rhetoric of children's folklore speaks also of their "own group traditions," which raises the question, Just what are the folk groups to which children belong? Folklorists have expanded considerably their definition of the "folk group." No longer reserving this term for isolated rural community or urban enclave, most folklorists would agree with Alan Dundes's view that a folk group consists of two or more people who share something in common—language, occupation, religion, residence—and who share "traditions" that they consider important to their shared sense of identity (Dundes 1965, 2). Folk groups should be small enough that each member has, or could have, face-to-face interaction with every other member. That means that folk groups could be fairly large, but the definition excludes "groups" that are mere aggregations of individuals who share some element but never interact so as to develop group traditions.

Children's folk groups, therefore, can be many and overlapping. The smallest folk groups can be composed of playmates. These tiniest folk groups often develop rich traditions of interaction (Oring 1986). The family sibling group and the family itself are an important folk group, as folklorists are coming to see (Sutton-Smith and Rosenberg 1970). Moving out in larger and larger concentric circles, we see that the neighborhood, the street corner gang, the play group, the school class, the Cub Scout den or Brownie troop, the organized sports team, the "secret club," and so on are all likely folk groups for the child and adolescent. And, as is true for adults, the child's constellation of folk groups likely consists of a mix of the informal and the formal. As several of the following chapters indicate, one feature of children's culture is the increasing organization of their folk groups and folk-group activities by adults. And just as common is the child's resistance to that organization. The folklorist, for example, more readily assumes that he or she will find a folk group at the "pickup" softball game at the neighborhood sandlot than at the Little League stadium game. But, as Fine shows in his work, the Little League team *might* constitute a folk group in spite of its "artificial" formation by adults (1987). Indeed, kids often form folk groups in such settings precisely because they want to assert their own group culture against the adults' definition of the group.

In other words, the apparent circularity of Dundes's definition—that a folk group exists where there are folk traditions, and that folk traditions are the expressive communications a group shares—is not meant to avoid the need to define our domain. Rather, the circularity tells the folklorists that a folk culture is a dialectical process, the group and traditions defining one another, and that it is *always* an empirical question whether a given group is a folk group. The folklorist must look at the group, observe their culture, and decide whether this is a folk group. To paraphrase the old joke, If it looks like a folk group, acts like a folk group, smells like a folk group, and tastes like a folk group, it must be a folk group.

This dialectical process between group and tradition poses a peculiar problem of organization for the editors of a sourcebook for children's folklore. Most older textbooks in folklore and folklife organized the subject matter by *genre,* devoting individual chapters to songs, jokes, riddles, dance, crafts, and so on. Toelken's textbook (1979) stands alone in its organization around contexts and folk groups. The editors of this *Sourcebook* combined these approaches, commissioning some chapters on genres, method, settings, or theory. This solution is no more completely satisfying than the solitary genre or solitary contextual approach, but our aim is to remind the reader of this underlying complexity of the folklorist's constantly shifting perspective between group and tradition, between "context" and "text." Perhaps we can argue that our very diversity need not be seen as a lack of coherence, but is rather emblematic of the ever-present multiplicity that characterizes cultural events, especially in the post-modern view of scholarship.

In the rest of this section we turn to Grider to answer the question, Who are the folklorists of children? What we print here are edited and revised excerpts from an article in which she introduces a special issue of *Western Folklore* in 1980 and celebrates the Year of the Child in 1979. We conclude our introduction with her reminder to the reader of the dialectical situation within which children live and that we are dealing with here:

> Ladles and jellyspoons,
> I come before you to stand behind you
> To tell you something I know nothing about
> The next Wednesday (being Good Friday)
> There will be a mother's meeting
> For Fathers only.
> If you can come please stay at home.
> Wear your best clothes
> If you haven't any.
> Admission free (pay at the door)
> Take a seat but sit on the floor.
> It makes no difference where you sit
> The man in the gallery's sure to spit.
> The next number will now be
> The fourth corner of the round table.
> We thank you
> For your unkind attention.

1 WHO ARE THE FOLKLORISTS OF CHILDHOOD?

Sylvia Ann Grider

Most scholars date the serious study of children's folklore to two nineteenth-century collections of children's games: *The Traditional Games of England, Scotland, and Ireland: Tunes, Singing-Rhymes and Methods of Playing According to the Variants Extant and Recorded in Different Parts of the Kingdom* (1894–98) by Lady Alice Bertha Gomme and *Games and Songs of American Children* (1883) by William Wells Newell, the first secretary of the American Folklore Society.

Lady Alice was married to the distinguished British scholar Sir George Laurence Gomme, and together they formed a successful research team. Consistent with Victorian mores, she limited her studies almost exclusively to children's games while her husband's interests ranged much more widely. The two of them intended to edit a multivolume *Dictionary of British Folklore with Traditional Games* as Part I, but the project was never completed. The Gommes were part of the intellectual milieu that adhered to the theory of cultural survivals, and *Traditional Games* reflects that discredited bias. Lady Alice regarded the games in her vast collection as remnants from the ancient past that reflected the ideas and practices of primitive peoples. She arranged the games alphabetically, which, as one historian has pointed out, "camouflaged Lady Gomme's primary intent, to reconstruct the evolutionary ladder of children's pastimes" (Dorson 1968, 27). For example, she decided that the game of "Sally Water" originated as a pre-Celtic "marriage ceremonial involving water worship," and that "London Bridge" echoed an ancient foundation sacrifice. She gathered her data from a network of retrospective adult correspondents rather than from direct fieldwork. Dorothy Howard writes the following in her introduction to the 1963 edition:

> The games in her *Dictionary*, it must therefore be inferred, are games belonging to Lady Alice's childhood or earlier and not necessarily

current among children at her time of reporting; the descriptions came from the memories (accurate or otherwise) of adults and not from observation of children at play. The games reported represent the play life (or part of the play life) of articulate, 'proper' Victorian adults (of Queen Victoria's youth) reporting on 'proper' games. Lady Alice, if she had any inkling of improper games lurking in the memories of her literate adult informants, gave no hint of it. And she chose to ignore the games of Dickens' illiterate back alleys and tenements though she could hardly have been unaware that they existed. Since, according to statistics, Dickens' children far outnumbered well-fed-and-housed Victorian children and since psychological excavators have dug up evidence to indicate that nice Victorian children were often naughty, we can only conjecture that Lady Alice's *Dictionary* might have run to twenty volumes, had she undertaken a different study with a different point of view. (Howard 1964, viii)

Although *Traditional Games* is her most significant work, Lady Gomme published other works on children's games, including *Old English Singing Games* (1900); *Children's Singing Games* (1909–1912), a schoolbook co-edited with the distinguished folksong collector and educator Cecil J. Sharp; and *British Folklore, Folk-Songs and Singing Games* (1916), in which she collaborated with her husband, Sir George.

Games and Songs of American Children was first published in 1883 by American folklorist William Wells Newell, eleven years before Lady Alice's work in England; it was enlarged and reissued in 1903. As the preface to the 1963 edition points out, "It was the first systematic large-scale gathering and presentation of the games and game-songs of English-speaking children. More important still, it was the first annotated, comparative study which showed conclusively that these games and their texts were part of an international body of data" (Withers 1963, v–vi). A literary scholar, poet, and translator who was also the first editor of the *Journal of American Folklore*, Newell "gathered the melodies, formulas, rules, and prescribed movements of the games both from the memories of adults and by observing and interviewing the children who played them. He set them down with tenderness and extraordinary sensitivity to the imaginative qualities of childhood and with a surprising amount of surrounding social circumstance to illuminate their use. . . . He accomplished his descriptions of children's pastimes with many literary and other testimonies to the antiquity and tenacity of childhood tradition. Since Newell believed—somewhat wrongly—that the games were vanishing so rapidly in a general ruin of popular traditions that they would soon be wholly extinct, the book conveys an elegiac quality of lament." He categorized his games according to function, or how they were used, instead of arbitrarily, as Lady Alice did later by alphabetizing hers; there are few games in her collection that he had not already documented. Both of these Victorian compendia are still valuable to students of childlore today, in part because of the vast amount of well-documented raw data they contain.

Although these two monumental studies are probably the most important studies of childlore, they were not the first. The predecessors included Joseph Strutt, *Sports and Pastimes of the People of England* (1801); Robert Chambers, *Popular Rhymes of Scotland* (1826); James Halliwell, *The Nursery Rhymes of England* (1842) and *Popular Rhymes and Nursery Tales* (1849); and G.F. Northall, *English Folk-Rhymes* (1892). Consistent with the late-Victorian interest in collecting and organizing novelties was the 1897 publication of *Golspie: Contributions to Its Folklore* by Edward W.B. Nicholson, librarian of the Bodleian at Oxford. Nicholson asked Scottish schoolchildren to write down descriptions of their traditional lore and awarded prizes for the best essays. These essays are the basis of the book, and the names of the seven young prizewinners are listed as coauthors. The subject matter ranged from legends and ghost stories to songs, rhymes, games, and superstitions. [In 1952–53, Golspie Scottish schoolchildren filled out a special questionnaire for the Opies based on the items in the books, and thus provided some valuable comparative data (Opie and Opie 1959). The results predictably indicate considerable stability of these traditions over time.]

By World War I, interest in children's folklore became more and more diversified. Researchers sought more than conventional and socially acceptable games and nursery rhymes. Various journals on both sides of the Atlantic featured a spectrum of articles. In 1916 Norman Douglas published *London Street Games*, which, according to one authority, is a "pioneer work and social document of first importance. . . . Written by a fastidious literary craftsman, and based on genuine research amongst young cockneys, it records the secret joys of the gutter in a finely printed limited edition for the bibliophile. Even so, the book might have been a success if it had not been almost incomprehensible to anyone but a street arab. It is a skillful prose-poem fashioned out of the sayings and terminology of Douglas's urchin friends" (Opie and Opie 1959, v). Like Newell before him, he wrongly believed that all of the games he recorded were on the verge of extinction and so he wanted to preserve an accurate account of them—whether his reading audience could understand the esoteric argot or not.

A radical change in the approach to collecting, interpreting, and publishing children's folklore came about in the 1950s with the work of the English husband-and-wife team of Peter and Iona Opie, who were greatly influenced by the pioneering work of the American Dorothy Howard (Cott 1983). Two decades earlier, Howard successfully experimented with collecting traditional materials directly from children without the filter of adult memory (1937, 1938). Unlike the Opies, however, her work never reached a wide international lay and professional audience (1937, 1938). Howard's approach was also paralleled by the work of Brian Sutton-Smith, who used this direct technique in his fieldwork in New Zealand in 1949–51 (1954), although his direct approach was influenced by current trends in cultural anthropology (Beaglehole 1946). He says that he remembers meeting Peter Opie in a London pub in 1952 after his own thesis on games was complete. At that time the Opies had just completed their work on nursery rhymes (1952).

The Opies are recognized today as the world's foremost authorities on the traditions associated with childhood. Their works are consulted by specialists from museums, libraries, and universities regarding details about children's books, toys, games, and beliefs. The Opie home, not far from London, is a veritable museum and library of childhood. Their first major book, *The Oxford Dictionary of Nursery Rhymes,* was published in 1952 and has been reprinted eleven times. The *Dictionary* led to *The Lore and Language of Schoolchildren* in 1959, *Children's Games in Street and Playground* in 1969, and *The Singing Game* in 1985. As one reviewer stated, "*The Lore and Language of Schoolchildren* for the first time, uncovered and thoroughly explored 'the curious lore passing between children aged about 6–14, which . . . continues to be almost unnoticed by the other six-sevenths of the population. Based on the contributions of five thousand children attending seventy schools in parts of England, Scotland, Wales, and Ireland, the Opies' book presents the riddles, epithets, jokes, quips, jeers, pranks, significant calls, truce terms, codes, superstitions, strange beliefs, and rites of the modern schoolchild, examining and commenting on them with fascinating historical annotation and comparative material that suggest the extraordinary continuity of the beliefs and customs of the tribe of children" (Cott 1983, 54).

The Opies were leaders in refuting the premise that literacy and the pervasive mass media are destroying the traditions of children, and of course we know today that the media even help to diffuse many traditions (Grider 1976, 1981). As they remark in the preface to *Lore and Language,* "The modern schoolchild, when out of sight and on his own, appears to be rich in language, well-versed in custom, a respecter of the details of his own code and a practising authority on self-amusements. And a generation which cares for the traditions and entertainments which have been passed down to it is not one which is less good than its predecessors" (Opie and Opie 1959, ix). The Opies speak of the continuity of children's traditions:

> No matter how uncouth schoolchildren may outwardly appear, they remain tradition's warmest friends. Like the savage, they are respecters, even venerators, of custom. And in their self-contained community their basic lore and language seems scarcely to alter from generation to generation. Boys continue to crack jokes that Swift collected from his friends in Queen Anne's time; they play tricks which lads used to play on each other in the heyday of Beau Brummel; they ask riddles that were posed when Henry VIII was a boy. Young girls continue to perform a major feat of body raising (levitation) of which Pepys heard tell . . . , they hoard bus tickets and milk-bottle tops in distant memory of a love-lorn girl held ransom by a tyrannical father; they learn to cure warts (and are successful in curing them) after the manner in which Francis Bacon learnt when he was young. They call after the tearful the same jeer Charles Lamb recollected; they cry "Halves!" for something found as Stuart children were accustomed to do; and they rebuke one of their number who seeks back a gift with a couplet used in Shakespeare's day. They attempt, too, to learn their fortune from snails, nuts, and apple parings—divinations which the poet Gay described nearly two and a half centuries ago; they span wrists to know if someone loves them in the way that Southey used at school to tell if a boy was a bastard; and when they confide to each other that the Lord's Prayer said backwards will make Lucifer appear, they are perpetuating a story which was gossip in Elizabethan times."(Opie and Opie 1959, 2)

Other folklorists, of course, were turning their sophisticated attention toward children's lore in the 1950s, leading to a major assault on the "triviality barrier" (Sutton-Smith 1970a). In 1953 the influential *American Non-Singing Games* by Paul Brewster was published. Then in 1959, the same year as *The Lore and Language of Schoolchildren*, the University of California published the first major work by Brian Sutton-Smith, *The Games of New Zealand Children*. According to Dorothy Howard, "Dr. Sutton-Smith, working in a folklorist's paradise (two small isolated islands with a total population of two million people) spent two years (1949 and 1950) in the equable climate traveling, sleeping in a sleeping bag, watching children play and recording what he saw and heard. The study is a unique gem" (Howard 1964, vii). In the twenty years or so since the Opies popularized the trend, innumerable studies of children's lore have been published, including a popular American analog to *The Lore and Language of Schoolchildren* entitled *One Potato, Two Potato: The Secret Education of American Children* by the husband-and-wife team Herbert and Mary Knapp (1976). The subtitle of the book was changed in later editions to *The Folklore of American Children*. The most recent significant contribution to the field is the extensive and thoroughly annotated collection of children's folklore compiled and edited by Simon J. Bronner and aptly entitled *American Children's Folklore: A Book of Rhymes, Games, Jokes, Stories, Secret Languages, Beliefs and Camp Legends for Parents, Grandparents, Teachers, Counselors and All Adults Who Were Once Children* (1988).

In general, contemporary international scholarship dealing with children's folklore tends toward limited, specialized case studies based on meticulous ethnographic fieldwork. Significant work is being done throughout Scandinavia, Germany, and Australia. Two important reference books, *Jump-Rope Rhymes: A Dictionary* (1969) and *Counting-Out Rhymes: A Dictionary* (1980), have been edited by the American folklorist Roger D. Abrahams. Scholars also finally are investigating previously taboo topics such as children's use of obscenity and scatalogical materials. Graduate students at major universities throughout the country have written dissertations dealing with children's folklore. Brian Sutton-Smith, long an international leader in the field, has focused his work primarily on games and play behavior. In 1975 he helped organize The Association for the Anthropological Study of Play (TAASP) in order to facilitate communication among researchers. His most recent work in children's folklore, *The Folkstories of Children* (1981b), however, departs from games and play and turns instead to narrative, using a phenomenological approach radically different from that of previous studies. *Speech Play: Research and Resources for the Study of Linguistic Creativity* (1976), edited by Barbara Kirshenblatt-Gimblett, is an extensive investigation of the application of linguistics to the study of children's verbal lore.

In conclusion, we see that the field of children's folklore is interdisciplinary, depending heavily on cross-cultural, comparative systems that have been worked out through generations of research. Folklorists have stayed in the research forefront because their discipline is the best for documentation and analysis of traditional materials of all kinds. The triviality barrier probably will be a continuing concern in the study of children's traditions, at least for some segments of the academic community. Even so, folklorists have not abdicated their responsibility to the enrichment of knowledge just because the subject matter happens to concern children. Specialists throughout the world are continuing to document and investigate the traditions of childhood in an attempt to understand this integral aspect of our common cultural heritage.

OVERVIEW

HISTORY OF CHILDREN'S FOLKLORE

Brian Sutton-Smith

This section continues to be centrally concerned with who the children in children's folklore are. It approaches that question through two reviews of the field of children's folklore. The first, by Zumwalt, is about the history of the concept of the child; the second, by McDowell, is about the way in which folklore gets transmitted.

In order to set these chapters in context some further remarks on the history of childhood are needed. In recent scholarship the notion has become widespread that childhood is a modern and invented concept. This brilliant idea, attributed to Philippe Ariès, has had a powerful impact on the recognition of how relative many of our current twentieth-century ideas about childhood are, although many historians have been dubious about the simplicity of the picture that Ariès has drawn (Wilson 1980). What does seem worth stressing is that, with the industrial revolution, children became increasingly separated from the work world and gradually accrued more and more markers as a distinctive subcultural group. Their acquisition of special clothes, special literatures, and special toys, particularly in the late seventeenth century, is taken by some historians as evidence of a change toward a special status (L.J. Stone 1977). Over the next two hundred years a series of steps brought this group into coordination with the rest of the sociopolitical system. Universal schooling was introduced, and, in our own century, the ever-increasing organization of children's recreational time, at first through games and sports and subsequently through television and the mass marketing of toys. Through these two hundred years children also organized themselves, within a variety of subcultures of street and playground and neighborhood (see chapters by Mechling, Mergen, and Beresin). As they became free from apprenticeships in village and town, they roamed their neighborhoods and streets, both exploring and engaging in the traditional pastimes, once shared by all ages, related to the seasons and the festivals that characterized life in the Middle Ages. Thus the children in children's folklore were a group dis-enfranchised from the economic machine by the events of the industrial revo-lution; they then reconstituted themselves as a distinct subculture, associat-ing themselves with such leisure activities as had already been prevalent in their own societies. They took upon themselves the traditional leisure-time customs that they could reconstitute according to their own more elemen-tary capacities, gradually honing them down to the kind of dimensions with which we are now familiar. Complex adult sports, such as Prisoner's Base, which is said to have been a popular adult game of the 1100s, were aban-doned for the simpler versions, such as King on the Mountain; the more com-plex linear forms of Nuts and May were given up for the simpler circular pleasures of Farmer and the Dell (Sutton-Smith 1959b). For some hundred or so years these traditions have persisted in childhood, while the adults of modern society have gradually adopted the spectator activities and mass-participation forms that have become the leisure culture of modern society (R. Williams 1979). Children, still a distinctive group in most respects, de-spite some claims to the contrary (Postman 1982) have increasingly found an antithesis in mass cultural phenomena (parodies of commercials, distinc-tive play with Barbie dolls, topical graffiti, rhymes, etc.) and in persisting earlier elements from adult expressive behavior (e.g., hopscotch).

This brief description is a considerable over-simplification of the great changes that have taken place in Western civilization and the distinctive role of children in those changes. It may serve, however, as a corrective to the notion that children's folklore has always been the same and is of a univer-sal character. That is unqualifiedly not the case. The concept of childhood varies not only historically but also anthropologically, and, as children's sta-tus varies within different groups, so does their distinctive subcultural tra-ditions. In most respects child subculture is not different from any other sub-culture. A group that senses itself to be distinct usually develops character-istic customs and ceremonies, many of which express opposition to those of the hegemonious surrounding culture. In these terms children's folklore is the product of a kind of generational subculture instigated by a society that requires quasi-dependence and quasi-independence in the young.

But whatever the larger economic and sociological processes, philo-sophical reactions to this process have led to many other and often contrary descriptions of this novel subculture. Some descriptions attribute subordi-nate qualities to the child group, such as primitive, prelogical, synaesthetic, atavistic, irrational, and disenfranchised; these are characteristics that until recently have been thought to be shared with savages and women. The same condition has been romanticized by those who have spoken of "noble savages" and childhood as especially imaginative, idyllic, and innocent. Some-times this innocence carries with it the moral power attributed to childhood by Rousseau, and sometimes it carries the bowdlerized fancifulness so char-acteristic of much twentieth-century children's literature. Childhood as dis-continuous from adulthood comes to be used as a projective screen for ei-ther aspiration or despair (Covenay 1957).

These issues are central to the chapter by Zumwalt, in which she con-trasts some of these older views of children, as savage or innocent or simple, with her own discoveries of their actual complexity. She contrasts the ideal and the real behavior of girls who are on the one hand portraying themselves in their play as obedient, domestic, and romantic and yet, at the same time, often covertly, also portraying themselves as sexually provocative, manipu-lative, scheming, and rebellious. She opens up the issue of what Fine (1980b) has called Newall's paradox—how it is that children can have such a repu-tation as creatures of tradition, as conservers of child culture, and at the same time be known for their innovative fantasies and novel behaviors. Zumwalt's emphasis on these complexities calls into question the more simplistic no-tions of childhood that often prevail.

In Grider's earlier chapter we have already seen that some major schol-ars have always seen children's folklore as a conservative event (Gomme, Opie) whereas others have reckoned it an innovative (Douglas) or changing historical series of events (Sutton-Smith 1981a). In his chapter John McDowell attempts a reconciliation of these differences in terms of a modern "performance" theory of cultural transmission. Children, he says, have reason for conserving some folklore elements because they are partially appropriate to their needs or are particularly satisfying aesthetically. Other elements, however, do not meet those needs, or are changed because of childish perceptions, fantasies, ambivalences, rebelliousness, misunderstanding, or creativity.

There is an interesting conceptual transition between chapters one and three that is not unlike the transition that folklore has itself undergone in this century. Grider expresses some of the traditional concerns of the field: origins, cultural survivals, the tenacity of tradition on the one hand and lam-entations over its disappearance on the other. Zumwalt advocates putting aside these ideas, in which the child is compared with the savage, and sug-gests instead a focus on the meaning of folklore to the children who engage in it. Her concern is a combination of psychogenic functionalism (Wolfenstein), sociogenic functionalism (Malinowski), linguistic structural-ism (McDowell), and social structuralism (Goodwin after Goffman). Whether this approach be described as anthropology, ethnography, or dis-course analysis, it has been among the major "semantics" within which folklore has been construed in the past fifty years. McDowell on the other hand, with his focus on the child player as a performer constantly generating his play material as an emergent function of his own limitations, perceptions, and strengths; his ambivalences, phonic subversions and parodies; as a function of the utility and aesthetic value of the material to the performer as well as a function of his response to the group; is highlighting concepts about folklore as performance, as contingent "activation," which have had more appeal in recent theorizing. There is in McDowell, however, as much of a romantic attachment to the generating power of the young performers as there is in, say, the Opies to the constancy of their texts and the continuity of historical materials. They seek the universal and the constant; he seeks the specific and the emergent. McDowell gives sufficient examples to set the stage for a study that will seek to distinguish the genres of the durable from those that are ephemeral, and to seek accounts of those differences in terms of place, historical circumstances, and the special character of the players.

While this is undoubtedly a valid quest, in recent play studies by Meckley it has been discovered that among preschoolers the two phases are virtually indistinguishable (1994). Studying and video-taping the play behavior of twelve four-year-old children over a six-month period, she discovered that while some children were more innovative than others, whatever they invented immediately became a tradition for all of the children in the group—not just the ones that had initiated the play. So that when a group of children played what had been the game of another group, they always repeated it largely in the way it was done before. What was amazing was how much shared knowledge there was across this group of children of the play forms of all the other children.

Admittedly, just as only a minority were strong innovators, there was also a minority who seldom knew what was going on. This led to the generalization that as innovation hit the ground it immediately crystallized so that everyone knew how to continue it. That is, play no sooner appeared in their group life than it was ritualized so that all could participate. Play and ritual were, at this embryonic stage of play development at least, a biphasic phenomenon.

What is also particularly appealing in McDowell's account is the way in which he shows us that children sometimes go well beyond the antitheses (real-ideal, mimicry-mockery, conservative-innovative, play-ritual), for example, when they engage in flights of playfulness that are a cascade of nonsense or silliness. The playful idiosyncratic content is often so bizarre it could never be conserved even if the performance of being bizarre does itself become a ritualized kind of nonsense within the playing group.

2 THE COMPLEXITY OF CHILDREN'S FOLKLORE

Rosemary Lévy Zumwalt

When I first started work in children's folklore, I dutifully asked my five-, six-, and seven-year-old informants all the prescribed questions: Where did you learn that? Why do you think it's funny? What do you call it? They would, after the weeks passed, bear this with strained patience. With their heads cocked to one side and their eyes narrowed, they would answer, "I didn't learn it from anybody. I made it up!" "Can't *you* see why it's funny? It's funny, that's all!" I would persist and get the answers I needed for my collection.

Now, years later, as I look back at this initial study of children's folklore (Zumwalt 1972, 1976), I am struck with the richness the children were offering me. At the time, the rhythm, the lyrics, and the image captivated me. I focused on symbol, the ideal little girl in folklore. And I emphasized tradition, the creation and continuity of this image. I likened it to the formation of stalactites, the concentrated accretion over centuries, a drop at a time, forming a multifaceted image. The ideal little girl in folklore could, according to the refraction of light from her crystalline image, shine with innocence, glitter with enticement, or gleam with lust.

The ideal little girl was present in the folklore, and she was important. Yet, coupled with this ideal little girl portrayed in the texts was the real little girl who performed the jump-rope songs:

> I am a Pretty Little Dutch Girl
> All dressed in blue.
> And these are the things
> I like to do:
> Salute to the captain.
> Curtsey to the king.
> And show my pants to the U.S. Marines!

This was the same little girl who would throw down her jump rope and run to the baseball diamond to play what she classified as a boy's game.

The children in my early folklore study were presenting me with the complexity of their lives. That I chose to study one aspect, the image as revealed in the text, is understandable. Part of the leverage one needs to launch an undertaking is just such a focus. That I now recognize the text *and* context, the ideal *and* the real, the conservative *and* the innovation, adds to my wonder of the child's world of folklore.

I would like to reflect on what I see as the complexity of children's folklore, a complexity that has sometimes been overlooked for a simpler view. An approach that was predicted on the simple nature of the child was nineteenth-century cultural evolutionary theory. In this framework, the child was equated with the savage. In much twentieth-century literature on children's folklore, the equation remains. For an understanding of cultural evolutionary theory as it pertains to children, we must turn to the works of Charles Darwin, Herbert Spencer, and Edward Burnett Tylor.

Charles Darwin, in *The Descent of Man and Selection in Relation to Sex* (1871), extended the evolutionary theory developed in *On the Origin of Species* (1859)—one focused primarily on natural selection—to the evolution of the sexes and of social behavior.[1] In Darwin's framework, the male and female child are equal, mentally and physically. At puberty, the inequality between the sexes begins to develop. The male grows to full intellectual and physical capacity. The female, retaining aspects of the child, is arrested in development between the child and the adult male. This was attributed to the evolution of the species and the sexual maturation of the individual.

Of the "Mental Powers of Man and Woman," Darwin concluded, "man has ultimately become superior to woman" (Darwin 1871, 2:382). During "primeval times," men had to compete with rivals for "the possession of the females." This competition led to "the greater intellectual vigor and power of invention" in man (Darwin 1871, 2:382). It also led to "the greater size, strength, courage, pugnacity, and . . . energy of man in comparison with the same qualities in woman . . ." (Darwin 1871, 2:382).

Coupled with the results of an evolutionary selection for a male of superior strength and intellect were the effects of sexual maturation of the individual organisms. In childhood, the male and the female are equal in intellectual capacity. At puberty, there is differential development of the intellect according to sex. In support of his position, Darwin notes "that eunuchs remain throughout life inferior in" mental faculties (Darwin 1871, 2: 328–29). This disparity in intellectual capacity between the sexes has been mitigated by "the law of equal transmission of characters to both sexes"

(Darwin 1871, 2: 329). Without this law, Darwin says, "it is probable that man would have become as superior in mental endowment to woman, as the peacock is in ornamental plumage to the peahen" (Darwin 1871, 2: 329).

Herbert Spencer—a man who influenced Darwin and was influenced by him—discussed the evolution of mental complexity in *The Comparative Psychology of Man*, an address delivered to the Royal Anthropological Institute. Spencer endeavored to establish the evolution of the intellect and to link it with the development of mankind from savagery to civilization. To establish the degrees of intellectual capacity, Spencer compared the child's mind with the adult's. This contrast, between the child and the adult mind, is analogous, Spencer said, to that between "the minds of savage and civilized" (Spencer 1977 [1876], 9). To support his position Spencer notes that "the sudden gusts of feeling which men of inferior types display" are like "the passions of childhood" (Spencer 1977 [1876], 12).

Following the evolutionary scheme of Darwin and Spencer, man, woman, and child could be arranged hierarchically: Man is rational, physically and emotionally strong, civilized. Woman is irrational, physically and emotionally weak, and childlike. The child is weak and unformed, with a need to be emotionally nurtured by the mother and physically strengthened by the father. The child, then, is the living link with the savage past.

Edward Burnett Tylor continued in Darwin's theoretical footsteps. For Tylor, folklore was the remnant of the intellectual past, just as the fossil was the remnant of the physical past. The survival of the primitive was preserved in children's folklore. Rhymes, songs, games, and toys of children "reproduce, in what are at once sports and little children's lessons, early stages in the history of childlike tribes of mankind" (Tylor 1929 [1871], 1: 74).

Cultural evolutionary theory in the nineteenth century was, in the literal sense of the word, progressive. It was predicated on the notion of progress, of development from the simple stages of savagism to barbarism and to civilization. It was also progressive in terms of its representation of human potential, that moving toward increasing complexity. Within each individual infant and each infant race, there is a potential to develop out of the state of savagism. Certain savage races might need the assistance of the civilized races to speed up the evolutionary process. Again, there is the parallel between the child and the race. Just as the child is raised by the parent, so can the savage be pulled out of the primitive state by the representatives of the civilized nations.[2]

In this theoretical framework, the child recapitulates the development of the race. As Alexander Chamberlain says in *The Child and Childhood in Folk- Thought*: "Ethnology, with its broad sweep over ages and races of man, its searchings into the origins of nations and of civilizations, illumined by the light of Evolution, suggests that in the growth of the child from helpless infancy to adolescence, and through the strong and trying development of manhood to the idyosyncracies of disease and senescence, we have an epitome in miniature of the life of the race . . ." (Chamberlain 1896, 3).

A.R. Radcliffe-Brown in *The Andaman Islanders* draws the same parallel between the development of the individual and the development of the race. As he explains, the primary task of the child is to bring order to his social world. The same process is at work in primitive society where, Radcliffe-Brown says, "the supreme need" requires that the primitive bring order to the world around him. "Just as the child organises and develops his experience by treating inanimate objects as if they were persons . . . , so primitive man, in exactly the same way, organises and develops his social experience by conceiving the whole universe as if it were the interaction of personal forces" (Radcliffe-Brown 1948 [1922]: 380).

Born in a state of nature, naked and vulnerable, the infant gradually is tamed, grows to manhood, acquires the manners of the civilized. If the child grows to womanhood, she never thoroughly outgrows the child. It remains within her, part of her essence, her childlike nature. Thus these three categories—man, woman, and child—reflected the hierarchical division of culture into civilized, barbaric, and savage:

man = civilized

woman = barbaric

child = savage

Cultural evolutionary theory did not just overlook the complexities inherent in children's folklore, it denied them. Children's folklore was simple; it was a direct link to the lower—and therefore simpler—stages of cultural evolution. In this vein, Karl Pearson reasoned, children's delight in nursery tales "arises from an unconscious sympathy between the child and the thought and customs of the childhood of civilization" (Bett 1924, 1–2; quoting Pearson).[3]

Following this approach, since the child is linked through an unconscious sympathy to the lower stages of evolution, it is understandable that we would find aspects of the savage and the barbaric in children's folklore. In *Counting-Out Rhymes of Children*, Walter Gregor remarks, "It is now an acknowledged fact that some of the games of children are survivals of

what was once the occupation of men in less advanced stages of civilization
. . ." (Gregor 1973 [1891], 9). Henry Bett, in *Nursery Rhymes and Tales; Their Origin and History*, points to the element of cannibalism in "our children's tales."

> Fee fi fo fum I smell the blood of an Englishman!
> Be he alive or be he dead,
> I'll grind his bones to make my bread! (Bett 1924, 31)

This, Bett said, was "simply a remembrance of times when primitive men were cannibals and ate their enemies, as some savages do today" (Bett 1924, 30).

Alice Bertha Gomme, the grand lady of nineteenth-century childlore studies, worked within this cultural evolutionary framework.[4] According to Lady Alice, children's games are "some of the oldest historical documents belonging to our race"; they show "man's progress from savagery to civilization" (Gomme 1964 [1898], 2: 461). In Lady Alice's work, this progress from savagery to civilization does not entail a movement from simple to complex. Though she was evolutionary in her approach to folklore, she was also ritualistic in her interpretation. Accordingly, children's games originated from complex traditions. As Lady Alice says, "If [children] saw a custom periodically and often practised with some degree of ceremonial importance, they would in their own way act in play what their elders do seriously" (Gomme 1964 [1898], 2: 142).

Such was the case in the game "Round and Round the Village." The children in their play retained the ancient custom of "the perambulation of boundaries, often associated with festive dances, courtship, and marriage" (Gomme 1964 [1898], 2: 142).[5] As evidence of this early origin, Lady Alice refers to the ritual in southeast Russia. On the eve of her wedding, the bride goes round the village and kneels before the head of each household. In India, the bride and groom are both transported round the village (Gomme 1964 [1898], 2: 143). Lady Alice concludes that "the Indo-European marriage-rite contained just such features as are represented in this game" (Gomme 1964 [1898], 2: 143). Further, she says, "the changes from rite to popular customs, from popular custom to children's game" show the usefulness of folklore study.

To her credit, Lady Alice did not reduce children's folklore to a single theoretical approach. The games were not merely a survival from a past age. Nor were the games simply a key to past rituals. Children's folklore was a living tradition—a link to the past, to be sure, but also a vibrant force in the present.

The identification of children's lore with survivals from earlier stages of cultural development is no longer part of contemporary interpretation. Now the giant's chanting "Fee, fi, fo, fum, I smell the blood of an Englishman" might be interpreted as the dreaded father-figure. As Alan Dundes says, "Up in the beanstalk world, there is a cannibalistic giant who often in some vague way is linked with Jack's father . . ." (Dundes 1980, 41). By extension, the cannibalistic element could be interpreted as the child's fear of the father's brutal strength and oral power.[6]

Still, while the literal interpretation of child's lore as survival has been discarded, the fundamental equation between child and savage remains, at least as a metaphor, in much work on children's folklore. The child has become the savage in our midst. Iona and Peter Opie, in the introduction to *The Lore and Language of Schoolchildren*, remark that "the folklorist and anthropologist can, without traveling a mile from his door, examine a thriving unself-conscious culture" which is as unnoticed and untouched by "the sophisticated world . . . as is the culture of some dwindling aboriginal tribe living out its helpless existence in the hinterland of a native reserve" (Opie and Opie 1959, 1–2). Sylvia Ann Grider, in her editorial statement to *Western Folklore*'s special issue on *Children's Folklore* makes a similar observation: "In this day of inflated costs and shrinking grants, there is no need for the folklorist to scour the outback of Australia in search of aborigines, for all he needs to do is glance into his own apartment complex courtyard or neighborhood playground to find a cooperative group of informants whose private worlds are dominated by tradition" (Grider 1980, 162).

Iona and Peter Opie conclude their remarks on the child as the savage in our midst by quoting Douglas Newton: "The world-wide fraternity of children is the greatest of savage tribes, and the only one which shows no sign of dying out" (Opie and Opie 1959, 2, quoting Newton). Sylvia Grider, after suggesting the affinity between the Australian aborigines and children, denies the savage nature of children: "And these little folks are not savages either . . ." (Grider 1980, 162). Thus for the Opies, the child is like the aboriginal in the hinterland. For Grider, the child offers the exotic of the outback, but has the advantages of not really being savage.

In his discussion of children's riddling, John McDowell notes the "tendency to despise the products of childish cognition." To recognize the intellectual sophistication of child's lore, McDowell suggests that we borrow from Claude Lévi-Strauss's cerebral savage, "whose primitive speculation represents another, not a cognitively inferior, science" (McDowell 1979, 144). "The time may be ripe to turn our humanistic energies to those savages among us and discover at our very portals the cerebral child, concerned in his or her verbal art with complex matters of rationality, logic, sociability, and aesthetics" (McDowell 1979, 144). In his analysis of a children's riddling session which focuses on the differences between animals and machines, McDowell suggests that the children "are working through basic anomalies in their cultural apparatus, much as primitives examine apparent contradictions through the logical tools of mythology" (McDowell 1979, 145).

In suggesting the analogy between the cerebral child and the cerebral savage, McDowell is not stressing the simple nature of children or of primitives. Rather he is stressing the complex nature of the intellectual system, that the riddles of the child and the mythology of the primitive serve to order their cognitive universe. Even with his recognition of the complexities in child and primitive lore, McDowell is using the basic equation of cultural evolutionary theory. The child is equal to the savage. The frame he uses is Lévi-Strauss's: The cerebral child is to the cerebral savage as children's intellectualization is to primitive speculation, as children's riddling is to primitive mythology.

The groundrock of this system is Tylor's. According to Edward Burnett Tylor, comparisons could be made between groups widely separated in space and time. This could be done because of one common factor, the psychic unity of mankind. The results of Tylor's comparative study were arranged on an evolutionary ladder, from the simplicity of savagery to the complexity of civilization. Lévi-Strauss and McDowell lay this ladder on its side and eliminate the notion of progress from simple to complex. Savage thought is complex; children's thought is complex. But for all three, the common factor that allows comparison is the same, the intellectual capacity of humankind. For Tylor, it is psychic unity; for Lévi-Strauss, *la pensée sauvage*; for McDowell, the cerebral child.

In this survey of cultural evolutionary theory, we have gone from the classic form of the nineteenth century, when it was thought that the savage state survives in children's folklore, to the twentieth-century equation between savage and child. Scholars in children's folklore would do well to examine the assumptions underlying cultural evolutionary theory. The first step would be to scrutinize the concept of *the simple*.

It is past time to recognize that children are not simple, nor are societies simple. The child is a complex individual, not a simple adult, or a link to the savage past. And the savage past cannot be exemplified by savage cultures in our midst, except those of our own making.[7]

The term *savage* carries with it the weight of the cultural evolutionary theory. The whole world rises on the shoulders of the savage—be it the Australian aborigine or the African tribesman. Whether used in Lévi-

Strauss's clever turn-of-phrase, *la pensée sauvage*—the savage thought or the wild pansy—or McDowell's offspring of the cerebral savage, the cerebral child, the term denotes the wild, untamed, uncivilized. This equation between the child and the savage, whether intended in the literal or the metaphorical sense, is a disservice to the folk group, its culture, and its folklore. What is needed is a recognition of the complexity and the integrity of cultures *and* of children.

The child-as-savage, the child-as-exotic, has also been used as a justification for studying children's folklore. The reasoning is as follows: There is no need to go to faraway lands when the exotic is within, in our own households. This need to justify the study of children's folklore could be avoided if we simply accept the obvious—that children's folklore is a legitimate and an important area of study.

A major theoretical shift has occurred between the nineteenth and the twentieth centuries, from a search for origins to a search for meaning. As we have seen, in the nineteenth-century cultural-evolutionary framework, children's folklore provided a link with the past. In contemporary approaches, children's folklore provides a key to understanding the crucial, unstated elements in a child's life. This stress on meaning is apparent in the psychological, functional, structural, and symbolic theories.

Martha Wolfenstein's *Children's Humor* shows just such an attempt to arrive at the underlying, unconscious meaning of children's jokes. She anticipates the criticism that she has given undue emphasis to the trivial. She counters, "But when one hears one child after another repeat these same apparently trivial witticisms, and sees what value they attach to learning and telling them, one feels that there is a discrepancy between the intensity of their interest and the seeming triviality of the content. This gap can be filled in if we reconstruct the underlying meaning of the joke" (Wolfenstein 1978 [1954], 14). In Wolfenstein's psychological approach, the underlying meaning of the joke is directly related to the basic motive of joking, "the wish to transform a painful experience and to extract pleasure from it" (Wolfenstein 1978, 18). This Wolfenstein calls "the wish to joke" (Wolfenstein 1978, 25).

The release of anxiety through joking is a constant, as Freud has shown in *Wit and Its Relation to the Unconscious*, but the joking forms themselves change according to the developmental stages of the child. It is Wolfenstein's attempt to correlate the different forms of humor with the different age levels of children that makes her work unique.[8] Wolfenstein follows the psychoanalytic scheme of emotional development, the Oedipal, latency, and adolescent periods. For example, Wolfenstein discusses verbal play in which a child changes the sex or name of another child. A three-year-old makes a joke by calling a girl a boy, or vice versa (Wolfenstein 1978, 19, 89), and the child of four does the same thing by changing proper names. These children are playing with verbal ambiguity; underlying this is the question about sexual identity and individual identity. As Wolfenstein says, this joking behavior carries a powerful message, "I change your sex; I change your name; I change your meaning" (Wolfenstein 1978, 82).

The moron joke cycle, for Wolfenstein, marks the latency period of children, from six to eleven years. At that age, the children are greatly concerned "with the issue of smartness and dumbness." The riddles ". . . serve in part the function of demonstrating that they are smart and the other fellow, who does not know the answer, is dumb" (Wolfenstein 1978, 20). This contrasts with the endless fantasies of the Oedipal children and the artful anecdotes of the adolescent. The joking riddle makes a parody of questions and answers. As Wolfenstein says, "The question posed is trivial or absurd; the solution is nonsensical" (Wolfenstein 1978, 94). This is linked to the concern of the latency period, the child's repressed curiosity about his/her parents' sexuality (Wolfenstein 1978, 95). This curiosity reveals itself in the joking riddle: "Beneath this verbal formula is a latent meaning which has been drastically condensed and disguised. The child values the joke's concealment of material which he is anxious to repress. He also strenuously denies that the joke has any relation to himself" (Wolfenstein 1978, 138).

In the introduction, Wolfenstein notes that she, at times, ventures on "not too certain ground" when she relates a frequent theme from psychoanalytic observation to "other subjects in other circumstances" (Wolfenstein 1978, 18). It is her analysis of the repressed sexual meaning of the moron jokes which seems so strained. For example, Wolfenstein analyzes one of the most popular moron jokes: "Why did the moron tiptoe past the medicine cabinet? Because he didn't want to wake the sleeping pills." The clue to the joke's meaning lies in the action of the moron and the function of the pills. The moron tiptoes and the pills induce sleep. As one child explained to Wolfenstein, the joke is funny because "sleeping pills put you to sleep. They don't sleep themselves" (Wolfenstein 1978, 105). She continues: "The same thing could be said about the parents at night. Thus there is here what we might call a latent riddle: Why are the parents at night like sleeping pills? The moron in the joke is a fool because he doesn't know that they put you to sleep and don't sleep themselves" (Wolfenstein 1978, 105). Wolfenstein concludes her analysis of this joke by pointing out that the moron might not be quite such a fool. He is after all tiptoeing around to find out what his parents are doing in the night.

While her analysis of this joke is penetrating, it does seem that Wolfenstein has, under the rubric of the latent riddle, created and analyzed a different joke from the one initially given. This search for the latent meaning in children's humor takes us on an unnecessarily circuitous path through the child's world of the subconscious. The children themselves—the very ones whom Wolfenstein would place in the latency period—provide a much more direct route to the sexual meaning of their humor through explicit sexual jokes (see Zumwalt 1976 and Gaignebet 1974). The foregoing is not a dismissal of Wolfenstein's work. She has compiled a rich and detailed analysis of children's humor. And her use of the psychoanalytic approach has given us access to the hidden meaning of children's folklore, which lies below the conscious level. As Dundes remarks, hers is "a neglected classic . . . a landmark in the study of wit and humor" (Dundes 1978, 8).

While with psychological analysis the intent is to arrive at the hidden, subconscious meaning of the folklore, with functional analysis the emphasis is on the use of folklore in the social setting. Malinowski, in his writings on functionalism, emphasized the transformation of the biological individual into the cultural individual. Part of this transformation comes about through the socialization of the child. Within this theoretical framework, folklore functions to create a social being, and to reinforce cultural values.

In *Shonendan: Adolescent Peer Group Socialization in Rural Japan*, Thomas Johnson provides a detailed description of peer-group socialization. The *Shonendan*, a boy's club, is of crucial importance for the boys from the fourth grade through junior high school. The club provides the center of their activities and the focus for their interests. To protect the *Shonendan* from adult intervention, the boys made it a point "to appear to be doing things as the adults would wish them to, regardless of what was actually happening" (Johnson 1975, 253–54). This point is reiterated at every weekly meeting. As Johnson says, the result is that "They have set up a kind of peer group tyranny enforcing conformity to the boys' perception of the adult social code for children, and they have done this in the name of freedom from adult interference" (Johnson 1975, 254).

This enforcement of the social order for the good of the whole, for the good of the *Shonendan*, perpetuates the values of the community. As a mark of their success in the enforcement of order and the perpetuation of values, the members of the *Shonendan* learn how to break the rules and avoid detection: "While there is certainly behavior of which the adults would disapprove—some drinking, sexual explorations, etc.—the boys themselves recognize that these are disapproved actions and are very careful to conceal them from the adults" (Johnson 1975, 254). The leaders guard against exposure by excluding the younger, and therefore less cautious, members from such covert activity. The *Shonendan* provides effectively for peer-group socialization, a major function of children's folklore cross-culturally.

The structural approach to folklore examines both surface (morphology) and underlying (deep) structure. The attempt is made to find a key to the meaning of the material in the components of the structure and in their combination. In *Children's Riddling,* John McDowell thoroughly examines both surface and deep structures of riddles. Discussing one surface form, "What kind of X is a Y?" McDowell suggests that this is a construction of a system of classification. This surface structure, or morphology, in its essence is based on classification, for it categorizes or types. In the riddle "What kind of head grows in the garden?" [A head of lettuce], two tokens which are not generally classified together are brought into relation with one another (McDowell 1979, 68). The descriptive routines of children reflect, McDowell says, "the scientific discoveries of the children" (McDowell 1979, 65). In their riddles, children can communicate their increasing knowledge of their world. He lists three categories for these descriptive routines: "what is—understandings of diagnostic qualities; what has—understandings of possessed qualities; and what does—understandings of habitual behavior."

From an examination of the content of the riddle corpus, McDowell is able to construct a taxonomy for the categories. The taxonomy reveals the oppositions of culture vs. nature, animate vs. inanimate, mankind vs. other forms of life, and artifact vs. artifact (McDowell 1979, 104–5). Of these, McDowell finds the nature-culture theme to be predominant, with the others ranking below it in importance. McDowell concludes: "The children's riddling, taken as a single and complete unit of discourse, thus delivers a cosmos as the children perceive it, placing man in the center of the universe, exploring his technological capacity, and contrasting him with other significant entities in the natural world" (McDowell 1979, 105). By examining the structure of the riddle, McDowell is able to suggest that riddles both organize the child's universe as a form of classification and play havoc with the order by taking the familiar and rendering it strange (McDowell 1979, 87).

An innovative and provocative approach to children's conversation and play is put forth by Marjorie Harness Goodwin. In "The Serious Side of Jump Rope: Conversational Practices and Social Organization in the Frame of Play," Goodwin examines play activity within the game of jump rope as "continuous with that outside the play frame" (Goodwin 1985, 315). She looks at the process of negotiation of what is often considered to be set rules. For Goodwin, play provides an important dimension for serious negotiations.

In her work on children's conversational activity (1985, 1990), Goodwin examines, in minute detail, texts of conversational activity. The transcription symbols indicate overlapping, simultaneous speech, elapsed time, sound production, and volume. The children speak for themselves in these scrupulously transcribed tapes. What they tell us, through Goodwin's elucidation, is of the creation and continuation of social structure through conversation. In this approach, there can be no arbitrary domain of traditional play which would be classified as folklore. Instead, Goodwin uses the terms of Goffman to describe the play frame, "situated activity system" and "focussed gathering" (Goodwin 1985, 317; Goffman 1961b). Certainly Goodwin situates the activity within the ethnographic setting and draws out the complex play of forces, showing what is at stake in a game of jump rope.

THE IDEAL AND THE REAL

Initially, in my work with little girls' folklore, I was concerned with the ideal little girl as she was represented in the folklore. I found her reflected in the texts of the jump-rope songs, hand-clapping songs, counting-out rhymes, taunts, jokes, and catches. She emerged from the pages of my collection, teased out by symbolic analysis, and she stood before me, the image of the ideal. I chose to highlight her. Still, beside her stood the real little girl. How was it that I brought forth the ideal and let the real remain in the background? First, my analytical lens was focused on structure and symbol. I viewed folklore as a symbolic code which the children used to organize their universe. Second, I looked to the content of the folklore as a source for these symbols.[9] The ideal little girl is present in these selections, as is the mirror image of the little boy. I will analyze a few selections to draw out the image of the ideal.

The nature of boys and girls is stated in the following hand-clapping song:

My mother, your mother
Lives across the street
1617 Mable Street.
Every time they have a fight,
This is what they say:
Boys are rotten,
Made out of cotton.
Girls are dandy,
Made out of candy.
Icka-bocka soda bocka

Icka-bocka boo.
Icka-bocka soda cracker
Out goes you![10]

This conclusion about the nature of boys and girls—that boys are rotten and girls are dandy—is given validity by the source, "my mother and your mother."

The good little girl and the bad little boy clash in the following jump-rope song:

Down by the ocean,
Down by the sea,
Johnny broke a bottle,
And he blamed it on me.
I told Ma.
Ma told Pa.
Johnny got a lickin'
So ha, ha, ha!
How many lickins
Did Johnny get?
1, 2, 3, 4, 5 . . .[11]

True to his rotten nature, Johnny has broken a bottle. Then, instead of accepting the act and its consequences, he blames it on his sister. The little girl tells Ma. Ma in turn tells Pa. And then Johnny gets it! The little girl is the innocent one, unwilling to accept the blame cast on her. Instead of direct action, a verbal or physical fight, the little girl turns to her mother. And apparently the mother accepts without question the little girl's story. Just as the daughter avoided direct action, so does the mother: She passes the responsibility to her husband. Her husband, accepting, as his wife did, the son's guilt and the daughter's innocence, punishes the son without further question. The father, in contrast to his wife and daughter, is direct and physical in his treatment of Johnny: He spanks him. The little girl is vindicated and she gloats over her victory. She is not satisfied to have Johnny punished. She must count the lickins, and laugh at the spectacle.

The little girl in "Down by the Ocean" is indirect. She appeals to someone with more authority for help. By going to her mother, she is proving herself to be an obedient daughter who respects her parents. She is contrasted with her brother, who shows his disrespect for authority by his doubly antisocial act of breaking the bottle and blaming it on his sister.

35

In the case of the little Dutch girl in the following hand-clapping song, a pretty face is at a premium and brings substantial reward:

> I am a pretty little Dutch girl,
> As pretty, as pretty can be, be, be.
> And all the boys in my neighborhood
> Are crazy over me, me, me.
> My mother wanted peaches,
> My father wanted pears.
> My father wanted fifty cents
> To mend the broken stairs.
> My boyfriend gave me peaches.
> My boyfriend gave me pears.
> My boyfriend gave me fifty cents
> To mend the broken stairs.
> My boyfriend gave me peaches.
> My boyfriend gave me pears.
> My boyfriend gave me fifty cents
> And kissed me on the stairs.[12]

The little Dutch girl attracts the attention of every boy in the neighborhood for one reason only: She is pretty. Her looks alone supply her family with their needs, since her faithful boyfriend grants her every wish, just for a kiss on the stairs. She is definitely dependent on him, however. When a fight breaks off relations between them, her family is left in need:

> My boyfriend gave me peaches.
> My boyfriend gave me pears.
> My boyfriend gave me fifty cents,
> And threw me down the stairs.
> I gave him back the peaches.
> I gave him back the pears.
> I gave him back the fifty cents,
> And threw him down the stairs.
> My mother needed peaches.
> My father needed pears.
> My brother needed fifty cents
> To buy his underwear!

Since the aid of a boyfriend is an economic necessity, the little girl searches diligently for him. In the jump-rope song "Ice Cream Soda," she jumps to find out his identity:

> Ice cream soda.
> Delawarie punch.
> Tell me the initials
> Of your honeybunch.
> A, B, C, D . . .

When she misses, she calls out a name that begins with that letter:

> Danny, Danny,
> Do you love me?
> Yes, no, maybe so.
> Certainly![13]

In another version of "Ice Cream Soda," the first verse is the same, except that the name is determined in place of the initial:

> Ice cream soda.
> Delawarie punch.
> Tell me the name
> Of your honeybunch.
> A, B, C, D . . .

In the second verse, instead of determining whether or not the "honeybunch" loves the little girl, their marriage is divined:

> Danny, Danny,
> Will you marry me?
> Yes, no maybe so.
> Certainly!

It is assumed natural in both versions that the little girl will have a lover. His existence is not in question, only his initials or his name. Once these have been established, the question is simply whether or not he loves her, or whether or not he will marry her. Apparently the man of these jump-rope songs has an option to love or not to love, to marry or not to marry. For the little girl, this choice is not available.

When the little girl finds her love, it is likely that she will greet him with the kiss that is peppered throughout folklore. This kiss has different connotations. Sometimes it is a feminine tease; sometimes a precursor to marriage. "Missed me, missed me! Now you gotta' kiss me!" is called out to the person who is "it" in a game of tag. The children of the following taunt find that the kiss holds greater import:

> Nancy and Bobby
> Sittin' in a tree.
> K-i-s-s-i-n-g.
> First comes love.
> Then comes marriage.
> Then comes Nancy with a baby carriage.[14]

The little girl's orientation must be directed toward the home, for this is the center of her activity. Even her address is decided. As my informants said, "My mother, your mother, lived across the street, 1617 Mable Street." This is also rendered, "My mother, your mother, lives across the way, at 514 East Broadway" (Abrahams and Rankin 1980, 154). This leaves no doubt where the little girl will be found. She is in the home. She will probably be hanging up the clothes, as in the following counting-out rhyme:

> My mother, your mother
> Hangin' up the clothes.
> My mother punched your mother
> Right in the nose.
> What color was her blood?
> Blue. B-L-U-E spells blue.
> And you are not it![15]

Or maybe she will be drinking coffee or tea, as the little girl is in the following jump-rope rhyme:

> I like coffee.
> I like tea.
> I like Janie
> To jump in with me![16]

Part of her work will certainly follow the command:

> Wash the dishes.

Dry the dishes.
Turn the dishes over![17]

When the baby arrives, he must be fed. The method of obtaining food and preparing it for baby's consumption is a task of divided labor:

Fishy, fishy in the brook.
Daddy catch him on the hook.
Mommy fry him in the pan,
Baby eat him like a man.[18]

Daddy brings the food home, mommy prepares it, and baby eats it. This chain is continued with baby's eating, for he is urged to "eat him like a man." Presumably this means that baby will keep trying to be a man as he eats his fish, until he grows up and is a food-provider for his wife and baby.

The little girl of folklore emerges as a creature of variation. At times, she is a good little girl who obeys her parents, uses her good looks to get a boyfriend, and then makes sure that he ends up as her husband. At other times, she is manipulative and scheming; sometimes, provocative and rebellious. The image of the ideal in folklore is the little girl who is *usually* obedient and submissive.

This ideal little girl has the power to influence through repetition and suggestion. The girls who jump to "I am a Pretty Little Dutch Girl" do not necessarily identify with her on a conscious level. Yet they do hear the message of this jump-rope song encoded at many other levels of their lives. It is this reenforcement that folklore imparts to already existing values that gives these symbols their potency.

To stop here in our analysis, however, is to give a distorted picture of the little girl, her folklore, and her social values. Next to the ideal little girl stands the real little girl. This real girl of flesh and blood is responsible for the continuation of the tradition and the re-creation of folklore in performance. She is also a girl who lives in a society where the ideal has been challenged. And she is aware of this challenge.

In his classic remarks on fieldwork, Bronislaw Malinowski advised the ethnographer to record both what people say they do and what they do. The ethnographer will then have "the two extremes within which the normal moves" (Malinowski 1922, 21). It is likely that what people say will yield the ideal; and what they actually do will reflect the real. In my work with children's folklore, the ideal is revealed in the texts and in the formal interviews. The children tell me how it *should* be. In their actions—both in the performance of the folklore and in their daily lives—they show me how it *really* is. It is of crucial importance to elicit the ideal *and* to observe the real. Often the tension between the ideal and the real reveals an area of cultural stress, of shifting cultural values.

The real little girls from my folklore study return to me in all their complexity. There is Sara, aged eight, who ran into my kitchen to perform with delight and accentuated pelvic thrusts:

> La-la-la boom dee a,
> They took my pants away.
> They left me staying there
> Without my underwear.[19]

It was also Sara who explained to me that men should open doors for women, because men are strong and women are weak. Yet Sara was the one who suggested the formation of the women's lib group. This followed the creation of mod maidens, a club jointly created by Sara and Hillary that focused on dressing-up and playing with Barbie dolls.

Jacqueline, aged ten, and Hillary, aged eight, revealed another apparent discrepancy between the ideal and the real. The two explained to me the division between boys' and girls' games. Boys play tether ball, Greek dodge ball, dodge ball, kick ball, and baseball. Girls play hopscotch, jump rope, tree tag, and they play on the rings at school. In narrative folklore, girls and boys, for the most part, say different rhymes. As they stressed, boys would never say "I am a Pretty Little Dutch Girl." There is an overlap occurring mainly in the nasty jokes. When I was questioning Hillary and Jacqueline about the games played by the boys and girls, my inquiries brought an incredulous response from Jacqueline:

> RZ: What about other boys at school? Do they play hopscotch?
> Girls: No.
> RZ: Do they play jump rope?
> Girls: No.
> RZ: Do they play on the rings?
> Jacqueline: Oh, Rosemary, you must be kidding!

To Jacqueline, this division was so clear that my questions seemed absurd. It was most interesting in Jacqueline's case that she saw baseball as a boy's sport because she played it constantly and was in great demand as a team member. As she explained it, "Girls can play it, but it's a boy's game."

In her approach to boys, Jacqueline was a combination of the seductive and the aggressive. At the age of ten, she had considered herself married for over a year to her boyfriend, Brian. Brian's younger brother, Jimmy, performed the wedding ceremony in which a "diamond" ring from a bubblegum machine was given to Jacqueline by her "husband." This wedding ceremony was in keeping with the image of the ideal little girl. Yet Jacqueline's more aggressive behavior was at the other end of the spectrum. She would chase and tackle Brian, covering him with kisses as she wrestled him to the ground. Often this was done with the help of her girlfriends, accompanied by delighted laughter from the girls and screams of help from Brian.

How does the image of the ideal little girl mesh with this real little girl, aggressive and demanding in her behavior toward her boyfriend? And how do we resolve the seeming contradiction between the little girls' classification of boys' and girls' games and their actual participation in the games? What do we do about Sara, who expects men to open doors for the weaker sex but founds women's lib groups? Perhaps rather than expecting a blending or a merging of the ideal and the real, we should attempt to see the intertwining layers in the children's lives. We need not expect simplicity and consistency. We will not find it.

CONSERVATISM AND CREATIVITY

Much work in children's folklore has focused on its conservative and traditional nature, the manner of transmission, from child to child, without the aid or knowledge of adults. It also has to do with the remarkable continuity and stability of narrative texts.

Children's folklore is part of the insular world of the child. In comments about my research, principals, teachers, and parents would say, "Children's folklore, interesting. But does it exist?" or "Rope jumping? Do children still do that?" As Mary and Herbert Knapp said in *One Potato, Two Potato*, "Most adults simply assume that today's children don't play traditional games any more" (Knapp and Knapp 1976, xi). Iona and Peter Opie remarked on the adult's ignorance of children's folklore: "The schoolchild's verses are not intended for adult ears. In fact part of their fun is the thought, usually correct, that adults know nothing about them. Grown-ups have outgrown the schoolchild's lore" (Opie and Opie 1959, 1). The body of children's folklore, shared so enthusiastically among children and unknown to adults, certainly strengthens the bonds between children and sets off a safe territory, free from adult restraints.

Stone and Church in *Childhood and Adolescence* discuss the period of middle childhood, which encompasses years six to ten: "The middle years are perhaps the age adults know least about. One reason for this is that during the school years children turn their backs on adults and actively shut them out from much of the world of childhood. Beyond the family-centered school-based life of earlier years, children join a separate, neighborhood- and school-based society of their peers, forming groups along lines of age and sex" (Stone and Church 1957, 202). The desire to protect and sustain the group fosters the conservatism of children. Innovation in dress, manners, and speech is suppressed. The urge to be like other children is the motivating factor in choosing what cereal to eat for breakfast and what clothes to wear to school.[20]

Alice Bertha Gomme attributed a mystical force to this conservatism in children's folklore. As she says, "There must be some strong force . . . potent enough to almost compel their continuance and to prevent their decay" (Gomme 1964 [1898], 2: 514). Lady Alice identified this as "the dramatic faculty of mankind."

In addition to the continuity of form, there is also a conservatism within the corpus of children's folklore. In the course of my research, I encountered only one or two selections of folklore that were not part of my own repertoire when I was a child growing up in Napa, California, in the 1950s. There was one item that appeared new on the scene and enjoyed wild popularity for a few months. It was used as an insult or taunt:

God damn you
Mother-fucker
Titty-sucker
Two ball bitch!

When the girls in my study decided that swearing was bad, they changed this to "Oh, you M-F, T-S, T-B-B!" Gradually, even the abbreviated version was dropped by the children. At the time, I suggested that a radical new element in children's folklore might attract excited attention for a time. But the values and aesthetics of the group would militate against radical change, splintering off sharp corners to maintain the rounded body of oral tradition (Zumwalt 1972, 50). John McDowell, in writing of the poetic quality of riddles, uses the metaphor of the rounded body: "They are like the polished stones, rounded off through the incessant action of a brook's water, as their continuous rehearsal on the tongue of the folk endows them with an increasingly graceful and rounded contour. At the same time, this grace of form ensures their perpetuation, rendering them pleasurable and memorable" (McDowell 1979, 57). This rounded body of folklore, this enduring form, has to do with the content of the folklore. The conservatism of the children, then, is highlighted in their folklore repertoire.

In accord with the Opies, Sutton-Smith attributes the retention of children's games to the conservatism of children. As he notes, between the ages of six and nine, children have "relatively unorganized personalities" and participate in a "very precarious" group life (Sutton-Smith 1972a, 45). The games provide the children with a reliable structure, a means of control in their otherwise powerless state. As Sutton-Smith says, "The children's conservatism (their jealous regard for the rules of the game) has its basis in their need for structure in social relationships . . ." (Sutton-Smith 1972a, 45–46). Through guarding the games and assuring a tradition of continuity, the children exercise control over a portion of their world. One might add that while they are controlling this portion of their lives through playing a game, the children are simultaneously being controlled by the game. So they have the freedom to choose and the constraints of the choice in the same moment. Their world of play is a microcosm of the adult world.

Along with the duality of freedom and constraint, there is conservatism and innovation. As Sutton-Smith remarks, "In seeking to understand children at play . . . we must hold in mind the dual fact that children are *innovative* as well as *conservative* . . ." (Sutton-Smith 1972a, 65). Mary and Herbert Knapp also stress this: "While children are remarkably conservative in preserving their traditions for generations, they are also very flexible in adapting their lore to present concerns" (Knapp and Knapp 1976, 14).

This dual orientation was present in William Wells Newell's *Games and Songs of American Children* (1963 [1883]).[21] Chapter four of this work is entitled "The Inventiveness of Children" and Chapter five, "The Conservatism of Children." Newell refers to "the legacy of other generations and languages" present in children's folklore. He poses the rhetorical question "Should we then infer that childhood, devoid of inventive capacity, has no resource but mechanical repetition?" (Newell 1963, 22). To answer this, he discusses children's fantasy play: A solitary girl transforms the city park into a place filled with make-believe companions; two young girls conduct elaborate lessons at their imaginary boarding school. Newell also mentions the creativity of secret languages. Children's "love of originality finds the tongue of their elders too commonplace; besides, their fondness for mystery requires secret ways of communication" (Newell 1963, 24). He gives the reader instructions for "Hog Latin," a secret language of New England: "It consists simply in the addition of the syllable *ery,* preceded by the sound of hard g, to every word. Even this is puzzling to older persons, who do not perceive that 'Wiggery youggery goggery wiggery miggery' means only 'Will you go with me'! Children sometimes use this device so perpetually that parents fear lest they may never recover the command of their native English" (Newell 1963, 24). Forever inventive, when they tire of this secret language, Newell says, the children simply create a new one.[22]

While recognizing the force of innovation, Newell is pulled back to the lodestone of tradition. In the conclusion to the chapter on "The Inventiveness of Children," he remarks that the majority of children's games have existed for centuries with "formulas which have been passed from generation to generation." "How," Newell asks, "are we to reconcile this fact with the quick inventiveness we ascribe to children?" (Newell 1963, 27). The inventiveness, Newell tells us, yields localized games—the fantasy play of the lone child, the "gibberish" of a group of children—which fade when interest lags. Traditional games have passed the test of time—they have survived— because they have an appeal broader than that of passing innovation: "The old games, which have prevailed and become familiar by a process of natural selection, are usually better adapted to children's taste than any new inventions can be; they are recommended by the quaintness of formulas which come from the remote past, and strike the young imagination as a sort of sacred law" (Newell 1963, 27). In his notes to the first edition, Newell singled out the emphasis on tradition in his work: "It is devoted to formulas of play which children have preserved from generation to generation, without intervention, often without the knowledge of older minds" (Newell 1963, i). Newell found "something so agreeable in this inheritance of thought kept up by childhood itself" (Newell 1963, 12). The imminent disappearance of these rhymes is "a thousand pities" (Newell 1963, 12).

One might caution here against an overly arbitrary division between inventiveness and conservatism. While Newell posits a division between these two types of play, children do not—for is it not possible to play a traditional game with innovation, to chant rhymes centuries old with fantasy of the moment? Thus even these two forces in children's folklore twine together in complex interplay. As one individual in her reading of my work has pointed out, "Innovation has also survived the test of time." Just as children share in traditional games, so they share in fantasy play. In this sense, innovation has the same depth in children's folklore as tradition. It was present in the past, it adds intricacies to the traditional games of the moment, and it will remain a force in the culture of childhood.

Yet still in accord with Newell on this point, might we find "something so agreeable" in the tradition of children's folklore, and something so pleasing in the creativity? The challenge is to broaden our grasp, to encompass the complexity of children's folklore—to reach for the text and the context, the ideal and the real, the tradition and the creativity. Still, in our endeavor to encircle all this, we must not expect fully to succeed. There is the magical in children's folklore that will never be captured. And here we might learn from the anthropologist who went to Dublin, Ireland, to study a leprechaun. In 1957, as the story goes, a mechanic from the Vauxhall Factory captured a leprechaun in Phoenix Park. People came from all over to see the leprechaun, and among these was the anthropologist. For four or five days, the anthropologist observed the leprechaun. On the fifth day, the leprechaun took on the appearance of a tiny, shriveled root and died.[23] So with children's folklore, the voice on the wind, the creativity of the moment, cannot be fully captured. The fluid world of the child eludes the static state of the printed word. Their mirthful nature will not be pinned down by our sobriety. That is fair; it is part of the rules of the game. The children have, after all, warned us that they do it all "just for the fun of it!"

NOTES TO CHAPTER TWO

1. Darwin's twentieth-century descendants in the social sciences are wont to connect Social Darwinism with others. John Friedl in *The Human Portrait* says, "Although Darwin did not mean for his theory of evolution to be applied to human social and cultural change, it was proposed by many social scientists that cultures evolved in a struggle for survival, just as animals did. This doctrine, inappropriately called 'social Darwinism,' was ultimately used to justify white supremacist policies of Western nations . . ." (Friedl 1981, 116). In spite of Friedl's sympathetic interpretation of Darwin's work, Darwin did not wait for others to create social Darwinism. The seeds were present in *Journal of Researches into the Natural History and Geology of the Countries Visited During the Voyage of H.M.S. Beagle Round the World* (1852). It blossomed in his masterwork, *On the Origin of Species* (1859), and took firm root in *Descent of Man* (1871). It is well to keep in mind the reality of our historical antecedents in theory. For a discussion of the *Forerunners of Darwin: 1745–1859*, see Bentley Glass 1968.

2. The cultural evolutionary orientation was opposed to the theory of degenerationism. Archbishop Whately, the major advocate of the latter theory, represented the savage as the end point of the fall from grace. From this perspective, to propose an evolution from savagery was blasphemy. There could be no development from the savage state, since that ran counter to the biblical account of creation. The savage represents not the childhood of the race but the depths of degradation. For a detailed discussion of the theory of degenerationism, see Margaret Hodgen's *Doctrine of Survivals* (1936). For a discussion of evolutionary theory, see Frederick Teggart's *Theory and Processes of History* (1977 [1941]), and Kenneth Bock's *Acceptance of Histories* (1958). See also Dundes's "Devolutionary Premise in Folklore Theory" (1969a).

3. Karl Pearson (1897) *Chances of Death*, London: Edward Arnold. 2:53–54.

4. Alice Bertha Gomme's two-volume work, *The Traditional Games of England, Scotland and Ireland*, was originally published as part one of George Laurence Gomme's intended but not completed *Dictionary of British Folklore*. Volume 1 was published in 1894; Volume 2, in 1898. The Dover edition is an unabridged republication of this important work. See Dorothy Howard's introduction to the Dover edition for remarks on Lady Alice's cultural evolutionary theory.

5. Alice Bertha Gomme's treatment of "Round and Round the Village" is an

45

example of her thorough scholarship. First she presents the music, then she provides nineteen versions with informant and geographic designations. There follows a description of how the game is played with accompanying diagrams. Lady Alice includes directions for *each* version. She then provides a four-page chart that lists the segments of the rhyme with coordinates for geographical area and version. This facilitates what she refers to as the analysis of the game rhymes. And finally she discusses the game in relation to the custom of perambulation of boundaries, with citations to other pertinent sources. This is just one game in her two-volume work, which considers more than two hundred games.

6. For differing interpretations of Aarne–Thompson Tale Type 328, "Jack and the Beanstalk," see Humphrey Humphreys's "Jack and the Beanstalk" (1965 [1948], 103–6); William H. Desmonde's "Jack and the Beanstalk" (1965 [1951], 107–9); and Martha Wolfenstein's "Jack and the Beanstalk: An American Version" (1955, 100–113). For the solar mythological approach, see the summary of Angelo De Gubernatis's interpretation in Dorson (1955). All of the foregoing articles are reprinted in Dundes's *Study of Folklore.* See also Dundes's "Projection in Folklore: A Plea for Psychoanalytic Semiotics" (1976a, 1510–11).

7. For an examination of the origin theory as it relates to narrative, see Brian Sutton-Smith's "The Origins of Fictions and the Fictions of Origin," *American Ethnological Society Proceedings,* 1984, 117–32. In relationship to cultural evolutionary theory, it might be that a culture has a simple technology, but that is not the same as a simple cognitive system. The Australian aborigines—who from the nineteenth century to the present have been the choice of the evolutionary anthropologists as the simplest, most primitive culture—do, indeed, have a simple stone-tool technology. But they have a kinship system so complex that it is a point of dispute still among kinship experts as to how to describe it. The result of the myriad of ethnographies written during the nineteenth and the twentieth centuries has been to present the complexity of cultures; and this complexity is apparent even though the cultures might be described in these same ethnographies as simple, savage, or primitive.

8. See Dundes's foreword to the 1978 edition of *Children's Humor* for an appraisal of Martha Wolfenstein's contributions.

9. In the winter of 1971, I began a collection of jump-rope and hand-clapping songs that I gathered from children at an elementary school and from children living in an apartment complex in Santa Cruz, California. One year later, I broadened the scope of the project to include the children in two other elementary schools. At this point, I was still limiting my search to jump-rope and hand-clapping songs. Then, as serendipity would have it, I recorded some "nasty jokes" from my three major informants. As I listened to the jokes, I heard the same message threading through the jokes that bound together the jump-rope and hand-clapping songs. From that point on, I attempted to study the full gamut of children's folklore.

10. Collected from a six-year-old Caucasian girl in Santa Cruz, California, February 1971. The informant had learned this two years earlier when she attended school on the Navajo reservation in Window Rock, Arizona. She used it as a jump-rope song and she said that the girl jumping rope ran out on the last line.

11. Collected from an eight-year-old Caucasian girl in Santa Cruz, California, in 1971.

12. Collected from a six-year-old Caucasian girl in Santa Cruz, California, in 1971.

13. Collected from an eight-year-old Caucasian girl in Santa Cruz, California, in 1971.

14. I used this rhyme to taunt my older sisters when I was a child growing up in Napa, California, in the 1950s. I also heard it chanted endlessly by my informants in Santa Cruz, California, in 1971–72.

15. Collected from a six- and an eight-year-old Caucasian girl in Santa Cruz, California, in 1971. The two learned this from an eight-year-old boy.

16. Collected from a ten-year-old black girl in Santa Cruz, California, in 1972.

17. I performed this rhyme with my two sisters when we were young. The two participants join hands and swing their arms back and forth on the first two lines. On the last line, they attempt to twist around, back-to-back, while still holding hands. A favorite time to perform this was at the kitchen sink while doing the dishes.

18. I learned this as a child; I also collected a version in 1983 in Columbia, South Carolina, that is exactly the same, except that the baby is urged to eat "like a lamb."

19. Collected from an eight-year-old Caucasian girl in Santa Cruz, California, in 1972. The rhyme is performed to accompanying pelvic thrusts. On the first "la," the pelvis is thrust to the right; on the second, to the front; and on the third, to the left. As my nine-year-old informant said, "On 'boom dee ay,' you stick your butt out in the back." The final word, "underwear," is executed with a pelvic thrust to the front.

20. The tradition and continuity in children's folklore is illustrated in *The Lore and Language of Schoolchildren*. Iona and Peter Opie record several versions of the jump-rope song "Not Last Night but the Night Before," spanning the years from 1835 to 1959. (See Opie and Opie 1959, 23.) Clearly in their examples, variation does occur in the text, but the overall form remains intact throughout the years.

21. Gary Alan Fine refers to the dual concerns of conservatism and innovation as "Newell's paradox." Fine suggests a partial resolution for the division of these two forces. This involves viewing children's folklore from three analytical perspectives. In the first (which he calls *thematype* analysis), the folklore is analyzed according to theme or structure. In the second (which he calls *ecotype* analysis), the folklore is analyzed according to the social environment. And in the third (*egotype* analysis), the performance of the folklore is highlighted. Fine notes, "Any item of folklore can be analyzed from any and all perspectives, although most folklore approaches focus on only one" (Fine 1980d, 180).

22. For a Japanese version of pig latin, see Thomas W. Johnson (1975, 232–33) See also Berkovits's "Secret Languages of Schoolchildren" (1970).

23. Folklore Archives, University of California, Berkeley. Collected by Susan Rush from Penola Campbell in Oakland, California. The informant first heard this legend in 1968 when she was living in Ireland; it was told to her by her husband, who had lived all his life in Dublin.

3

The Transmission
of Children's Folklore

John H. McDowell

The transmission of children's folklore naturally falls within the broader question of the transmission of folklore in general. Every conceptualization of folklore must contain a theory, whether explicit or implicit, regarding the transmission of folklore, since folklore is universally recognized as an inherently social phenomenon. While these issues have not always received the attention they deserve, folkloristic theories of transmission nonetheless abound in the literature. To gain a grasp on these theories, I suggest the following two categories: theories viewing folklore transmission as a superorganic, mechanical process; and theories emphasizing its serendipitous and emergent character.

Folklore transmission viewed as a mechanical process figures prominently in those theories of folklore taking their inspiration from the philological roots of our discipline. Jakob Grimm, in his studies of Germanic and Indo-European languages, identified systematic laws of phonological shift that operate, for all intents and purposes, outside the immediate arena of concrete speech events. The Grimm brothers considered folklore "only a higher and freer speech of mankind," and hypothesized that laws similar to sound shift laws could be discovered to account for the persistence of traditional items and their variants through time and space (see Crane 1918). Their theories accounting for Märchen as broken-down Indo-European myths are perhaps the main fruit of this orientation. The realm defined by their compelling aphorism, *das Volk dichtet*, "the people, as a whole, composes poetry" (Kittredge and Sargent 1904), transcends the sphere of grounded human interaction.

This superorganic orientation persists in the work of the historic-geographic folklore scholars. Kaarle Krohn (1971, 98) argues that "it is the mechanical laws of thought and imagination that prevail in the rich variation of oral tradition." In a sequence of chapters entitled "The Influence of

Faulty Memory," "The Impulse Toward Expansion," and "Laws of Transformation," Krohn discusses a series of "laws of thought" capable of producing the observed differences among variants of a migratory folklore item. But these laws are strictly conjectural, founded on the examination of texts, rather than on the examination of living folkloristic "cultures." Folklore transmission, in this frame of reference, becomes an impersonal process to be inferred and reconstructed on the basis of exclusively philological evidence. The status of these "laws of thought" is quite analogous to that of Grimm's laws of consonant shift, founded on the impersonal forces of language change.

Krohn sought to embody the "mechanical laws of thought and imagination" in two models, portraying the spread of folklore materials in the manner of waves on the water emanating from a central source of disturbance, and in the manner of a stream welling forth in a certain direction. C. W. von Sydow rejects these models, introducing elements of an alternative theory of folklore transmission. Retaining the same essential goals as those held by Krohn, von Sydow introduces the concepts of *active and passive bearers, mutation,* and *oicotypification.* "The dissemination of a tale," von Sydow contends, "is desultory to a high degree." "Only a very small number of active bearers of tradition equipped with a good memory, vivid imagination, and narrative powers do transmit the tales. It is only they who tell them. Among their audience it is only a small percentage still who actually do so. Most of those who have heard a tale told and are able to remember it, remain passive carriers of tradition, whose importance for the continued life of the tale consists mainly in their interest in hearing it told again" (von Sydow 1965 [1948], 231).

The commitment to folkloristics as a philological inquiry is evident in the key construction here, "the life of the tale." Yet at the same time, von Sydow delves beyond the impersonal forces of language and culture drift to enfranchise the individual performers and audience members in his general theory of folklore transmission. Krohn had spoken of bilingual border populations, and "temporary visits by hunters, fishermen, craftsmen, merchants, sailors, soldiers, pilgrims, and other wanderers" (Krohn 1971, 59), but von Sydow's concept of active and passive bearers locates folklore transmission directly in the immediate context of the folklore performance.

Von Sydow introduces the term *mutation* to refer to specific alterations of narrative materials as storytellers constantly reinterpret a narrative tradition. The language he uses here creates a juxtaposition between the superorganic framework of folklore transmission, and a more situated, human-oriented approach: "An original motif may be superseded by a new mutation, but a new mutation may also yield to the older form, being unable to assert itself at its expense. If a motif is particularly popular, this very fact may induce various narrators to mutate it in different ways" (von Sydow 1971, 234). The process envisioned here is still somewhat mechanistic, yet the term *mutation* admits an element of caprice, since the precise moment and direction of a mutation cannot be foreseen with any certainty. The concept of mutation presupposes recognition of the immense range of potential inherent in any act of folklore transmission.

One possible result of mutation in the folklore transmission process is "a certain unification of the variants within one and the same linguistic or cultural area on account of isolation from other areas," a result referred to by von Sydow as *oicotypification* (von Sydow 1971, 238). He observes that oicotypification might result "from the circumstance that one mutation has prevailed over the rest so as to become the oicotype of the tale within the area concerned" (von Sydow 1971, 238). In this manner, the demands of scientific generalization are reconciled with recognition of the autonomy of each individual instance: the individual cases, autonomous in themselves, nonetheless are thought to pattern into configurations describable in terms of scientific laws. In the end, von Sydow remains a voice of loyal opposition within the camp of philologically inspired folklorists.

In recent years, folklorists have developed approaches to folklore transmission amenable to the groundwork laid in von Sydow's critique of overly mechanistic models of transmission. The work of these scholars readily incorporates von Sydow's notions of active and passive bearers, locating folklore transmission within finite communicative contexts, and mutations, pointing to the unique, unpredictable quality of any given instance of folklore transmission. Perhaps the key word is *emergence,* indicating a fortuitous result achieved through the continuous interaction of all relevant components in a given folklore performance. According to Richard Bauman, "The concept of emergence is necessary to the study of performance as a means towards comprehending the uniqueness of particular performances within the context of performance as a generalized cultural system in a community" (Bauman 1977a, 37). The theory of folklore transmission residing in the performance-centered approach is one concerned with "the interplay between communicative resources, individual competence, and the goals of the participants, within the context of particular situations" (Bauman 1977a, 38).

In a theory centered on the creation and re-creation of folklore through performance, the term *transmission* becomes extremely problematic. The very notion of the "item" of folklore, with its demonstrable "life history," is no longer entirely tenable. The folklore text, formerly thought to embody the empirical foundation for folklore studies, becomes, in this light, a pale and in many ways a misleading reflection of the performance it purports to record (McDowell 1982).

If it is no longer possible to hold that folklore is "transmitted" in the manner of a mechanical signal, then how are we to speak of that critical moment when folklore enters into an interactional format, finding articulation in the speech or action of one individual, yet leaving a trace in the short- or long-term memory of another, eventually to spring forth as a performance that in some sense repeats the original? How are we to account for the persistence of form and content in folklore over time? And what constraints, or patterns, can we identify in the extensive capacity of performers to shape and reshape folkloric routines that have entered their repertoires? These are the central issues in the construction of a modern theory of folklore transmission, a theory intended to address the stable, generalizable aspects of the process in question, as well as its more capricious, serendipitous aspect.

The domain of children's folklore is a good place to begin formulating such a theory. The world of the child is in some sense more contained, and thus more accessible to study, than the multifarious world of the adult. In the child's realm, we can often specify with some precision the sources of the routines we observe, and thereby gain a better handle on the processes of transformation and preservation operative therein. In short, the child's processing of folkloric materials can be taken as a microcosm of the process of folklore transmission in general, and, as such, can provide some provocative clues of relevance both within and beyond the realm of children's folklore.

What is it, then, that happens when one child performs a folkloric routine in the presence of another child, or group of children? Speech act theory, with its emphasis on perlocutionary effect (Austin 1962), would suggest isolating one complete interactional node as the focus of our analysis, but we must go one better, to incorporate the arrival of a "repeatable" message to the position of a third individual:

child A	child B	child C
1 (encodes a message)	2 (decodes the message)	5 (decodes a message)
	3 (processes the message)	
	4 (reencodes the message)	

This model draws attention to five discrete moments in the process of folklore transmission. The first moment, when child A encodes a message, initiates a string of events culminating in the arrival of that message to a third child, who then proceeds to decode it. Clearly, the boundaries of this model are arbitrary, but we may nonetheless utilize it as a tool for identifying the basic structure of one finite instance of folklore transmission among children.

STAGE ONE: CHILD A ENCODES A MESSAGE

In the initial formulation of the message, child A draws on previous experience in the world to produce a message containing the kinds of features we identify as folkloric. While there is no consensus on this point, we can generally mention features such as provenience from a common store of communicative resources lying outside the official, institutional channels; possessing a formulaic quality, something I have referred to elsewhere as an accessible rhetoric (McDowell 1979); and in some way betraying a grounding in the ethos of some finite, operative human community. In short, child A produces an item of folklore.

The inspiration for this initial action need not proceed from a folkloric source. In many instances, children do draw on these folkloric resources, the forms so richly documented by Opie and Opie (1959) and elsewhere. Yet even the briefest exposure to children's folklore reveals the almost amoebic ability of children to incorporate extraneous materials into their expressive competencies. Along these lines, I would mention two particularly important tributaries: materials proceeding from the folkloric repertoires of adults, yet suitable for child consumption (for example, fairy tales, riddles, nursery rhymes, and lullabies); and materials proceeding from popular culture sources, of major importance in the expressive behavior of contemporary children (Sutton-Smith 1971a).

When adult folklore or popular culture is assimilated into the realm of children's folklore, changes take place that are most revealing of childish attitudes and concerns. These extraneous materials undergo a sea change, to eventually display the contours of perception and conception characteristic of the child's mind. The distance between the original material and the child's revamping of it thus stands as an indication of the difference between the child's cosmology and that of the adult. Consider the following narrative, produced by an eight-year-old child of Mexican descent:

Hey, you know that little girl, she had a, she had a mother but the mother was witch, and the mother had said:

"Go get apples and don't give anybody one."
So that lady had turned into a witch, and she went up there, and she said:
"Can I have an apple? I haven't eaten for years and years."
And she goes:
"OK."
So that lady had eat it and turned into her mother again, and she said:
"Didn't I tell you not to give anybody an apple?"
"Mom," she said, "she never eat for—"
Then her mother had killed her.
Then her little brother had pulled her hair:
"Brother, brother, don't pull my hair;
Mother had killed me for a single pear."
And then he ran and go called her father. Then her father pulled her hair, she said:
"Father, father don't pull my hair;
"Mother had killed me for one single pear."
And her father killed that lady.[1]

There is a strong sense of the presence of the Märchen in this story. The pattern of interdiction-violation, the poetic couplets, and the familiar motive of the informing corpse, all testify to an origin in the adult fairy tale corpus. Yet this is a rather odd performance by adult standards. The shift from apples to pears is unsettling, and in general the plot is too skeletal, rushing to the denouement without fully exploiting the available sources of tension and ambiguity.

Abandoning the adult perspective momentarily, the most remarkable aspect of this story is its manifest assimilation to the world of the child. The child is placed in the center of the action, the protagonist of a story developing a cruel and fatal conflict: Either the child denies food to a starving person or the child transgresses the command of her mother, thus to pay the ultimate price. The transformation of the mother into a witch is a telling, indirect portrait of the ambivalence inherent in mother-daughter relationships, as well as the ultimate extension of the nightmare wherein all familiar things crumble before our eyes into strange and evil forces.

A similar adaptation of external materials to the consciousness of the child can be observed in reference to popular culture. Consider the popular ditty associated with the cartoon figure Popeye. The original text, so far as I can recall, is as follows:

I'm Popeye the sailor man,
I'm Popeye the sailor man,
I'm strong to the finish
'Cause I eats me spinach,
I'm Popeye the sailor man.

Now consider the following two parodies of this ditty, the first ubiquitous among North American schoolchildren, and the second found among children of Mexican descent in Texas:[2]

I'm Popeye the sailor man,
I live in a garbage can,
I eat all the worms
And spit out the germs,
I'm Popeye the sailor man.

Popeye nació en Torreón	Popeye was born in Torreon
Encima de una sillón,	On top of a toilet seat,
Mató a su tía	He killed his aunt
Con una tortílla,	With a tortilla
Popeye nació en Torreón.	Popeye was born in Torreon.

Two features are especially striking in these transformations. For one thing, the content of the original message, an instance of exemplary behavior in respect to eating habits, is radically altered to produce a message subversive of standard, adult-imposed decorum. Each parody creates a fictive world that stands as a miniature rite of rebellion, a vision of a counter-factual world inhabited by worm-eating garbage-can residents, and tortilla-wielding aunt killers. The exemplary Popeye is converted into an anti-Popeye, exhibiting filthy and murderous qualities obviously anathema to the conventional etiquette.

The second feature of interest here is the scope given to the child's poetic muse, which reverses the dominance relationship between phonological and semantic elaboration obtaining in adult verbal creations (Sanches and Kirshenblatt-Gimblett 1976). In these parodies, the semantic thread is a bare one indeed, subservient to the phonological attraction of such lexical items as *worms/germs,* and *tía/tortílla, Torreón/sillón.* In reference to style as well as to content, the parodies transform the original material into vessels expressing the child's sensitivities.

The communications we are concerned with are primarily lodged in the verbal and kinesic media, and thus are perishable upon performance. The words spoken by child A, or the folkloric activity performed, vanish rapidly as a physical presence, leaving behind only a trace in the memory of those who were witness to them. Under these conditions, the decoding of the message must, of course, be a precipitous affair, without recourse to a permanent or perduring record. As a result, there is no guarantee that the message encoded by child A is the same message after decoding by child B. Imperfectly perceived material, or material not familiar to the recipient, may be assimilated into gestalts (frameworks) already present in the mind of child B.

In the section titled "Wear and Repair During Transmission," the Opies (1959) provide a number of characteristic examples, including the delightful recasting of the old hymn:

> Can a woman's tender care
> Cease towards the child she-bear?

A great many studies in folklore have shown how traditional materials adapt in this fashion to their new environments, and, indeed, this is one of the sources of "mutation" recognized in the theories of von Sydow (1971). In the absence of a written record serving as a check to this process of mutation, there exists in every instance of folklore transmission the possibility for text modification due to spontaneous assimilative processes. The child's world, so little affected by written constraints, offers an excellent field laboratory in this respect.

STAGE THREE: CHILD B PROCESSES THE MESSAGE

In the model directing our discussion, there ensues a period, however brief or protracted, dedicated to the activity of conceptual processing. The message has been received and decoded by child B, perhaps already in modified form due to the rigors of instantaneous registration of a perishing stimulus. At this point, the message as received must be digested, that is, broken down into information units compatible with the child's concept of the world and his or her aesthetic proclivities. The assimilative processes initiated at the moment of message reception are accelerated, as the new information is stored through association with familiar archetypes. Theories relating to this stage have been quite celebrated in the history of folklore studies, and include such prominent constructs as Max Müller's *disease of language*, and the irrepressible construct *faulty memory*, to be found in the writings of

Kaarle Krohn (1971), among others.

Alan Dundes (1969a) has noted, I think quite correctly, the degenerative bias in most of these constructs. It is just as plausible to cite the creative, generative dimensions of this message-processing stage. We have already seen, in reference to materials received by children from outside sources such as adult folklore and popular culture, that these assimilative processes refurbish the materials received, endowing them with their inimitable fidelity to the outlook and expressive preferences of the communities in which they circulate. The exuberant and unbounded give-and-take of children's play ensures the continuous reworking of traditional materials; yet strikingly, children have shown themselves to be among the most dedicated supporters of tradition, as folklorists have often noted. A theory of folklore transmission must allow for each of these possibilities, the retention of traditional models, and the piecing together of new models out of traditional materials.

Stage Four: Child B Reencodes the Message

Any theory of folklore transmission must at some point take into account the moment of composition, generally occurring without the use of artificial aids to the memory such as scripted texts or plans. Folklorists have developed important perspectives, such as Albert Lord's theory of composition during performance (1960), and Ruth Finnegan's alternative model of rehearsal and performance (1977), with its greater weight on memorization as a factor in folklore transmission. The work of Parry and Lord and their followers indicates that in many folklore traditions a type of spontaneous poetic composition takes place, a process comparable to linguistic performance (capable of creating an unlimited number of novel utterances on the basis of internalized linguistic structures), but operating at a higher, extra-sentential, poetic level.

Children's folklore performances amply exhibit the effects of both rote memorization and improvisation on the basis of traditional models. In the verbal genres capable of stimulating a field of discourse, that is, a sequence of related items, the children frequently first exhaust their store of traditional items, and then move on to novel items, spontaneously composed on the model of familiar traditional items. The following sequence of interrogative ludic routines, taken from a riddling session among middle-class North American children, illustrates some facets of this process:

1. What did the big chimney say to the little chimney?
2. What did the Aggie say to the other Aggie?
3. What did the three Aggies say to the other four Aggies?

4.   What did the rug say to the floor?

5.   What did the dead penguin say to the live penguin?

6.   What did the rug say to the floor?

7.   What did the ten Aggies say to the one Aggie?

8.   What did the one Aggie say to the zero Aggie?

9.   What did the blue whale say to the duck?

10.   What did the whale shark say to the great white?

11.   What did the live duck say to the other live duck?

12.   What did the baby say to the cradle?

13.   What did the blue whale say to the great white?

14.   What did the (burping noise) say to the great white?

15.   What did the uhhh say to the great white?

16.   What did the burp say to the great white?

17.   What did Spiderman say to Ironman?

18.   What did the Martian say to the human?

19.   What did the man say to the store?[3]

The pace of this session was so rapid that the children did not pause to provide answers to the questions posed. The traditional items here are numbers one, four, and six, and they establish the framework for the surrounding and subsequent improvisations. These models provide the canonic form, What did the X say to the Y? as well as the following set of rules for acceptable formulations:

1.   The question specifies two entities in conversation.

2.   Neither of these entities is normally included in the category of speech participants.

3.   A motivation for dialogue must exist, either in the form of a shared identity (little chimney, big chimney) or habitual proximity (rug and floor).

Using this traditional framework as a point of departure, the children collectively undertake an excursion through the orders of their cosmology, coming to rest on such improbable conversants as humanoids (the Aggies, numbskull figures in Texas popular culture), animals (penguins, whales, ducks), inanimate objects (cradle, store), physical processes (the burps), and conceptual constructs (the zero Aggie). This riddling session can be viewed as a virtual symposium on childish ontology, isolating as it does a set of entities contrasting on the values *material, objective, animate, human, age of reason* (McDowell 1979). This riddling excerpt not only demonstrates the important enculturative dimensions of children's folklore, but suggests as well that scholars anchored to a perspective enfranchising only the transmission of traditional texts may well be missing most of the point in regard to children's folklore.

STAGE FIVE: CHILD C DECODES A MESSAGE

The small transmission circuit we have been concerned with here is complete with the arrival of the message to the position of child C in the model. The form and content of this message may remain unchanged throughout the entire process, so that the message encountered at stage one is identical to the message encountered at stage five. By the same token, one or more of the transformational devices we have mentioned might intervene to create a radically different message. Both results are possible; the text of the message is emergent in the context of child-to-child communication. A large number of factors, including the mood of the interaction, the capacities of the performers, the form or genre of folklore involved, and the rhetorical purposes of the performers must be taken into account in investigating the relative stability or lack of stability of messages in the crucible of folklore transmission.

The foregoing analysis would suggest that only by attending to the appearance of folkloric routines in finite, particular situations can we adequately project the destiny awaiting an item of folklore moving through minimal transmission circuits. Some kinds of folklore, for example, what the Opies (1959) refer to as the "Code of Oral Legislation," and children's rhymes and ditties, are retained in standard versions as far as possible, since they are valued by the children for their instrumental and aesthetic properties, respectively. The performative efficacy of phrases like "Finders keepers, losers weepers," or "Sticks and stones will break my bones/but names will never hurt me," depends in large measure on the verbatim repetition of the formula at the appropriate moment. Yet even in respect to these forms, children will produce free and fantastic parodies or recastings, as the spirit moves them. In other genres, such as riddling, the juvenile peer group may attach little value to the precise repetition of a traditional item, placing as much or more importance on the ability to formulate spontaneous improvisations along the line of items conveyed through oral tradition.

In the realm of children's folklore, then, we must rethink the notion of tradition, a concept much used but perhaps not fully understood in folkloristic discourse. In the first place, tradition must be conceived of as persistence through time and space, without any a priori constraints on the *duration* of the time involved, or on the *extension* of this physical space. Children's folklore does produce those fabulous instances of repeatability over long stretches of time and across immense geographical expanses that have always captivated the folklorist and the folk. Think, for example, of the well-known hand-clapping rhyme, "Patty Cake, Patty Cake," attested as far back as 1698 in D'urfey's comedy *The Campaigners,* which portrays "the affected tattling nurse" speaking as follows to her sucking babe:

> Ah Doddy blesse dat pitty face of mine Sylds,
> and his pitty, pitty hands, and his pitty,
> pitty foots, and all his pitty things, and
> pat a cake, pat a cake baker's man, so I will
> master as fast as I can, and prick it, and
> prick it, and prick it, and prick it, and
> throw't into the oven. (Opie and Opie 1952, 341)

The counting-out rhyme beginning with the line, "Eeny, meeny, miney, mo" constitutes an even more striking example, since by and large it is children alone who have been responsible for its perpetuation, and as Henry Bolton (1888) has shown in his classic study, it is of great antiquity and widely distributed throughout the European diaspora.

By the same token, there can be little doubt that many of the folkloric traditions of children are much less long-lived, and at the other end of the spectrum, could be better characterized as local and transitory. Within a neighborhood gang, for example, forms of folklore may thrive for a time but then perish as the children mature and their families move on to other residences. The items of folklore performed in this context may not enter the folklorist's most narrow construction of tradition, but they are certainly perceived to be traditional by those who create and maintain them. The world of children's folklore draws attention to the inherent relativity of the concept denoted by the words "persistence through time and space."

Further modification of the folkloristic construction of tradition centers on the notion of repeatability. When traditional items function primarily to guide innovative folkloric production, as in the riddling session considered above, then we should speak of a traditional competence rather than a set of traditional items. What persists through time and space, in these instances, is the capacity to formulate appropriate folkloric items, as much as the traditional items themselves. Longitudinal studies reveal the gradual acquisition of competence in the traditional forms of children's folklore, whereby narratives are given artistic shape and poignancy, and riddles eventually incorporate authentic kernels of linguistic or conceptual ambiguity (McDowell 1975). Exposure to children's folklore tends to redirect the folklorist's focus onto the persistence of traditional modes of self-expression, and the transmission, not necessarily of traditional items, but of traditional competencies.

The present discussion of the transmission of children's folklore has served primarily to complicate the notion of "the transmission of folklore" in general, and that may be its essential contribution to folkloristic dialogue. The drift of the argument has been in the direction of discrediting the conventional preoccupation with the transmission of particular folklore items. Individual items of folklore do occasionally persist through time and space, and therefore must in some sense be "transmitted" from one person to another. But I would suggest that this result is one possibility among many, and not really the privileged member of the set. It is just as likely that the item of folklore will perish, either through neglect or through transformational processes operating at the various moments of encoding, decoding, and reencoding of messages. The term introduced by von Sydow, mutation, if taken seriously and carried to its logical conclusion, adequately captures the character of these events.

Viewed in this perspective, the concept of "the transmission of folklore" can be interpreted as a metaphorical instrument appropriate to a particular historical moment in the evolution of folkloristic theory. Its roots lie in philology, perhaps most concretely in the mechanical process of producing a new manuscript by copying an earlier one. It conjures up images of a superorganic process, a perpetuation of "items" with their peculiar "life histories," quite external to the everyday communicative exchanges of ordinary human beings. There is no question that this serviceable metaphor has usefully informed folklore studies, by enabling a systematic hermaneutics of that one possibility it attends to, namely the preservation of a message intact, or only moderately changed, as it filters through finite communicative networks.

But the robust world of children's folklore forces the folklorist to confront the creative potential of every folkloric transaction, the capacity for new forms and items to emerge from traditional competencies. These creative factors are regenerative rather than degenerative, facilitating the continuous emergence of folkloric materials freshly coined in response to the experiences and needs of their hosts. It is this facet of folklore that lends the materials we study their authenticity and vitality, as trenchant markers of individual and community identity. The folkloric messages that persevere intact over time are nonetheless revalidated with each performance as suitable vessels for the expression of local concerns. And of equal importance, innovative messages are formulated, as traditional items and competencies are adapted to these same requirements.

These considerations lead to the suggestion of a neutral term, perhaps the *activation* of children's folklore, to refer to the processes set in motion as traditional competencies enter into finite communicative settings among children. Within this constellation, transmission intact or in recognizable variants would remain as one possible outcome, but the folklorist would be alert to the creative, transformative potential of all such encounters. A theory regarding the activation of folklore is necessarily grounded in particular instances of situated human intercourse, and retains an essential bias toward emergence as its central paradigm. Two rather different sorts of children are envisioned in the "transmission of children's folklore" and "the activation of children's folklore." In the former instance, the child (and, by extension, every human being) serves primarily as a repository and conduit for the exchange of traditional items possessing a destiny all their own. The items are literary, but there is no process of literary composition, save for the romantic notion of "the people as a whole composes poetry."

In a theory of the activation of children's folklore, the items recorded may or may not evince significant literary value, but the child emerges as the genius of composition, a complex cerebral and sentient locus of a serious effort at self-expression and communication. This latter perspective drives folkloristics in the direction of an aesthetics of the ordinary, a grounded theory of artistic composition engaged with the fundamental human requirement of self-realization through artistic performance. In the end, the child (and by extension, the human being) projected by this paradigm is a much more interesting figure, one immersed in real-life contingencies, and not a mere cipher in a superorganic device.

NOTES TO CHAPTER THREE

1. I recorded this narrative in a peer-group setting, in Austin, Texas, during the spring of 1974. The child who performed it had a large repertoire of Märchen-like stories drawn from traditional Mexican sources. For more details on this item and the other children's folklore included in this paper, see McDowell 1975.

2. The English variation on the Popeye ditty was widely distributed among Austin schoolchildren in the mid-1970s. Chicano children performed both the English and Spanish parodies, setting them to the familiar Popeye tune.

3. This riddling session was recorded among Anglo-American school children in Austin in 1974, as a part of the Texas Children's Folklore Project, supervised by Professor Richard Bauman. Four children were present, two girls and two boys, all aged six years. Interestingly, it was the girls who performed the three traditional items, while the boys collaborated in producing the freshly coined items.

SECTION II

Overview

Methods in Children's Folklore

Brian Sutton-Smith

In this section we begin our study of methods in children's folklore by presenting two studies of children at play. The first is by Ann Richman Beresin, who conducted extensive video fieldwork in a multiethnic urban playground. The second, by Linda A. Hughes, is her report on several years of study of a group of elementary-school girls playing the game of foursquare. Both are unique insofar as these kinds of methods with children have seldom been used, and yet they are also relatively "modern" investigations in their attempt to capture as fully as possible the ongoing performance of being a child player. Subsequently, we present an overview by Gary Alan Fine of the different kinds of methodology that can be used by workers in this field. He announces several ethical principles that should be kept in mind in doing child folklore research and then gives a number of examples that some will find controversial.

But there are two other foci that are predominant in this section also. The first two chapters not only use particular methods but in their content they are about play and games, and for that reason alone could have been placed in the following section on children's concerns. Again, as in chapter 2, they are both about the play of girls. And this in itself is somewhat unusual, there being very few studies exclusively about the play of girls (Sutton-Smith 1979c). In this introduction then we will discuss, in order, some background considerations and references on play, on games, on girls, and on methodology.

PLAY

While games have been a regular subject matter within children's folklore since Newell and Gomme, informal play has not. In general play as a subject matter has more often been the concern of psychologists and to a lesser extent of anthropologists and biologists, as a number of surveys and general studies attest. It is fundamental to realize that despite the record of history and anthropology, showing that play has often been thought of as a devilish or useless pursuit, the cultural attitude to play in this century has been predominantly positive, even idealized. Scholars vie with each other to proclaim the functional values of this or that kind of play, paying little attention to the abundant evidence that play and games are sometimes dysfunctional and dangerous to life, limb, and integrity (Fagen 1980). The preference for the romanticized view of play as voluntary, intrinsically motivated, and fun (Rubin, Fein, and Vandenburg 1983) over the antithetical view of play found in this volume as rebellious, hierarchical, and passionate is a distinction in general between the psychological view of play and the folklore view of play. Clearly there is at present no general widespread acceptance of any particular definition of play, so that it behooves us to pay attention to the multiple meaning the phenomenon has attracted throughout its history. Any adequate definition, for example, would need to take into account the following dimensions.

1. That play is often associated with *irrational, impulsive, and random* behaviors is clear from mankind's addiction to games of chance and gambling and children's practices of many kinds, involving risk taking or "deep play" (Geertz 1973). More money is spent on games of chance or gambling than on any other kind of play. Many contemporary play theorists try to manage this anomaly simply by repudiating the idea that games of chance are forms of play. They may allow that play involves risks, physical risks, loss of victory, and loss of face but not loss of money. Other will agree with R. Caillois (1961) that chance is a fundamental form of play, not to be ignored when play is being defined. If that premise is granted, chance becomes a form of play unlike many others where the players are not in control of their fate and where the outcomes can have a material importance to their welfare. Much the same could be said of professional sports, although admittedly the player's own mastery plays a greater role.

2. The leading culturally acceptable kinds of play from the Greeks to the modern Olympics have been some kind of *physical or intellectual contest* (Huizinga 1955 [1950]). Chance and contest are, therefore, mankind's two major play obsessions . Any play theory that does not begin with these empirical monsters is probably making some kind of special pleading for a select group (for example, children) or a select connotation (for example, a twentieth-century notion of optimal experience).

3. The dominant Western epistemologies since Plato have emphasized philosophy, logic, and science as the sources of knowledge and have discred-

ited the arts, literature, and play as such sources. Play, in consequence, has had in Western society a two-thousand-year history as trivial or useless, or as acceptable only when imitative of the more substantial forms of knowing (Spariosu 1989). In many cultures, on the contrary, play is often seen as a sacral, not a profane or unimportant matter (Turner 1974; Schechner 1988).

4. Some forms of play are associated with trickery and deception as their major modality as in games of strategy and in the many kinds of teases, riddles, and pranks that are recorded in the pages that follow. Such kinds of_deception and flexibility_ seem critical to many kinds of play (Sutton-Smith and Kelly-Byrne 1984).

5. What is missing in much modern play theorizing is the highly repetitive, ritualized, even compulsive character of much play. This is true both of animal and human play. The players seem driven from within by impulse or from without by the motifs of the game. The emphasis on free choice in modern theorizing, if ever appropriate, seems to have more to do with the original decision to begin playing in some situations of contemporary leisure than with what happens thereafter. Most tribal play games are obligatory, not voluntary (V. Turner 1974a). All members of the appropriate age, gender, and skill are required to participate in these important events. Even in modern, solitary play, one can argue that individuals are drawn into their play by important internal compulsions. What is important is not so much their choice of the play as their being driven by the passionate idiosyncratic pleasure to themselves of those choices. It is not the voluntarism but the compulsion or desire that tells us most about the play.

6. The modern view of play as voluntary, free, intrinsic, and imaginative borrows its major connotations from the Romantic movement of the nineteenth century, from which the subject matter of children's folklore also has its source. It was at that time that the faculty of the imagination was conceptualized as a critical human function intervening between rational thought and sensory experience. It was said that the play of imagination was essential to human freedom, delivering mankind from the compulsions of both logic and experience (Spariosu 1989). The modern consumer psychology of freedom as a form of choice probably also plays a part in this rhetoric. The most famous expression of this idealized view of play is that presented by Huizinga in the work _Homo Ludens: A Study of the Play Element in Culture_ (1955 [1950]), a work on play that has had probably more influence on interdisciplinary scholarship than any other in this century. Huizinga states that the "essentials" for play are that it be a free activity, quite consciously outside "ordinary" life, "not serious," but at the same time absorbing the

player intensely and utterly. It must be an activity connected with no material interest, from which no profit can be gained. It must proceed within its own proper boundaries of time and space, according to fixed rules and in an orderly manner. It must promote the formation of social groupings that tend to surround themselves with secrecy. And players must stress their differences from the common world by disguise or other means (1950, 13).

While the notion that such a set of "essential" and static characteristics has been much criticized in the play literature as owing more to the history of philosophical idealism and to the sociology of the doctrine of "Amateurism" than any universal state of mankind (Gruneau 1980; Duncan 1988), it is also devastated by the empirical subtleties and intricacies delivered here in the chapter by Hughes on the game of foursquare. The relationships between the real and the irreal that she reveals are so complex that this Huizinga set of qualitative abstractions of the irreal appears to have a quite limited validity. Even if the message is that the game she studies, foursquare, is play, Hughes says, that is only the beginning of the entanglements and real contingencies and consequences that then emerge. In her account, many of Huizinga's characteristics are at best only a "mask" for what is actually going on underneath. The players are as much constrained by each other and by the social contingencies of their group life as they are free. The struggle for one's group or one's position in the hierarchy that tries to dominate the game is a very ordinary and yet a quite serious form of social life. The girls are most intense about their dedication to the supremacy of their own claque. The profit of their participation is social acceptance and prestige. As she says: "Their actions in the game had clear social consequences outside its bounds." The boundaries of time and space, fixed rules, and orderly manners are not as definite as Huizinga implies but are as mutable as anything else going on. Nothing is beyond the gaming manipulations of the players. The play does maintain and promote social groupings, as Huizinga contends. This is its main cooperative thrust and motive, according to Hughes. When secrecy and disguise occur here it is within the game, rather than in its external relationships.

Perhaps Huizinga would respond to these criticisms of his components of play's formal definition by saying that Hughes's girls are not really playing because they do not play the game for the game's sake and Hughes doesn't analyze the game for the game's sake. Instead, the girls seem to manage the play of the game entirely for the advantage of their own social group. Alternatively, Huizinga might say that Hughes is talking about social matters, not really about games at all, and that these social matters can occur anywhere, not just in games. He might also argue that females aren't much interested in games in any case, so that all we see here is a case of game sabotage. Now it is true, paradoxically enough, that Hughes does not much talk about the acts of the game itself. For example, although she talks about the play action of "slams" at great length she doesn't talk ludically about "slams"; she talks rather about the social control of or subversion of "slams." I think Hughes would then respond that, on the contrary, she could show that the same kind of behavior is quite typical in all kinds of play, including the example she gives from adult ice hockey. What is clear is that from now on any definition of play has to measure up to her informal characteristics as well as those formal ones offered by Huizinga. His formal characteristics can certainly be found to illuminate some play and games here and there, but these characteristics come and go along with many others, and we will probably never be able to ice down and factor these changing clusters of variables until we have many more concrete studies of the kind given us here by Hughes.

7. The theory of evolution has contributed in turn its own argument that play and growth are essentially related, and has led to the great body of rhetoric trying to show that when children play they develop some kind of useful skills. Unfortunately, the biologists are not agreed about what specific functional values play serves in animals, even though the greater neural complexity of the high players, and the relative ineptness of those within primate groups who cannot play, has led to the feeling that there must indeed be some functional connection between play and growth (Fagen 1980). The emphasis that there must be such growth is, however, more clearly rhetoric than science. As mentioned, Western culture has often opted for the view that play is useless rather than useful.

8. Modern psychology has added the empirical finding of relationships between play and novelty, play and creativity (Berlyne 1960). Bateson (1972) has proposed that all these elements of play history (play as irrational, as competitive, as useless, as deceptive, as free, as growth, and as novel) can be reconciled within a theory that sees play as basically a kind of communication used by both animals and humans. It is neither good nor bad in its own right, but serves primarily as a primitive and paradoxical form of expression and communication in which both primary and secondary processes are united in a way that is relatively safe for the participants and unites them in a social community temporally transcending their ordinary ambivalences (Sutton-Smith 1985). Not surprisingly, many of the less civilized of human motives (irrationality, risk, lust, aggression, deception, contest, antithesis in general) here find acceptable expression. Not surprisingly either, this expression is often banned by hegemonic culture and must mask itself and hide itself away in order for

this expression to be achieved. When it is achieved, a considerable degree of license may ensue, as well as venturesome and novel combinations of thought and behavior. It is important to emphasize here also the steadily increasing *solitarization* of affluent children in their play over the past fifty years. Whether one measures that play through children's increased time alone with toys, through their increased time in private bedrooms, in single-child families, or in front of the television set (consequently not on the streets) the predominant fact about children's play in this century as compared with the last, is its solitariness (Sutton-Smith 1985).

For overviews of the functional views of play in the psychological literature we suggest Bruner, Jolly and Sylva (1976), Herron and Sutton-Smith (1971), Sutton-Smith (1979b), Smith (1984), Yawkey and Pellegrini (1984), and Hellendorn, van der Kooij and Sutton-Smith (1994). In anthropology, Helen Schwartzman's *Transformations: The Anthropology of Children's Play* (1978) has become the classic. In biology, the classic is Robert Fagen's *Animal Play Behavior* (1980). Within folklore, the only scholarly works about play are generally about speech play as in the Opies' *Lore and Language of Schoolchildren* (1959), and Barbara Kirshenblatt-Gimblett's *Speech Play* (1976b). In recent years, probably as an indirect result of the feminist revolution in behalf of family history, a number of volumes have appeared on the history of children's play. These are Dominick Cavallo's *Muscles and Morals* (1981), Gary Goodman's *Choosing Sides* (1979), Bernard Mergen's *Play and Playthings* (1982), David Nasaw's *Children of the City* (1985), and Brian Sutton-Smith's *History of Children's Play* (1981a). Bernard Mergen's own chapter in this *Sourcebook* covers these latter volumes. Perhaps the best single source of information on play in recent years has been the publications of the Association for the Anthropological Study of Play, whose annual volumes since 1974 and more recent journals *Play and Culture* (Champaign, Ill.: Human Kinetics Press) and *Play Theory and Research* (Champaign, Ill.: Sagamore Press) have been the most comprehensive sources for students of play. In the past several years, the book-length studies in play emerging from the State University of New York Press have also been a major source.

In sum, we do not have any adequate definition of play, despite our need for such precision in scientific advancement. Play is a fuzzy concept and implies a changing family of concepts that include dreams, daydreams, fantasy, imagination, solitary play, games, sports, festivals, carnivals, television, video games, virtual reality, and so forth; the concepts change as we shift from one culture to another, as some of the above references indicate. Play is like the arts in being the name of a manifold colligation of human activities. It is like sex also in being mainly a source of pleasure and perhaps only occasionally a source of function. Undoubtedly there is some ultimate neural wiring that differentiates this kind of species transformational process from others, but at this point we are not very near to what seems to be its distinctive conative and affective subjunctivity. In evolution, play is a more primordial language than speech but like speech is neutral as to content, and like speech can both be communicative or enactive in function. All we can be sure of is that it suddenly catapults the survival of species from reflexive behavior into enactive contemplation.

GAMES

Both Beresin and Hughes offer us small-group methodology involving various kinds of observations and interviews. More important, however, is the radical shift that Beresin and Hughes announce in the study of games. Building on the work of Kenneth Goldstein and Erving Goffman, these young scholars show that most earlier research has been too limited because it was largely confined to surface descriptions of the action in games, a description confined to the official rules or the idealized statements of the players. Their critique is largely true if leveled at the work in folkgames, though it is less true of game studies in anthropology and psychology, where a much greater sensitivity to the hidden agendas of games is more manifest. An example is Firth's account of the dart game in Tikopia (1930) or in Redl, Gump, and Sutton-Smith's extensive work with the game playing of disturbed children. (Avedon and Sutton-Smith 1971, chapters 18 and 19). Furthermore, without disparaging Hughes's general position in favor of contextualized studies, the quite abstract game categories of Roberts, Arth, and Bush (1959)—those of chance, strategy and physical skill defined in terms of the attribute determining the game outcome (randomness, intellectual decision, or physical skill)—have nevertheless been amazingly revelatory of cultural game patterns throughout the world. Despite the obvious differences in the way in which these games are played in different societies, each has statistically significant relationships with other cultural variables: chance with responsibility training, nomadism, and economic uncertainty; strategy with obedience training; and social complexity and physical skill with achievement training. These findings have contributed enormously to bringing games into serious consideration in modern scholarship within structural-functionalist theoretical rhetorics.

Like Zumwalt in chapter two, Hughes argues that the child players are much more complex than has been assumed in prior folklore study. By not being concerned with the living context of particular games, but of games in general, earlier researchers tended toward a more separatist view of games than appears in the Hughes record, where games are embedded in everyday social interaction. Other recent researchers who have been similarly concerned with the social interaction actually occurring in the midst of games and its similarity to everyday life are Denzin (1977), Schwartzman (1978), Garvey (1977), Von Glascoe (1980), and Goodwin (1985). Goodwin's approach in particular raises the contrast between the treatment of games as frames set apart from ordinary experience and transcending that ordinary experience, and the treatment of games as illustrating the social interaction and communication norms of ordinary experience. The danger of either polarity is that at one extreme we may get the philosophically "essentialist" view of games as illustrated by Huizinga above (Gruneau 1983); at the other, the games are reduced to an epiphenomenon of sociolinguistics (Goodwin 1985). Games need to be accounted for both as continuous and as discontinuous with everyday experience. There is a real sense in which games are a quite "different" experience from everyday life, being where one can safely engage in all kinds of actions that would not be allowed elsewhere; at the same time it is true that the social interaction, the rule systems, and the players' temperaments are also continuous with everyday life.

Furthermore, while on the one hand we can say with Bateson (1972) that the play in a game is "the nip that means the bite but not what the bite means," on the other hand general success and esteem in play count enormously in childhood success. Not to be able to play is to fail childhood. Play and games are not separate from life but are interwoven within it in multiple ways, which are now beginning to be approached by workers such as Beresin, Hughes, and Goodwin. What may be of ironical interest is the possible coincidence between a typical male researcher's focus upon the actions in the games that men play (discontinuity) and female researchers' interest in the etiquette by which the games women play are sustained (continuity). In female researchers it is as if the game might be an incident in a prolonged conversation, whereas in the studies of males it is as if a conversation may be an interruption of an ongoing gaming activity. It has taken the largely female investigators mentioned here to bring these differences to light (Mechling 1985).

For general reviews of prior research and thought on games we can recommend Avedon and Sutton-Smith (1971), Caillois (1961), Goffman (1961b), Huizinga (1950), Jones and Hawes (1972), and Sutton-Smith (1972).

GIRLS

Play and games have throughout Western history been largely the preserve of men and boys. The variety of games available to boys yesterday and of toys today far exceeds in complexity and range those available to girls. Some writers have even suggested that recreation has simply not been central to the life of women and girls in Western society (Wimbush and Talbot 1988). Others have argued that the play of women and girls is much less obvious because it tends to be verbal and private rather than physical and public (Schwartz-man 1978). This would parallel cross-cultural sex differences in the display of humor, where men more generally have access to public and women to private forms of such expression (Apte 1985). The historical sex-role shift within children's folklore, however, is that although the nineteenth century might show more folk gaming activity by boys, the contrary would be the case today. With their greater access to sports organizations, the playground play of boys has become increasingly homogenized throughout the century and increasingly under the sway of modern adult interests in coaching and sports. The relative neglect of girls, particularly girls in lower socioeconomic orders and minority races, has left them as the legatee of children's folklore. Thus jump rope, hopscotch, and jacks continue to flourish with girls, while marbles, momley peg, and prisoner's base are seldom seen in boys' folkplay any longer. When girls' games are contrasted with those of boys (team sports) their games appear to be much less complex, less active, less intrusive, more confined, less competitive (Sutton-Smith 1979b). Some have written that, as a result, girls may not develop the large group collaborative and competi-tive skills that are essential to their success in modern organizations (Lever 1976). The papers by Zumwalt and particularly those by Beresin and Hughes raise questions about that line of interpretation. The complexity of the girls' game organization is a complexity in the meta levels of the play. Several so-cial functions are being accomplished at the same time. It is as if the girls are using the game to reaffirm their small group ties and to maintain their collaborative networks in the midst of competitive activity. They do play the game and abide by its rules, and yet they are also "gaming" the game in terms of their own social rules of nice versus nasty, and further interpenetrating these rules with the preexisting coalitions to preserve their favorites. There is a subtlety here that is ignored in most attempts to compare the role of games in the lives of boys and girls, men and women. Lever's notion (1976) that girls break up their games in the presence of argumentation, whereas boys go on arguing with each other until they finally resume the game again is countered by this evidence of girls' persisting collaboration by Hughes and collateral evidence from Goodwin and Von Glascoe (1980). Given Gilligan's (1982) position of women having a "different voice," a concern, as much with collaboration as competition, there is evidence here of just that concern in the method of play. Still, we need to have care here. Hughes's girls were studied in a Quaker school that had its own particular ethos of cooperation, exercised, one presumes, more coercively than in most places. It could be that some of the differences now appearing between the findings about girls by Hughes and Goodwin and those of Lever might be due to the location of the study and the relative familiarity of the girls with each other. Still, the general fear that girls are underprivileged in their school playground life continues and it is increasingly suggested that this has a lot to do with the way in which the rough and tumbling boys dominate the playground space in a physical way, thus disadvantaging the girls (Thorne 1993).

METHODS

Again in the Beresin and the Hughes studies we have quite intensive investigations of one particular focus. These studies and those of the prior section contrast methodologically with the questionnaire and interview techniques carried out with large numbers of students, more typical in earlier work in children's folklore. Hughes gives some indications of the step-by-step process by which she proceeded from observations to interviews. In these kinds of exploratory studies the investigator cannot know beforehand just what is to be studied, and must remain open to all kinds of possibilities if the ultimate outcome is to be of any potential worth. Going beyond Hughes's assertion that the "*gaming* of the game is as important as the game," Beresin suggests that in a variety of ways the larger community also affects what occurs in the game (for example, commercials, school recess rules). Beresin's use of video and audio recording reveals a host of contingencies beyond the text that are relevant to the life of the game in an urban elementary-school playground. In short, Beresin's study demonstrates the intricate ways in which a game functions in the context of playground space and the players' age, gender, and ethnic grouping, and how the commercial world and the school's rules enter from the outside, thus having their own influence on what goes on. Once again games are not so separate from life as has often been suggested.

What is remarkable about Fine's overview is first his enunciation of a series of principles of ethical procedure (informed consent, credit to informants, lack of deception, lack of harm to subjects) and then his pursuit of examples, many of which some readers will find controversial. With an admirable openness Fine details his own ad hoc responses on a number of difficult questions, and we are left with a clear impression that when one is attempting to gather the often arcane and antithetical lore of children, the phenomena of racism, obscenity, cruelty, gifts, and gender can arise and leave the researchers in a highly ambiguous position between wanting to uphold public morality and retaining the confidence of their informants. Not everyone will agree with the "solutions" that Fine adopts here, but we can applaud his courage in telling us about them, and we can realize that these are very real problems because children's folklore is often about culturally antithetical matters. Subject matter that might be incidental to orthodox socialization research can be central to children's folklore and cause ethical problems perhaps beyond neat solution.

4

DOUBLE DUTCH
AND DOUBLE CAMERAS

STUDYING THE TRANSMISSION OF CULTURE

IN AN URBAN SCHOOL YARD

Ann Richman Beresin

It can be said that within the children's game lies an entire cosmos. For Jean Piaget, the study of marbles uncovered the wrestlings of the moral judgments of the child. For Brian Sutton-Smith, the flexibility of children's games revealed play itself as a process of invention and reversal. For John McDowell, the riddle texts unfolded an array of themes reflecting that of the children's lives as a whole. (Piaget 1965; Sutton-Smith 1976b; McDowell 1979). This paper will examine the complex world of double dutch jump rope as practiced and performed by third- through fifth-grade girls in an urban, public, working-class, racially integrated elementary school yard in Pennsylvania. It will be argued here that the study of the game reveals complex, overlapping cultural worlds, and that if we can attune our eyes to the game beyond the basic game text, that the potential meaning of such study goes beyond the collection of interesting rhymes.

Unlike the classic studies of jump-rope rhymes which have privileged the texts of the rhymes over their actions (Abrahams 1969; Butler 1989; Delamar 1983; Gomme 1894; Newell 1883), in this paper I seek to explore the interaction around the game in addition to its texts, and to examine its relationship to the specific context of the urban school yard. I suggest not only that the school yard shapes the game—and it is indeed inseparable from it—but that the privileging of game texts by collectors of children's folklore has been directly related to the available methodologies for folk-game study. Rhymes and songs were written down by observers of children, and these rhymes were then compared with older rhymes and rhymes from different regions in order to examine cultural uniqueness and distribution. It was not until recently that the invention of the audio tape recorder enabled the student of games to capture verbal nuances, cadence, and rhythm, thus allowing for the preservation of detail beyond the mere text.

Although it is hard to imagine folk song collectors today not using a tape recorder to capture the details of song, the use of visual media in game study is virtually untapped. Like dance ethnography, the study of folk games could greatly benefit from the preservation of actual game performances on film or videotape, in order to examine the game in its rapid-fire detail, and then, perhaps most significantly, to replay the game for the participants to get their expert views.

Prior to the use of audio and video equipment, students of children's folklore made use of historical documentation and oral history to extract meaning from rhymes and games. The Opies' extensive use of written documentation and Sutton-Smith's vast collection of oral history around folk games have emphasized the shifting temporal context of the games (Opie and Opie 1959, 1969; Sutton-Smith 1981a). Although collections from Gomme to the Opies have included musical notation in singing games, the jump-rope literature has, to this day, typically emphasized the poetic meter, and done so sparingly, leaving the impression that jumping rope was something one does perhaps sitting down with one's mouth (Butler 1989). The first in-depth interactionist study of the game of jump rope is Goodwin's 1985 article "The Serious Side of Jump Rope: Conversation Practices and Social Organization in the Frame of Play," which, by using audiotaped transcripts of talk around the games, allowed for the capturing of variation in actual rope games as they were performed in the streets of Philadelphia. Although still emphasizing the verbal interaction around the game and implying that the game of rhythmic foot work, known as jump rope, was primarily a verbal art, this provided a step into the study of the game as more than fixed text. Goodwin's study demonstrated that the game was a framework, as Bateson and also Goffman have suggested, for other kinds of dramas (Bateson 1972; Goffman 1959, 1974). For more on the significance of the inclusion of the larger social context and folk interaction, see Bauman 1982; Briggs 1988; and Kendon 1990.

The majority of the folk-game literature can be said to be either a micro or a macro survey, leaving us with often uncomparable details, as Schwartzman has noted, or acontextual lists of separate events, as is popular in the general books on American children's folklore (Bronner 1988; Knapp and Knapp 1976; Schwartzman 1978). For years the historical comparative methodology when used in combination with fieldwork provided the only way to merge the two perspectives. But, given our relative access to the technology of wide-angle and close-up footage, this is no longer the case. Rivka Eifermann's massive study of Israeli Arab and Jewish children's games serves as perhaps the closest prevideographic model of combined micro and macro study; she utilized hundreds of simultaneous observers within the same play area. (Eifermann 1971, 1979). In this manner Eifermann was able to amass a wealth of detail in survey form and to compare children of different social classes, locales, and ethnicities. Although the published versions of her study do not illuminate the important details of the folk games within its survey, it stands as a marker in the careful examination of the meaning of children's games in the larger culture.

THE USE OF FILM AND VIDEO

Gregory Bateson and Margaret Mead pioneered the use of film in *Learning to Dance in Bali,* as they captured the nonverbal stylistics of a cross-cultural dance lesson. Reels of unedited film recorded the instruction of cultural forms. Film documentary, which by definition is an edited process of graphic storytelling, has its own fascinating history, but what is relevant here is not the use of film and video as storyteller, but rather as presenter of art forms.

Helen Schwartzman's encyclopedic text *Transformations: The Anthropology of Children's Play* includes in its final pages a listing of ethnographic films, ranging from Bateson's own 1954 film of river otters at play to Bess Lomax Hawes and Robert Eberlein's *Pizza Pizza Daddyo* in 1969, a film about a special performance of favorite African American singing games. It is in these films that the details and nuances of the games emerge, and the texts can be placed in perspective, as verbal expressions of bodily forms.

What is being proposed in this paper is the use of film or video as witnessing or documentation, so that when a game is described in transcription or in actual videographic presentation we can see the phenonemon being discussed. Unfortunately, this chapter is itself limited to the paper medium, but with careful description of a few minutes of actual footage, it is hoped that the reader will begin to see and hear details of the game. As microethnographers Adam Kendon and Frederick Erickson advocate, through the use of such documentation we can begin to be more consistent about our study of social phenomenon, in this case the cultural transmission of folkgames, and build upon a collection of real cases involving real human beings (Kendon 1979; Erickson and Wilson 1982). We have the possibility of checking them, and rechecking them, long after the fieldwork is over, in slow motion and in fast forward, with sound on and sound off, to see things not possible in the quick blur of the moment. And we have the possibility of the local experts sharing their specific insights on their own folk process, well after the moment of concentration is past. The very field of children's folklore expands before us, and it has the potential to become the study of children's cultures and folklife, in all its richness and complexity.

When this author set out to study the games and rituals of one multiethnic working-class school yard in 1991, it became clear that one pair of eyes would not be sufficient to capture the details or the larger boundaries of school-yard interaction. In the summer months, the principal of the Mill School was approached for general permission to spend time at the daily fifteen-minute recess periods, and eventually to use audio and video recorders. Permission was granted, as no individuals were being targeted in the study, and student anonymity was assured. General information letters were sent in the fall to one class in each of the third, fourth, and fifth grades on which the fieldwork was based. In mid-fall, a stationary videocamera was placed in a second-floor window facing the school yard, and set on a wide angle. This was done to capture the basic traffic zones and play spaces, and as an aid in the locating of field observations within the larger picture. The principal was supportive and accepted such a plan, as the individual faces were obscured, and he, too, was curious to learn what kinds of interaction were occurring. Recess had been canceled by his predecessor out of fear of school-yard violence, and the status of recess time was uncertain. Such documentation, to be shared with him and his staff at the end of the year in report form, was of interest and had policy implications.

On the first day of school, daily nonparticipant observation fieldnotes were written, and it was not until rapport was firmly established with the children and staff that audiotaping commenced. From January to May, daily audiotapes were made, overtly, with many texts collected, rules explained, interactions noted, and nonverbal information described. It was not until May that the researcher felt ready to ask the children if a mobile video camera could be set up on the school yard to record their games directly. A deep rapport had developed by that time, and their response was universally positive. They were quite excited, as it had been our agreement that they could see themselves on video later in the month. At that time, they were to tell me what they thought about the games they played. Small group interviews with the three classes under study had been conducted since the beginning of the year, so this would be another round of interviewing, also considered a pleasant task.

In sum, the methodology included ongoing small group interviews, daily fieldwork, gradual inclusion of audio recording, seasonal wide-angled videotaping from the second-floor window, eventual close-up or micro-video footage, and then the presentation of samples of the footage to the participants. A total of thirty-three videotapes were recorded, covering twenty-seven days of recess. Nineteen tapes of wide-angled footage were made, and fourteen tapes of close-up micro footage were made. Fifty-one days of live audiotape were also recorded.

One hundred and four third-, fourth-, and fifth-grade boys and girls were observed, audiotaped, and videotaped during recess. Forty-seven children served as native experts and provided their own commentary as they watched themselves at play on videotape. Occasionally younger and older children were included in the taping process, if they were part of a game being studied and played by the core participants.

Although not the first study to utilize videotaped games of children in this manner, this study is among few to share the footage with its participants in this age group (see also Sutton-Smith and Magee's "Reversible Childhood" [1989a], on the use of reflexive video ethnography with young children). Although this is not the first study to examine school-yard games and the transmission of culture in one place (See Parrott 1972; Sluckin 1981; Hart 1993), it is unique in its deliberate emphasis on a public, multiethnic school. Studies of urban play, such as Dargan's and Zeitlin's extensive photo essay *City Play* (1990), capture bits of the cultural crossover visible in urban street games, but in the following transcriptions we can see it emerge in the school-yard games themselves. Such cultural crossover is significant in the light of the emphasis on school desegregation so important to the American public-school system, and in the light of the potential elimination of recess as school policy (Sutton-Smith 1990b).

Several games were studied in this larger exploration of the folklore of the 1991–92 Mill School yard, including the games of the third- through fifth-grade boys. This paper, however, will serve as a window to the specific game worlds of the double dutch players. (For a complete view of the larger study, which includes handball, folk basketball, hopscotch, step dancing, and play fighting, see Beresin 1993.) Double dutch was perhaps the chief peer-led activity for African American girls at the Mill School, and provided a performance focus for a mobile audience of both girls and boys in the school yard.

DOUBLE DUTCH

A fast-paced, polyrhythmic jump-rope style, double dutch utilizes two ropes, typically turned inwards, egg beater fashion, by two girls who have "the ends," while a single jumper executes specific steps to a specific song or chant. It is almost exclusively an African American girls' tradition in urban Pennsylvania, and has been virtually ignored in the jump-rope literature. There has been so little written on double dutch in the folklore literature, and in the collections of African American folklore, that it could even have been said to be skipped over.

Singing game and street game collections like those of the Opies have described larger game traditions but excluded rope singing. American children's folklore, as in the works of Bronner and Knapp and Knapp, have homogenized the ethnicity of their young experts and have given us only single rope traditions; the African American collections of general folklore have rarely even mentioned the lore of young girls (Kochman 1972; Jackson 1967; Whitten and Szwed 1982). With the exception of Jones's and Hawes's *Step It Down* (1972) and *Black Girls at Play* (1975) by Bauman, Eckhardt, and Brady, the games of African American girls have been rendered practically invisible, and these collections have examined only the stepping and clapping forms. Abrahams's *Jump-Rope Rhymes: A Dictionary* (1969), a text called "the most thorough recent compilation of these (jump rope) rhymes for English-speaking children" (Schwartzman 1978, 36), lists a handful of articles relevant to double dutch but, with the exception of his own useful 1963 article, all deal with it only in passing.

Even when only a single rope was available—it was typically one brought by a child from home—it was utilized in the style and steps of double dutch. Two girls hold the ends and turn for the girl who is jumping, and often it is expected that one must turn for someone before getting the chance to jump. Occasionally the "double Irish" or "double orange" style of rope turning was observed; that is the term for the turning of the ropes outward, egg beater style. This method was considered more difficult and sometimes occurred by accident when the turners changed direction. More typically, there would be two turners rapidly turning the rope inward, left, right, left, right, swaying rhythmically to the slapping beat as the rope brushed the ground. The jumper would dance the steps associated with the song or rhyme, and a group of singers, ranging from the turners to nonparticipants to would-be participants, would dance a minimal version of the game in place. This was considered both a fun thing to do while you await your turn, as well as a chance to practice the sequence.

The game was competitive, with jumpers vying to be the one who could not only stay in the ropes the longest but could progress the furthest in the particular rhyme. Someone would shout "She got foot" or "She got turn." And one would often hear the cry of "Saved!" or "Saved by one!" meaning that the person shouting had progressed farther than the jumper who had just tripped on the turning rope. Steps were parodied, styles imitated, and occasionally corrected in order to ensure that the jumper did the job right. Turners could be accused of turning too rapidly, or of intentionally "flicking" the rope to make it more difficult, and high-status jumpers, usually the more skilled fifth and sixth graders, claimed first jumps, while the younger, less experienced players would be the turners. The chance to jump first, and if one was skilled, stay in the spotlight, was often called long before the game started, in the hallway, in the classroom, or at the end of one round for the round the next recess.

Double Dutch Style

Count 2 turns
left hand
clockwise

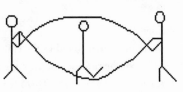

Count 2 turns
right hand
clockwise

Count 1 turn
right hand
clockwise

Count 1 turn
left hand
clockwise

Immigrant Chinese and Haitian girls, representing a small minority of this officially racially desegregated school, also occasionally did individual, single jump rope. Two Chinese girls sometimes jumped in two parallel ropes and, in their own ropes, looped circles around each other, sort of a couple dance while jumping. The Haitian girls sometimes jumped with a second girl in the same small rope, either face to face or back to front. Regardless of form or ethnicity, jump rope was almost always competitive, either by endurance, elaborateness of steps, or frequency of turns.

The European American girls would often be observers of the double dutch games, and on only rare occasions do individual ropes themselves. When they did so they would compete to see which of them could jump the most times. They would not sing or chant, just count the number of continuous jumping steps. One girl was up to 230 and still jumping. Unlike the African American girls, who stayed in one place or rotated their positions slightly to be out of the bright sun, or the immigrant girls, who stayed in one place with their individual ropes, the European American girls did a running jump rope step and would, one at a time, run around the entire yard counting. Like their hand-clap games, which were also done to numbers or counting, the European American girls had clearly distilled their games and no longer had an active jump-rope singing tradition at this school. The singing jump rope game, and for that matter the singing hand-clapping game, had become predominantly an African American tradition.

Many double dutch songs included the same sequence of steps or commands: foot, bounce, hop, turn, criss (crossing), clap, with "foot" or "footin" being the basic right, left, right, left running step over the quickly turning ropes. "Bounce" involved a lighter touch of the foot while doing the running step; "hop" a one-footed airborne step. "Turning" and "crissing" involved the most skill and only the most advanced jumpers were able to do those steps. Taisha, a particularly graceful fifth grader, was known to add turns to all of her steps, in every sequence, just for the challenge of it.

THEMES OF THE JUMP-ROPE TEXTS

Much like the world of themes found in the children's riddling studied by John McDowell (1979), the recorded texts of the rope games were spheres of the African American girls' culture. There were "1,2,3 Halleluya" and "Hey, D. J., let's sing that song," and "Boom Boom Tangle"—a rhyme about rap artists. Plus there were "All in Together," "Hey Consolation, Where Have You Been," "Girlscout, Girlscout, Do Your Duty," "Juice Juice, Let's Knock Some Boots," "D-I-S-H Choice, Do Your Footsies," "Challenge, Challenge 1,2,3," and "Kitty Cat Come, Gonna Be on Time, Cause the School Bell Rings at A Quarter to Nine." But these themes, the ones of religion, region, pop music, of group entry and exit, schooling, and even of plain step display in menu form, were out-shouted by "Big Mac," a commercial for the McDonald's Corporation.

As Cheyna, a fourth-grade African American girl had said, "Want to hear my favorite?" (Snap fingers on down beat. Accented syllables are capitalized)

> Big MAC, Fillet FISH, Quarter POUNDer, French FRIES, Ice COKE, Milk SHAKE, Foot
> Fillet FISH, Quarter POUNDer, French FRIES, Ice COKE, Milk SHAKE,
> BOUNCE
> Fillet FISH, Quarter POUNDer, French FRIES, Ice COKE, Milk Shake,
> HOP
> Fillet FISH, Quarter POUNDer, French FRIES, Ice COKE, Milk Shake,
> TURN
> Fillet FISH, Quarter POUNDer, French FRIES, Ice COKE, Milk Shake,
> CRISS

Big Mac appeared in twenty-three out of fifty-six live unrequested recordings of double dutch chants, closely followed by a follow-the-leader game, "Challenge Challenge, One, Two, Three." This contrasted with the rest of the active repetoire, of which two or three versions were recorded of each. First observed in mid-October, "Big Mac," and its occasional partner "Challenge Challenge," were the only chants jumped at recess until February. Most of the other rhymes did not appear at all until April. "Big Mac" represented forty percent of all the songs sung for double dutch, with "Challenge Challenge" representing thirty percent.The remainder totaled three to six percent, tallying another thirty percent. "Big Mac" was therefore not only the first jump-rope rhyme to appear in the school yard and not only the most frequently jumped, but, as we will see, also the one used for learning how to play the game of double dutch itself.

Collectors of jump-rope games have typically emphasized the antiquity of the games and rhymes, in part because of the archive methodology available, as discussed, and in part because of the inherent romance in finding things old. Paradoxically, the most significant rhyme for the players of this game was the newest one, invented by the McDonald's Corporation as a menu chant. Again and again the local jump-rope experts—the third-, fourth-, and fifth-grade girls—claimed that the "Big Mac" rhyme was commercial and approximately ten years old, but that the game was learned from their mothers and sisters. The dating of this particular chant was confirmed by the national public-relations office of the McDonald's Corporation, which indicated that the menu chants are periodically placed in local papers as part of a contest. It is significant that McDonald's has been a national sponsor of double dutch competitions since the late 1970s and that the only other long commercial text that emerged was in an interview setting: This was "R-E-E-B-O-K do your footsies the Reebok way." Reebok is also a national sponsor of double dutch competitions.

All of the new attempts at double dutch recorded in the school yard were done to the "Big Mac" rhyme. When Isha, a fifth-grade expert jumper, was asked what was the easiest rhyme, she answered, "Challenge Challenge," because "you just had to imitate what was done before you." When asked why the younger girls and the ones new to double dutch started with "Big Mac," she answered, "Because they don't have nothing else." Commercial culture is, for the kids of the school yard, the most basic of common culture.

The commercial is easily learned: It's short, it's quick, and it's "fun in the mouth." Children who are bused in from all sections of the city know it, and children from all economic levels have access to it. It may have been introduced by the corporate-sponsored leagues and ad campaigns and may be a future classic example of the "invention of tradition" (Hobsbawm and Ranger 1983), but it would not have continued if it did not serve some function. Adam Kendon, in his book *Conducting Interaction* (1990), talks about "movement coordination in social interaction" and the use of ritual to facilitate synchrony. The sound bytes of "Big Mac" may well serve to speed up the ritualization of entry into the game in a recess period that allows only fifteen minutes for play in this city.

In an environment where raw materials are inaccessible and consistently removed from the play time, it appears that the African American children from poorer neighborhoods, rich with an oral tradition, are teaching non–African Americans what can be done, as Isha says, "when you don't have nothing else." This is especially true of the play of girls, which is particularly repressed in the school yard by the institution of school itself. Here it is commercial culture that is the common denominator, both within an ethnic tradition and across ethnic traditions.

One of the most relevant texts on this topic is Newell's 1883 book *Games and Songs of American Children*. His essays "The Inventiveness of Children" and "The Conservatism of Children" address the dynamics inherent in play study, the idea of play as being both traditional and transitional, and the idea that children reconstruct and reinvent performances relevant to their complex lives. The key word is relevant. Valuable things are reused and recycled and retold. And as we will see, the repetition of the commercial rhyme may be fixed, but the variation and creativity in the game can be found in the foot work. In a sense, the folklorist begins with the text, but cannot stop there.

VIDEO TRANSCRIPTIONS OF DOUBLE DUTCH

The following are transcriptions of actual footage of the "Big Mac" game, filmed on two days in the spring of 1992. The clips are unique in that they capture two incidences of non–African American girls participating in the African American tradition of rope jumping. The first example is the first time R., a European American third grader, actually got a chance to jump, although she had been a turner of single rope African American games previously. The second example is an overt lesson in the art of double dutch itself, as given by African American girls to an immigrant girl from Hong Kong, and also to a Polish American girl.

The transcriptions show a basic diagram of the rope, and list a running time imprinted on the videotape in hours, minutes, and seconds. In this manner the transcript reflects specific frames of videotape and can be cross-referenced by time. The cross referencing of tapes by time turned out to be rather significant and is a topic to which the concluding pages will be devoted.

The action is described in the middle column, and the audible conversation and game text is listed in the right-hand column. Following the principle, but not the style, of Ray Birdwhistell's kinesics, and Adam Kendon's studies of nonverbal communication, it was considered important to at least describe the basic body motion as a line of communication separate from the speech (Birdwhistell 1970; Kendon 1981). Actual kinesic transcriptions, from Birdwhistell to Laban, have proved too complex for most readers and, in a sense, give us more detail than is necessary for this level of analysis. (For an example of Laban's system of movement notation, see Hutchinson 1977). The advantage of video ethnography is that the footage is there to be reanalyzed over time, as more and more detailed levels of analysis become of interest. (For more on the recent attention given to the body in folklore studies, see Young 1993.)

Example A: The Single Rope Version of "Big Mac"

In the following transcription there is a demonstration of non-double dutch and double double dutch styles utilizing a single rope. Third- and second-grade girls Q., V., and S., all African American, and European American girl, R., took turns jumping. One to two singers sang as they jumped without doing any particular steps. A more experienced jumper joined in and the two jumped at once, facing each other, laughing. The last jumper performed the "Big Mac" steps and sang all the way from foot to criss, with a stop in the middle. She was angry when another girl tried to do joint jumping with her. They jumped past the honking bell, and this episode ended angrily when she was interrupted by another attempt at joint jumping.

Diagram	Time	(Action)	Voices
	10:40:15	(Q. jumps single rope, both feet, not double dutch style)	(no singing)
	10:40:27	(R. gets a turn, jumps, same way)	
	10:40:29	(A second African American girl, V., jumps in; they stop)	
	10:40:30	(R. again jumps)	"No, no,no"
	10:40:36	(Joint jumping of R. and V.)	Laughter of R. and V.

10:40:38	(R. tries again)	"Hey come on!"
10:40:43	(S. begins turn)	
10:40:51	(S. sings to herself)	"Quarter pound-er, french fries, ice coke, milk shake, foot"
	(jumps non-d-d style)	
10:41:02	[school bell rings]	(Sound of bell, screams)
10:41:04	(V. jumps in to joint jump)	
	(A., a turner, yells)	"No, don't jump in."
	(S. gets angry, starts again.)	"Quarter pound-er, french fries ice coke, milk shake, turn quarter pounder, french fries ice coke, milk shake, criss"
	(S. does required motions)	
10:41:17	(V. jumps in; they miss. S. gets angry. R. tries to collect the rope)	

There were several variations from the typical game here, reminding us that no game really is typical. The text itself was varied and began with "Quarter pounder, french fries," creating an even syncopation of the usual rhyme, making it slightly easier for this younger player. The format itself was different as a single rope, not a double rope, was being used. The style was different, as both before and after the double dutch style was being jumped a second player attempted to do joint jumping. And the intensity of the game itself was shaped by the honking of the bell.

Example B: The Double Rope Version of "Big Mac"
Here we have a distinct double dutch lesson, utilizing two ropes. Second-through sixth-grade girls, all African American, were instructing a Polish

American and immigrant girl from Hong Kong in the art of double dutch. Neither got very far, and the sixth grader instructing them had the others learn by standing in the middle of the ropes while trying to turn in a way that made it easy for them. The rope itself was flimsy and the wind was strong. As each got stuck, a young girl in the front jumped up and down shouting "Saved! Saved!" indicating that she had gone farther than these older girls in the overall competition. When the bell rang, there was much shrieking and shaking, and the young immigrant from Hong Kong was knocked over and began to cry.

Diagram	Time	(Action)	Voices
	10:46:50	(K., a second-grade Chinese immigrant is trying to learn double dutch)	"Big Mac fillet fish"
		(she misses)	
	10:47:01	(Second-grade African American girl, who has ends, dances, turns to her audience, and points out)	"Saved! Saved!"
		(Three second graders dance in place)	
	10:47:05	(Polish American sixth grader, enters) (She is told, nonverbally, to stand in the middle and lift her feet in place. She does. The other turner, her instructor, also a sixth grader, is checking to see which rope should be raised first)	
	10:47:12	[Off camera]	"One, two, three."
	10:47:15	(Girl steps in place, in the middle of the rope; fourth grader	Sixth grader says, "Do it again."

	on side nods that the right side should be turned first)	
10:47:20	(She jumps high, both feet together, and misses)	"Big Mac"
		Instructor says "I told you not to come down!"
10:47: 27	[School bell rings] (Girls jump up and down. A nearby boy jumps in front of the camera and shakes his whole body. The Chinese girl gets knocked over.)	(honk)

Of interest in this clip is the capturing of cultural transmission from ethnicity to ethnicity, something undiscussed in the literature of the school yard, and also of the banging of one culture—school yard culture—into that of school instructional time (Pellegrini 1987; Hart 1993). The video camera captured not only the teaching of the game, and the competitive reaction of many of the players as they gauged their relative status, but the context of the school yard and how it affected the players themselves. The visible time stress at the ringing of the bell, which caused one observer to shake while another player was knocked over, thus emphasizes the utility of using a popular culture rhyme, such as Big Mac, for the sake of quick negotiation. At the same time, this also indicates the need to examine the reasons for the bell as a significant part of the game itself.

Both video clips captured variation in game text, language specific to the game, and examples of direct and indirect instruction. Both indicate that there is something about the timing of the ringing of the bell that shapes the game and the interaction around it and that can be said to be unique to the culture of the school yard.

BEYOND THE GAME: THE SECOND CAMERA

In order to make sense of patterns across these games, we can compare similar transcripts, as we did above, and then also comb through the footage of the wide-angle camera. With this survey of the macro footage, an interesting larger pattern emerged.

Consistently, at the end of the recess period, violent interactions were visible on the wide-angle screen. In glimpses from the micro footage, one can clearly see a definite rippling of anger, kicking, punching, and fighting during the transition back to the classroom. Typically within two minutes of the ringing of the bell, an almost palpable tension is trackable. In the macro footage alone, eight out of nine sample tapes showed distinctly violent conflict in the lining up transition, with six out of the eight violent interactions occurring less than one minute before the bell, and the other two occurring within two minutes of the bell. In more than half of the micro footage, taken of a variety of games, there are incidences, indirectly captured, of real fighting or direct violence. And, in all of these images, with only one exception, the tension occurs within a minute and a half of the ringing of the bell.

Victor Turner, symbolic anthropologist, has spent much of his career analyzing the liminal, in-between moments in rites of passage in tribal cultures (Turner 1974a). Although some attention has been paid to transitions in the sociology of face-to-face communication as studied by Goffman, the attention of folklorists to transitional times has been minimal. Some attention has been paid in the folk game literature to opening rituals like counting out rhymes (Goldstein 1971; Opie and Opie 1969; Sluckin 1981; Sutton-Smith 1981a), but these are usually viewed as pregame ceremonies, rituals designed for the facilitation of games' beginnings. The phenomenon under discussion presently is the lack of ritual in the school yard and its associated lack of transition at game's end.

The second camera allows us to see how the context shapes the game, beyond the interaction around the text. The study of the one genre, then, leads to the understanding of the ecology of the larger context. The advantage of extended ethnographic fieldwork in one place is that it allows us to see the significance of the place on the game, and the patterning over time. Superficial folk-game surveys that are panoramic mask larger contextual issues and indeed the crossing of ethnic boundaries, which are perhaps only visible over time. It was apparent that the children needed the entire school year to reach a point of intimacy with each other, as well as the researcher's needing that much time to observe the big picture in that place.

BEYOND THE CAMERA

The camera is seductive, as it seems to provide a form of documentation with less debate and more data. Yet, even when the editing is kept to a minimum and the shots are taken at the widest angle possible, no camera is objective. It too is the manifestation of decisions made by the photographer, ranging from angle to height to light to the very decision as to when the tape begins and ends. The goal is not to present a new objectivity in folk game presentation, but rather to present the performances on the film or video back to as many participants as possible in order to collect yet more stories about the folk games as cultural markers.

When the adults at the Mill School viewed the above clips, several of the staff responded that the tapes were "too happy" and performance oriented, and many shared that they had never observed anything but "misbehavior" during recess. Many of the staff did become nostalgic about the games they had played during their childhoods; they noticed that although some were the same, many were different with new and different rules. The comment about misbehavior is significant, given that the staff generally had the opportunity to come to the school yard only in the last few minutes of recess, which I have documented as the time of most conflict. They indeed missed all the constructive cultural expressiveness and sharing that occurs in the earlier parts of the play period.

When the third- through fifth-grade girls, both African American and European American, viewed the clips, their reaction was delight, pride, and outright laughter. For several it was an opportunity to reflect upon their own process of learning how to "do double dutch." For Tanya, a fifth grader, it was a chance to comment on the misdirection of the above double dutch lesson. She had been taught to enter the ropes and begin by jumping in near the ends. In the above clip, the immigrant child from Hong Kong and, later, the Polish American girl, were being instructed in the middle of the rope, with the rope being turned from a stationary position around the jumper. This was considered to be much more difficult, indicating that there is an acknowledged art to instruction as well as performance.

Tanya, like many of her expert double dutch friends, started learning "how to jump" when she was six or seven years old. Her training, like theirs, was intensely visual and often meant observation without direct participation. "I started in like, first, or second grade, got to be first or second, because my, I never knew how to jump, but my cousin was in, my cousin was in the eighth grade and my cous used to always play rope, and I used to always jump in they (sic) rope, and they used to get mad at me, and kick me back to my line." For Rica, an African American fourth grader, the process also involved the observation of older girls, and had to do with her "catching on" to the new songs. "This is how I learn because when people, like older people start jumping, yeah, like I catched on to the song, like Tamisha's sister, she'd be singing all these bunch of songs I don't know. And the next (day) they'd have two of them."

If we are going to be able to understand the process of the transmission of culture within the boundaries of one place, such as the school yard, as well as across the boundaries of that place, and across time, such reflections can be most insightful. The study of children as tradition bearers within an ethnic tradition and in a multiethnic setting sheds light on children's folklore as an area of cultural study, and not just cultural collection. Their process is more than aural, it is kinesthetic and intensely visual, and our process as fieldworkers can parallel it.

5 CHILDREN'S GAMES AND GAMING

Linda A. Hughes

Most studies of children's folk culture are based on collecting and analyzing items of folklore like rhymes, jokes, riddles, and games. Few describe or analyze the ways children use their folklore, or how its form and function vary across social contexts (J. Evans 1986; Factor 1988). In this chapter, I explore some important conceptual and methodological issues involved in shifting the focus from collecting children's folk games to describing how children play them, and contrast the very different images of children that can emerge from these two types of studies. I will focus first on developing a model of game rules that allows players to mold their games to the demands of social life in particular settings, and, second, on adopting the play episode, not the game, as the basic unit of analysis.

GAMES AND GAMING

Kenneth Goldstein (1971) long ago demonstrated that there can be significant differences between the characterizations of children's folk games and the actual games. In his observations of children playing counting-out games such as the "game of chance," Goldstein recorded a range of familiar practices that were not consistent with common characterizations of the game (Roberts and Sutton-Smith 1962). In fact, much of what Goldstein observed, such as choosing rhymes with different numbers of beats depending on the number of players and tagging on additional rhymes if the initial outcome was not the one they wanted, appeared to be designed to *minimize* the role of chance in determining outcomes. Their activity, he argued, was as much a "game of strategy" as of chance. And to Goldstein that made a difference in how we analyze this game, and especially in how we characterize the experiences and skills of its players. It led him to caution that "the rules which are verbalized by informants and which are then presented by collectors in their papers and books for our analysis and study are . . . the rules by which people should play rather than the ones by which they do play" (Goldstein 1971, 90). Few studies of children's folk culture since have heeded this caution.

Denzin (1977) and Fine (1983) have proposed the term *gaming* to describe the processes by which players mold and modulate the raw materials of their games into actual play. This is not simply a matter of creating variants of the rules of a particular game, as many folklorists have assumed. The same rules can also be understood and used in qualitatively different ways by different groups of players. As Maynard (1985, 22) has observed, "[T]he *way* a rule is used in a group may be more important than the content of the rule in describing a local group's culture. . . . [C]ultural objects [including rules] need to be approached not by way of previously established content but by way of how they emerge and function in the communication patterns of a particular group." Game rules can be interpreted and reinterpreted toward preferred meanings and purposes, selectively invoked or ignored, challenged or defended, changed or enforced to suit the collective goals of different groups of players. In short, players can take the same game and collectively make of it strikingly different experiences.[1]

The conceptual and methodological framework I will be developing approaches children's folk games not as sets of game rules, but as highly situated social contexts in which real players collectively construct a complex and richly textured communal experience. I will begin by describing three different rule systems that are implicated whenever games are actually played: game rules, social rules, and higher-order gaming rules governing the interplay between game structure and social process. I will then contrast several qualities of games with qualities of the social episodes in which they are embedded in the playing. Throughout, I will draw on my own observations of how one group of girls played the common ball-bouncing game foursquare to illustrate implications of the framework being developed for actual studies of child culture. A brief description of this study can be found in the appendix.

GAME RULES, SOCIAL RULES, AND GAMING RULES

The study of children's gaming begins with the assumption that most games in the playing, and certainly the vast majority of folk games in childhood, are, as Goldstein (1971) suggests, something more than a listing of their rules. They are richly textured, and highly situated instances of social life. Playing games is something of a very different order than describing them (Collett 1977), and it always requires that players know something more than the rules of the game.

To play competently and well, for example, players usually need at least some degree of physical or strategic skill (Avedon 1971). They also need social knowledge and skill, however, and it is this aspect that will be of primary concern here. Players incorporate general cultural knowledge about such things as fairness, cheating, and being a good sport or a team player into their playing. They also display a more situated social/interactional competence (Speier 1976) or knowledge about such things as initiating and sustaining complex interactional sequences, and generating and regulating appropriate, responsible group conduct.

A primary goal of gaming studies is to describe how the social worlds of players are integrated with the stated demands of particular games to generate qualitatively different versions of the same activity. They are concerned, therefore, with at least three primary domains of meaning: the rules of the game (the game text), the rules of the social world in which that game is embedded in the playing (the social context), and the additional domain of shared understandings that is generated out of the interaction between game structure and social process in particular times and places (gaming rules).

Gaming rules are not of the same logical type (Bateson 1972) as either game rules or social rules. They are higher order "rules for rules" (Shimanoff 1980) that derive from the need to manage and negotiate the interplay between the game and other contexts of everyday life (Collett 1977). They consist, among other things, of shared understandings about (1) when and how the rules of the game ought to be applied, ignored, or modified; (2) which of many possible interpretations is most appropriately applied to specific instances of the same or very similar actions; (3) which of many possible courses of action is to be preferred over others in particular circumstances; and (4) what are the limits and consequences of acceptable conduct in the game.[2]

Gaming rules, like other rules of the social world, have a critical evaluative dimension, and this is reflected in phrases like "ought to be," "preferred" and "acceptable." We often judge some ways of accomplishing the same ends to be qualitatively different (nice or mean, fair or unfair, respectful or disrespectful), and to view some of them as more or less acceptable or appropriate in particular contexts (Fine 1987; Roberts 1987). This quality is a major methodological concern in studies of children's gaming.

All of this implies, as Goldstein (1971) proposed, that what players do when they play games is not fully described by reference to the rules of the game. This runs counter to the commonsense view that rules, and perhaps especially game rules, tell us what we can and cannot do, and thus needs to be explored in greater detail. In the following section, I will outline an alternative way of thinking about rules, including game rules, that permits the kinds of interpretation and negotiation that characterizes episodes of social life like playing a game.

RULES AND RULES FOR RULES

We commonly think of rules, and perhaps especially game rules, as being rather rigid and explicit, as primarily prescriptive and proscriptive in function (Shimanoff 1980). This contrasts with the perspective commonly adopted by those who describe social life in terms of rules, and who think of rules as highly ambiguous, largely implicit, and essentially productive or generative in function (Harre and Secord 1972; Hymes 1980; Shwayder 1965). The former conception, which has appropriately characterized most studies of games, emphasizes the many ways rules *confine* the range of actions available to players. The latter conception, however, stresses how rules help us *choose* among the many possible courses of action available to us in the course of everyday life (Brenner 1982; Gruneau 1980). It rests upon an analogy with the grammatical rules of language, which do not explicitly and rigidly determine each and every utterance we make, but instead guide our construction of novel yet meaningful and appropriate action.[3]

Game rules do strongly shape what happens within a particular game. To borrow from Goffman (1959) and Burke (1945), game rules typically set a *scene* by identifying an appropriate setting, a set of necessary props, and game roles. They then outline a sequence of game *action,* which is usually cyclical and repetitive (L. Hughes 1983, 1989). At another level, game rules also create distinctive domains of meaning (placing a ball in a hoop, for example, has particular meaning within the context of a game of basketball), and specify a typically nonpragmatic relationship between means and ends (one does not approach the task by using a ladder).

Game rules still leave substantial areas of ambiguity, however, and a central task in gaming studies is to describe players' perceptions of areas of ambiguity and how they go about managing them. Game rules do not rigidly and explicitly specify each and every move in the game or, as Goffman (1974, 24) observes, "establish where we are to travel or why we should want to, . . . [they are] merely the restraints we are to observe in getting there." One does not, as Shwayder (1965, 243) notes, "succeed in getting into a certain chess position by following the rules of chess." There are many ways of accomplishing the same ends within the general "restraints" of the rules (Brenner 1982; Collett 1977; Gruneau 1980).

There is also another very important sense in which game rules provide an ambiguous framework for player action. In the social world, we do not respond simply and objectively to what people do, but rather on the basis of what we take actions and events to *mean* (Harre and Secord

1972). Translated into the world of gaming, this means that while game rules may tell us what we can and cannot do, they do not also tell us what is to count as an instance of that "doing" (Brenner 1982; Harre 1977). The same or very similar actions can be taken to mean very different things to different players and in different contexts of occurrence. This is perhaps the most central tenet of the study of children's gaming. It can be illustrated, however, in the most formal of gaming contexts, professional sports. "(National Hockey League) referees must have an *instinct* for which violations to call and which to ignore. They themselves talk of 'good' penalties (flagrant violations such as tripping the player with the puck) and 'bad' ones (minor offenses such as hooking a player who doesn't have the puck late in a tight game). 'You *could* call a penalty a minute,' says referee Ron Fournier. 'But *that's not what we're supposed to do.* You call a guy for a minor infraction and even though you cite the rule number, he just looks at you and says, "What's that?" *It doesn't earn you respect*'" (Shah 1981, emphasis added).

Competent hockey players and referees are clearly expected to know what a "hook" is, and what are the rules about "hooking." But they are just as clearly expected to know that all "hooks" are not to be understood or responded to in the same way. These types of understandings are often implicit (thus the appeal to an "instinct," not to the rule book for hockey), they are subject to choice and evaluation ("You could . . . but that's not what we're supposed to do"), and they lead to social, rather than game-prescribed, consequences (the referee just cited is concerned about winning or losing "respect," not about winning or losing the game). All of these qualities are clear markers of gaming rules.

Children make similar distinctions. The players I observed responded very differently to the same move in different contexts of performance, and they recognized important differences between what you could do under the game rules and what you were supposed to do as a socially competent member of a play group. Their actions in the game had clear social consequences outside its bounds, and this strongly shaped the meaning of actions under the rules of the game. Their treatment of the common act of "slamming the ball" will illustrate.

In the game of foursquare, as in many other ball-bouncing games, a "slam"[4] is a hard bounce high over the receiving player's head. "Slams" are difficult to return, and thus constitute one way players can try to eliminate another player from the game. They were usually understood to be prohibited by "the rules" among the players I observed.

Despite this prohibition, however, "slams" were very regularly used without any indication that players perceived a game rule to have been violated. This was possible because whether the same or very similar "move" was taken to constitute a "slam" was not a simple matter of assessing what a player had or had not done. At one level, these players felt obliged to consider such things as the heights of the particular players involved, their relative skill levels, and their degree of engagement in or distraction from play. A low, easy bounce might constitute a "slam" to a short, inexperienced, or temporarily distracted player, but not to an older, more skilled, or attentive one.

At another level, players' interpretations of "slams" were also influenced by relationships among the players involved, and even by who would come into the game next if a "slam" was successful. A very hard bounce among "friends" was understood quite differently than the same "move" among members of different social cliques. A "slam" was far more likely to be interpreted as a "real slam," and not "just an accident," when its effect was to bring a friend rather than a nonfriend into the game.

Maynard (1985) has observed that one has to know the history of relationships among children in order to understand what is going on in their disputes. The same is also true of understanding what is going on in their games. There are rules among children for who can appropriately do what to whom (Davis 1982; Eder and Sanford 1986; Thorne and Luria 1986), and actions under the game rules are often interpreted within this additional domain of social obligation and responsibility.

The example of "slams" illustrates this point particularly clearly. The players I observed were generally much more concerned about the intents and purposes underlying a particular performance of a "slam" than they were about the outward form of the action itself. Both were essential to perceptions of whether a "rule" had been broken or not, and to generating an appropriate response (Hughes 1988, 1989, 1993). As noted above, friendships provided a primary context for assessing motives and their appropriateness, and this in turn strongly shaped players' judgments of the acceptability of actions under the rules of the game. Even their terminology for differentiating among different types of "slams" reflected the importance of motive over form. There were "minislams" and "nice slams," and there were "rough slams" and "mean slams." Each called for a different type of response.

Incorporation of social criteria like motives into judgments about the status of particular actions under the rules of the game can have far-reaching consequences. Motives are notoriously difficult to prove and impressions of one's intentions can be actively managed and manipulated. Among the players I observed, this created substantial areas of ambiguity that were then subject to both playful and serious manipulation for strategic purposes.[5] They could, for example, violate the stated rules against such moves as "slams" and still be treated as though they were acting in a totally appropriate and acceptable way. This was because strict adherence to the game rules did not allow them to fulfill critical social obligations to their friends. In fact, the gaming rules, which did incorporate rules concerning the responsibilities inherent in friendships, often required "slams" to nonfriends even when they were very explicitly prohibited by the game rules. I will return to this example below, as it provides a particularly clear illustration of the highly significant subtleties of meaning that can be generated out of the need to reconcile the (sometimes competing) demands of social structure and game structure.

"Basic Rules" and the Rules of Play in Particular Settings

Having stressed the importance of attending to how groups of players *interpret* the rules of their games, I should note that play groups also *elaborate* the rules of their games in ways that are important to understanding the principles underlying play in particular settings. The players I observed clearly distinguished between the "basic rules" of foursquare, those that correspond to the rules presented in printed descriptions of this game, and a variety of other types of rules they used in playing the game (Hughes 1989). The "basic rules" (Table 1) were only a small part of what players listed as the rules of their game (Table 2), and they were not even included among what they called the "real rules" of the game. In fact, these "basic rules" did not seem all that important to players. They almost never mentioned them when asked about the rules of their game, and when queried about them, they dismissed them as "just things you had to do." Players were far more interested in the rules they generated and controlled, and that they could use to introduce excitement, variety, strategy, and fun into the game. These are precisely the kinds of rules and practices that rarely make their way into descriptions of games, despite their apparent importance to the players themselves.

Table 1. The "Basic Rules" of Foursquare

Hit a ball that lands in your square to another square.
Let the ball bounce once, but only once, in your square.
Don't hit a ball that lands in another square.

99

TABLE 2. The "Real Rules" of Foursquare

AC/DC	Front Spins	One-Two-Three-	Slow Ball
Babies	Frontsies	Four	Smitty Rules
Baby Bottles	Getting Out on	Part-Rules	Special Rules
Baby Stuff	Serve	Poison	Spins
Backsies	Goody Rules	Practice	Takeovers
Backspins	Half Slams	Purpose Duckfeet	Taps
Bishops	Half Wings	Purpose Stuff	Teenie Boppers
Bops	Holding	Randi Rules	Three Square
Chances	Interference	Ready	Time In
Comebacks	Kayo Stuff	Regular Ball	Time Out
Country and	Knee Balls	Regular Rules	Times
City	Lines	Regular Spins	Tough Rules
Donna Rules	Low Ball	Regular Square	Trades
Double Taps	Main Rules	Regular Volley	Tricks
Duckfeet	Mean Slams	Rough Ball	Two Square
Fair Ball	Mean Stuff	Rough Slams	Untimes
Fair Square	Medium Ball	Rough Square	Volley Round
Fakes	My Rules	Saves	the World
Fancy	Nice Ball	Saving Places	Volleys
Fancy Day	Nice Slams	Secrets	Volley Regular
Fast Ball	Nice Square	Slams	Wings
Fish	No Outs	Mini-Slams	
Friends	One-Handed	Mandy Slams	

Table 2 also illustrates the widespread borrowing of rules and terms across games, including many practices like "interference" and "time out" that these players assumed to apply to all games. Many of the core concerns of this group of players, like motive, are also apparent in their terminology. Terms like "mean," "nice," "friends," and "purpose," for example, are extensively used to label game "moves." Documenting and then exploring players' categorizations of their game rules provides another important window on principles underlying play in particular settings.

GAMES AND GAMING EPISODES

The basic unit of analysis in gaming studies is the play episode, not the game, so I will now turn to several important distinctions between qualities of games and qualities of the episodes in which they are embedded in the playing. I will begin by contrasting the stated point of the game with the purposes of its players (Sabini and Silver 1982), and then consider, in turn, the significance of nongame prescribed action to the creation and maintenance of gaming episodes, the relative roles of competition and cooperation in the study of games and gaming, and the interplay between the interpretive "frame" defined by the game (Bateson 1972; Goffman 1974) and players' own "framings" of what occurs within its bounds.

The Points of Games and the Purposes of Players

Games usually have some clearly stated objective or point, almost always stated in terms of criteria for determining winners and losers. Participants in the game, however, have purposes, and these may be shaped not only by the game but also by the social matrix in which it is embedded. Players may incorporate a variety of goals or purposes beyond those specified by the activity (Brenner 1982; Collett 1977; Maynard 1985), they may define "success" very differently than the game defines "winning" (Simon 1985), and they may further reinterpret "winning" in light of a variety of agendas that are totally extrinsic to the game itself. Whenever we judge some ways of winning to be more or less appropriate than others, we recognize that success may be something more than meeting the criteria of the game. A six-foot tall adult who defeats a child at basketball, for example, would normally be viewed as winning in a very different sense than when he competes with someone of similar size and skill.[6]

The issue can be much more complex, however. Players' own criteria for success may differ from, and even conflict with, the game's criteria for winning. The girls I observed provided a particularly striking example. They played within a social matrix that demanded that they help and protect their friends, or at least make an appropriate display of doing so. This demand for a *collective* orientation interacted with a game that defined winning as an *individual* achievement in a variety of interesting and significant ways (Hughes 1993). For example, players who played the game according to its rules, competing as individuals, were treated as though they were acting in a totally inappropriate and unacceptable way. They were quickly eliminated from the game. This was because the *gaming* rules among these players required that they sustain the impression that they were "mean" *only* to help and support their friends, not for their own personal gain. Players themselves were quite clear about this discrepancy between how the game was supposed to be played and how it actually was played.

Amanda:[7]	It's supposed to be that you treat everyone equal and no one's your friend and no one's your enemy. . . . Everyone is just all for yourself. That's the way it's *supposed* to be. It's like one on one. It's not *supposed* *to* be team on team.
Janet:	It's not *supposed* to be (laughs).
Author:	You make it sound like lots of times it *is* team on team, though.
Chorus:	It *is!* (laughter) (Fieldnotes 4/27/81. Emphasis in original)

Regardless of what the game rules said, these players still played foursquare like a team game, with groups of friends vying for control of the game. In fact, much of what happened in the playing of this game would be totally inexplicable in the context of individual competition, even though this game has long been categorized that way.

Activities and Episodes

Just as players need not always be primarily oriented toward game-prescribed procedures and outcomes, what happens during gaming episodes need not always be primarily defined by the game. An episode defined as "playing the game" may incorporate a great deal of action that is in no way defined by the activity itself, even though it may be strongly shaped by its occurrence within one type of social episode rather than another. There are many possible breaks in, or overlays upon, the action specified by the game. There may be time-outs, fights, discussions, interruptions, interference, stalemates, "side-plays" and "side-involvements," changes in "keying" or "footing" (Goffman 1963, 1974, 1981). Some are woven into and concurrent with action that is primarily defined by the game. Others are perceived as clear breaks or interruptions in the game (Denzin 1977).

All of this can be ignored when the purpose is to describe games and their rules. When the purpose is to describe how players understand and collectively negotiate a particular instance of gaming, however, close attention must be paid to all of the activity that is woven into and around the game. Players need to understand and manage transitions among activities that are defined primarily by the game and those that are not, and they need to integrate the flow of action across those boundaries in meaningful ways. Many important gaming rules deal with these issues, and a great deal of communicative activity among players concerns their management.

Incidents of this type tend to cluster around transitional junctures in the game, (Erickson and Shultz 1981), as players partition it into emic units (Clarke 1982) of game-related and non-game-related action, and then integrate these units into a single episode of play. Systematic mapping of what can and must occur at these various slots and nodes (R. Lindsay 1977; von Cranach 1982) provides critical information concerning basic principles underlying play in particular settings. Figure 1, for example, illustrates the basic episodic units defined by the game of foursquare. In contrast, Figure 2 more closely approximates the episodic structure as I saw it played in the setting I observed.

Mapping the structure of the gaming episode is critical because it creates highly repetitive units for analysis and because players often display their understandings of actions and events more explicitly during breaks in the game itself (Collett 1977; Grimshaw 1980; R. Lindsay 1977; Marsh 1982). When things go smoothly, the principles organizing an exchange may not be apparent at all. When something goes wrong from players' perspectives, however, or when interpretations of actions seem to require a great deal of management, those principles may become the explicit topic of discussion. When players are accused of inappropriate conduct and must defend or excuse their actions, or when players stop play to fight over the finer points of what did or did not happen in a particular exchange, they provide a window on their own interpretations of actions and events, and on the processes by which they collectively negotiate and renegotiate those interpretations as new circumstances arise.[8]

The players I observed very clearly illustrated the methodological importance of identifying and attending to such "contexts of justification" (Harre and Secord 1972; Much and Shweder 1987), many of which occurred outside of what players perceived to be "playing the game." Challenges to actions under different types of rules, for example, only occurred at certain junctures. Players only selectively challenged actions under some types of rules and not others. And they employed only a few types of responses to such challenges: "I couldn't help it," "I didn't mean to," and "I didn't know." Analysis of the types of accusations that were made or not made and under what circumstances, and especially of the conditions under which they succeeded or failed, provided a very important entree into the basic principles underlying play in this setting. They were an important clue, for example, to the underlying concern for motive noted above, and they illustrated very clearly how the difficulties inherent in assessing motive could be managed and manipulated to a variety of ends.

The form of accusations, denials, and excuses, and especially their contexts of use, for example, helped explain why players were called out for

FIGURE 1. Structural model of the game of foursquare

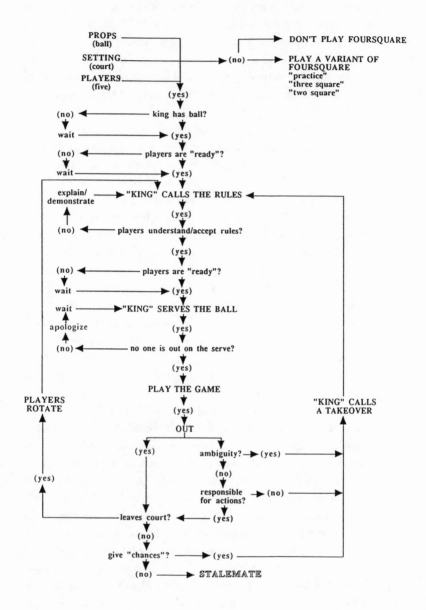

FIGURE 2. Structural model of an episode of playing foursquare

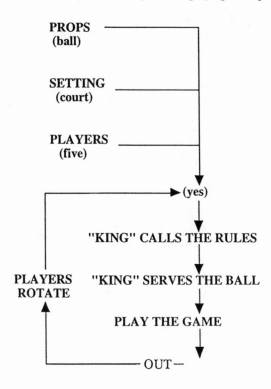

PROPS
(ball)

SETTING
(court)

PLAYERS
(five)

► (yes)

"KING" CALLS THE RULES

PLAYERS   **"KING" SERVES THE BALL**
ROTATE

PLAY THE GAME

OUT —

violating only some types of rules and not others, despite players' stubborn insistence that they would be out for violating any of them. It seems useful to develop this example in somewhat greater detail here, because the principles involved are so fundamental to gaming in this setting and thus critical to further discussion.

The players I observed recognized a number of different types of game rules. Motive was essential to assessing the status of actions under only *some* of them, and their ways of responding to perceived violations varied accordingly. The game rule "no holding" will illustrate the basic workings of this system and how it affected play at many levels in this setting, though all of what these players called the "real rules" of their game operated in much the same way (see L. Hughes 1989 for a full description of rule taxonomy and use among these players).

Players generally understood that there was "no holding." That is, players were supposed to hit the ball, not catch it and throw it to another player. In practice, however, this was interpreted to refer not to the action of catching and throwing but to its context of use. As one player put it, "no holding" means "you can't just stand there and *decide* who to throw it to" (Fieldnotes 5/5/81. Emphasis in original).

> Randi: (In my rules) you can't hold the ball. . . . You have to hit it. You can't pick it up.
>
> Author: Do you really call people out if they throw the ball instead of hitting it?
>
> Randi: Uh huh.
>
> Author: I didn't see that happen too much.
>
> Randi: Well, like if they . . . just grab it for a second and then throw (that's okay). But if they hold onto it, . . . just do it deliberately, like then they're out.
>
> Author: It's okay if you just do it quick, but you're not really supposed to?
>
> Randi: Instead of hitting it like this *(demonstrates tapping the ball with her fingertips)*, they sort of pick it up, sweep it up like this. But you can't really call that holding because they didn't *really* hold it. (Fieldnotes 5/7/81. Emphasis in original)

These players' treatment of "holding" is reminiscent of the NHL referee's treatment of "hooks." The same action could be variously interpreted as "holding," "not holding," or "holding that was not *really* holding," depending upon its context of use and especially on a player's reason for "holding." The "no holding" rule did not prohibit "holding" per se, but only "holding" for particular purposes.

The only type of "holding" that was of serious concern among these players was "holding" that was "*really* mean," that is, "holding" for the purpose of deliberately eliminating another player from the game. Actions that had the effect of getting another player out were "*really* mean" only if they were also intentional, and "purpose stuff" was "*really* mean" only if it was directed at getting a player out. To complicate matters even further, players also interpreted "holding" differently depending upon whether it was used against a friend or a nonfriend. While it was expected that such "moves" would be directed toward nonfriends, their use in exchanges with friends was an extremely serious violation of gaming rules among these players.

In practice, as noted above, distinctions among "moves" based on the perceived motives of players are highly ambiguous. For this reason, players had to monitor and manage their actions very carefully. This was a power-ful constraint on what players could do in the game, but it was also a po-tent resource for play. Ambiguity of intent was actively generated and ma-nipulated to a variety of ends.

For example, the issue in trying to call someone out for violating rules like "no slams" or "no holding" was not simply what a player had or had not done, but whether it was "*really* mean." Would-be accusers were very aware of the likely outcome of making such a serious charge, even implic-itly. "Meanness" would surely be denied, and accusers then had only two choices for further action, neither of which was very appealing. They could either suffer the embarrassment of backing down, and appear "mean" them-selves for having falsely accused another, or they could risk a serious esca-lation of conflict by further accusing the offender of lying. Needless to say, players who understood this system rarely, if ever, took the risk of directly calling someone out for violating these types of rules.

Players who "slammed" or "held" the ball, in turn, routinely worked this system to their own advantage. They acted with relative impunity be-cause they knew that if they were challenged, they did not have to deny that they had done something (though this often was the apparent topic of dis-course). They only had to deny that they had a "mean" purpose ("I didn't mean to"), a "mean" intent ("I couldn't help it"), or the kind of foreknowl-edge necessary for a truly intentional act ("I didn't know").[9] Often they only had to express sufficient outrage that someone could think so "meanly" of them to quite effectively stave off the challenge.

Would-be accusers were clearly at a disadvantage here, and one re-sult was that these players almost never attempted to call someone "out" for violating rules like "no holding" or "no slams" that incorporated an assessment of underlying intent. They were not lying, however, when they steadfastly maintained that players would be out for using these actions in "mean" ways. It was the mode or style of enforcement, not the principle, that was ultimately at issue. Rather than trying to call a player "out" for "slams" or "holding," players usually tried to precipitate a less ambiguous "out" under a different kind of rule, like failing to hit the ball into another square. Since this did not involve an exchange among players and motive thus was not an issue, this was the preferred mode of enforcing the rules. Even if such actions were challenged, the player(s) who precipitated the "out" had recourse to the same highly effective set of excuses and denials: "Gee, I'm sorry. I didn't mean to."

A full explication of this scheme is clearly impossible here. This brief introduction, however, will illustrate how criteria for evaluating actions in the social world, like motive, can constrain and shape player actions in ways that the game rules alone do not, while also providing players with significant resources for playful and strategic manipulation. Games, as they are actually played, invoke multiple frames of reference. Players' choices among various courses of action will be explained only rarely by reference to a single rule or principle. Their decisions usually involve a process of weighing, balancing, and finally integrating a variety of concerns and agendas.

COMPETITION AND COOPERATION

Another important issue arises in the relative emphasis given to *competition* and *cooperation* in studies of games and gaming. Games are prototypically competitive, but social life is prototypically cooperative (Hymes 1980). Cooperation, therefore, is taken as the more fundamental organizing principle in gaming episodes. Participants in face-to-face interaction must coordinate their actions to sustain the exchange and the projected definition of the situation upon which it is based, even though their expected roles, underlying purposes, and motives may be quite different (Goffman 1959). Simply put, a great deal of cooperation is required to sustain a competitive exchange.

I have found this notion to be particularly useful in resolving apparent contradictions between what players say and what they do. Statements may be true about the game yet false about the process of playing it, as well as the reverse. For example, I observed many instances when players collectively ignored violations of game rules or consistently failed to pursue effective strategies for "winning," even though they insisted that this was not what they did or were supposed to do. If I had interpreted these observations purely in terms of the game, I would have concluded (as Gilligan 1982; Kohlberg 1966; Lever 1976, 1978; Piaget 1965; and others have) that these girls cared very little about games and their rules.

When viewed in the context of the gaming episode, however, these same actions were actually indicative of what Borman and Lippincott (1982, 139) have called the "press to maintain the game." Players understood that continuing the game depended on sustaining the social episode in which it was embedded, and further that threats to the episode arose primarily from perceived failures to fulfill responsibilities to friends. They thus cooperated in framing competition in a way that would not threaten the episode, even when this meant bending the stated rules of the game. When players all acted as though the ball landed on a line when it clearly did not, or acted as though a "slam" was accidental when it was clearly quite deliberate, they were often dealing with a critical boundary beyond which strict enforcement of the game rules would have threatened continuation of the episode, and ultimately the game itself.

Attempts to directly enforce those types of rules that required an assessment of motive provided a particularly clear example of players' need to balance the demands of playing the game with the demands of sustaining the episode. Competent players knew that such attempts were far more likely to make players mad than they were to make them out. They also knew that making players mad in certain kinds of ways could, in turn, easily escalate into an extended stalemate in the game (L. Hughes 1988). Regardless of their roles or interests in a particular exchange, therefore, they usually opted for courses of action that were more likely to accomplish the desired outs without also bringing to the foreground inherently awkward issues of who was being *"really* mean." Those rare instances when a stalemate did occur, of course, were highly revealing of what was at stake in those choices, and thus of what these players perceived to be beyond the limits of negotiation.

Frames and Framings

Finally, it is important to make a general distinction between games as *frames,* which mark off what occurs within their bounds from other possible realms of experience (Bateson 1972; Goffman 1974), and gaming as a process of *framing* what occurs within that domain. I have already noted a number of ways that games do act as interpretive frameworks for what occurs within a gaming episode, as well as some important limits to the resources they provide their players. It is still important, however, to place the players, and not the activity they are engaged in, firmly at the center of the gaming process.

The literature on games has often extended the notion that games grant distinctive meanings to actions and events to suggest that they also communicate an attitude toward those events. A shove on the basketball court, for example, is not supposed to mean what it would normally mean if we were not playing a game. This is a type of meta-communication about how actions are to be interpreted that Bateson (1972) has called "the message this is play."

The distinctive domains of meaning constituted by games should not be confused with gamers' communications about such things as "playfulness," however. They do not eliminate the need for players to communicate their attitudes toward actions and events in the game. Games probably do invoke a general expectation that events will not be taken too literally, but frames are notoriously leaky affairs (Goffman 1974). There is nothing about games per se that dictates players' attitudes toward events, whether they are to be understood as fun or serious, competitive or cooperative, work or play, "nice" or "mean," fair or unfair. This is a matter of framing, not the frame.

Regardless of the fact that they are playing a game, players must and do communicate about how their actions are to be interpreted, about how they understand the actions of others, and about the conditions under which everyday meanings will and will not be allowed to permeate the game. While the relative need for such communications will vary with circumstances and events, they constitute another important entree into the principles players use to organize their play. They also can be a highly significant factor in the distinctive quality or style of gaming in different settings (Harre and Secord 1972).

A further elaboration of how the players I observed handled performances of "slams" will illustrate. They often seemed to work very hard to make their play look far more hectic and difficult than it actually was, especially when potentially "mean" moves were being used. Even rather easy "slams" were often accompanied by very exaggerated reaching and bending, cries of "whew!" and mopping of brows. Either I did not understand the physical demands of this game, or players perceived something very important to be at stake in the *style* of their performances.

Something very important was at stake. Players were very concerned that if they got someone out (especially a friend), or even used a move that *could* be interpreted as "mean stuff," this might be understood as a real act of exclusion or personal affront. This could have very serious consequences for the gaming episode, as well as for relationships among players more generally (L. Hughes 1988). They responded by orchestrating the style of their performances toward alternative, more acceptable interpretations.

One way they did this was by overlaying rather easy exchanges with the possibility that their exaggerated performances *could* be indicative of the physical challenges of the game. The logic was rather simple, and again centrally concerned with perceived motive. In the heat of a fast-paced exchange, players might not be totally in control of their actions. If they were not in control, their actions could not be truly intentional and they could not be held fully accountable for their consequences. In short, they could not be "*really* mean."

Players constantly and redundantly reinforced this perspective on events. They followed almost every instance of "outs" resulting from actions that would be "mean" if deliberate with "Gee, I'm sorry. I couldn't help it. I'll get you back in." What might be understood as "meanness" was thus recast as something very different and far more acceptable, an accident. Or just before a "mean slam" they would call out to a friend in line, "Sally, I'll get you in!" recasting that "slam" as "nice" to a friend rather than "mean" to its recipient. Or they would frame accusations of unacceptable conduct in extended "yes you did/no you didn't" exchanges, thus embedding "meanness" in a playful frame.[10]

It is important to note that the purpose of these kinds of elaborate framings of actions was not deceit. The real, and often patently "mean," motives of players were almost always totally transparent, regardless of the style of performance, and highly likely to shape the exchanges that followed. Instead, these elaborate framings of actions derived from the ambiguities inherent in simultaneously applying multiple frames of reference to the same action, and from the resulting need to carefully manage actions that, under some circumstances, would constitute a serious breach of standards for acceptable conduct. As one of my players put it, "You have to do it with style."

GIRLS' GAMES AND GIRLS' GAMING

Having outlined a number of important conceptual and methodological issues in the study of children's gaming, I want to conclude by illustrating how gaming studies might enrich our understanding how folklore functions in the daily lives of children. Just as Goldstein (1971) found a "game of strategy" in a "game of chance," I found some interesting counterpoints to the prevailing wisdom concerning girls and their games in the stereotypically feminine game of foursquare.

The foursquare study focused on a naturally occurring play group, so it is not surprising that gender was a major factor in the gaming patterns identified. This reflects an important bias in children's experiences during the elementary-school years, when boys and girls tend to play in separate play groups and also to play stereotypically different types of games (L. Hughes 1988; Lever 1976, Maltz and Borker 1982; Sutton-Smith 1979c). Since gender is also, and for the same reasons, a highly significant factor in the more general literature on children's games, I will use this area of overlapping concern to briefly illustrate how gaming studies might enrich our current understanding of children's traditional culture.

A variety of differences have long been noted between the types of games preferred by boys and girls, and in the structure of boys' and girls' play groups (L. Hughes 1989, 1993). Girls' games, for example, are often characterized as less complex than boys' games in regard to rule and role structures, and as less competitive than boys' games, more often involving competition among individuals rather than teams. I have already illustrated that at least one group of girls can generate a highly elaborate rule structure, and can play in groups larger than the dyads and triads commonly associated with girls' play. Some further comment is due, however, regarding the notions that girls are not competitive, and that when they do compete, they prefer individual over team competition.

It has been proposed that girls avoid the more highly competitive games common among boys because their potential for conflict and divisiveness is incompatible with girls' concern for establishing and maintaining close, intimate relationships with small groups of friends (Gilligan 1982). The foursquare study suggests that game structure and social structure may not be so simply related. While the players I observed did care a great deal about "being friends" and "being nice," they also competed quite aggressively and quite well. They did not fear or avoid competition, but they did prefer certain *ways* of competing.

Given the current notion that girls avoid competition because of concerns about friends and "niceness," it is interesting that the players I observed used these same concerns to define acceptable, and even expected, competition among players. This was possible because foursquare, as I saw it played, was a large-group activity, often involving a dozen or more players and thus more than one group of close friends. This meant that while players expressed an ideal obligation to "be nice" to everyone, they were, in fact, obligated to "be nice" to only some of the other players. This social structure, and not the structure of the game, provided the primary framework for competition among players.

Appropriate ways of competing in this group rested on players' shared understanding that close friends would "be nice" to each other, helping each other get into the game and remain there. As long as "mean" actions were perceived as *primarily* aimed at fulfilling these important obligations to friends, and only *incidentally* at deliberately eliminating or excluding someone else from the game, players did not regard them as "*really* mean," but as something far more acceptable, "nice-mean." Appropriate ways of competing among these players, therefore, were not a matter of "being *really* nice." They all knew that this was impossible because almost anything you could do to "be nice" to friends was by definition also "mean" to someone else. Rather, it was a matter of avoiding being perceived as "*really* mean." This required very careful management, especially when players' relative obligations to others were subject to subtleties of interpretation.

The examples of players' framing their actions cited above, in which they constantly and redundantly cued the preferred ("nice") interpretation of their actions, reflect the importance of managing this important boundary between "nice-mean" and "*really* mean." When players shouted to a friend in line just before slamming the ball, "Donna, I'll get you in!" the message was: This "meanness" is not "*really* mean" because it is *primarily* oriented toward helping a friend and only *incidentally* toward eliminating another player.

The degree to which competition among these players depended upon their relative obligations to friends and nonfriends is even more clearly illustrated by the following excerpt from fieldnotes. Donna, the "king" in this exchange, is a highly skilled and competent player. Under almost any other circumstances, she would have played a very active role in determining who was out. In this case, however, each of the remaining three squares was occupied by a player to whom she had important, though very different, social obligations outside of the context of the game. The effect was very striking. Donna was unable to compete at all.

> Donna is king. Her younger sister, Pam, is in square #3; a boy she has been trying to impress, John, is in square #2; and her best friend, Sally, has just come into the game.
>
> Donna calls, "times," and takes her sweater off. Her sister, Pam, also calls, "times," and fixes her hair. Someone in line comments, in a slightly sarcastic tone, "*Everyone* has times."
>
> Donna calls, "untimes," and bounces the ball back and forth with John. Her friend, Sally, takes her sweater off and ties it around her waist as Donna has just done. Her sister, Pam, does the same.
>
> Donna finally calls, "Fairsquare," a call meaning that no one is supposed to try to get anyone else out. She serves the ball to John, and then immediately calls, "times." She bends down to fix her shoe laces, as the others bounce the ball among themselves. She calls, "untimes," hits the ball once, and then calls, "times" again, this time to fix a barrette.
>
> Donna fiddles with her hair until Sally tries a slam past John, but the ball lands outside his square. Donna calls, "untimes," and then turns to Sally, "Sorry, Sally, I'll get you back in." (Fieldnotes 4/30/81)

Donna and Sally's teacher cornered me in the lunchroom the next day to ask if I had any idea why Sally was suddenly refusing to speak to her best friend.

In this case, Donna had equal, though different, social obligations to all of the other players. This deprived her of a framework of friends and nonfriends, and she was left with no basis for appropriately competing with the other players. Interestingly, she could not solve her dilemma by frequently calling "times" to fix her hair and fiddle with her clothes. Within the logic of play in this group, it was not simply *acceptable* to "be mean" in order to "be nice" to your friends. It was *expected* that players would "be nice" to their friends. It was "mean" *not* to "be mean," if, as a consequence, you were *not* "nice" to your friends. Sally was angry because her best friend had not affirmed their special relationship by eliminating someone else from the game.

It is also interesting to note the implications of this way of competing for another common notion about girls and their games, that they prefer games based upon competition among individuals rather than teams. The nonteam structure of foursquare is typical of girls' games, but it would have grossly distorted the social reality to describe its playing in terms of individuals vying with other individuals. The friends versus nonfriends framework these players used to set the boundaries for appropriate and expected ways of competing meant that all actions were embedded in, and evaluated within, the context of *groups* vying with other *groups*. These may not constitute teams proper, but neither are they entirely different, at least from the players' perspective: "It's not supposed to be team on team . . . but that's not the way they do it" (Fieldnotes 4/27/81).

This illustrates particularly clearly the significance of Goldstein's (1971) distinction between "the rules by which people should play" and "the ones by which they do play" with which we began this chapter. Any analysis of play in this setting that was based purely upon the stated rules and structure of the game of foursquare would have been highly misleading about very fundamental qualities of its playing. Competition among individuals is not the only alternative to competition between formal teams, and this is a distinction that probably does make a difference. If I were to speculate about girls' apparent preference for nonteam games based upon the current observations, for example, I might conclude that girls do *not* like competition among individuals any more than they like competition among teams. Instead, I might propose that girls, perhaps unlike boys, prefer activities where they, and not the activity, determine who will vie against whom, and where competing parties represent meaningful social divisions rather than more arbitrary or skill-determined groupings. This explanation would appear to be at least as plausible as the rather convoluted argument that girls prefer to act as individuals in their games because they value close friendships.

In this chapter, I have outlined some conceptual and methodological issues involved in shifting our attention from children's games to their playing. Along the way, I have tried to provide support for Goldstein's (1971) concern that studies of what children play, rather than how they play, have limited, and perhaps even distorted, our understanding of children's folk culture. I would add that gaming studies have much to recommend them, both theoretically and practically, as highly useful vehicles for increasing the subtlety and richness of our understanding of child culture. Folkgames are not only both controlled by children and readily accessible to adult observation, they also possess a degree of explicitness in their stated rules that is unusually conducive to comparative study. Few other genres of traditional culture, at any stage in the lifespan, allow such ready access to variations played on the same basic interactional structure across such broad stretches of time and place. Nothing could be more central to the core issue of variation within tradition that stands at the heart of folklore studies.

NOTES TO CHAPTER FIVE

1. Further discussion of interpretive approaches to game rules can be found in Brenner (1982), Collett (1977), J. Evans (1986), Factor (1988), Fine (1987), Polgar (1976), and Roberts (1987).

2. D.D. Clarke (1982) presents a more detailed discussion of probable, permissible, proper, and effective sequences of action.

3. The rule metaphor being applied here is modeled, of course, on Chomsky's (1965) transformational rules of grammar. More detailed discussions of this conceptualization as it is applied to social life may be found in Harre and Secord (1972), Shwayder (1965) and Hymes (1980).

4. Foursquare players' own terminology is enclosed in quotation marks. See L. Hughes (1989) for a more detailed glossary and taxonomy of game rules and terminology.

5. Eisenberg (1984) and Grimshaw (1980) discuss the important functions of creating and managing ambiguity in everyday life. Eder and Sanford (1986) provide examples of its use among early adolescents to manage awkward issues of responsibility for one's actions.

6. See Goffman (1961a) and Csikszentmihalyi (1975) for more complete discussions of this issue.

7. Pseudonyms have been used for all players.

8. Austin (1962, 1970), Goffman (1967), Garfinkel (1967), and E. Hall (1977) present various views on this perspective and its methodological implications.

9. Von Glascoe (1980, 229–30) reports very similar patterns among a group of girls playing the game of redlight in Southern California: "A surprising order to philosophical inquiry emerges in the course of [resolving disputes between the director and the other players]. Arguments are grounded in terms of player-members' doctrines about intentional acts, unconscious acts, "accidental" acts, goal-directedness of acts and fate-determined acts. A summary of director's arguments is expressed in the following paradigm: I saw you move, and your move was intentional and goal-directed, therefore you must return to the start line. A summary of the player's response would be: "I didn't move, and if I did, it wasn't goal-directed, and if it was goal-directed, it

wasn't intentional, and if it was goal-directed and intentional, you didn't see me." Goodwin and Goodwin (1983) and M. Goodwin (1990) also present highly detailed accounts of interaction within and between black boys' and girls' play groups in urban Philadelphia, and report very similar patterns.

10. These kinds of exchanges, and others like apologies ("Gee, I'm sorry") and accusations ("You're being mean." "No, I'm not." "Yes, you are") can also become highly ritualized and thus somewhat detached from their meaning in other contexts of use. They can, for example, become the subject of "playfulness" among players or a topic for comment or gossip among players in line. The interplay of meanings among different contexts of use remains highly significant, however, and can be used to methodological and analytical advantage.

APPENDIX: THE FOURSQUARE STUDY

The examples in this chapter are drawn from an ethnographic study of approximately forty children who played the game of foursquare during recess at a Friends (Quaker) school in the western suburbs of Philadelphia. I observed these children over a period of two years, from the fall of 1979 to the spring of 1981, and subsequently interviewed ten regular players about the game and its playing. I will only briefly describe this study here, and only selectively draw upon its findings. More extensive descriptions of this game and its playing, and of the methodology used in this study, can be found in L. Hughes (1983, 1988, 1989, 1991, 1993).

The Players

The children who were most intensively observed in this study (twenty-seven girls and twelve boys) represented a naturally occurring play group, entirely self-selected by their spontaneous participation in the game of foursquare. The regular players were predominantly fourth- and fifth-grade girls (twenty of the twenty-seven girls observed); they were white and from middle- to upper-middle-class families. Younger and older children, boys as well as girls, were also observed. Approximately twenty percent came from Quaker families.

The Game

I chose to focus on the game of foursquare for a variety of reasons. In the setting observed, this game has been almost exclusively child-initiated and sustained for at least twenty years. It is played year-round with very few seasonal diversions, and it is played in a relatively small, well-defined space at each playing (a court painted on a paved area of the playground). This allowed for easy observation of the same game over an extended period of time with no need for research manipulation. Further, the structure of this game required explicit statements about the rules prior to each round of play, allowing ample opportunity to explore relationships between stated rules and action.

Foursquare is a relatively common and widely distributed playground game. It was apparently first introduced via physical education classes (see Farina, Furth and Smith 1959; Fait, 1964), but it has long been a folk game in many settings (see, for example, Lindsay and Palmer 1981). Foursquare would generally be categorized as an individual (nonteam) ball-bouncing game, with a "leader" or "central person" (Gump and Sutton-Smith 1955), whose outcome depends upon a mixture of skill and strategy (Roberts and Sutton-Smith 1962). In the setting observed for this study, the game would be described as follows:

Foursquare is played with a large, red, rubber ball on a square court, approximately twelve feet on a side, which is further divided into four equal squares. It may be played by any number of players, with a minimum of five (four active players, one of whom occupies each of the four squares, and a fifth player who replaces any player who is out of the game).

The first player to arrive for recess commonly stands in one of the squares, called the "king" square. When the remaining squares have been filled, any additional players form a line next to the court. They enter the game in order as the active players are out, leave the court and join the end of the line.

The game begins when the player occupying the "king" square calls a set of rules for the round of play that follows. Calls may invoke a set of rules ("my rules," "Debbie rules," "regular rules"), or selectively allow or prohibit one or more specific actions ("wings," "no spins," "duckfeet is out"). After calling the rules, the "king" serves the ball to one of the other players by bouncing the ball in that player's square. The ball is bounced from player to player until one of the players fails to return it to another player's square, or until the ball bounces more than once in a player's square. That player is out, leaves the court, and goes to the end of the line of players waiting to get into the game. The remaining three players rotate toward the "king's" square, filling in the vacant square, and the first player in line enters the game at the square farthest from the "king." The "king" again calls the rules and serves the ball to begin a new round of play.

Methods

I conducted this study in two distinct phases (observations followed by interviews), and employed a wide range of methodological techniques. This was designed to allow conclusions based not only upon participant and observer, but also upon a confluence of evidence derived from multiple perspectives on the same events. During both phases, I placed primary emphasis on eliciting children's own terminology, and on understanding events, as much as possible, as they did.

Observations

I observed a total of twenty-three half-hour recess periods; foursquare was played during fourteen of these sessions. I dictated my observations into a tape recorder for transcription and elaboration immediately following each session. All entries included the identities of individual players, their roles in the game, the order in which players entered and left the game, and the rules in effect for each round of play.

I focused on different aspects of play during different sessions. These included patterns of ball movement among the players; the kinds of talk that occurred during play, while waiting in line—in disputes, discussions, and demonstrations; the conditions under which players were "out" versus given a "takeover"; attempts to modify the rules, successful and unsuccessful; and photographic documentation of nonverbal communication. I always paid particular attention to disputes, and to other contexts in which players were called upon to explain or justify their actions. I also informally queried players about events in the game, and occasionally played the game myself. I regularly visited classrooms and the staff lounge to gather information about the broader school context.

Interviews

In the spring of 1981, I intensively interviewed ten girls representing "regular" foursquare players in nine sessions of a half-hour to an hour. I always interviewed the players in groups, rather than individually, to allow discussion among participants, encourage the use of shared terminology, and allow the kinds of side-exchanges that often reveal private meanings. I also took care to interview girls from the same social cliques both together and in combination with girls from different social circles, to encourage challenges to any one interpretation of what happened in the game. Interviews ranged widely over topics spontaneously raised by children, as well as focusing more narrowly on the rules of their game and its play. During the interviews, different groups of players also were asked to sort various game rules, written on 3" x 5" cards, into categories, and to explain their criteria for distinguishing between different types of rules.

Analysis

I used the juxtaposition of information derived from field observation, participant observation, and interviews, along with informant evaluations, to generate and check my understanding of principles underlying the playing of foursquare in this group. I transcribed all observations and interviews and indexed them for mention or occurrence of particular players, rules, and roles, and for instances of disagreements, apologies, excuses, explanations, demonstrations, and instruction in which players were called upon to somehow explain or justify their actions.

I constructed a structural model of the game to represent meaningful gaming units (such as "calls," "serves," and "outs") as a network of nodes (von Cranach 1982) or junctures at which alternative courses were possible. I further characterized each unit and juncture in terms of variations in player actions and players' responses to those variations, in order to identify what players perceived to be acceptable versus unacceptable conduct in the game (see Fig. 2). I also constructed an elaborated glossary and taxonomy of game rules (L. Hughes 1989) based on the rule sorts conducted during interviews (see Table 2). Players' own criteria for distinguishing among various rule types and functions provided additional evidence concerning general principles underlying play. Further analyses focused on relationships between stated rules and action, the rhetoric and politics of actual rule usage, and issues of strategy and style as performances are managed and modulated toward preferred interpretations.

6

Methodological Problems of Collecting Folklore from Children

Gary Alan Fine

Most chapters in this *Source book* cover some aspect of childlore, providing a descriptive account of the range and content of that genre. This chapter has a different goal. I wish to describe techniques for effectively collecting children's lore of all types. While no absolute methodological rules exist, there are guidelines with general validity.

Because of social, cognitive, and physiological differences between children and adults, the techniques of collecting from children are not necessarily identical to the techniques of collecting from adult informants. Unfortunately, the major methodological guides to folklore collecting either do not discuss collecting from children (Ives 1974; Dorson 1972) or only briefly cover the topic (Goldstein 1964, 150–54). General research dicta do not cover the special challenges faced by those who collect childlore.

Folklore has traditionally relied on multiple methodologies. Among the most prominent of these techniques are reminiscences, interviews and diaries, surveys and questionnaires, observation, and experiments.[1] Ideally, a multimethod approach generates the most complete and richest analysis, although researchers recognize that this is not always possible because of financial and time constraints.

In describing each methodology I will discuss its ethical implications, and how research can be conducted to protect the rights and dignity of informants. Three criteria are essential for an ethical research technique: (1) no harm must be done to the subject, physical, social, or psychological; (2) the subject must not be deceived by the researcher, unless such deception is an integral and necessary part of the research; and (3) subjects must be given informed consent as to the nature of their participation, giving them the freedom to withdraw at any point if they choose. Most universities and colleges have established Institutional Review Boards to examine ethical issues in research with human subjects; folklorists affiliated with a college or university who are planning to conduct research should contact these committees to gain their approval before collecting data. Although university regulations differ, committee approval is generally required. Most federal grants require official approval of research procedures, but even unfunded research is often subject to the same requirements. Although this may appear to be an impediment to research, such collective validation of one's research techniques prevents personal desires from obscuring ethical concerns. Further, and of more pragmatic importance, with institutional approval comes university sponsorship and insurance. The University of Minnesota, for example, will cover investigators for up to three million dollars per subject for any injury caused during research. Any folklorist who has transported a group of rowdy children in heavy traffic can appreciate the protection offered.

Research with children poses ethical issues, because children have not reached the age of consent and because of the dynamics of role relationships between adults and children. Most discussions of ethical issues are based on the assumption that the research relationship is among peers; this research fiction cannot be maintained when working with children, however. One must recognize the legitimate roles of parents and guardians.

REMINISCENCES

Many early folklore researchers interested in children's traditional culture have asked adults to recall the games that they played when they were young. While some collectors also observed and interviewed children, they were particularly interested in adult reminiscences. It is difficult to determine the proportion of the games and variants collected by Lady Gomme and W.W. Newell (or for that matter later by the Opies and the Knapps) that derived from adult reminiscences, since none of these admirable works specified their informants, an unfortunate tradition in studies of children's folklore. Memories of the activities of childhood, however, play a major role in most collections of childlore.

Why should this be so? There are reasons, both pragmatic and theoretical, for relying upon adult memories. Pragmatically, adult collectors can easily obtain information from their peers. Often this information is not collected through face-to-face contact, but through correspondence. The folklorist can efficiently obtain a large sheaf of childlore at little cost. Collecting from adults through the mail also encourages a geographically diverse collection of material without the burdens of travel. This research technique also provides data in usable form, as most of the correspondents will communicate in serviceable prose. Since adults are being asked directly for information, ethical issues are minimized.

Collecting from adults also has theoretical justifications. If one believes that folklore is disappearing or disintegrating (Dundes 1969a), folklorists are obligated to collect material rapidly, particularly emphasizing traditions of previous generations. In collecting from parents rather than their children, one uncovers traditions from a time in which children's traditions flourished to a greater extent than they currently do. The older one's informant, it is believed, the better will be the quality of one's data. Although this belief is discredited today, especially in childlore, it explains why reminiscences were considered valuable data.

A second theoretical justification for using adult reminiscences is based on Hans Naumann's theory of *gesunkenes Kulturgut*. Supporters of this theory argue that folklore is transmitted downward in social hierarchies. The traditions of the rich become the traditions of the poor, and the traditions of adults eventually become the traditions of children. This perspective, also no longer widely accepted by contemporary folklorists, suggests that by collecting children's lore from adults one might be able to obtain less corrupted versions of childlore.

A possible third justification for collecting adult reminiscences, although not currently posited, is that this method might generate an important research tradition of its own. By collecting data from adult informants one can examine the structure of memory: How do adults recall their childhood (and "childish") activities and how do they express these activities? While such research is limited because of the difficulty, if not the impossibility, of obtaining records of how adults actually played these folk games when children, we do have descriptive studies of the games of the previous generation.

Despite the potential for research, most folklorists are hesitant to use reminiscences as their sole methodology in any reasonably complete study of childlore, although reminiscences may be a valuable source of supplementary or confirmatory information.

INTERVIEWS AND DIARIES

Interviewing children is a common technique for collecting folklore. This methodology can be as straightforward as a conversation. Children are either asked to explain their traditions (essentially through free association) or they are given topics (games, jokes, riddles) and then asked to expand on these through directed recall. Interviewing can be conducted with individual children or with a group (McDowell 1979), and can be focused on one genre or can cover several. The competent interviewer must establish and maintain trust with the informant. Often folklorists strive to collect traditions that children communicate to each other away from adults (Fine 1981). That proves particularly thorny when one is interviewing children with whom one is not acquainted and when the interview involves "sensitive"—obscene or aggressive—subject matter. Despite this difficulty, important interview studies of children have been conducted (Grider 1976), and some obscene material collected (R. Turner 1974).

Parallel to the interview is the directed performance or the "induced natural context" (Goldstein 1967b; Goldstein 1964, 87–90). In collecting verbal lore such as riddles, one can simply ask one's informants to perform them. But what about folk genres that involve acting—or example, games, and folk drama? Here the folklorist may gather a group of children and request that they demonstrate their traditions. Elizabeth Tucker (1977, 1980a) asked the members of the Girl Scout troop she led to act out stories in order to earn merit badges. Although the girls created the skits, they did so at the behest of the researcher. Researchers who request that children play a particular game transform an interview into a "dramatic" event. This differs from naturalistic situations that characterize observation and ethnography (see the chapters by Beresin and Hughes in this volume).

Folklorists working with children may ask their informants to keep a diary of their activities. This technique is similar to a written interview or reminiscences telescoped in time. Rather than asking the children what they did in the past, they are asked to write down what they do as they do it. To the extent that children take this task seriously, one can examine how folk activity is situated in time and space. The diary writing skills of children may depend on their age, maturity, and motivation, but, if all one requests is a documentary record of who did what when and with whom, diaries are useful.

Ethical issues are typically not pressing when conducting interviews because deception is rarely involved and little or no harm can result. Still, one must consider "informed consent." Fortunately it is relatively easy to explain to child, parent, guardian, and supervisor what one hopes to collect. By describing the genre and the need for studies of children's traditions, both child and adult can be informed of the value of participation. Researchers who wish to collect obscene or aggressive lore, however, may find that their options are limited. Here the researcher may be deliberately vague about what is being collected by stating that what is wanted is the "full range of children's traditions," hoping to gain the child's trust and that the adult will not be within earshot. That skirts the edge of ethical acceptability. Although scholars should not oppose collecting obscene lore, one might object to secretive strategies that do not involve the consent of parents or guardians. One technique of avoiding the problem is to avoid the topic unless one's informant spontaneously raises it. Even though the folklorist does not raise sensitive topics, some parents may object to the researcher who does not prevent the child from expressing this material.

Another ethical problem, perhaps more significant for folklore studies than for any other discipline, is that of confidentiality and attribution. In most social-scientific research, one explains to informants that their names will never be used. Occasionally, when the information is unique (as in psychiatric case studies or life histories of deviants), attribution could harm the informant. In contrast, in the humanities one assumes that all informants will be fully identified and may even share in the royalties. It would be ludicrous to publish a poem or reproduce a painting without identifying the poet or painter—even if the artist is a child. People deserve credit (and financial rewards) for their creations.

A discipline squarely situated between the humanities and the social sciences, folklore occupies an awkward position. Material collected from informants might, under certain circumstances, be harmful or embarrassing, and yet, simultaneously, might be an aesthetic performance that deserves credit. Although folklorists do not often consider the ethical ramifications of their work, a hidden and painful contradiction exists. Folklorists know of the psychological and social harm that even well-intentioned publicity can cause a folk informant, even when that folk informant requests that the work be identified. Fame can be a harsh taskmaster. When one deals with adults, and particularly when one's research focuses on a few informants, probably the most ethically justified stance is to allow the informants to choose how and where they will be identified. The folklorist should point out the foreseeable advantages and drawbacks, perhaps signing a contract that permits remuneration. With numerous informants, informants are not usually identified by name because no individual's contribution is so central as to become the focus of attention.

In conducting research with children the ethical problems are more difficult, because children may not have the competence to foresee what is best for them. In instances in which a small number of children is highlighted (particularly in those studies that emphasize "artistic" genres—a fiendishly difficult judgment) parents might be asked, with royalties placed in a trust fund (royalties, for example, from record albums or published life histories). The standard practice when collecting from many children should be to avoid using the children's names, but only their age, sex, place of residence, and, sometimes, ethnic background. Although this procedure denies "credit," most folklorists would agree that it is an ethically defensible position.

We most frequently think of surveys as election-year devices for measuring the public mood. A survey is essentially a structured interview given to a large number of individuals. Often the questions require the respondent to select among a limited set of options,[2] although that is not always required. Surveys can be carried out face-to-face, over the telephone, or by written respondent responses. The basic advantages of the survey are that one can collect a lot of data quickly and, depending on the circumstances, it can be done with minimal effort. One may employ a random or representative sample. If one asks questions that require numerical answers or that have categories of answers, statistical tests are possible (see Fine 1979a). One should at least be able to compare answers or among groups, something not always possible with the smaller number of participants in most in-depth interview studies.

Some surveys are quite extensive. Mary and Herbert Knapp (1976) in their study of American childlore collected questionnaires from children throughout the United States. An even more extensive national survey was conducted in Finland:

> [I used] as my main material unstructured descriptions written by children and young people. The material used in this book is taken largely from the results of a collective effort organised in Finnish schools in 1969, in which over 30,000 writers, mostly aged between ten and eighteen, took part. This body of material is not suitable for statistical analysis, but it gives a vivid and many-sided picture of the life of the tradition and its social basis. . . . For instance game-starting situations are described in writings which had as title "How a game starts in the yard," play-languages are described under the heading "How I learnt the secret language," and so on. . . . Teachers were asked to emphasise that the writers were free to write as they wished, without worrying about grammar or spelling. They were also asked to write truthfully, directly, without embellishment, and using slang and swear words where necessary. Many of the writers delighted in taking advantage of the freedom thus offered them. (Virtanen 1978, 10)

Although the author does not detail the nature of the sample or how this sample was selected, this research is an example of national surveys found in Europe produced with the support of a national folklore commission. Such studies are useful in delineating the range of folklore within a nation.

Surveys that depend on numerical or categorical responses allow folklorists to estimate how frequently a folk tradition is performed, how many perform or know of it, the characteristics of active or passive tradition bearers, and the occasions on which this tradition is performed. The open-ended questionnaire does not permit this type of systematic analysis, but it does display what is performed and how it is performed. The technique seems particularly appropriate for obtaining texts of short or fixed forms, such as riddles and folk speech.

The basic problem with these approaches is that the researcher is limited by the questions asked. Anyone who has conducted open-ended interviews is aware that the answers one receives direct the next questions. That is impossible in a structured survey in which the order of questions is predetermined. When one is questioning hundreds or thousands of informants, some structure is necessary. A related problem is that questionnaire responses, even those based on open-ended questions, are not very detailed, and one may not learn about what folk traditions mean for one's informant. The researcher receives a description of the content, form, or even context of the folk tradition, but its personal or communal significance is absent.

Researchers must ensure that children understand the questions asked them—an obvious but sometimes overlooked point. It is crucial when the survey is designed to be completed by children of various ages. One wonders about the scope or utility of a questionnaire that can be understood by children between the ages of eight and eighteen. Such a questionnaire must be designed for the youngest child; as a consequence, one loses valuable information from older children.

The ethical problems in survey research are relatively straightforward, similar to those of interviewing. Neither deception nor possible harm are significant dangers, as long as confidentiality is maintained. Informed consent may be a troubling issue for those questionnaires distributed in school, where it is not always possible for parents to be made aware of what their children are asked to complete.

OBSERVATIONAL METHODOLOGIES

The methodologies I have described above ask children (or adults) to talk about things, rather than do things (excepting the performance interview). In contrast, in observational methodologies the field researcher views children interacting in their "natural" environment. A long tradition of observational work in folklore (Newell 1903 [1963]), in psychology (Sherif and Sherif 1964), and in sociology (Thrasher 1927) exists. Indeed, observation is likely the most popular methodology for research on children's culture. Through observation one feels that one is learning what children "really" do, and not what they can be made to do or say.

Researchers conduct observational studies in several ways, enacting different roles. Some researchers, particularly those examining child development, observe "systematically." They have a predetermined category system, and every time a behavior occurs that is covered by their categories, they make a notation. This approach, appropriate for certain research questions, is rarely applicable to children's culture because it doesn't allow researchers to capture the meaning, content, or context of the child's behavior. Category systems are generally too confining for folklore research.

More relevant to the collection of childlore is what has been variously called "ethnography," "participant observation," or "unsystematic observation." Here the observer attempts to capture what children are doing as accurately and as completely as possible (Fine and Sandstrom 1988). The children's performances are rarely directed, so one weakness of observation is that one may have to wait a long time for anything interesting to happen.

The adult "participant" observer can select one of several roles. They include that of the supervisor, leader, observer, and friend (Fine and Glassner 1979; Fine 1980a). The role that the adult researcher adopts affects acceptance by the children as well as the content and context of children's culture that can be observed.

FIGURE 1. Roles of Adult Researchers in Observational Settings With Children

Direct Authority		Present	Absent
Positive	Present	Leader	Friend
Contact	Absent	Supervisor	Observer

From Fine and Glassner 1979, 156.

Supervisor

The supervisor is a researcher who has direct control over the child, yet lacks positive contact. Supervisors may be teachers, camp supervisors, or religious instructors. This role provides access to a relatively limited range of children's culture. The preadolescent must follow the orders of the authority when under observation; as a result, behavior often differs when the supervisor is absent. Children carefully manage the impressions that adults have of them (Fine 1987). Although the observed behavior may be natural, it does not represent the *range* of behaviors of preadolescents. With this research role, many barriers between adults and children cannot be eliminated. Supervisors will be uncomfortable collecting sensitive traditions from children, although they may be confident in their authority.

Leader

The leader is essentially a supervisor with positive contact, a friendly teacher, Little League coach, or scoutmaster. A wider range of childhood behaviors are displayed in front of a leader and, even if preadolescents overstep the line, some tolerance typically will be shown by the adult; the frame of reference for all behavior when the leader is present, however, is that of the adult. Preadolescents may feel constrained to act "politely" so as not to embarrass their adult leader, and that may prevent them from behaving in "naughty" ways, which may be precisely what the researcher wishes to observe. Their respect is a barrier for the adult who wishes to understand childlore.

Observer

The observer role is the inverse of the leader role. The observer is an adult who lacks both formal authority and affective ties, who rather stands back and watches. Although preadolescents do not try to gain this person's approval, neither do they admit the observer into their confidence. Children know which of their activities upsets adults, and may avoid them when strangers are present. Some preadolescent groups watch out for adults and change their behavior accordingly. The pure observer has no more right to observe preadolescent behavior than has any member of the public, although that depends on how the observer presents the research. Because of the absence of positive relations, questioning preadolescents about sensitive topics is difficult. The observer witnesses behavior, but its meanings and motivations are frequently opaque.

Friend

The fourth major research role in observation studies involves befriending one's informants. No adult can ever completely achieve peer status because of age and power differentials. Differences between adults and children can be made less salient, however, leading the adult to the hidden recesses of children's culture. Friendship is conducive to the development of trust between researcher and subject, although this trust must be cultivated. Children may set aside their normal reserve at first, but this extraordinary relationship takes time to develop. During my research with Little League baseball players I was once awarded the title of "honorary kid" to recognize my special role—a role that allowed them to talk freely in my presence (Fine 1987). The key to the friend role is the explicit expression of positive affect combined with lack of authority and a desire not to direct behavior.

Each of these methodological roles has value for collecting children's folklore, although for the folklorist who is interested not only in observing but also in understanding, the roles of leader and friend seem to be most effective. For successful observation, the researcher must witness a wide range of behavior, and must be concerned with rapport, access, and trust.

One's choice of role affects what one learns (Vidich 1955); most observers desire access to as many aspects of the child's world as is feasible. Generally this access can be most easily achieved when the observer is relatively passive and nonjudgmental (Bogdan and Taylor 1975; Schatzman and Strauss 1973). Yet, the observer's presence affects the situation in subtle and unpredictable ways (McCall 1969). Adults are always salient in children's societies by virtue of the authority that is implicit in their status, and all data collected from children by adults must be examined for effects arising from their presence.

Two techniques may increase rapport and access. The first is for the adult to adopt the behavior and values of the children—having the adult become, as much as possible, a peer. The second is for the adult to provide social rewards and material gifts to promote acceptance.

Access Through Adoption of Values and Behavior

Although the adult participant observer can not completely "go native," some researchers mimic the behaviors of the children and adolescents whom they study. Hollingshead describes his classic study of Elmtown's youth: "We 'ganged' and 'clowned' with the adolescents in their 'night spots' and favorite 'hangouts,' after the game, dance, or show" (Hollingshead 1975, 15). He courteously refrained, however, from observing lovers' lanes.

A thin line separates what is appropriate and what is awkward for both parties. In general, one should avoid behaving in ways that make one feel uncomfortable. Because of the difference between acceptable adult behavior and acceptable child behavior, this discomfort may be particularly evident when the adult attempts to be a peer. Children sense whether a researcher seems a good bet as a friend (Cottle 1973a) and can spot those who attempt to be something they are not.

Although being approving, sympathetic, and supportive promotes rapport, a false attempt to be "with it" may backfire. For example, children's slang is hard for an adult to master, and even when learned correctly often sounds strange when uttered by an adult. Knowing what one is not and what one cannot be is as important as knowing feasible role possibilities. Children frequently guard their privacy; by preadolescence, presentation of self is highly developed, particularly as it relates to adults. Any intimate, sharing relationship takes time to develop, and may never develop if pressured.

Access Through Rewards and Gifts

Because of the adult's greater access to social resources, particularly though not exclusively monetary, a researcher may feel that it is advantageous to employ some of these resources to gain rapport with a group. This approach, although sometimes quite successful, may lead to difficulties. There is a wide range of possible services that a participant observer may be expected to perform, including companionship, providing educational expertise, complimenting, sharing food, and loaning money. One useful rule of thumb whenever the researcher is being a friend is that one should behave as any friend might. When in a role with some authority one must be careful to avoid misusing that responsibility merely to curry favor.

Loaning money may produce tension in the relationship (Whyte 1955; Wax 1971), but there are some situations in which loans may be necessary to gain rapport and trust. One must ensure, however, than it not be expected that loans will be forthcoming. I resorted on occasion to claiming that I had no money when it seemed that demands for loans were becoming too frequent. I always insisted that the loan was for that one time only, and thus had justification for refusing to loan money to that same person in the future. Monetary involvement can be a particularly tricky aspect of fieldwork (Goldstein 1964).

There is a danger in providing any services, even those that do not relate to money. Researchers may become accepted for what they can provide, not for what they are. They will be seen as useful only so long as they provide rewards. I learned this when I first studied preadolescents. The first few days I brought sticks of chewing gum, eating them in public view. I was more than happy to share gum with whoever asked. This unfortunately led to an insistent demand for gum that was counterproductive to my research goals. After a few days on which I "forgot" to bring gum, the requests halted.

Trust

The observer of children, like the researcher who studies deviant groups, finds that trust is essential. Polsky (1962) argues that a researcher who wishes to be accepted by a criminal group must (1) be willing to break some laws (if only as an accessory to crimes and not reporting information to the authorities); (2) make his or her contacts believe these intentions; and (3) prove that these acts are consistent with relevant beliefs. In the case of children, the issues are similar. The participant observer may be tested, as I was. This testing appears to be a precondition for acceptance in private settings. One key area in which this testing occurred was in determining my reaction to rowdiness, including shouting, shoving, fighting, insulting, and arguing (see also Glassner 1976). Repressing my adult desire to intervene at the slightest provocation led to my being allowed to observe on other occasions, as an adult who knew how to behave around children.

Once I was in a park with a group of preadolescent boys who, over five weeks, had begun to trust me. Suddenly, these boys spotted a group of girls they did not know, seated around a park bench near a thermos of water. One boy decided that it would be great fun to bother them (and simultaneously pay attention to them). He and his friends plotted to rush them, steal their thermos, and pour out the contents, disrupting their gathering. After a short period of insults between boys and girls (mostly about physical attractiveness), the plan was put into effect—with the expected screaming and squealing by the girls. At one point, several of the girls turned to me (busily taking notes and appearing, I assume, furtively guilty) and asked me, as the adult presumably in charge, why I didn't stop them. This reasonable question placed me in a difficult situation. Since no serious harm seemed to be occurring, and since I felt that the behavior was not being done for my benefit, I didn't intervene and said only that I had no control over their behavior. The boys were gleeful at hearing this and soon left the scene of battle. In retrospect, this occasion was a major step in my acceptance. I indicated to the boys that I would not excessively restrain them and that I knew "my place." After that episode the boys told me more about the aggressive and sexual dimensions of their traditions.

The Key Informant

Often crucial to a researcher's acceptance in a field setting is a "key informant." This individual gives time, energy, and prestige to help the researcher understand what is going on and to get others to reveal sensitive matters. Within a group, several potential key informants may be found. One criterion for this position is that the individual have a central position in the social structure of the group, with access to persons or knowledge. I differentiate two components of the key informant's role: that of sponsor and source. These two components need not necessarily be embodied in the same person. Other adults may help in acting as sponsors in making introductions to children, and low-status children may be the source of much valuable information, although they provide little aid in gaining entry into their group. The convergence of ability and willingness to supply the researcher with information and entry is the mark of the key informant. This willingness is connected to security in one's social position; those boys who became my key informants were socially self-confident, leaders in their group, and gregarious. They were preadolescent teachers willing to suggest how I should act or react; they were willing and able to invert the normal adult-child relationship. Of course, the relationship is not entirely one-sided. These children reap status and material rewards from their association with the adult researcher. One develops exchange relationships that are essentially balanced, even though different sets of commodities are exchanged.

ETHICAL ISSUES OF OBSERVING CHILDREN

Ethnographic observation poses an array of challenging ethical issues. In most ethnographic investigations research depends on relationships among peers—actual or theoretical equals. One cannot, however, pretend that either adults or children would be comfortable in a situation in which equality was expected. The age-based power differential can never be eliminated, and adult researchers must recognize the immaturity of their subjects. Although issues of direct harm or overt deception do not occur frequently, ethical issues do arise, and one must also consider how to achieve "informed consent." I consider three substantive ethical issues in this section: (1) the responsibility of the adult in managing potentially harmful situations; (2) the implications of the adult "policing" or disciplinary role; and (3) problems of explaining the research in a clear and comprehensible fashion. In considering ethical issues, programmatic rules are not possible.

Adult responsibility

When one deals with children in situations without a clear authority structure, difficulties may arise. Children are mischievous, sometimes aggressive, and on occasion cruel. What is the responsibility of the researcher in such situations? Clearly, researchers have an ethical requirement to protect their subjects from harm, particularly since on some occasions the observer's presence increases aggression (Polsky 1962; Glassner 1976). The researcher should remember that other adults, who might intervene if the adult researcher were not present, will refrain, feeling that the children are already under adult supervision. The adult cannot be entirely passive, even though he or she alters the behavior of the group.

Fortunately few situations are clearly dangerous. Boys get into fights, and on occasion girls do as well. Many children's groups contain members whose roles include breaking up fights and minimizing physical danger. In one group one child acted as a sort of medic, providing paper tissues for bloody noses, counseling for hurt feelings, and companionship during emergencies (Glassner 1976).

If a fight is sufficiently serious, however, intervention is necessary, and steps must be taken to end the dispute. If the fight caused permanent damage to one or more participants, the observer would properly have been held morally responsible, and had the observer been in a position of responsibility, legally responsible as well.

Other situations develop that, although not physically dangerous, involve behaviors generally condemned by adult society, such as racism or theft. I vividly recall the day I escorted some preadolescent friends for ice cream, and discovered to my acute discomfort that they were stealing candy. My first reaction was to stop them and insist that they return what they took. This emotion was partly attributable to ethical concerns and partly to the fear that I might be blamed or held responsible. I also realized that if I made a public display I would likely not alter their behavior, but only ensure that I was never privy to such behaviors again. Also, since I had by this time developed attachments to many of these children, I was afraid that I might cause them embarrassment or legal trouble. I decided to do nothing—a decision as much from indecision as from ethical concern, although in retrospect the decision was probably theoretically sound. As we were driving home, the boys discussed what had occurred, and by nonevaluative probing I was able to learn of stealing in other situations. This episode indicates the difficulty of making moral decisions in the fast-moving events of the real world.

Adult policing role

Should adult researchers allow themselves to police children? Authorities often hope that researchers will perform their job for them (see, for example, Geer 1970). No difficulty, however, is more serious than for the researcher not to be considered an "honest broker." The adult must prove him/herself worthy of trust. Most researchers working with children will not be accorded trust at first; only after a series of "tests" does trust develop (see Fine and Glassner 1979; Glassner 1976). In attempting to pass these "tests," however, adult researchers can sometimes get in trouble with adult authorities (Birksted 1976).

The conflict over the policing role is most clearly evident when the researcher desires positive relations with his/her subjects and also avoids authority—the "friend" role. The "observer," because of role distance from the subjects, is rarely asked to police—the "leader" and "supervisor" are supposed to be in charge. Yet, it is essential in all cases that the precise nature of what this policing entails be made clear to all parties. Elizabeth Tucker (personal communication, 1976), for instance, found herself called before a local Girl Scout council for not adequately disciplining her troop (in the council's view), while researching the informal behavior of preadolescent girls. Although Tucker was eventually cleared, the period was difficult for her and the parents were involved. The solution for the researcher who wishes to avoid responsibility seems to be to emphasize to both adults and children that one will not be a disciplinarian, and to back this up with consistent behavior. Whenever the adult feels it imperative to intervene, it should be made clear that the intervention is being done as an individual and not as an agent for society or the institution.

Informed Consent

When the participant observer is not in a formal position of authority (and even in some cases when he or she is) the observer must inform the subjects of the research intent. The need for informed consent has perhaps not been sufficiently recognized in ethnographic research. When the adult has little authority, an honest explanation of the research is important (Konopka 1966). Yet, even a well-meaning explanation will not adequately convey to children what the research entails. When I studied Little League baseball teams I was asked if I were a reporter, writing a movie like *The Bad News Bears*, working with Little League headquarters, or selling drugs. During the time I was in graduate school I could convey the purpose of the research by saying I was a student and this was homework; later I explained that I was writing a book. These did not answer every question, but they seemed to work reasonably well (Fine 1987).

Although explanation is important, actions are the main way in which children learn the intentions of the researcher. The questions asked, and the situations during which the observer scribbles furiously or fiddles with the tape recorder, provide clues to the observer's true interests. Informed consent, while a goal toward which we must always strive, will frequently be only partially achieved.

EXPERIMENTS

A common methodology in several branches of the social sciences, most particularly in psychology, is the experiment. Although this approach is not common in folklore, some suggest that experimentation is an appropriate methodology for folklorists (Goldstein 1967a). Most experiments that have been conducted using folkloric materials have been attempts to understand the processes of diffusion (Bartlett 1932; Anderson 1951; Wesselski 1931). Some of this research, such as that of Wesselski, used children—in his case elementary school girls. The girls were told a version of Sleeping Beauty, and in their retellings changes were noted, confirming Wesselski's view that oral tradition was unreliable and that the Märchen were transmitted primarily in printed form. This experiment, and others similar, do not directly address children's folklore content, but they do indicate the processes of change of children's lore.

More directly relevant to the use of experimentation for researching children's traditions is Paul Gump and Brian Sutton-Smith's examination of differences between "high-power" "it" roles and "low-power" "it" roles— the games black Tom and dodge the skunk respectively (Gump and Sutton-Smith 1955). Applying folklore to social work, these researchers discovered that when children played high-power "it" roles they were more successful and, further, that the high-power "it" roles led to fewer negative reactions of the playing group to "it," and more positive feelings by the "it" toward himself. This was particularly significant for those less skilled boys who were able to exploit the power edge inherent in the high-power "it" role. Gump and Sutton-Smith could make these claims because they had each child play every role and could compare reactions across conditions. This suggests the greatest value of experiments: They permit the systematic comparison of groups under controlled conditions. One observes what happens in a speci-fied situation, and compares this to a second situation with other constraints. Experimentation also permits a random or systematic selection of subjects, often permitting statistical analysis.

An experiment is a technique in which the researcher manipulates some aspect of a subject's experience in order to determine its effect on be-havior or attitudes. Typically this involves comparing groups that each have been manipulated, or comparing a manipulated group with a nonmanipulated group—a "control group." The major weakness of this approach stems from the experimenter's control—it is an artificial situation, since it is controlled or created by the researcher. Before we become too criti-cal, however, remember that the same is true of surveys and interviews. For some research problems, such as comparative analysis, and for confidence based on statistical evidence, the experiment may be the research method of choice.

Much has been written about the ethical problems faced by experi-mental researchers. Since experimentation has not become a major meth-odology in folklore, it is not necessary to discuss the ethical issues in the same detail as discussed for interviews and observation (see Diegner and Crandall 1978). I have previously discussed how one obtains informed consent with children and their guardians, and this problem remains in experimentation. Although potential harm may exist in experiments (particularly in the medical domain), it is unlikely that any experiment on children's folklore is likely to cause irreparable damage. Of more significance is the legitimacy of deception. I refer to the situation in which the experimenter tells his/her subjects that the experiment is testing something that it is "really" not testing, or simply (as in the Gump and Sutton-Smith study) not informing subjects that they are being studied.

Even when harm is not done directly by the experimental deception, some researchers (for example, Kelman 1968, 211–21) argue that deception by its nature raises serious ethical problems. Is it justified to deceive a person, even though during the experiment that deception will not cause harm? Doesn't deception, once uncovered, undermine the confidence that subjects have in social science and decrease the confidence that individuals have in one another? Do we wish to reside in a world in which deception is legitimate behavior? Are we willing to do to our friends that which we willingly do to our subjects: lie, make promises we don't intend to keep, deceive them about the purposes of the interaction, or withhold relevant information? The experimenter-subject relationship is, after all, a real relationship. Some answer these fears by pointing to the value of the information which is gathered. Further, some of the information might not have been collected if the subjects knew what the experimenter wanted. If the children tested by Gump and Sutton-Smith knew that the researchers were interested in influencing their self-esteem through the games they played, they might have responded quite differently. Further, some might question whether deception is uncommon or harmful. Might deception not be viewed as similar to the "little white lies" that are common elsewhere in life? Children, in particular, are deceived constantly for their own good. A child who is told not to go out at night because "the goblins" may get him or through similar threats (see Widdowson 1977) is being deceived and may not be disabused of these ideas for years. No fiat can be given, but it is essential that the researcher consider the special responsibilities that derive from the choice to work with children.

CHILDREN AS COLLECTORS

Although most childlore has been, and will continue to be, collected by adults, children can serve as folklore collectors in certain circumstances. The most publicized example of this phenomenon is the books, edited by Eliot

Wigginton, in which high-school students collected lore from neighbors of their North Georgia school. There has been debate as to the proper role of these books and their imitators in folklore (Dorson 1973a; Wigginton 1974), but there is no doubt that they teach adolescents (as later projects taught preadolescents) the value of traditional beliefs. Although Dorson and Carpenter (1978, 7) refer to these works as "journalism projects," and a scholarly reader must admit that the quality of the material collected varies, some of what is collected is valuable material for even the serious scholar. Children can also be used to collect material from themselves and from their peers and near-peers. This collection, when the young collectors are properly trained, can be useful in obtaining information that might be very difficult for adults to collect. While I didn't use preadolescents as miniature ethnographers, I did loan several of them my tape recorder, and was rewarded by tapes about fartlore and a recording of a mutual masturbation session.

One must insure that preadolescents do not become exploited in this process. They should not substitute for paid workers as a means of cost saving. Second, they should be properly trained, and their research tasks should be limited to the extent of their training—limits that vary with age. Third, children should not be placed in situations in which they could be in danger or in which they might be condemned by others. This means that the collection of obscene lore by children is ethically sensitive. If the child is being instructed to collect obscene material, or material which the investigator has reason to expect to be obscene, then relevant adults should be apprised of this fact. Some adults, including some researchers, feel that children should not be involved in collecting—or performing—obscene material, while others are more open. Both positions should be respected. Despite these problems, children can collect folklore, with educational benefits to themselves and to the discipline.

The Challenge of Collecting Children's Folklore

The other chapters in this volume demonstrate that the study of childlore is an intellectually important pursuit. My purpose is different. I hope to demonstrate that conducting folklore research with children is difficult, but that these difficulties can be surmounted. Whether the issue is the development of trust, the linguistic or intellectual barriers between children and adults, or the special ethical concerns that come from working with minors, unique problems affect this scholarly domain.

Childlore can be collected in several ways. No one methodology has the monopoly on success or failure (see Table 1). The best research is often research that does not rely on a single methodology, but blends several techniques, a process of "triangulation." While there is much more to be said—about the subtleties of working with children of particular ages, for instance—texts can only get us so far as methodological tools. Ultimately no piece of writing can ever substitute for the personal experience.

TABLE 1. Selected Advantages and Disadvantages of Childlore Methodologies

	Advantages	Disadvantages	Examples
Reminiscences	1. easy to collect 2. historical or comparative	1. not current, based on recall 2. words, not behavior	Knapp and Knapp 1976 Gomme 1894.
Interviews (induced performances)	1. sense of what respondent feels 2. ability to ask follow-up questions	1. time-consuming 2. talk, not natural behavior	Piaget 1932 Tucker 1980a
Surveys	1. large or random sample 2. statistical or comparative analysis	1. surface answers 2. no follow-up 3. talk, not natural behavior	Fine 1979a Virtanen 1978 Knapp and Knapp 1976
Observation	1. inexpensive 2. natural context	1. lack of control 2. often unsystematic 3. labor-intensive	Fine 1979b Goldstein 1967b
Experiments	1. control of variables 2. statistical or comparative analysis	1. artificiality 2. ethical issues of deception	Gump and Sutton-Smith 1955

NOTES TO CHAPTER SIX

1. I exclude historical or library research, not because it isn't valuable for learning about childlore but because the methodological and ethical issues are substantially different from those discussed here.

2. Participants in surveys are typically called respondents rather than informants.

OVERVIEW

CHILDREN'S FOLKLORE CONCERNS

Brian Sutton-Smith

Children's folklore concerns are much more extensive than have been dealt with in folklore research. Indeed most of the chapters that follow in this central section of the *Sourcebook* are about some form of speech play, whether rhymes, songs, riddles, teases, or tales. This focus on speech play has its source in the predominant influence of the "ethnography of speaking" in folklore research during the past twenty years. Increasingly in those years folklorists have become interested in the social basis of human communication in how individuals actually communicate at particular times and places and in particular groups. Within folklore the leading scholars who have had the greatest influence, direct or indirect, upon the chapters that follow are Dell Hymes (1969), Richard Bauman and Joel Sherzer (1974) and Barbara Kirshenblatt-Gimblett. In particular, *Speech Play* by Barbara Kirshenblatt-Gimblett, (1976b) with its bibliographic survey of children's play, word play, nursery lore, nonsense and limericks, play languages, numbers, letters, mnemonics and counting-out rhymes, names, humor, joking relationships and interaction, verbal contests, obscenity, proverbs and speech metaphor, riddles, and narrative and audio-visual resources, is the essential forerunner and complement to the present volume. A central position must be given also to John McDowell's *Children's Riddling* (1979), which is unique in establishing the viability of research on a particular genre of a particular children's group. With only recent exceptions (L. Hughes 1983; Beresin 1993), most researchers of childhood consider the notion of dissertation work on, say, the jump rope of one group of players, or hopscotch, or jacks of a specific group too trivial to be worth considering. McDowell's *Children's Riddling*, and Hughes's and Beresin's work in the present volume, exposes the scholarly shallowness of that adultcentric attitude.

   A comparison of the chapters in this section with the list of topics in the introduction imparts some idea of what is missing here, and probably as well what has been little researched. In approaching play and games in this work only by two highly specialized studies, we ignore the many different ways of playing and games that children get into, though this omission is in part remedied in the writing of Mergen, Bronner, and Mechling in the next section. Still, we lament the lack here, for example, of material on folk games, pregame ceremonies, rule making in different kinds of games, cheating, or performances in singing games, or play and games on traditional occasions. In the meantime the reader might find some solace in the very useful popular accounts of Mary and Herbert Knapp in *One Potato, Two Potato: The Secret Education of American Children* (1976), *Children's Games in Street and Playground* by Iona and Peter Opie (1969), and Bronner's *American Children's Folklore* (1988).

Although the chapters that follow give us many examples of language play, as well as useful categorizations and accurate knowledge of different kinds of playful discourse, what we miss here is any real certainty about the underlying relationships between play and language. This is not, of course, the authors' fault, because there is very little research on these relationships. What the literature does seem to support is the finding that in the earlier stages of childhood the phonological elements of language are played with much more than are the semantic, syntactic or discourse elements. As children develop, however, these later elements increasingly become the center of attention. Thus younger children will enjoy the nonsense of sounds, but by seven or so years, children in their riddling are showing increasing interest in word meanings and their proper categorization, as well as using words in a social way as in teasing rhymes and pranks. Barbara Kirshenblatt-Gimblett has suggested, following Jacobsen, that much of the younger children's verbal play with sounds, although different from adult poetry, may well be its precursor. The fine ear for the sounds of the language that such play may exercise, prepares one for poetry and literature, she says.

What stands out in the chapters that follow with respect to all kinds of verbal play, sounding or otherwise, however, is the strong association that it has with the children's own peer socialization pressures (dominance, scapegoating, legislation, judgments, teasing, pranks, parodies). The record of these chapters is that the usage of the children's verbal play is largely antithetical to the normative intentions of adult socialization in behavior or words. It is an example of the paradoxical way in which the children express their hostilities, wishes, and resentments with minor danger to themselves.

What is generally overlooked in much theorizing about language and play relationships, is that play language has a semiotic character quite different from that of language as used in everyday communication. Put briefly, the more players play together, the more elliptic and esoteric their dialogue tends to become. They develop their own peculiar argot, which would certainly not score very well on standard measures. In short, the important connection between play and language may have to do with the peculiar uses of language in play, rather than between play and language ordinarily considered. Play is itself a caricatural or schematic activity ("galumphing" as some have called it), and when it moves verbally it breeds analogous and elliptic usages of language perhaps familiar only to those who are a part of the "secret" community. Thus the ellipsis may serve to mask what is going on from those who are not members of the play group. Perhaps more important, the ellipsis helps to establish the players as a play community (McMahon 1993).

In the chapters that follow, Sullivan introduces us to children's songs and rhymes, the latter of which he prefers to think of as poems, because they resemble the poetic character of the ancient oral traditions of the world. He distinguishes here also the tradition of parental nursery lore (lullabies) from the traditions of children themselves (game lore), which in adolescence includes parodies of nursery lore. He categorizes children's rhymes in terms of the functions they fulfill in children's groups for legislating outcomes, as an expression of power relationships between children, for making judgments about each other, and for humor's sake. In all of this material the formative role of the verse is the establishment and maintenance of the peer group in its antithetical relationship to adult conventions; in particular, the use of phonology for the political purposes of childhood subversion rings out loud and clear. It is intriguing to think of the subculture of childhood moving against its adult overlords with a phonological armamentarium.

Roemer's work on riddles benefits from the sociolinguistic tradition to which we have referred above. Those who work within this tradition in this *Sourcebook* are generally at an advantage from a systematic and scholarly perspective in the interpretation of verbal folklore. In addition, works on riddling are themselves a well-established tradition of study within folklore and anthropology yielding a rich and suggestive array of cross-cultural as well as modern examples. What is even more important is that Roemer supplements the work of Hughes in showing riddling sessions to be an ongoing achievement at any moment and not merely a reflex of tradition. Indeed tradition is the historical context of the semantic field from which the social construction of the riddling occasion begins. As Denzin argues, children's worlds of play are "not just given or handed down; rather they are constructed worlds that are interpreted, negotiated, argued over, debated about, compromised" (1977, 173). It is a contrast between papers presented throughout this sourcebook that those who deal only with recorded folk-lore necessarily make folklore appear to be a matter of tradition, while those who have gotten their material directly from children's behaviors see folklore very much as a matter of life construction. Newell's paradox may owe some of its power to the difference between these approaches to scholarship.

Tucker deals with children's narratives and legends and in doing so clearly indicates some of the enthusiasm that adult collectors borrow from their child informants. Indeed her chapter is in some ways most valuable for her own "contagious" involvement with her subject matter. She also manages to blend an interdisciplinary tolerance for psychological studies of children's stories with a more folkloristic analysis of the traditional tales and legends that she and others have collected. That "psychological" explanations should serve mainly for the stories of younger children and folkloristic explanations for the tales and legends of older children seems largely to be an accident of scholarly history. What Tucker's essay does demonstrate is that although oral storytelling does not compare in its strength among children with the transmission of games, jokes, and so forth, it is nevertheless still more alive than one would expect from what goes on in schools. Literacy has diminished but not entirely quelled the traditions of child-transmitted stories even in the urban middle class.

With Jorgensen's essay on pranks, the verbal subculture of the first three chapters in this section begins to take on a more physically antithetical character and with it a cultural seriousness perhaps lacking in the others. Unlike rhymes, riddles, and tales, pranks overflow into adult culture in an intentionally disruptive fashion. This is partly due to their practical rather than their verbal character, and partly to the older age of the perpetrators. Jorgensen's central thesis is that pranks, tricks, teases, and taunts are about victimization, some of which are malevolent and deceptive and some of which is straightforward and benevolent. More important, however, she describes their roles as kinds of communication. Her article brings into the forefront some of the less pleasant aspects of the culture of childhood. In thinking of children's folklore as the material for the politics of childhood we need to accept that there is often nothing very romantic about these politics.

In sum, in these four chapters we have a sample of the concerns of children. Here are some of the phenomena that are part and parcel of the way in which they establish relationships among themselves and in so doing differentiate themselves from other age groups in modern society. As with any subculture, some of their effort goes into building their own culture and some of it into distancing their culture from the conventional adult culture around them.

7

Songs, Poems, And Rhymes[1]

C. W. Sullivan III

Poetry and song came early in the development of Western civilization. Much of what we have left to us of the earliest literary works—*Beowulf* or Homer's *Iliad* and *Odyssey*—were probably recited in chanted or sung versions long before they were written down, their forms and places fixed forever in literary history. Moreover, many of the narratives that came later, whether they appeared first in oral or written form, were poetic rather than prose. So, too, poetry and song come early in the lives of children. Before they begin to attend school and even before they begin to associate with others of their own age, they encounter poetry and song. Although much folklore is passed on from older to younger members within a generation, whether it is a generation of college students or a generation of "neighborhood kids," the first traditional poetry and song a child hears comes from another generation. The child's mother, usually, but more often these days the father, too, talk, chant, and sing to the child almost from the moment he or she makes an appearance in the world. Much of that chanting and singing is functional; that is, it is used by the parent to soothe a restless child, to help the child drift off to sleep, or to interest the active or fussy child. One parent that I know sang the alphabet to her older child when he was small so that he would hold still while she changed his diapers.

Much of what is sung to these infants is not traditional in the truest sense of the word. For example, because it is most often associated with school—day school, kindergarten, or first grade—few will argue that the alphabet song is a traditional folk song. And many of the other poems or songs recited or sung to children have known, often literary, sources. Folklorists, at least, know that "Mary Had A Little Lamb" was composed by Mrs. Sarah Josepha Hale of Boston in 1830, and many of the other popular rhymes recited to young children—"Little Miss Muffett," "Peter, Peter, Pumpkin Eater," "Little Jack Horner," and the rest—can all be found, with some small variation from text to text, in any Mother Goose collection. But there are two other considerations here. First, this material, even though its sources are known, is often passed on in the same dynamic way that all folklore is passed on. Parents often recite poems or sing songs to their children that were recited or sung to them a generation back by their own parents; all of the parents busily passing on "Mary Had A Little Lamb" are transmitting it in a traditional way to their children and, perhaps indirectly, to future generations. And if there is a Mother Goose collection of nursery rhymes in the house, it is probably consulted by the parents for additional material or it is available for the pictures that will amuse children when they are being read to or when they are looking at the book themselves.[2] A second, and more indirect, consideration here is that the material the child learns is not forgotten as soon as the infant or tot stage is past. Children will remember this material and use it, for example, as the basis for parodies in future childhood years. And the rather innocent Mary and her lamb becomes

> Mary had a little lamb,
> She also had a bear;
> I've often seen her little lamb,
> But I've never seen her bear.[3]

In oral tradition, of course, the "bear" of the last line of the parody is heard and understood as the homonymous "bare." Thus, there is a great body of material which, if not originally of the folk, is certainly passed on in the same manner as any other traditional materials and which does, shortly, become intertwined (as in the parodying of "Mary Had A Little Lamb") with materials (in this case, the parody) that are generated within and transmitted from older to younger members of the folk group—children.

It is also important to note here that the parents are teaching by example. That is, when they recite or sing to the child, the child gains an awareness of poetry and song as genres and learns about rhyme and rhythm, stanzaic or episodic structure, and all of the other technical details, inherent and unnamed, of oral performance. The child will then be able to recite, chant, and/or sing his or her own material at a later date. Thus equipped, the child ventures forth into a peer group where much of the activity will involve, if not be governed by, poetry and song.

SONGS AND RHYMES AND OTHER THINGS

Organizing and studying almost anything in the humanities according to generic classification can be quite difficult because generic boundaries are never absolute and seldom firm. At best, generic categorization allows us to group similar things together on a temporary basis, recognizing all the while that almost all of those things could just as easily be placed in one or more other categories. This is especially true of folklore, where songs and legends and tales often blend together, where foodways are sometimes inseparable from festivals, and where songs and poems seem to be a part of almost everything.

Traditional gatherings and festivals and celebrations almost always include songs, and if the official song is not traditional among the folk celebrating the event, there is often a parody of the official song. "Happy Birthday," though perhaps not a traditional folk song, is certainly passed on to children in traditional ways as a part of the birthday celebration, and there is no question that the parody of the birthday song,

> Happy Birthday to you,
> You live in a zoo,
> You look like a monkey,
> And you smell like one, too.

is the property of the children who sing it, and others like it, after or in lieu of the official song. The same situation occurs on other days as well. On St. Valentine's Day, one can hear innumerable parodies of "Roses are red . . ." initiated by and passed on among children, and the parody of that well-known rhyme is seldom as complimentary as the original. While children are playing at having a wedding, or attending the event itself, they are likely to sing or chant

> Here comes the bride,
> Short, fat, and wide,
> Look at her wobble,
> From side to side.

And should a child try to pull an April Fool joke on someone on April 2, he or she is likely to be told, "April Fool has gone past/You're the biggest fool at last."

Children's games, too, often include rhymes and songs. In fact, before the game is started, there may be a counting-out rhyme to determine who bears the onus of being the first one to be "it." Of all game rhymes, probably the jump-rope rhyme has been the most widely collected. The Knapps suggest that, while jump-rope rhymes exist about almost every topic (school, movie stars, politicians, history, bumblebees), the largest group concerns familiar domestic situations:

> Mable, Mable, set the table,
> Don't forget the salt, vinegar, mustard,
> *Pepper!* [the signal to turn the rope as fast as possible]

Or,

> Mix a pancake, stir a pancake,
> Pop it in the pan.
> Fry the pancake, toss the pancake,
> Catch me if you can. (Knapp and Knapp 1976, 112)

There are also numerous songs and rhymes for clapping games and for ball-bouncing games. For all of these, the song or rhyme serves to regulate the rhythm so that the rope turners and the jumper, the clappers, or the ball-bouncers, are all operating in unison. Some other songs, songs that date back to the play-party games of the Colonial Puritans, actually structure the dramatic action of the game itself. In a game called "Marriage," a boy and a girl pledged their love to each other in song, passed under an arch of their friends' arms, declared themselves married, and then kissed (Newell 1963 [1883], 59). More well known and still collectable from children outside schools or day-care are "London Bridge" and "Ring Around the Rosie." And there are many others.

Simpler play situations may also be structured by songs or rhymes. Among a child's first experiences with rhyme may be "This Little Piggy Went to Market," a rhyme taught by the parent to establish a routine in which the child is entertained and also in which the child is encouraged, as he or she gets a bit older, to participate. Later, a child may be taught this verse:

> Here is the church,
> Here is the steeple,
> Open the doors,
> And out come the people.

In this routine, various hand and finger positions are used to represent the church, the church with a steeple, and the people coming out of the church.

Although much of children's riddling seems to be moving away from the true riddle and toward the riddle joke, there are still rhymed riddles and catch questions that can be collected. One of the early riddles a child learns is a rhymed catch question:

> Railroad crossing
> Without any cars;
> How do you spell it
> Without any *rs*?

A similar riddle from Australia asks

> I saw Esau
> Sitting on a seesaw,
> How many Esaus is that? (I. Turner, Factor, and Lowenstein 1978, 103)

The first line of that riddle is certainly familiar to folklorists as the beginning of the title of *I Saw Esau: Traditional Rhymes of Youth* by Iona and Peter Opie (1947). In their *Lore and Language of Schoolchildren* (1959), the Opies recorded more than a dozen different rhymed riddles collected from British children. Riddles in this group included the Sphinx's riddle to Oedipus as told by a fifteen-year-old girl; "four riddles which were known in Charles I's time; and four which, although apparently traditional, do not seem to have been previously recorded, for they are not included in Archer Taylor's comprehensive collection" (Opie and Opie 1959, 76).

The same power that poetry and song have always had in religious ritual manifests itself in children's rhymes and songs that are a part of their superstitions or folk beliefs. Small children who want to play outside during inclement weather know enough to chant

> Rain, rain, go away,
> Come again another day,
> Little _____ wants to play.

When it is not raining, the children walking along the sidewalk know that stepping on a crack can "break your mother's back." And there are many, many jump-rope rhymes that, besides setting the pace for the game, are also ways of divining the future. There are jump-rope divinations to reveal the name of a girl's boyfriend or future mate, the number of rooms in the house the girl will live in when she is grown and married, the number of children she will have, and much more.

The initial or seminal studies of children's folklore recognized or assumed that rhymes are a part of games, celebrations, superstitions, and the like. W.W. Newell's *Games and Songs of American Children* (1883), Lady Alice Gomme's *Traditional Games of England, Scotland, and Ireland* (1894–98), and Norman Douglas's *London Street Games* (1916) all contain rhymes—although rhymes are mentioned in none of the titles and only Newell's title mentions songs. Of that era, Henry Bolton's *Counting-Out Rhymes of Children* (1888) is one of the few that addresses itself directly to rhyme, even though the rhymes are, in essence, rhymes that have to do with games.

More recent collections—with or without any accompanying criticism—have followed this lead. Popular and well-known collections of children's folklore such as Iona and Peter Opie's *I Saw Esau: Traditional Rhymes of Youth* (1947) and *The Lore and Language of Schoolchildren* (1959), Sandra McCosh's *Children's Humour* (1976), Mary and Herbert Knapp's *One Potato, Two Potato* (1976), Turner's *Cinderella Dressed in Yella* (1969), Iona and Peter Opie's *The Singing Game* (1985), and Amanda Dargan and Steven Zeitlin's *City Play* (1990) have tended to present rhymes as a part of or related to some other subgenre of children's folklore, especially games, and have commented on the rhymes themselves, as rhymes, in only very limited ways. Turner, for example, suggests that rhymes associated with games tend to live longer than rhymes of amusement because "game-rhymes are required to regulate the games themselves, while amusement-rhymes are able to respond quickly to cultural changes and the events of the day—and are at least in part required to do so" (Turner et al. 1978, 162). And the articles of children's rhymes and songs that have appeared in various journals have, by and large, followed suit.

We know, however, that the spoken syllables "na-na-na-na-na" mean very little to a child; whereas, those same syllables, chanted or sung with the proper inflections, have the power to enrage that same child. More complex versions of the same taunt, such as "Johnny kissed a girl" or "Johnny is a fairy" seem easier to account for. The name-calling or action-attribution could certainly annoy or anger "Johnny," but that does not account for the ability of the nonsense syllables to do the same thing. It is too easy to say that the hearer imagines the unarticulated words; there must be something in the intonation, the rhythm, the actual notes themselves, that contributes to this effect.

A few critics have tried to assess the rhymes as rhymes, and these critics have, at the very least, come up with some interesting findings. In an afterword to *A Rocket in My Pocket*, Carl Withers suggests that the rhymes are important precisely because they are rhymes: "Through the ancient device of rhyme, and the still more ancient ones of furious alliteration and assonance, they have found a way to comment incisively, and often in a very up-to-date fashion, upon the world of adults and upon other children" (Withers 1948, 204). Dorothy Howard, the very next year, commented on the "progressive intricacy of the rhythm patterns" of ball-bouncing rhymes collected from chronologically sequential age groups (Howard 1949, 166). And in 1966, in an article in *American Anthropologist*, Robbins Burling compared nursery rhymes in English, Chinese, and Bengkulu in some detail and found them all to have a four-line, four-beats-per-line structure. Burling suggests that more in the way of comparative metrical analysis needs to be done before the universality of this pattern can be ascertained, but he does speculate about what such a universality might imply. "If these patterns prove to be universal, I can see no explanation except that of our common humanity. We may simply be the kind of animal that is predestined not only to speak, but also, on certain occasions, to force language into a recurrent pattern of beats and lines" (Burling 1966, 1435). Burling wonders if this translinguistic patterning might also be true, at least in part, of "sophisticated verse." More recently, efforts like Howard Gardner's articles, especially "Metaphors and Modalities: How Children Project Polar Adjectives onto Diverse Domains" and "Style and Sensitivity in Children," and Peter Jusczyk's doctoral dissertation, "Rhymes and Reasons: The Child's Appreciation of Aspects of Poetic Form," have dealt specifically with the poetic devices children use and appreciate, devices whose technical functions children will not be able to understand until much later in their lives. In *American Children's Folklore* (1988), Simon Bronner treats songs and rhymes in their own chapters and discusses the social and cultural functions of the various subgenres, especially gross rhymes and song parodies, arguing that children's folklore adapts to changing times and comments on them (page 27).

RHYMES AND SONGS: A FUNCTIONAL BREAKDOWN

The definitive work on the nature of rhyme and the manner in which children's traditional rhymed and metered materials achieve their effects has yet to be written. Until it is, perhaps the closest we, as critics, can come to an understanding of how poems and songs work is to observe their effects on the people who use them. In other words, what we can do is look at the ways in which poems and songs function as children's folklore.

As I have already mentioned, many rhymes and songs have been collected as parts of children's games where they function as *legislation*. That is, many of the rhymes and songs found in games are there as the legislative structure; rhymes and songs are used to set up the game and get it under way, to provide the rules for the game as it proceeds, and in some cases, to determine the winner of the game when it is concluding. Before many games can get started, it is often necessary to decide who will start the action—who will be the first jump-rope jumper and who will be the twirlers, who will be the first "it" for hide-and-go-seek or tag, or who will make the first move. Often this is determined through a counting-out rhyme. A counting-out rhyme is necessary in this situation because the first person to be "it" is doing so freely and not as a penalty for having been caught or having his or her hiding place spotted. The counting-out rhyme provides an impartial way of selecting the first "it." And some critics have suggested that the counting-out rhyme dates back to much more serious and ancient sacrificial situations in which the person chosen was a literal sacrifice in a religious ritual. In any case, the children accept the results of the counting-out rhyme as impartial and impersonal so that there is no suggestion that the first "it" is of any less stature than the other people in the game.

As the game gets started, a chant may be employed to state some of the rules. When the "it" person for hide-and-go-seek finishes counting, he may add, still in the chanting rhythm of the count, "Anybody around my goal is it!" This means that no one can stand right beside the spot where the counter is standing and tag the goal just as the counter finishes. Should the counter forget to add that qualification, however, that rule does not apply.

Any game may contain everything from the occasional rule-making rhyme to a rhyme or song that continues as long as the game is played. Within chasing and hiding games, one can occasionally hear rhymes like "One, two, three/Get off my father's apple tree" (Knapp and Knapp 1976, 29). This two-line rhyme is designed to get a "base-hugger" to leave the safety he is sticking too close to. If the "it" in hide-and-go-seek stays around the goal too long, he is likely to hear the chant, "Goal sticker, goal sticker/ _____ is a goal sticker." These rhymes and chants, however, appear only sporadically in chasing and hiding games; in games of jumping rope, rhymes and songs often last for the duration of the game. It must be noted that these rhymes and songs may have only one or two verses and then a long enumeration that continues until the jumper misses and is, temporarily anyway, out. Rhymes like

> Cinderella, dressed in yella
> Went downtown to buy some mustard.
> On her way her girdle busted,

> How may people were disgusted?
> 1, 2, 3, 4, . . .   (Turner et al. 1978, 14)

could, conceivably, go on forever, counting off the number of times the person jumping makes it successfully over the rope. In fact, the twirlers usually increase the speed as the game goes on so that the jumper will eventually miss. There are, of course, other rhymes that have a specific duration, and the jumper is required to stop when the rhyme is over and exchange places with one of the twirlers or one of the waiting bystanders/observers.

In addition to jump rope there are other games that have rhymes or songs that structure them and also continue for the duration of the game. Many clapping and ball-bouncing games use rhymes or songs, and the familiar songs, "London Bridge" and "Ring Around the Rosie," last all through the games they structure. Most of these children's games do not have over-all winners or losers. They generally conclude when most of the participants feel like stopping rather than at some predetermined point in the game. External factors such as darkness, homework, supper, and bedtime are much more likely to conclude a game than the crowning of an absolute winner. In the case of a game like jump rope, however, the number of jumps totaled up in the chant might suggest that one jumper is better than the others.

A second category of children's rhymes and songs, and one which is very close to the first category, contains rhymes and songs used for *power*. Certainly teasing rhymes like "na-na-na-na-na" give the user some power over the one at whom the rhyme is directed, and in its more complex versions, like "Nanny, Nanny, boo-boo/Stick your head in doo-doo," its power to make the victim angry is impressive. As children get older, they acquire a number of rhymes which give them the power to physically abuse another child. To be caught in one of these situations, the victim must have never heard the rhyme before, and so these tricks are often played on newcomers.

> Adam and Eve and Pinch Me
> Went down to the river to swim;
> Adam and Eve got drowned.
> Who was left?

When the victim answers this question—as he or she must, or lose considerable face in the group—the person who said the rhyme can then pinch away. Only a slightly more subtle rhyme instructs the victim to "Look up, look down/ Look at my thumb/ Gee, you're dumb." This rhyme, all by itself, is not a rhyme of physical abuse, but a later variation of it says

This is my finger,
This is my thumb,
This is my hand,
And here it comes.

As the last line is recited, the reciter steps closer and slaps the victim on the cheek. Other tricks play on the word "duck," so that the victim thinks the word refers to a bird while the trickster interprets it as an instruction; when the victim does not duck, he or she is slapped by an immediately apologetic trickster who says, "But I told you to duck."

The fascinating aspect of these rhymes of physical abuse is that seldom is a fight started. The victim realizes that he or she has been tricked. The victim also realizes that there is a whole crowd watching the trick and waiting for a reaction. The only thing the victim can do at the moment is take it like a "good sport." He or she may plot revenge and get back at the tormentor with a similar trick at a later date, but the victim is more likely to use the trick that was played on him or her to trick someone else. The victim thus becomes an insider looking for a new outsider to prey upon.

There are various other rhymes used by one child to establish his superiority over another. Among young children, tricking someone into looking at or for something that is not there is followed by this rhyme:

Made you look,
You dirty crook;
You stole your mother's
Pocketbook.

In general, victims seem much more willing participants in their own downfall when they are made to say a line or response that will eventually reflect badly on them. At the end of one such series, the victim—after saying, "I am a gold key," "I am a silver key," and "I am a brass key"—must then announce, "I am a "monk key" (that is, a monkey). Once again, the victim must accept the humiliation and wait to play the trick on someone else.

A third category of rhymes and songs suggests quite strongly that children develop a sense of what is or is not acceptable at an early age, and when they see another child acting in an unacceptable way, they often have a rhyme or song of *judgment* for the occasion. One group of judgmental rhymes is directed at children who are incorrectly dressed. Should someone not have assembled his or her clothing carefully, he or she might hear

I see London,
I see France,
I see _____'s
Underpants.

Exposed underwear and open zippers seem to be primary targets for this rhyme and others like it, but the clothing standards that such rhymes reinforce are adult standards. The child who uses this rhyme is aware of "proper dress" and is passing judgment or trying to correct the child who is unaware of the standards or who has slipped.

There are other ways a child can violate the group's standards, and there are rhymes for such occasions. A child who has been discovered to be a liar is quite likely to hear "Liar, Liar/Pants on fire/Hanging from the telephone wire." The liar has violated the group's trust, and the insulting rhyme is a judgment on the liar's actions. Other children whose actions set them apart from the group—notably tattletales, crybabies, and teachers' pets—will also have insulting rhymes directed at them. The child soon learns not to act this way if he or she wants to remain a member in good standing.

Children with noticeable differences have always been singled out by the group. In the past, children with glasses or braces were persons of ridicule to their peers; that, however, seems to have changed, and braces are even becoming a status symbol in certain parts of the country. Other obvious differences, especially the physical ones, still attract attention. Adults who were overweight children may never forget

Fatty, fatty, two by four,
Couldn't get through the bathroom door,
So he did it on the floor.

"Skinny" children, at the opposite end of the size spectrum, get similar treatment, as do redheads and children who are especially funny/ugly.

This quickness to recognize differences makes children particularly susceptible to racial and ethnic prejudice. To be sure, they are quick to pick up and promulgate views that their parents have (so that there are staunch eight-year-old Democrats and Republicans), but their recognition of physical and behavioral differences, already noted, suggests that the rhymes and songs about blacks, Jews, and Asians that the Knapps collected for *One Potato, Two Potato* (1976, 190–203) function only partly as racial material. Some of the impetus for the transmission of these materials must come from the group's sense of itself as a group, a sense that is certainly developed, in part, by recognizing others that are not a part of the group—and racial differences are easy to recognize. This does not make these rhymes of prejudice any more acceptable, but it does enable us to understand a bit more clearly why children are so quick to use them.[4]

The fourth category, which may well be the largest and which also crosses into other categories from time to time, consists of rhymes and songs that contain *wit* and *humor.* A great deal of material in this category is derived, ultimately, from the adult world. Children seem to have little respect for even the most traditional nursery rhymes, the most serious television commercials, or the most sacred songs. Parodies of "Mary Had A Little Lamb," as well as parodies of other nursery rhymes abound. Television commercials extolling the effectiveness or the quality of some new or well-known product become rhymes or jingles disparaging the product. In the 1950s, the Pepsi-Cola slogan, "Pepsi-Cola hits the spot," became

> Pepsi-Cola hits the spot,
> Smells like vinegar, tastes like snot;
> Pour it in the kitchen sink,
> Five minutes later, it begins to stink.

And more recently, commentaries concerning the use of Comet cleanser have been collected.

> Comet, it makes your mouth turn green;
> Comet, it tastes like kerosene;
> Comet, it makes you vomit;
> So get Comet and vomit today.

Not only do children seem quite willing to parody television commercials, but they also seem quite willing, unlike most adults, to make jokes about "snot" and "vomit."

Songs, too, are readily parodied by children and the children do not seem to be at all upset that songs adults consider important—whether secular political songs or sacred church music—are being violated. And so, "The Star-Spangled Banner" becomes

> Oh, say can you see,
> Any bedbugs on me?
> If you can, take a few,
> 'Cause I got them from you.

And there are similar parodies of "America," "Yankee Doodle," and "America the Beautiful." Church music is certainly not immune from parody. Generations of school children have sung variations of a parody of "The Battle Hymn of the Republic" through which they get some psychological revenge on the educational system by describing "The Burning of the School" and enthusiastically singing one variation or another of the chorus:

> Glory, glory, hallelujah,
> Teacher hit me with a ruler.
> I bopped her on the bean
> With a rotten tangerine,
> And her teeth went marching on.

Similar parodies exist of "We Three Kings," "Jesus Loves Me," "Hark! The Herald Angels Sing," and many more. In the same vein, there are parodies, in the appropriate rhyme and meter, of various prayers, from "Grace" before meals to "Now I Lay Me Down to Sleep." The children's answer to the old cliché "Is nothing sacred?" would seem to be a resounding "No!"

Another large segment of humorous rhyme and song is also derived, albeit indirectly, from the adult world. Children begin to learn quite early that there are "unacceptable" or "dirty" words in the English language, words that they should be especially careful not to say in the presence of adults. That, of course, makes those words all that much more delicious to say—if only within the peer group. In *One Potato, Two Potato*, the Knapps place these rhymes and songs in a larger category that they call "shockers" (Knapp and Knapp 1976, 179–89). And it is a shock to many adults to discover that children know and joke about body parts, bodily functions, sexual differences, and sexual activities. Art Linkletter may not have realized it, but kids will also say the grossest things. "Great Green Gobs of Greasy, Grimy Gopher Guts," a song that usually ends with the line "And me without a spoon," is not a song that most adults would enjoy; children—especially boys (but that may be role-playing)—love it. And there are any number of rhymes, some of them parodies of nursery rhymes, that focus on bodily functions or the products thereof:

> In 1944,
> The Monkey climbed the door;
> The door split,
> And the Monkey shit,
> In 1944.

And what Jack burned when he missed his jump over the candlestick is almost too painful to think about. Adults seem to have conveniently forgotten that they ever knew and passed on such materials, and when it comes to the rhymes and songs about sexual matters, they "can't imagine" how the children know such things. The Knapps collected the following parody/shocker from a ten-year-old: "Now I lay her on the bed/I pray to God I'll use my head." And the following song parody, also collected by the Knapps, exhibits a somewhat more sophisticated knowledge:

> My Bonnie lies over the ocean,
> My Bonnie lies over the sea,
> My daddy lies over my mommy,
> And that's how they got little me.
> (Knapp and Knapp 1976, 172, 185)

The children, for their part, are more perceptive than the adults concerning this humor; the children are aware of how the adults would react and, therefore, keep these materials generally among themselves.

There are a great many reasons why children find humor in these materials, and defiance of adult prohibitions is probably the least important reason of all. Certainly one of the reasons children use these words (and a reason they will later be eager to try cigarettes, alcohol, and sex) is to feel like adults. By using these materials, the children are like the adults whom they have very likely heard saying the same words or talking about the same topics. In addition, sexual humor—whether a parody or a song or rhyme in its own right—is a way of dealing with a topic of considerable anxiety in such a way that the anxiety is largely removed. Laughter, after all, is a way of dealing with fear and nervousness as well as a way of expressing delight. There is, in fact, a considerable amount of work to be done in mapping the development of children's sexual humor, work that should show that the humor changes—in topic as well as understanding—as the child grows older and more aware of first his or her own sexuality and then sexuality in relation to the sexuality of other people.

The last category is, of course, *miscellaneous*, and in it are lumped rhymes and songs that might be considered in one or more of the other categories but do deserve some mention on their own. Certainly there are humorous parodies and rhymes of judgment among autograph rhymes, but the occurrence of the specific item, the autograph rhyme, is the result of an autographing situation rather than a joke-telling session. And many of the rhymes, like the one that follows, could be nothing but autograph rhymes:

> Remember Grant,
> Remember Lee,
> But most of all,
> Remember me.

And other traditional rhymes, like "Roses are red . . . ," are changed to include sentiments about friendship.

Topical rhymes and songs, focusing on political figures, cartoon heroes, movie stars, and the like are also passed on among children in traditional ways—although the length of such a rhyme's popularity may well depend on the duration of the popularity of the subject of the rhyme or song. The Opies, the Knapps, and Turner, Factor, and Lowenstein were all able to collect rhymes involving Adolf Hitler as recently, in some cases, as the 1970s; but it is unlikely that any of the parodies of "Davy Crockett" that were sung in the 1950s are being passed on in the 1980s. Some of the topical rhymes and songs that circulate among children are also parodies; the resulting combinations can be quite interesting:

> My peanut has a first name, it's J-I-M-M-Y
> My peanut has a second name, it's C-A-R-T-R
> Oh, I hate to see him everyday
> And if you ask me why I'll say
> 'Cause Jimmy Carter has a way
> Of messing up the U.S.A. (Sullivan 1980, 9)

This parody of an Oscar Mayer commercial jingle is also, and perhaps foremost, an example of topical, political children's folklore—and it may be an interesting evaluation of Jimmy Carter as a president.

Some Concluding Comments

This article merely scratches the surface of a vast and interesting topic. Children will make up songs and rhymes about anything and everything. I obtained some insight into the process while chauffeuring my sons and their friends to various activities. They attempted take-offs or parodies on whatever fell within their range—on the radio, on billboards, or on store windows. Nearly all of what they created was almost immediately discarded; it was not very original, clever, or funny. Some items were tried out in several ways before most of them, too, were given up. In fact, I can remember them keeping only a very few items for much longer than it took for the item to be said and evaluated. But if this sort of activity goes on all the time among a great many elementary schoolers, some new things will be created, kept, and circulated right along with that great body of material that has been in circulation for generations.

This small study, larger studies like *One Potato, Two Potato, The Lore and Language of Schoolchildren,* and *Cinderella Dressed in Yella,* and the encyclopedic collections like Roger Abrahams's *Jump-Rope Rhymes: A Dictionary* (1969), can, after all, only point to and provide examples of the immense body of traditional songs and rhymes being passed on among children.

NOTES TO CHAPTER SEVEN

1. For the purposes of this article, the terms "poem" and "rhyme" will be interchangeable when used to refer to the rhymed and metered items in children's oral folklore.

2. Elementary-school teachers are reporting a sharp drop in their students' familiarity with even the most commonly recited nursery rhymes. Collectors of children's rhymes, and especially collectors of parodies, might begin to notice a decrease in the amount of traditional nursery rhyme material they gather.

3. Examples of children's rhymes and songs, unless otherwise noted, are from my own collections.

4. A similar group identification process takes place among elementary-school children as they begin to become aware of the sexual group to which they belong. Boys and girls each think that their group is the best, that members of the opposite group are unpleasant and objectionable.

8 RIDDLES

Danielle M. Roemer

In this chapter, I survey four areas relevant to the study of children's verbal and nonverbal riddling. The first of these sections involves situational and interactional contexts. The second considers common rhetorical strategies of English-language riddles. The third takes up developmental concerns, reviewing the literature on children's acquisition of productive competence. The concluding section treats some of the interactional functions of children's riddling. Because of the bias in the literature, the discussion throughout the chapter necessarily emphasizes verbal riddling.

Riddles are a type of solicitational routine (Bauman 1977b, 24). As such, they are characterized by a speech act that elicits a response; that is, they are marked by an implied or stated question posed by the initiating participant. The second participant answers the question. To be sure, types of solicitational routine other than the riddle can be found in children's repertoires. Among these are directive catch routines and knock-knock routines. Directive catch routines call forth a gestural or otherwise physical response, rather than a verbal reply. For their part, knock-knock routines, though containing questions, do not solicit solution-oriented responses. Instead, the respondent replies to the speaker with formulaic utterances. For these reasons, directive catch routines and knock-knock routines are omitted from the discussion.[1]

CONTEXTS AND PROCEDURES OF RIDDLING

Questions of when, where, how, and with whom children's riddles have been addressed in the folkloristic and anthropological literature, but they have rarely been answered in depth. Prior to the 1960s or so, collecting standards allowed considerable latitude in the recording of contextual and interactional data. Many researchers simply ignored the information. Others sketched out basic parameters, but too often their observations tended toward the obvious and the dominant. For example, researchers have tended to regard community members as a homogeneous group, thereby assuming that whatever was true for adult riddling held equally well for children's. Or, they viewed children themselves as undiversified, thereby bypassing differences in riddling due to youngsters' ages, or, in urban areas, their ethnic heritage. Especially problematic has been information about settings and interactional events that encourage or inhibit riddling. Though fieldworkers' sensitivity to context and dynamics has increased markedly in the past three decades, descriptions as specific as Manuel's of Bagobo riddling in the Philippines are not yet commonplace: "Riddle making . . . may start with younger folks or children, during some kind of activity like playing house, chatting around the fireplace, waiting for a turn to pound rice, fetching water, occupations of no strenuous nature, or while people are at rest after lunch. After the impulse is set by young people, the older folks may get stimulated to participate, depending on what they are doing otherwise" (Manuel 1962, 125; McDowell 1979; also Glazer 1982, 91–115; Bronner 1988, 186–99).

Despite this unevenness in the literature, enough information is retrievable to at least hint at some cross-cultural trends. As the first of these, we can identify two broadly different tracks that communities take with regard to the appropriateness of distinct groups' engaging in riddling. First, there are groups that treat riddling as an activity open to both adults and children. Among the Anang of Nigeria, for instance, both adults and children may pose and answer riddles (Messenger 1960; also Jetté 1913 and Manuel 1962). Secondly, and in contrast to groups like the Anang, communities may limit active involvement according to the age (or perhaps, the social status) of the potential participants. In some cases, riddling is seen as an adult prerogative. Though riddles may be posed occasionally to children for specific purposes, such as testing the youngsters' intelligence, they are not otherwise encouraged to participate (Bodding 1940; also Lindblom 1935). As an alternative to across-the-board restrictions based on age, other communities require children to simply remain silent when riddling occurs in adult social events. For instance, riddling at wakes may be appropriate for adults but not children. Although they are permitted to observe, youngsters are discouraged from joining in. Interestingly, though on such occasions children can overhear riddles that they later share with their peers (Roberts and Forman 1971, 195). Whereas the groups mentioned immediately above restrict riddling to adults, others regard the activity as a pastime for children. This appears to be the case in urban groups (for example, Basgoz 1965; Roberts and Forman 1971; Virtanen 1978) as well as in some tribal and preindustrialized societies (Hollis 1909; Doke 1927; Schapera 1932; Bascom 1949; Blacking 1961; D. Hart 1964; Fortes 1967; Upadhyaya 1970).

Within the literature, the most frequently reported occasions of adult-child riddling are those involving pedagogy and leisure-time activity, respectively. In pedagogic riddling, the adult takes on the role of teacher, the child the role of student. The interactions can occur in the home as well as in the school. To take the home environment first: Among the Chamula of Central America (Gossen 1974, 115–16), mothers may use riddles in teaching their children to talk. In the Ozark mountains of the United States in the 1930s (Randolph and Spradley 1934), some parents regarded "workin' out riddles" as an intellectual discipline for children. They posed riddles to their children in the hope of training the children's minds. Similar motives appear to have been behind adult-child riddling in other areas of the United States (Potter 1949, 939) and in Europe (Goldstein 1963). By far, the most frequent reports of pedagogic riddling in the home come from Africa. There, riddling is used to amuse children while testing their wit and competence in culture-specific values (D. Hart 1964). With respect to pedagogic riddling in the school environment, several curriculum reports (for example, Cazden 1982; Scriven n.d.) have suggested that riddling in the classroom can aid youngsters' development of perceptual and descriptive skills. Although to my knowledge we have no ethnographic reports of pedagogic riddling within the mainstream classroom, there exists at least one report treating riddle use in formal, non–English language instruction. Diane Roskies (cited in Kirshenblatt-Gimblett 1978, 15) studied classroom activities in *Kheyder,* a Jewish primary school. There, a variety of verbal art forms were applied in the teaching of the Jewish alphabet. As one example of the pedagogic play, the children were encouraged to tell riddles dealing with the shapes of the letters.

In contrast to pedagogic riddling, leisure-time riddling is pursued as an end in itself. Entertainment is the primary goal. Generally speaking, leisure-time riddling between children and adults develops in the vicinity of the home, when practical obligations are few (L. Roberts 1959; Barrick 1963; Burns 1976, 145–47). Although parents and siblings appear to be children's most frequent coparticipants (McCosh 1976, 57), youngsters confronted by more distant relatives and other visitors may find that they can use riddling to communicate across the "small-talk barrier" (Jansen 1968; Knapp and Knapp 1976, 106). Of course, it is always possible that this arrangement can backfire. Proud of their "funny, clever" children, parents have been known to encourage the youngsters to "perform" riddles for the parents' friends (McCosh 1976, 129). Trapped, visiting adults may serve not so much as coparticipants but as spectators to the children's performances.

Though in-depth analysis is lacking, we have clues to the interactional parameters of adult-child leisure-time riddling. In such contexts, it appears, riddle subject matter can become problematic and speaking rights can be unequally distributed. As to the first point: It seems that youngsters in both Western and non-Western groups censor the riddles they tell adults. Among the Venda of Africa (Blacking 1961, 2), children tell certain riddles only in the company of their peers and never in the presence of their elders. Likewise, British and American youngsters delete sexual riddles from those they share with adults (McCosh 1976, 57). Secondly, turns at talking can be unequally distributed during adult-child riddling. In adult-child, nonriddling conversations, at least among American participants, children's speaking rights are often limited (Sacks 1972). A similar arrangement appears to be in effect during at least some adult-child riddling. David Evans's (1976) transcript of riddle interaction among four black men and two black boys provides a possible example. The interaction is dominated by the adults, particularly by the elderly man who poses most of the riddles. For their part, the boys try to guess some of the riddles but do not offer any of their own. On the whole, they are willing to watch and listen, allowing the adults to take charge of the interaction.

In comparison to adult-child activity, leisure-time riddling in children's peer groups has received even less documentation. Many of the reports merely state that such riddling occurs. Those that do investigate the topics tend to focus on formal riddle sessions. A *riddle session* (Burns 1976, 142) consists of a series of riddle acts, possibly interspersed with other performance material. The organization of a riddle session can be described in terms of (1) role relationships among the participants, (2) the conjoining of the interactional units that make up the sessions, and (3) restrictions or expectations influencing the selection of acts in one session relative to selection procedures in other sessions. To date, much of the research has adopted the first of these foci, summarizing the riddle session as a contest in African societies (Burns 1976, 147–53). One of the more detailed of these reports has been published by John Blacking.

According to Blacking (1961), there are not set rules for the composition of riddling teams among the Venda of Africa. Depending on circumstances, teams can be made up of girls, boys, or a combination of both. Age variables can be relevant, as when younger boys take on a team of older boys. The most important factor, however, is riddling competence. Since the Venda place a high positive value on the knowledge of words and on facility with formal language, the child who knows many riddles is much in demand.

Other youngsters may try to bribe their way onto the team of such a riddler, offering him or her oranges or bits of sugar cane.

Riddle contests among the Venda typically begin with some variant of the proposal *A ri thaidze!* ("Let's ask each other riddles!"). Once started, the contest develops in one of two ways: as the event *Thai dza u bulelana* ("riddles that you reveal to each other") or as *Thai dza u rengelana* ("riddles that you buy from each other"). Though Venda children use both types, they prefer the second. They explain that engaging in bartered riddles is less competitive, easier to play, and lasts longer than the alternate method. In addition, by being able to "buy" an answer with a riddle of one's own, children decrease their embarrassment at not knowing the answer to the opponents' question (pages 1–8). Blacking summarizes the organization of bartering contests as follows. The letters "A" and "B" refer to the two riddling teams:

> A asks B a riddle. B does not answer it; instead he "buys" A's answer by posing another riddle. A answers his own first riddle and then "buys" the answer to B's riddle by posing another riddle.

> B then answers his own first riddle and "buys" the answer to A's second riddle by posing another riddle.

> The game continues in this fashion, with the burden of questioning shifting regularly from A to B, until one side or the other is unable to ask any more riddles. (page 3)

Blacking's report represents one of the more useful investigations of competitive riddling among children. Though it would have been more informative if he had included excerpts from actual contests, the specifics he does provide contribute significantly to the value of his study.

In contrast to the riddle contests of the Venda, leisure-time sessions among Western urban children tend not to develop according to preset patterns. Instead, their sessions are seemingly diffuse. To a considerable extent, the apparent lack of organization derives from (as well as fosters) the occasions in which the riddling occurs. Usual settings for this riddling include (in the United States) the playground during recess, the cafeteria at lunchtime, anywhere on the school grounds before and after classes, the school bus, the street, the park, neighborhood backyards, and (in urban Finland) the courtyards that lie behind blocks of flats (McCosh 1976, 57; Virtanen 1978; McDowell 1979, 122). Typically, adult supervision in these areas is distant enough to permit peer group interests to hold sway. As a result, "contentious riddling" (McDowell 1979, 122) can develop. In such riddling, participants are verbally aggressive, take liberties with one another, and repeatedly test each other's social competence. The sessions seem to wander from riddling per se to material such as knock-knock routines, narratives, songs, name-calling, obscenity, and a variety of victimization procedures (McDowell 1979, 1980).

No doubt, the flexibility of contentious riddle sessions has discouraged their investigation. Until recent decades, fieldworkers have not had widespread access to adequate recovery tools, such as audio and video recorders, for dealing with emergent interaction. In addition, investigators did not have the analytic tools to cope adequately with conversation-like data. Only within the past two decades or so have relevant perspectives become available. One of these perspectives is known as the "ethnography of speaking" (Bauman and Sherzer 1974; Bauman 1977b; Roemer 1983). Another developed principally as a result of the work of ethnomethodologists. Primarily sociologists, these researchers study the organization of everyday talk (for example, Sudnow 1972; R. Turner 1974). One of their primary contributions has been to resolve an apparent paradox: that casual exchange is both structured *and* the result of the participants' active negotiation. In short, ethnomethodologists argue, everyday encounters do not merely happen to participants; they are achieved by them. For example, in everyday conversation speakers tend to explore topics by using immediately prior talk as a context for the shaping and understanding of subsequent talk. They establish the interconnectedness of their utterances and thereby give a sense of order to their interactions. The relevance of this organizational technique to children's leisure-time riddling follows.

In *Children's Riddling* (1979), John McDowell applies ethnomethodological perspectives to the study of children's riddle sessions. As members of their own peer group culture, McDowell argues, children possess a basic understanding of how to get things done in riddling. Although they are not self-consciously aware of the procedures employed, children nevertheless manage to accomplish an underlying sense of order in their riddle sessions. For example, they allow topically related riddles produced early in a session to influence the production and interpretation of riddles offered later in the same session. In other words, initial riddles establish a semantic field which the children continue to investigate in subsequent riddles. McDowell (1979, 136) illustrates this process with riddles that, taken from a single session, constitute a symposium on modes of locomotion. These riddles are given below in the order in which McDowell's informants delivered them:

1. What has eight wheels and rolls?—roller skates.
2. What has two wheels and pedals?—a bicycle.
3. What has four wheels, no pedals, and a steering wheel?—a car.
4. What has four legs and can run?—a mustang.
5. What has three wheels and pedals?—a tricycle.
6. What has four legs and can't walk?—a chair.
7. What has two legs and it can walk?—a monkey.
8. What has long legs and it's hard to walk?—a seagull.
9. What has two seats, four wheels, and they can roll?—a car.
10. What has lots of windows and they can fly?—airplane.
11. What are those little clocks and it's in your car?—a dragger.

In addition to exploring the semantic field of locomotion, this riddle sequence suggests a taxonomy, given below. The children supply the linguistic tokens (for example, mustang, chair) and points of contrast among the taxa (the major points of contrast are wheels, legs, and pedals; the minor points include wheels and legs, the effectiveness of legs, and so forth). The remainder of the taxonomic apparatus is implied. Nevertheless, McDowell (1979, 138) posits, the children put the concepts and tokens of locomotion in their logical places:

class of objects

locomotives						nonlocomotives
animals		toys		machines		furniture
run walk	walk hard	832		air	ground	legs
		wheels				
mustang seagull	skates bicycle		plane		car	chair
monkey	tricycle				clocks	
					dragger	

Focusing on what he terms the "cerebral child," McDowell argues for children's unself-conscious pursuit of deep-structuring principles. Though his analytic methods differ from theirs, McDowell's conclusions concerning riddle sessions are compatible with those of other researchers who have argued that youngsters are intrigued by play with classificatory principles (Sutton-Smith 1976b; Stewart 1978).

Elsewhere in *Children's Riddling*, McDowell considers a level of riddling organization more specific than that of the riddle session. In his chapter entitled "Negotiation," he examines the riddle act, the basic interactional unit of riddling. A *riddle act* (Burns 1976, 142) consists of all the interactional moves involved in posing and responding to a single riddle question. Riddle act organization can vary depending on the traditions of the culture in which the riddling occurs, the accepted practices of the peer group, and the situational conditions that impinge on the riddling during its course.

Following Tom Burns's survey (1976, 153–54) of the possibilities of riddle act construction, McDowell (1979, 112) identifies the following sequence as basic to the efforts of his informants. The children consistently drew on this sequence in developing their riddle acts, thereby indicating that it represented shared knowledge within the peer group:

1. riddle act invitation ("I've got one"; "I know one")
2. riddler's statement (the riddle proposition)[2]
3. riddlee's initial response (that is, a guess; declining to guess)
4. riddler-riddlee interaction in the contemplation period (requests for and the supplying of hints)
5. riddle answer sequence [3]

Each juncture in this basic sequence can be developed through one or more elaborative moves. After the riddler initiates a riddle act and the riddlee offers an initial response, McDowell (1979, 124–25) points out, certain elaborative moves become available to the riddler:

1. clue
2. rejection of unacceptable solution
3. affirmation of correct solution
4. delivery of correct solution

Supplemental moves may be used to consolidate the riddler's authoritative position:

1. encouraging the riddlee
2. refusing to supply requested information

For their part, respondents have access to at least the following basic moves:

1. request for clue
2. request for clarification
3. proposed solution

Supplemental moves available to respondents include:

1. request for solution
2. surrender
3. challenge

According to McDowell, the children did not regard either the basic sequence or its elaborative and supplemental moves as hard-and-fast conventions. Rather, the actual deployment of the sequence was negotiable, depending on the circumstances of the situation and the participants' individual and combined goals.

The following transcript excerpt illustrates the basic sequence and its elaborative moves. The excerpt is drawn from my own fieldwork, conducted during 1974–75 with five- through eight-year-old Anglo children in Austin, Texas. McDowell's study focuses on riddling among Mexican-American youngsters of similar ages in the Austin *barrio*. Despite differences in the ethnic heritage of our respective informants, McDowell's perspective can be applied effectively to the Anglo material. Though lengthy, the excerpt below represents a single riddle act. Each child's age is indicated in parentheses following the child's pseudonym. After presenting the excerpt, I consider the dynamics and the organization of the interaction:

1. [Maggie stands; the other children are seated on the ground]
2. Maggie (8): What runs all the way around the block an' [pause] yeah, what
3.   runs all the way around the block?
4. ———:   You!
5. Maggie: No.
6. ———:   People?
7. Maggie: No.
8. Cassi (7):   Clifford?
9. ———:   (?)
10. Maggie: [shouts:] No [pause] nobody knew it. Nobody knew it.
11. [presumably in response to Cassi's guess:] Yeah. [pause]
12.   Well, no.
13. ———:   Clifford.
14. ———:   Clifford.
15. Maggie: Raise your hand!
16. Susan (8):   Oh! [raises her hand]
17. Maggie: Susan.
18. Susan: Sidewalk?
19. Maggie: No.

20. ——: Clifford.

21. Maggie: No.

22. Lydia (5): Uh, a horse?

23. Maggie: No.

24. Cassi: Oh! I [pause] Clifford riding his tricycle.

25. Maggie: No.

26. Kathy (8): God [pause] I don't believe.

27. ——: A street?

28. Maggie: No. Give up?

29. Cassi: Oh! A streaker?

30. Maggie: No!

31. ——: Um, Clifford ridin' his bike?

32. Maggie: No.

33. Sharon (5): Uh [pause] a goose! Ah [pause] a goosey gander!

34. ——: A doggie?

35. Maggie: No!

36. ——: (?)

37. Maggie: Wha- [pause] um, no. Y'all get.

38. Kathy: [sarcastic tone:] A goosey gander!

39. Maggie: [shouting:] No, y'all are never going to guess it. Do y'all

40. give up?

41. ——: Yeah.

42. Maggie: Clifford's col-, I mean, Clifford's leash. It's so big it runs

43. all the way around the block.

44. Kathy: Oh, yeah!

45. ——: That was in the book, aha!

46. DR: Is *Clifford* a book that you read in school?

47. Maggie: No, it's a dog.

48. ——: I bought it [the riddle book *The Book of Clifford*]

49. [the next riddle act begins]

The role of riddler provides the participant with a certain authority. Here, the riddler, Maggie, calls attention to her authority in several ways. In terms of proxemics, she stands to deliver the riddle proposition (lines 1–3). The audience is thus "below" her, subordinate both in physical position and in knowledge of the answer. Secondly, she borrows a regulatory tactic from the classroom, demanding that potential respondents raise their hands and wait to be called on (line 15). In another authoritative move, she taunts the audience, and, at line 10, shouts gleefully that no one knows the answer.[4] And she extends her tenure in the riddler's role by permitting a lengthy series of guesses. For their part, the audience is willing to accept this arrangement, even to exploit it. They seem to enjoy coming up with guesses, so much so that their enthusiasm eventually threatens to diffuse Maggie's power. As the interaction progresses, Maggie's delight with the audience's involvement (line 10) begins to change to frustration. Her rejection of guesses becomes increasingly heated (lines 30, 35) and at two points she asks if the audience is ready to give up (lines 28, 39–40). Finally, the audience signals its surrender (line 41), Maggie delivers the correct solution (lines 42–43), and the audience verifies it (lines 44–45).

Borrowing McDowell's terminology, we can inventory the moves of this interaction as follows:

lines 1–3	riddle proposition (riddler)
4	possible solution (respondent)
5	rejection of solution at line 4 (riddler)
6	possible solution (respondent)
7	rejection of solution at line 6
8	possible solution (respondent)
9	possible solution (?) (respondent)
10–12	rejection of solution at line 8 and 9; taunting the respondents; equivocation and rejection of solution at line 8 and 9 (riddler)
13	possible solution (respondent)
14	possible solution (respondent)
15	regulatory directive (riddler)
16	compliance with directive at line 15
17	acknowledgment of respondent (riddler)
18	possible solution (respondent)
19	rejection of solution at line 18 (respondent)
20	possible solution (respondent)
21	rejection of solution at line 20 (riddler)
22	possible solution (respondent)
23	rejection of solution at line 22 (riddler)
24	possible solution (respondent)
25	rejection of solution at line 24 (riddler)
26	evaluation of the interaction (audience member)
27	possible solution (respondent)
28	rejection of solution at line 27; query concerning surrender

29	possible solution (respondent)
30	rejection of solution at line 29 (riddler)
31	possible solution (respondent)
32	rejection of solution at line 31 (riddler)
33	possible solution (respondent)
34	possible solution (respondent)
35	rejection of solution at line 33 and 34 (riddler)
36	possible solution (?) (respondent)
37	request for reiteration of solution at line 36; rejection of solution at line 36; attempt to limit further guessing (?) (riddler)
38	evaluation of solution proposed at line 33 (audience member)
39–40	attempt to prompt surrender; query concerning surrender (riddler)
41	surrender (respondent)
42–43	delivery of the correct solution (riddler)
44	confirmation of the correct solution (audience member)
45	confirmation of the correct solution (audience member)
46-49	discussion (riddler, audience members)

Outlined in this fashion, the organization of the riddle act is clear. The children draw from a limited pool of moves, repeating them as necessary. They share knowledge of the mover yet are aware that the moves can be manipulated for private goals. What might not have been apparent at first glance is thus revealed through analysis. The riddle act can be both an orderly and an emergent achievement. What remains for us as researchers is to become sensitive to children's accomplishments in riddling, both in their patterning and in their diversity.

RIDDLE STRATEGIES

Riddles are a particularly complex genre. Because they depend on a variety of communicative means, any comprehensive treatment of them must necessarily be multidimensional. The intensity needed for satisfactory treatment of these dimensions, however, either in integration or in balanced separation, is beyond the scope of this report.[5] My primary purpose here is to survey some of the ways common rhetorical strategies are illustrated in riddles. A secondary goal is to look briefly at the routines' relationship to codes for the construction of everyday reality. A third level of the routines' construction—that having to do with block elements and wit—is admittedly shortshrifted. Because of the linguistic apparatus required and because techniques of confusion have been discussed at length elsewhere (Petsch 1899; Georges and Dundes 1963; Abrahams 1981; Pepicello and Green 1984), I mention only a few blocks and consider these only in passing.

In the following survey, I regard rhetorical strategies as one reservoir of communicative means available for the framing and execution of riddles. The discussion is based on Kenneth Burke's concept of strategies for encompassing a situation (1941). In their solicitations, riddles point to some of the decoding work the respondent is to do. At the rhetorical level, this work involves the respondent's coping with common rhetorical strategies, among them description, comparison, contrast, narration, classification and definition, and cause and effect.[6] Although certain subgenres (for example, true riddles) have conventionally been thought of as characterized by a single strategy (for example, description), that characterization is not always accurate. The combination of strategies is possible within a single routine. Because of this potential for multiple framing, the present discussion is not limited to conventional taxonomic categories.

Relationships between riddles and rhetorical strategies has been considered in the literature (Abrahams and Dundes 1972; McDowell 1979). To my knowledge, however, the present survey is unique in the variety of forms it treats. Except where noted, all examples have been taken from children's oral tradition in the English language. English-language forms do not necessarily correspond to those found in other riddling traditions (Harries 1971). Therefore, I do not claim any automatic cross-cultural application for the points I raise.

VERBAL RIDDLES

Description

Verbal riddles making use of description present information about the appearance, qualities, activities, or nature of an entity, phenomenon, or event. This information may be supplied in the riddle proposition or via the riddle answer.

Some riddle propositions describe by enumerating attributes of an object. Too little information, however, is provided for the object to be recognized easily:

1.   What has teeth but no mouth?—a comb. (McCosh 1976, 165)

2.　What goes up when the rain comes down?—your umbrella. (McCosh 1976, 165)

3.　What has four wheels and flies?—a garbage truck. (Weiner 1970, 23)

The enumeration may be complicated by contradiction or grammatical ambiguity as in numbers 1–3 above. Or, it may engage in substitution, replacing commonplace descriptors with unusual ones:

4.　What has
　　Two lookers,
　　Two hookers,
　　Four down-hangers,
　　Four up-standers,
　　And a fly-swatter?—a cow. (Withers and Benet 1954, 72)

Instead of focusing on aspects of the referenced object, other riddles operate on a metalinguistic level. They divide the answer as *word* into syllables and give a description of each. Although Abrahams and Dundes (1972, 135) have identified the "word charade" as primarily a literary form of riddle, examples have been collected from children's oral tradition:

5.　My first drives a horse,
　　My second is needy,
　　My third is a nickname,
　　My whole is a bird.—whip-poor-will. (Withers and Benet 1954, 36)

In still other riddles, the enumeration is obscured by metaphor. The question provides the vehicle in a metaphoric comparison; the tenor is to be supplied in the riddle answer:

6.　What grows in winter, dies in summer, and grows with its roots upwards?—an icicle. (Opie and Opie 1959, 75)

The vehicle, of course, can vary the amount of descriptive information it provides:

7.　Little Nancy Netticoat,
　　Wears a white petticoat,

The longer she lives
The shorter she grows,
Little Nancy Netticoat.—a lighted candle.

8. Riddle me, riddle me,
    riddle me ree,
    I saw a nutcracker
    up in a tree.—a squirrel. (Opie and Opie 1959, 77)

Whereas the riddles surveyed above provide description in the proposition, others request that it be supplied in the riddle answer. The riddles below announce an explicit comparison or contrast and ask for a description of the ways in which the juxtaposed objects relate. The riddles are marked by versions of the formulas "Why is ____ like ____?" and "What's the difference between ____ and ____?" (Abrahams and Dundes 1972, 136):

9. Why is an alligator like a sheet of music?—because they both have scales. (Weiner 1970, 35)

10. In what way is a volcano the same as a mad person?—they both blow their tops. (Winslow 1966c, 170)

11. What is the difference between a cat and a comma?—a cat has its claws at the end of its paws and a comma has its pause at the end of a clause. (Opie and Opie 1959, 79)

As a variation of the comparison strategy, riddles can ask for a description of the circumstances in which one entity resembles another:

12. When is a boy most like a bear?—when he's barefoot. (Weiner 1970, 16)

Narration

Accounts of incidents occur infrequently in modern riddles, but some have been collected from children:

13. Whitey saw Whitey in Whitey.
    Whitey sent Whitey to drive
    Whitey out of Whitey.—Mr. White sent a white dog to drive a
    white cow out of his cotton field. (Withers and Benet 1954, 72; see

Rare in the English language but dealing in abbreviated narration, "dialogue riddles" (Abrahams and Dundes 1972, 135) quote the speech of characters in a fictitious interactional encounter. The respondent is asked to identify the speakers:

> 14. Crooked and straight, which way are you going?
> Croptail every year, what makes you care?—meadow to brook and the brook's reply. (Abrahams and Dundes 1972, 135; informant unspecified)

To my knowledge, dialogue riddles have not been collected from children. Narrational riddles, however, which are prevalent among youngsters reverse the pattern of this older form. Relying on the formula "What did the ___ say to the ___?" (Abrahams and Dundes 1972, 136), "Wellerism riddles" identify a speaker and an addressee and ask for a quotation of what was said:[7]

> 15. What did the big chimney say to the little chimney?—"You're too young to smoke." (Knapp and Knapp 1976, 105)

Using the formula "What did the ___ say when ___?" riddles related to no. 15 focus on a speaker's utterance in particular temporal or environmental circumstances:

> 16. What did the bull say when it swallowed a bomb?—"Abominable" (a-bomb-in-a-bull). (Opie and Opie 1959, 82)

> 17. What did the 500-pound mouse say when he came out into the street?
> —[bass voice:] "Here Kitty, Kitty, Kitty! Come, Puss!" (Jablow and Withers 1965, 257)

Definition and Classification

Riddles employing definition and classification techniques tend to fall into two groups. First, there are forms that borrow aspects of the negative definition. These indicate a category (such as doors) but immediately suggest that category's inefficiency relative to a specific member (a door that is not a door). The respondent is asked to resolve the dilemma by describing a circumstance when the contradiction does not obtain:

> 18. When is a door not a door?—when it's a jar. (McCosh 1976, 201)

Secondly, riddles can deal in definition by classification, that is, in logical definition. Information concerning genus (class), species (member), and differentiae (distinguishing traits) is manipulated. Examples 19–21 below provide genus and differentiae and request species:

> 19. What kind of money do people eat?—dough. (McCosh 1976, 186)

> 20. What kind of a plane has hair under its wings?—a Polack airplane. (McCosh 1979, 230)[8]

> 21. What do you call a monkey that eats potato chips?—chipmunk. (Weiner 1970, 35)

Alternatively, the strategy above can be inverted. Rather than supplying a descriptive definition and asking for a classificatory term, these provide the term and ask for its definition:

> 22. What is a dandelion?—a lion that dresses well. (Weiner 1970, 34)

> 23. What's the definition of agony?—a woman standing outside a toilet with a bent penny. (McCosh 1976, 182)

Cause and Effect

Riddles adopting the strategy of causation focus on a specific relationship between events in time. Often relying on the formula "What happened when ___?" some describe an event and ask for its consequences or result:

> 24. What happened when the cow jumped over the barbed wire fence?—utter destruction. (McCosh 1976, 188)

Others indicate an effect and ask for its cause:

> 25. Why did the window-box?—because it saw the garden fence.

(Opie and Opie 1959, 81)

26. What made Miss Tomato turn red?—she saw Mr. Green Pea.
(Knapp and Knapp 1976, 224)

NONVERBAL RIDDLES

Gestural Riddles

Although the data are scanty, gestural riddles appear to be primarily descriptive forms. The riddler describes the referent with various motions:

27. Hold your hands over your head and wiggle your fingers.
"What's this?"—"a midget playing a piano." (Levanthal and Cray 1963, 249)

Unfortunately for both respondents and riddle students, there exists no easily applied or widely accepted system for interpreting gestures. As they watch the riddler's motions, respondents might well wonder: What specific portions of the riddler's fingers should be understood as one semantic unit and which should be regarded as a combination of several? Ambiguities such as these are not always easy to resolve while the description is being produced. As a result, respondents may not merely be stumped as to the riddle answer; they may be baffled as to what constituted the description itself. Many of the same problems in observation confront researchers. Although serious attempts have been made to establish an analytic code for the study of gestures (for example, Birdwhistell 1970), gestural riddles remain elusive phenomena for investigation.

Visual Descriptive Riddles

As their name suggests, visual descriptive riddles depend on the strategy of description. Unlike analogous verbal forms, though, visual riddle answers are extremely difficult to anticipate. As one informant reported (Roemer 1982a), respondents rarely try to answer the riddler's verbal question "What is it?" because a riddle drawing "can mean almost anything."

Typically, a sketch gives only a minimal outline of the depicted object. The description is usually too brief for the respondent to recognize the object from the graphic evidence alone. Because the evidence is abbreviated, the sketch becomes susceptible to a variety of verbal answers. For example, among the college students I interviewed (Roemer 1982a), the traditional answer to Figure 28 was "a popcan lid seen from the inside":

28.

Other answers, however, would fit just as easily: "a baby crying," "someone inside a well looking up at the moon at night," or "someone inside a tunnel looking back at the entrance." Nothing about the sketch itself necessarily makes one of these explanations more likely than any of the others. Assuming that it can be made to fit the graphic data, the correct answer is quite simply the one that the riddler says is correct.[9]

Few visual descriptive riddles have been collected from American schoolchildren. There are indications, however, that this genre forms an active part of youngsters' riddle repertoires. Mary and Herbert Knapp (1976, 229) report that children sometimes exchange visual riddles in the classroom when the teacher's back is turned. In addition, college students (Roemer 1982a) have reported that they knew and told such riddles as children, exchanging them, for instance, on Scout bus trips.

At present, most of the published material on the genre has come from the European youngsters. In her study of Finnish "Children's Lore" (1978, 56–58), Leea Virtanen gives twelve visual riddles. To our loss, however, she provides the riddles without discussion:

---

29. Fɪɢ. Grandmother can't swim (Virtanen 1978, 57).

To date, the most extensive collection has been offered by Bengt af Klintberg (1980). Klintberg gained most of his material (seventy-five riddles) through questionnaires sent to sixth-grade students (twelve years old) throughout Sweden. The material returned showed "only insignificant" regional variations, suggesting that the tradition is relatively uniform across the country. Among Swedish schoolchildren, Klintberg reports, the riddles are most frequently termed *bildgåtor* ("picture riddles").[10]

The major strength of Klintberg's report is its discussion of historical and comparative issues. Klintberg traces much of the popularity of visual riddles in Sweden to American influence and particularly to the books of the American humorist Roger Price. A few of the riddles imported to Sweden have developed interesting quirks as the result of the language differences. Among American informants, Figure 30 is often explained as "a navel orange wearing a bikini." Because of translation problems, however, none of the Swedish riddles using the analogous Figure 31 have retained the "navel orange" answer. Instead, the Swedish orange is drawn without a "navel," and the usual answer is "orange in a bikini" (1980, 196):

---

30. Fig. A navel orange wearing a bikini (Roemer, unpublished data).

31. Fig. Orange in a bikini (Klintberg 1980, 193).

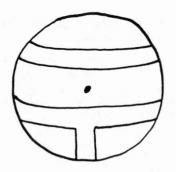

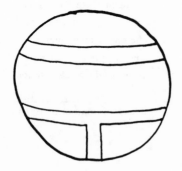

Although Klintberg's report provides very useful information, we as yet have no details on children's development of interest and competence in the use of the genre. Nor do we know if certain visual riddles are more appropriate among certain age groups. In addition, we have little information as to how the riddles are exchanged. Among American college students, visual riddles and rebuses are exchanged during the same interactional sessions

(Roemer 1981–82 unpublished data; Preston 1982). Does this hold true for sessions among schoolchildren? Similar points need to be raised concerning the other nonverbal genres surveyed in this section.

RHETORICAL IMPACT

True and Joking Riddles

Conventionally, the riddles treated in this chapter have been separated into categories depending on their solvability. Generally speaking, folklorists have termed riddles "true" if their answers could be reasoned out, based on information supplied in the riddle proposition and the respondent's adequate experience with recall of tropes, symbols, and other conventions shared within the particular culture.

What have been called "true riddles" are based primarily in description (for example, nos. 1, 2, 4, and 8) and have attracted considerable attention in the literature (Taylor 1951). In addition, they enjoy a measured popularity among American and British youngsters. Though some of the longer or more poetic forms (for example, nos. 4–8) remain current, urban children seem more attracted to riddles that are concise and brief. Mary and Herbert Knapp (1976, 109) cite children's tendency to abridge the longer forms (no. 32), creating brief and especially enigmatic descriptions (no. 33):

> 32. In marble walls as white as milk,
>   Lined with skin as soft as silk,
>   Within a crystal fountain clear,
>   A golden apple doth appear.
>   No doors there are to this stronghold,
>   Yet thieves break in to steal the gold.—an egg.

> 33. No doors there are to this stronghold
>   But thieves break in and take the gold.—an egg.

In addition, there has been a shift from statementlike descriptions to those using an explicit interrogative. Compared with the versions of the "egg" riddle above, no. 34 evidences both severe abridgement and interrogative form:

> 34. What house has no door?—an egg. (McCosh 1979, 165)[11]

The features of brevity and interrogative form are apparent in most of the true riddles found in urban children's repertoires. Indeed, one of the most popular of these demonstrates these characteristics:

35. What's black and white and red all over?—a newspaper.

The ubiquity of the "newspaper riddle" (Barrick 1974) has fostered a range of alternate answers: "a blushing zebra," "a skunk with diaper rash," "a bleeding nun," "an integration march," and "an Afro-American Santa Claus" (Knapp and Knapp 1976, 108; see also Weiner 1970, 37–38; McCosh 1976, 176–77; and Bronner 1988, 288–90 ff.). With these answers, the homonymic play in the question disappears and "red" is interpreted merely as the name of a color. When coupled with an answer such as "a blushing zebra," the interrogative shifts from the status of a true riddle question to that of a question in a joking riddle (discussed below).

Routines that interfere markedly in their own interpretation can be divided into two subgroups. Visual descriptive riddles and gestural riddles inhibit deciphering by the very flexibility of their codes. Outside of the orthographic code, which visual descriptive riddles do not address anyway, there exists no standard "grammar" for interpreting individual squiggles, dots, and blotches inscribed on a page. A line may mean one thing in one drawing and quite another in a second drawing. Furthermore, because it is the riddle answer that gives significance to the inscription, a riddle with a variety of answers can interpret its drawing in a variety of ways (for example, no. 28). Similar points can be raised with gestural riddles, but there the respondent must work not only with basically uncoded data but also with data that are kinesic and therefore highly ephemeral.

Joking riddles are the second category of forms that are extremely difficult of solution. To be sure, joking routines can differ in the quality of their humor, but, generally speaking, the propositions serve primarily as a setup for the punch line of the answer:

36. What is the worst weather for rats and mice?—when it's raining cats and dogs. (Leventhal and Cray 1963, 254)

37. What's tall and says eef eif [eof] muf?—a backward giant. (McCosh 1976, 176)

THE PARODIC IMPULSE

Parodic forms are not so much a distinct category of riddle as they are forms that extend the humor of joking riddles into absurdity and nonsense. Parodic riddles adopt the organizational strategies of more conservative forms.

What marks them as extensions is the degree of violence they do to assumptions of everyday life.

Parodic riddles are very popular among urban children, and various researchers have commented on this fascination. Alto Jablow and Carl Withers (1965) view the riddles as safety-valve mechanisms that enable youngsters to express their amused, angry, or frightened awareness of the fast-paced, violent, and often irrational world in which they live. If the routines are absurd and meaningless, Jablow and Withers argue, it is because urban society itself reflects those characteristics (1965, 252–55). For their part, Mary and Herbert Knapp (1976) agree that children may become connoisseurs of chaos in buffering themselves against modern life. The Knapps, however, also advance an alternate explanation. Urban children, they suggest, have developed sophisticated tastes in their folk humor. Because parodic forms deal in ambiguity and nonsense, they speak to children's almost insatiable fascination with complex and startling relationships (1976, 111).

Some parodic riddles can be used to challenge assumptions about what is possible in the everyday world. We can understand how an answer fits its question, yet what the riddle as a whole proposes is nonsensical given a conventional understanding of the "real" world. If what these riddles suggest were valid, we would need to reorganize our conception of the world around us. Examples of parodic forms include the following:[12]

Description:

38. What's big and grey with a purple spot in the middle?—an elephant hit by a Comanche grape. (Weiner 1970, 32)

39. What's green and flies from planet to planet?—an interplanetary cucumber. (Knapp and Knapp 1976, 110)

40. (Snap your fingers in the air several times, jerking your hand up and down.) "What's this?"—a butterfly with hiccups (or, a drunk butterfly). (Leventhal and Cray 1963, 249)

41. Fig. A clam with buck teeth (Roemer, unpublished data).

Contrast:

42. What's the difference between unloading dead babies and unloading bowling balls?—you can't use a pitchfork to unload bowling balls. (Knapp and Knapp 1976, 111)

Classification/Definition:

43. What do you call a werewolf in a Dacron suit?—a wash and werewolf. (Knapp and Knapp 1976, 110)

Effect/Cause:

44. Why do elephants have flat feet? —from jumping out of palm trees. (McCosh 1976, 224)

Catch Riddles

Using metacommunicative techniques, other riddles violate the conventions of riddling as a particular type of social exchange. No. 45 below challenges the expectation that a riddler's question will provide information relevant to the answer. Here, the respondents receive only part of the formulaic information characteristic of contrast riddles. Beyond that, the respondents are on their own:

45. A: What's the difference?
   B: Between what?
   A: On this one I'm giving you no clues. (Jablow and Withers 1965, 249)

Other riddles are iconoclastic in other ways. No. 46 begins with a descriptive question, the conventional way of initiating some of the most conservative of English-language riddles. It concludes, however, by challenging the assumption that riddlers know the answer to the questions they pose:

46. What's red, purple, green, yellow, gray, purple, sky-blue, and green?
   —I don't know, that's why I'm asking you. (McCosh 1976, 178)

A related surprise awaits respondents with no. 47. In addition to not supplying a satisfactory resolution, the riddle threatens the respondent's assumption of physical security:

> 47. A: What has six legs, fuzzy ears, and a long tail?
> B: What?
> A: I don't know, but there's one on your back. (McCosh 1976, 178)

In this and other catch riddles (Roemer 1977), the respondents are set up for victimization. By cooperating with what they *think* is the first speaker's intent, the respondents place themselves unknowingly in a vulnerable position. The trickster capitalizes on this vulnerability at the riddle's conclusion:

Description:

> 48. What word starts with *F* and ends with *CK*?—firetruck. (Winslow 1966c, 172)

Contrast:

> 49. A: What's the difference between an egg and an elephant?
> B: I don't know, what?
> A: If you don't know, I'll never send you to get eggs from the shop. (McCosh 1976, 178)

Cause-Effect

> 50. If you threw a white ball into a black sea, what would it become?—wet. (McCosh 1976, 181)

The Acquisition of Riddle Competence

Though research is still in its early stages, we have found that youngsters do not learn to riddle simply by memorizing and repeating set pieces. Instead, their competence proceeds through several stages and includes knowledge of riddle production as well as of riddle interaction. Below, I review this acquisition process and, reflecting the bias in the literature, focus on urban American children.

Made-up Routines

Youngsters acquire much of their knowledge of riddling in actual riddle interaction. Some exchanges may be conducted with adults; most often, they occur with peers. In American society, the peer group represents the single most important laboratory for youngsters' acquisition and exercise of riddling competence.[14]

When exposed to older children's riddling, young children (of around five years) notice question-answer sequences that call special attention to the asker. Although they find this sort of performance appealing, young children usually possess no ready stock of riddles to draw on. Wanting to participate, they make up their own, trying to imitate those they have heard. As I've shown above, riddles are based in common solicitational strategies. Young children depend on these strategies in making up their routines. Among McDowell's informants (1979, 59–68), the most frequently adopted strategies were those of cause and effect and description:

Causality:

51. How come the pig likes to get in the mud?—'cause he likes to take a bath in the mud. (McDowell 1979, 245)

Description:

52. What's red and white, and doesn't do nothing, and has a stick down its side, and the red and white thing is against the stick?—a flag. (McDowell 1979, 245)

By far, descriptive routines (like that in no. 52) appear to outnumber those based in other strategies (Weiner 1970; McDowell 1979).

Made-up descriptive routines enumerate the features or actions of some object.[15] Often, the referenced object or some reproduction of it is within the riddler's immediate environment. Like made-up routines based on other strategies, those of description do not contain a block element. Instead, the ideal routine—according to peer group standards (McDowell 1979)—is accurate and transparent, its answer easy to grasp. The respondent's correct answer signals that a "good" question has been asked:

53. What's big and has black stripes and white stripes?—a zebra. (U.T. Children's Folklore Project, unpublished data)[16]

54. What's real big and it grows in the ground and it's got leaves on it?—a tree. (U.T. Children's Folklore Project, unpublished data)

There is some evidence of cultural and regional differences in children's made-up descriptive routines. With respect to cultural differences, we can compare examples 53 and 54 above with those below. The former were obtained from Austin Anglo youngsters; the following, from Austin Mexican American children:

> 55. It's a little circle in your stomach.—belly button. (McDowell 1979, 244)

> 56. It's in a hole, what do you call it, in the zoo? —a guinea pig. (McDowell 1979, 244)

Though children of both groups used solicitations phrased as interrogatives, only the Mexican American youngsters in addition employed declarative solicitations (nos. 55, 56 above). This suggests that children from different cultural backgrounds may exploit linguistic resources differently in their riddle-making. These differences are suggested when we contrast material from the Austin youngsters (both Anglo and Mexican American) with material obtained in Massachusetts by Meryl Weiner (1970). Like the Austin children, the Massachusetts youngsters most often relied on the interrogative format. The youngest children in Weiner's sample, however, occasionally framed their descriptions as first-person statements. The riddler pretends to adopt the identity of the person, place, or thing being described:[17]

> 57. I have a tail. I have a body. I have a face. I am white and black. What am I?
> —a skunk. (Weiner 1970, 9)

This technique does not appear in the Austin material.

The Acquisition of Riddling Competence

The acquisition of riddling skills is essentially the acquisition of an artistic competence. Children just entering elementary school have mastered the basic linguistic resources of their native tongue. They have a rudimentary grasp of the cognitive systems in their culture. And, through their spontaneous play, they have gained practice with the "performance persona" (McDowell 1979, 187). In learning how to riddle, children learn to apply these acquired and developing competencies to the specific purposes of riddle interaction.

Although a number of developmental schemes are available (for example, Weiner 1970, Sanches and Kirshenblatt-Gimblett 1976, Sutton-Smith 1976b; Wolfenstein 1954), that proposed by McDowell (1979) and elaborated by Bauman (1977b) best suits our purposes here. In contrast to the others, this perspective treats riddle acquisition as a social interactional process.

During the initial stage in the acquisition process (around five years), youngsters learn the basics of riddle interaction. Through observing and participating, they learn that the poser of a riddle gains the floor, that the riddle contains both a question and an answer, that the respondent should be given a chance to guess, and that the poser should know the answer to his own question (Bauman 1977b, 26). Guided by these observations and stimulated by the riddles they hear from others, these youngsters make up their own routines (as discussed below); they also learn that the respondent's correct answer reflects positively on the riddler. By learning to present such "successful" routines, young children increase their understanding of the relationship between riddling and ego-enhancement.

At the second stage (around six years), children tend to modify their views as to what constitutes a "good" riddle. Now they come to believe that a riddle is a puzzling question with an arbitrary answer (Bauman 1977b, 27; Sutton-Smith 1976b, 115). Noticing that riddlers always seem to be right, regardless of the esoteric sequences they come up with, children at this stage are apt to initiate sequences like the following:

58. riddler: What color is blood?
    respondent: Red
    riddler: Nope, it's blue and black. (Bauman 1977b, 27)

"Potent elicitations" (Bauman 1977b, 27) such as this don't receive much peer group reinforcement. Since the relationship between the question and its answer is grasped only by the riddler (if indeed that), coparticipants aren't motivated to encourage similar routines. Faced with losing respondents, young riddlers once again modify their understanding of riddles. Though they still regard riddles as confusing, children come to assume that riddles must nevertheless be entertaining. As a result, they turn to the subjects of sexuality and scatology. If they weren't aware of it before, they soon realize that "dirt" sells:

59. riddler: What do you call people?
    respondent: I don't know, what?
    riddler: Doo-doo people. (Bauman 1977b, 27)

Toward the end of the second stage, children's interest in traditional riddles begins to surface. This burgeoning recognition, however, outstrips the young-sters' understanding of riddles' speech play. The children can't yet grasp all of the linguistic and sociolinguistic complexities in the riddles they try to repeat. As a result, some of their attempts are flawed:

> 60. What did the mean frog say to the nice frog?—"I hope you crick" (instead of "croak"). (Bauman 1977b, 28)

As children enter and proceed through the third stage (of around seven years), their production errors decrease markedly. Youngsters come not only to recognize the riddle as a traditional form, they are also beginning to ap-preciate it as such. As this shift is realized, the children increase their efforts to learn and to produce riddles as preset pieces, with a stable question and a fixed answer. The display of competence becomes a matter of demonstrat-ing one's knowledge of riddles within the peer group.[18]

In the final stage (at around eight years), children routinely succeed in the use of traditional riddles. In effect, they have gained mastery of peer-group riddling. The literature (Wolfenstein 1954; McDowell 1979) suggests that children maintain an interest in riddling until about the age of ten or twelve. After that time, they put their performance energies into other genres, allow-ing their interest in riddling to decline. Since most mainstream American so-ciety tends to regard riddling as a children's activity and thus as one inappro-priate for adults except under special circumstances (Roberts and Forman 1972, 182), we might say that youngsters between eight and twelve have prob-ably acquired as much competence in riddling as they will ever have.

Functions of Children's Riddling

Outside of the fact that it allows its participants to engage in social interac-tion, there is perhaps no single, universal function of riddling. At the least, riddle functions result from an interplay among the participants' perception of situational circumstances, their combined and individual goals, and their relative commitment to group and community standards. Documenting riddle functions depends on in-depth fieldwork and the analysis of riddles in individual communities, groups, and situations.

Below, I review some of the possible riddle functions based on the factor of social interaction.

Several researchers (for example, Roberts and Forman 1971; Sutton-Smith 1976b; Bauman 1982) have observed that in many urban groups rid-dling is a way of engaging in, representing, and commenting on the processes of questioning and answering.[19] Children have an interest in playing out and playing with interrogative formats. For example, riddling models the kind of interrogation that is ubiquitous in educational settings (Bauman 1982, 184). As a result, children's riddling may in part be an adaptive mechanism, allowing youngsters to come to terms with the participant structures of schooling. This perspective has several points that support it. Adult-child interrogation is characteristic not only of classroom interaction but also of interaction in the home environment. Parents routinely query children about the children's activities. It is not surprising, then, that children are attracted to an activity that allows them to serve in the role of interrogator. That role allows children some access to power. The children also become the focus of attention. And, in supplying the riddle answer, they enjoy "being right."

As an expressive model of interrogation, riddling also permits youngsters to manipulate the resources of communication. As I've shown, riddles are based on common solicitational strategies. As framing devices, these strategies serve as tools by which people orient and indicate their perceptions of the world. In riddling, such strategies facilitate the exchange of information, for example, by advising respondents of some of the cognitive and communicative work they are to do. Descriptive questions require that respondents notice details and generalize from them. Respondents to classification questions must indicate the categorization of experience. Comparison-contrast questions require information about similarities or differences in domains of experience. To be sure, riddles counterpoint these familiar strategies with a variety of disruptive techniques. True riddles have their block elements; joking riddles surprise with humor, and parodic forms startle with nonsense or victimization. These techniques complicate communication, whether the respondent's task is to solve the riddler's question or to relate its answer to assumptions of everyday life . The tension, however, is not irresoluble. The enigma of a true riddle can be solved, the humor of a joking riddle can be appreciated, and (except for the most drastic of the victimization forms) the absurdity of a parodic riddle can be dismissed as inconsequential to everyday concerns.

In concluding, I should point out that children are not likely to be self-consciously aware of the functions summarized above. For them, riddling is primarily a form of folk entertainment, one that also attests to the participants' competence in peer group and community traditions.

NOTES TO CHAPTER EIGHT

1. Catch routines, soliciting either a verbal or a physical response, are treated

in Roemer 1977. The interactional organization and developmental acquisition of knock-knock routines are discussed in Bauman 1977b. For an extensive collection of knock-knock routines, see McCosh 1976, 204–12.

2. The riddle proposition is the "question" unit of a riddle. It may take the form of an interrogative (such as riddle no. 35) or a statement (such as riddle no. 7).

3. Riddle act invitations are not unique to American children. Schapera (1932, 217) reports the following concerning the riddle invitation, proposition, and answer in children's riddling among the Bakxatla of South Africa:

The question is framed in the formula: *mpolêllê dilô o mpolêllê xore...ke eng?* (Tell me something, what is...?), the actual riddle appearing in the body of the formula. The answer follows simply: *ke*...(it is so and so). E.g., *mpolêllê dilô, o mpolêllê xore ntlo e tsweu ee senang mojakô ke eng? Ke lee.* (Tell me something. Tell me what is the white hut which has no door? It is an egg.) In practice, the formula is often wholly omitted once it has been used with the opening riddle, and the bare question is set; or else the word, *mpolêllê* (tell me), is placed before each of the remaining riddles.

We might also note that English-language true riddle (no. 8) incorporates a riddle act invitation ("riddle me") as part of its own rhyming structure. For an early description of a riddle act sequence in a traditional Native American culture, see Jetté 1913, 182–84.

4. Riddlers who taunt respondents who don't know the riddle answer have also been reported among Finnish children. In the first Finnish riddle collection, *Aenigmata Fennica* (1783), Christfrid Ganander wrote: "Lastly, one takes note that the young folks, boys and girls, test each other still at present with riddles in our province; it is shameful if the other cannot answer three riddles, and they then send [her] to the yard of shame (*hapiapiha*), and even wee children know still today how to say to each other, if the companion cannot answer three riddles: 'Go to Hyvola; may the dogs of Hyvola bark. Daughter, go to see who is coming there? A poor ragged girl all dressed in rags. A mouse is her horse, a ladle is her sleigh . . .'" (italics added), cited in Maranda 1976, 127.

5. Nor to my knowledge has anyone yet attempted such a comprehensive treatment, one integrating the various levels of the riddles' construction.

6. Although these are not the only rhetorical strategies upon which riddles draw, for reasons of space they must bear the burden of illustration here. One important strategy omitted from this chapter is that of instrumentality (for example, "Why did the man throw the clock out the window?—To make time fly" [Weiner 1970, 23; see also McDowell 1979, 64–65]). The use of instrumentality in riddles is particularly complex because it is is used strategically in both the riddle and the puzzle genres.

7. In its strictest sense, the term "Wellerism" refers to a quotation proverb such as "'Every man to his taste,' said the farmer when he kissed the cow." In British and American societies, the pattern of Wellerism proverbs is attributed to the literary figure, Sam Weller, who frequently used such sayings in Dickens's novel, *Pickwick Papers* (1836–37) (Taylor 1949, 1169–70). On Wellerisms recorded in the English language, see Mieder and Kingsbury 1993. Some folklorists have adapted the term Wellerism riddle to describe forms like nos. 15–17. For additional examples from children's tradition, see Opie and Opie 1959, 81-83 and McCosh 1976, 212–14.

8. Children's ethnic riddles and jokes are examined in Knapp and Knapp 1976, 191–205; McCosh 1976, 112–22, 226–55; Bronner 1988, 122–23, 292–94, n. 19.

9. And, of course, a visual sketch can be rendered in somewhat different ways depending on the perspective of the individual riddler. What matters is that the sketch presented accords with the eventual verbal answer. Ewa Östergren (1983) has offered sixty-six drawings that accord with the visual riddle answer "a giraffe passing a window." The sketches were produced by Swedish schoolchildren from three different classes. Of Östergren's collection, Bengt af Klintberg (personal communication) has commented: "What is interesting in [Östergren's] study is that she makes clear that the children learn the *idea* of the riddle and then visualize it according to their own

experiences. [In] other words, the Parry and Lord theory seems to be useful for children's pictorial riddling!" (italics in the original). My thanks to Professor Klintberg for making this information and a copy of Östergren's collection available to me. Other published versions of the "giraffe passing the window" sketch can be found in Klintberg 1980, 193 and Roemer 1982a, 183.

10. Klintberg (1980, 198) also reports that analogous forms are known in Germany (as *Drudel*) as well as in England. Relying on English and American data, McCosh (1976, 217) provides what appear to be traditional solutions (nos. 646–49) to visual riddle drawings. She neither identifies the statements as being part of such pairings, however, nor does she provide the drawings.

11. For a South African (Bakxatla) version of riddle nos. 32–34, see footnote no. 3.

12. Parodic forms often run in cycles. Some cycles popular since the early 1960s have dealt with elephants, grapes, bananas, and dead babies. See McCosh 1976, 60–65 for both English and American examples, and, for both texts and bibliography, see Bronner 1988, 125-27, 295–96 n. 22 on elephant riddles, as well as n. 23 on dead baby riddles. For studies of "sick humor" and the use of stereotypes in riddles and jokes, see Dundes 1987.

13. Sequences like this have been called "pretended obscene riddles." See Hullum 1972–73 and Brown 1973.

14. Though children learn most of their riddles from other children and, to a lesser extent, from adults, important popular-culture riddle resources include books, magazines, television programs, and artifactual material such as bubble gum wrappers and "Dixie" riddle cups.

15. McDowell (1979, 33–37, 59–66) uses "descriptive routine" as a catch term for a variety of spontaneously generated routines. I restrict the term to routines based on the technique of description only, or primarily such.

16. Between 1973 and 1976, the University of Texas Children's Folklore Project collected and investigated a range of folkloric forms used by Anglo, Mexican American, and black five- through eight-year-olds in Austin, Texas. Work produced by project members is reviewed in Bauman 1977b, 1982.

17. Description phrased in the first person is sometimes found in true riddles. Such riddles were occasionally used by the older children in Weiner's sample:

> The strongest man in the world can't hold me long,
>> yet I am lighter than a feather. What am I?

> —breath. (collected from a nine-year-old, as reported in Weiner 1970,
> 25; see also Taylor 1951, 667)

Though Weiner does not discuss the possibility, it may be suggested that the younger children borrowed this technique from hearing the older children tell "true" riddles.

18. As their interest in traditional riddles increases, children's concern with made-up routines declines. During riddle sessions, though, older children do occasionally fall back on made-up routines when they exhaust their ready supply of traditional riddles (McDowell 1979).

19. For a discussion of culturally based relationships between riddling (including that of children) and values of dialogism and polyphony in Madagascar, see Haring 1985.

9 TALES AND LEGENDS

Elizabeth Tucker

Children are natural storytellers, and collectors of folklore can get a great deal of enjoyment from recording their tales and legends. On playgrounds, at parties, and around campfires—especially on dark, spooky nights—the stories children tell are amazing in their variety. They range from brief, hastily mumbled renditions to impressively long tales with artistic sound effects: clicks, thumps, screams, and carefully timed pauses. Some children take a lot of pride in their storytelling abilities, while others give little thought to the tales they are telling. But in every case, children's folktales and legends teach us about the narrators' personalities, enthusiasms, and anxieties. They reveal community standards and cultural trends, as well as cross-cultural similarities; multinational studies of children's stories have revealed some striking parallel texts. Classifying the stories' origins and migrations can be an absorbing task, but delving into their deeper meanings is a process that has interested psychologists, sociologists, and linguists as well as folklorists.

For the collector setting out to gather children's stories, a number of options are available. Children can be interviewed singly or in groups, in their classrooms during school hours or in the midst of their free play and recreational activities. Each type of collecting yields a somewhat different kind of story. All alone with an adult researcher, a boy may be careful to give plenty of details but hesitant to broach taboo subjects; in the middle of her Scout group, a girl may laugh, shout, and skip from one subject to an-other as her peers' reactions change. Single-sex groups have different reper-toires than mixed groups, and classroom gatherings tend to have different atmospheres from get-togethers in less formal circumstances. In general, I have found that the more natural the setting is, the better storytelling is likely to be. Young people tend to relax in places they know well, and their sto-ries flow better with minimal adult interference. Even though unregulated gatherings get raucous at times, with children clamoring for turns to tell their stories, the results are much more interesting than those from carefully timed and disciplined sessions. Each collector must choose the type of collecting situation that she or he wants, taking all of these variables into account.

Once the stories have been gathered and the process of analysis begins, it is easy to start categorizing the tellers as representatives of their age, sex, and socioeconomic groups. It can be useful to think about "the adolescent boy," "the middle-class girl," or "the disadvantaged pre-schooler," but such abstractions should *not* interfere with attention to individual narrators. Each child has his or her own temperament, interests, moods, and idiosyncrasies; all of these individual factors are relevant to the process of storytelling. Of course, it isn't always feasible to get to know every child informant in depth—but the further the acquaintance goes, the more rewarding collecting is likely to be for both the storyteller and the researcher. Children cease to be mere representatives of categories when they are present, with all their quirks and challenges, over long periods of time. While their stories may fall into developmental patterns that have already been established, there are always surprises and deviations from the familiar trends.

In this chapter I will maintain a rough developmental sequence, beginning with very young children's stories and ending with the legends told by boys and girls on the brink of adolescence. Some clarification of the terms "tale," "legend," and "story" is necessary at the outset. The tale, or folktale, as it is more properly called, is a story with traditional content that has a certain kind of plot structure. This structure is clearly recognizable, from the "once upon a time" beginning to the "happily ever after" ending. While folktale heroines such as Cinderella and Red Riding Hood may suffer many misfortunes, we know that they will find happiness in the end. In the legend, on the other hand, disastrous conclusions are quite common; heroines and heroes have no guarantee of a happy ending. Often told as true stories, legends may be long and elaborate or brief and unadorned. They may be attributed to a definite place or person: "This happened in California," for example. If we hear of a poodle exploding in a microwave oven in San Francisco, our sense of geographic authenticity is heightened.

Legends and tales make up many of the narratives told by children, but not all; the rest can simply be called stories. "Story" is a general term that indicates a verbal account with some sequential development; one event follows another, and characters experience major or minor changes. Among the youngest narrators, "story" is often the best term to use. All legends and tales are stories, but not all stories lend themselves to classification by traditional folkloristic categories.

I will discuss story types that I have found to be typical of three age groups—two to five, six to nine, and ten to twelve—with quite a lot of attention to individual storytellers. I have thoroughly enjoyed gathering stories from children and supervising my students in their collecting projects; it has been difficult to choose among so many entertaining texts. I hope this sample will reflect some of the pleasure that comes from getting to know young narrators and hearing their favorite tales.

VERY YOUNG CHILDREN: TWO TO FIVE

When we think of children telling stories, we are likely to picture kids who are old enough to go to school, camp, and slumber parties—not tiny children whose ability to speak is still on the shaky side. It can seem strange to learn that two-, three-, four-, and five-year-olds are among the most candid and enterprising of storytellers. Their tales tend to be quite short, for obvious reasons of skill and attention span, but some four- and five-year-olds' stories go on at surprising length. Dreams, fantasies, and facts of everyday life merge in young children's narratives to form fascinating combinations that have their own inner logic. Folklorists have sometimes neglected this age group in favor of older children who can participate more fully in the "childhood underground" (Knapp and Knapp 1976), but psychologists have seemed more interested in tales told by the very young than stories circulated by groups of older children on the playground. Psychologists' collections from the 1950s up to the present have provided us with a valuable body of material; more recently, folklorists' collections have also proliferated.

The first systematic collection of young children's stories to be published was Evelyn Pitcher's and Ernst Prelinger's *Children Tell Stories* (1963). Based upon texts collected from boys and girls between 1955 and 1958, this study analyzes the psychodynamics of early childhood fantasy. The two authors tabulate frequent occurrences of settings, themes, and characters in order to show how fantasy tales differ by age and sex. All of their youngest narrators are preoccupied with falling down and breaking things, while the four- and five-year-olds are interested in a wider range of actions—very natural, when we consider how often two- and three-year-olds do fall down and hurt themselves! While the boys' stories differ from the girls' in some noteworthy ways (the boys', for example, having a wider spatial range and less domestic emphasis), all of the stories contain an intriguing blend of characters. Folktale personages such as Red Riding Hood, the Three Bears, and the generic "princess" intermingle with television figures like cowboys, Indians, space cadets, and pirates; even Bucky Beaver of the Ipana toothpaste commercial and the "eensy weensy spider" of nursery school songfests are part of this cast of characters. Of course parents, animals, and familiar objects are important inclusions too, and such seasonal figures as Santa Claus and the Halloween witch are given some prominence. All of this blending shows how rich the young child's fantasy life is and how close the linkage between fantasy and reality can be. While the differences between boys and girls make up a major portion of Pitcher's and Prelinger's analysis, we should keep their results in perspective; the role models and expectations for children of both sexes have undergone some significant changes since the mid-1950s.

A later study, Louise B. Ames's "Children's Stories" (1966), presents New Haven nursery school children's tales in an analytical framework derived from the Pitcher and Prelinger model. Ames differs in her approach, however, by focusing on the kinds of stories told at different ages rather than on the process of fantasy itself. Her results show a really remarkable preoccupation with violence at all ages from two to five; moving up in age, the form taken by violence changes from spanking to falling down and finally killing or dying. There are some fascinating minor points, such as the fact that only four-year-old girls tell stories about being thrown into the garbage (1966, 342). Folktale characters such as Red Riding Hood become major protagonists among the four- and five-year-olds, though there is still a lot of shifting from folktale contents to reality-based events in that age range.

The best collection of young children's stories by a folklorist is Brian Sutton-Smith's *The Folkstories of Children* (1981b). Sutton-Smith organizes the narratives of two- to four-year-olds under the heading of "verse stories," as opposed to the "plot stories" of older children up to the age of ten. These early verse narratives are rhythmic, repetitive, and often based upon a few key words; they tend to stress beginnings and endings rather than midstory development (1981b, 3–7). Among the stories chosen as examples, Sutton-Smith points out significant stylistic features that show individual differences. This is one of the important lessons of story analysis at the earliest age level: that very young children *do* have their own narrative styles, and that their stylistic proclivities come from both cognitive development and individual artistry.

In Sutton-Smith's study the older children's stories are best suited for structural analysis, the method used for identifying plot elements since the publication of Vladimir Propp's *Morphology of the Folktale* (1958). Nevertheless, children in the younger age group tell some stories with enough plot elements to make this kind of analysis worthwhile. Gilbert Botvin's scheme for fantasy narrative analysis includes such sequential categories as threat, deception, disequilibrium, alliance, defense, escape, rescue, and defeat (Sutton-Smith 1981b, 3–5; Botvin 1976). The youngest children's stories often stop at the disequilibrium stage, instead of moving on to a more positive and definitive resolution. Why this happens, and what we can learn from this tendency to leave characters in disarray, are problems that remain to be more fully explored.

What happens to the characters in young children's stories can be put in perspective by using a system developed by Elli Köngäs-Maranda and Pierre Maranda (1970). This system has four levels of confrontation that involve some sort of conflict between the central figure and the antagonist. At level one the antagonist completely vanquishes the weaker character; at level two the weaker one tries to respond, but fails; at level three there is a successful response to the antagonist's threat; and at level four the original threatening situation is so thoroughly changed that there is no further danger to worry about. Sutton-Smith applies this scheme to stories in his sample, finding that five-year-olds tell stories at a much lower response level than ten-year-olds, but noting that five-year-olds do occasionally tell stories at the fourth level (1981b, 20–24). Analysis by this four-level system can be very helpful in determining how the child narrator feels about himself: whether he feels secure and powerful, or whether he feels overwhelmed by adverse circumstances. Some of this response to threat seems linked to cognitive development, but the individuals' feelings of security are certainly relevant.

Recent research has focused on young children's storytelling within the framework of conversation. In her work with preschool children, Jean Umiker-Sebeok notes that there is a substantial difference between the intraconversational narratives children tell to adults and the narratives they tell to other children. When an adult is listening, stories grow longer and more complex (Umiker-Sebeok 1979, 106). This study and others indicate that children's intraconversational narratives reach their fullest development in familiar settings; unfamiliar surroundings or circumstances result in texts that do not fairly represent children's capabilities as narrators.

Further insight into young children's storytelling patterns comes from Judith Haut, who analyzes her son Bryan's stories between the ages of three and four. Haut states that, like other children, her son uses stories to entertain, influence conversations, and gain prestige. By narrating, Bryan is able to go beyond the kind of conversation adults expect from him and shift roles to gain the interest of his listeners (1922, 33–45). As collections and analyses of young children's stories have proliferated (see Preece 1987 and Paley 1990), it has been possible to understand narratives within a complex web of psychological and social motivations.

With all of these analytical alternatives, a look at a two-year-old's story can become quite a time-consuming venture—but it is sufficient here to give a brief analysis linked to knowledge of the child's personality. Here is a short narrative from two-and-a-half-year-old Janet, the daughter of well-educated parents in Binghamton, New York:

> Daddy cuts floor.
> Daddy gets boo-boo.
> Daddy go to doctor.
> Daddy get a band-aid.[1]

This story has the rhythmic, line-to-line structure characteristic of very young children's stories; the key word "Daddy" forms the basis of its development. While there are no definite indicators of time passing, such as the words "then" or "later," it is clear that some events precede others. Janet's father had just been repairing the bathroom floor and had gone to the doctor to get a bandage; all of these occurrences are retained in their proper sequence in the story.

Even from such a brief and factual narrative, we can see that Janet is an observant, sensitive child. She is concerned about her father's welfare and eager to understand what has happened to him; her story puts his frightening accident into a comprehensible framework. Just before telling her story, Janet spent some time alone in her crib. The collector overheard her saying to herself:

> Daddy play hockey? Yes!
> Mommy play hockey? *No!*

This is part of a monologue rather than a story, but it shows Janet's interest in all that characterizes and differentiates her parents. Since the publication of Ruth Weir's *Language in the Crib* (1962), bedtime monologues have been recognized as an important source of knowledge.

While real-life events provide a lot of material for stories, dreams furnish some of the most significant themes and plot elements. Young children may identify their narratives as dreams or, more commonly, tell what happened without mentioning that a dream was the source. Sometimes the dream may be about an experience the child has had recently; then the reason for its importance may be clearer.

Looking closely at young children's stories is sometimes just one facet of an evaluation and treatment process. Individual case studies by psychologists have drawn some important conclusions about children's self-expression, partly by analyzing narratives that emerge in a therapeutic setting. In one especially thorough study of stories told in a therapeutic environment, Richard A. Gardner used a technique of eliciting stories from his patients while telling stories of his own (1971). Therapy begins with a story told by the doctor; then, as treatment progresses, the doctor's stories develop from narrative material supplied by the patient. As the boy or girl grows more confident about telling stories and dreams, the doctor can use stories to focus on key aspects of the patient's feelings, convey messages about positive development, and bring about changes in behavior. When the child begins to tell stories that sound happier, more serene in their conclusions, the doctor knows that therapy can successfully come to an end.

Outside of a therapeutic setting, when four-, five-, and six-year-olds are asked to tell a story, their choice may well be a traditional folktale. "Hansel and Gretel," "Snow White," "Little Red Riding Hood," and "Cinderella" are all among the stories that I have found to be especially popular among young children. The reasons for this popularity are clear enough: Parents read the tales to their children, bookstores sell them in attractively bound volumes, and librarians include them in regular story hours. The term "fairy tale" is often used for these traditional folk narratives, although it most correctly applies to British tales about the small creatures known as fairies.

Many scholars have assessed the appeal and value of folktales for child readers and listeners, for example, Betsy Hearne (1989). In *The Uses of Enchantment: The Meaning and Importance of Fairy Tales* (1976), Bruno Bettelheim analyzes how folktales help children cope with psychological problems in order to move toward adulthood. "Hansel and Gretel," according to Bettelheim, provides children with a better understanding of starvation, anxiety, and desertion fears (pages 159–66). Critics of Bettelheim's psychoanalytical approach question the accuracy and appropriateness of this form of analysis. Jack Zipes, author of *Breaking the Magic Spell: Radical Theories of Folk and Fairy Tales* (1979), chastises Bettelheim for trying to put together "static literary models to be internalized for therapeutic consumption" (page 177). Alan Dundes questions Bettelheim's "uses of enchantment and misuses of scholarship" (1991) while Kay F. Stone explores controversies over the impact of fairy tales (1985). The most thorough assessment of these issues is Maria Tatar's recent work *Off With Their Heads! Fairytales and the Culture of Childhood* (1992). Criticizing Bettelheim for his "male developmental model" that "defines the self through separation and mastery" (pages 78–79), Tatar probes reworkings of traditional tales to reveal their hidden messages for children. Perrault, the Grimms, and others, Tatar says, have altered traditional stories so that they become lessons about the evils of disobedience, laziness, untruthfulness, and other behavioral traits perceived as dangerous by society. Close examinaton of reworked folktales can uncover substantial didactic content that has little to do with children's own priorities (see also Zipes 1983).

One fairly typical example of folktale retelling is a lively rendition of "The Three Bears" told by David, a boy who was almost six. David, who lived in Rochester, New York, at the time of collection, was thrilled to tell his story for the tape recorder. He laughed, hesitated a few times, and then began a long story that included the following: "This girl came along named Goldilocks. Okee, okeeee, okee, okee, okee. And, then Goldilocks came along and tried Papa-bear's porridge. That was too *hooooooo-o-o-ot!* She tried Mama-bear's porridge. That was too cold. She tried Baby-bear's porridge. That was ju-u-ust right. She ate it all up. Yum-yum-yum."[2] David is quite a creative narrator, especially with regard to sound effects. A few words are shouted, some vowels are extended for dramatic emphasis, and certain syllables are repeated to show intensified feeling, while some chains of syllables sound like speech play for the sheer pleasure of rhyming. In general, his version of "The Three Bears" shows a special sensitivity to the experimental possibilities that language offers him.

Perhaps the most practical reason why young children are so fond of telling tales like "The Three Bears" is that the structure of these stories lends itself so well to formulaic narration. There are so many repetitious lines, verses, and episodes that the child who is just learning to put together a story has a good chance of getting the sequence right. "Cinderella," "The Three Billy Goats Gruff," and "Snow White" all have numerous repetitions that ease recollection. Add to this feeling of competence the joy that the very young take in repeating actions and words—in speech play and games, for example—and you can see why folktale retellings are so popular. They offer a good chance to have fun with a story, develop narrative skills, and perhaps throw in a few original effects as well.

EARLY SCHOOL YEARS: SIX TO NINE

As children get a little older, they may care more about making fairy tales their *own* stories. Slightly different characters, a new setting, or a different ending can satisfy this need for personal manipulation. Kristin Wardetzsky (1990), drawing upon a data sample from the German Democratic Republic, suggests that children's own folktales differ markedly from the Grimms'. Their concepts of villainy go beyond the conventional witches and stepmothers, and their happiest ending is the return to a harmonious home (pages 157–76). I have also found in my own fieldwork that children's oral and dramatized versions of folktales teach us a great deal about the narrators' interests, needs, and storytelling skills (Tucker 1980a). One interesting text is eight-year-old Krystal's version of "Little Red Riding Hood." Krystal, a serious girl with a taste for sad stories, was attending day camp in southern Indiana when she told her story about a little girl going to her grandmother's house. Although the story's beginning made several listeners whisper "Red Riding Hood!" it soon became clear that Krystal valued her own ingenuity above traditional identification. Her villain was a "killer," not a wolf, and the only violent act that occurred was his removal of the little girl's hair with a knife. The story ended with the killer's threat: "'Every time I come to your grandmother's house, I'm gonna cut, I'm going to cut off your head and a finger, and a ear, and a nose, and a eye and a tooth,' and so she never came back to the house again. The end." This conclusion is reminiscent of some of the dialogue in the original "Red Riding Hood": "Why, Grandmama, what big eyes you have! . . . What a big nose you have! . . . What big teeth you have!" Besides containing these familiar terms of emphasis, Krystal's story follows the basic plot line of "Red Riding Hood" (type 333, *The Glutton,* in Aarne and Thompson 1961). Krystal must have known this narrative structure since her early childhood; it is straightforward and exciting, a good framework to use for creative story-building.

The most important question about Krystal's story is why she changed the ending so much. What motivated her to let the little girl get away so easily? One deceptively simple answer is that she needs to express her originality; this has to be her own story, so that she can feel proud of her work as a narrator. What seems especially significant in her story, however, is the sensitivity shown toward modern living conditions and dangers. In today's cities we measure a walk in blocks, not vaguely defined stretches, and we hardly need to feel worried about attacks from wolves. Burglars, rapists, murderers, and maniacs are far more threatening to us, and Krystal has chosen one of these frightening figures to use in her narrative. Her choice demonstrates Marianne Rumpf's point that the assailant in "Red Riding Hood" can be human or animal, supernatural or realistic; the story has adapted to different social requirements for many years, and its flexibility shows every sign of continuing (Rumpf 1955, 4).

Within the flexible network of children's storytelling, it has become increasingly common for children to build creative tales upon frameworks offered by movies and videotapes. Sylvia Grider's term "media narraform" is used to indicate a story based on a movie that the narrator has seen (Grider 1981). In my own research, I found that children about age six or seven enjoy using movie versions of tales like "Aladdin" and "Beauty and the Beast" as points of departure for their own imaginative stories. For example, the heroine of "Cinderella" becomes "Cinderella vampire" or "Cinderella tiger," as young narrators shift the frame to suit their fancy (Tucker 1992).

Another form of storytelling that has flourished in recent years has been the composition of a computer story. Teachers have encouraged their pupils to write and to print out their own stories with the help of a wide range of computer software. Programs such as Kidwriter and Explore-A-Story make it possible for young writers to create their own printed story texts, taking great pride in the creation process (Eltgroth 1988, 1989). Some computer programs combine art with writing, making story composition a delightfully multifaceted process (Summers 1988). In schools where children's creative stories and artwork are published, the researcher can discover narratives that reflect children's story-sharing as well as individual creativity.

In addition to stories based on folktale models, tales from oral tradition that begin frighteningly and end happily are very popular among children in the early years of elementary school. These tales differ from those of folktale origin in that they are generally transmitted from child to child, rather than from parent or teacher to child. The first and second grades are years of discovery in many forms, and one of these is storytelling apart from adult influence. At recess, after school, and at parties, boys and girls share the stories they have recently learned—often from somewhat older friends or siblings. In this manner a story like "The Golden Arm" or "One Black Eye" can remain fresh from one generation of schoolchildren to the next, constantly being rediscovered and passed on to new recruits.

My favorite term for traditional tales that end happily, in spite of a worrisome start, is "funny-scary story." Many of the second- and third- graders with whom I worked in the summer of 1976 used this term; it seemed to re-assure their listening friends that a story would be "not *really* scary." I found that these youngsters, new to the sharing of stories, found it very hard to listen to frightening tales that didn't end with some kind of happy resolution. They were beginning to experiment with fear, just starting to understand the pleasure of "a good scare," and constant reassurance was necessary.

One especially venerable funny-scary story is the tried-and-true "It Floats"; I heard it myself at camp in the late 1950s. Seven-year-old Stacy, one of the quieter girls at the camp in southern Indiana where I worked, told the story with much enthusiasm: "I got a funny-scary story. One time this boy and girl were walking home from their uncle's house, 'cause they stayed too late, and they were walking past this house and people say it was haunted. And then they stopped to look at it and they heard something say,

'It floats! It floats!' And then the little girl was real scared, she said, 'What floats? What floats?' And he said, 'Ivory soap floats'" (Tucker 1977, 122–123). From the reaction of the other children to Stacy's story, it seemed that "It Floats" had lost some of its topical appeal since the time of my own camping experiences. There was not much laughter, and some of the children were downright confused about the punchline; what did it matter if the soap floated? In the 1950s and early 1960s, when the manufacturers of Ivory Soap put the slogan "It floats" into a lot of their commercials, the story had much more appeal. Today Ivory Soap is known for its purity and its history of being passed down from mother to daughter (according to the television commercials). As advertising changes, storytelling may undergo adaptations.

One noteworthy aspect of Stacy's story is the fact that the girl, not the boy, has the courage to ask the disembodied voice, "What floats?" Even though she is "real scared," she takes the risk of confronting the voice and thus wins reassurance. We can see a close identification of the narrator with the protagonist in this story and other variants, such as the one collected from Jim, a ten-year-old boy, by John Vlach. In Jim's story three boys discover a haunted house in the country; two of them get killed, and the third asks the voice what floats (Vlach 1971, 101–02). Another contrast between Jim's story and Stacy's is the absence of any real expression of fear in the former compared to the fright in the latter. Since Jim is three years older than Stacy, he can reel off a funny-scary story without any trepidations; and besides, admitting to being scared seems less common in boys' funny-scary stories.

"It Floats" is just one of the many stories that belongs to the Aarne–Thompson tale type 326, *The Youth Who Wanted to Learn What Fear Is*. The essence of this plot structure is a confrontation with a spooky, often disembodied apparition; it may be a voice or some other kind of peculiar noise, like rapping from a cupboard. The Grimms' tale that gives type 326 its name is about setting out to learn fear, with a silly conclusion to the quest: The hero learns to shiver by having some slippery minnows poured down his back (Magoun and Krappe 1960, 12–20). Not all variants of type 326 end with a shiver, but they all have to do with encountering the unknown and getting control of one's own feelings. This process is exactly what the funny-scary story is all about; the form of the ghost matters very little.

"Bloody Fingers," another very popular variant of type 326, sometimes has a victorious baby as its central character. Young narrators enjoy identifying with this small hero, who responds to a ghost more bravely than adults do. Sometimes the one who answers the ghost is a hippie, and other times it is a teenager, a man, or a woman. As in "It Floats," the only noise made by the ghost is a monotonously repeated phrase. The ominous wail

"Bloody Fingers!" may come from a bathroom, a basement, an attic, or a telephone, depending on the whim of the storyteller. The punchline also has many forms, from the polite "May I have a band-aid?" spoken by the ghost himself in eight-and-a-half-year-old Jennifer's version (Tucker 1977, 268) to the more cocky "Cool, man, cool. Go get a band-aid!" in the tale told by ten-year-old Kenny (Vlach 1971, 100). All of these versions are united by a simple goal: to have the ghost verbally put in its place by a person—usually a very young person—who has complete control of the situation.

Perhaps the oldest and most beloved funny-scary story is "The Golden Arm," a camp and slumber party classic. Samuel Langhorne Clemens wrote an essay about the delicacy of delivering this story's punchline at exactly the right moment (Clemens 1897), and many other people have raved about its shocking "jump ending" during the past century. When the story is told well, the narrator grabs whoever is closest to him and shouts, "YOU GOT IT!" "I GOTCHA!" or some such fitting phrase to make the climax complete. A thorough bibliography of "Golden Arm" variants can be found in Sylvia Grider's dissertation, "The Supernatural Narratives of Children" (Grider 1976, 557–83).

While "The Golden Arm" still flourishes as a frequently told story, its climax is often mangled or misunderstood by child narrators. The main development of the story is usually much the same, with a severed arm, a golden replacement, and a ghost's walk to reclaim the arm after death. Ten-year-old Patricia's version is characteristic: "Okay, this one about a golden arm. There was this man and this woman, they got in a automobile accident, and this lady, they had to go to the hospital, and, um, they had to chop her arm off, 'cause it looked like a, you could see her bones and everything, they had to chop her arm off and they gave her a golden arm, and then when they, when they went home, she died of some disease, and the man took the arm off to remember her by. And every night she'd come back and say, 'I want my golden arm, I want my golden arm,' and um, he got *real* scared." So far, so good, but Patricia finishes the story off with the surprising words "he found her golden arm hanging up by a rope in the, um, garage" (Tucker 1977, 491–92). I have heard other children in the first few years of elementary school say a soft "I gotcha" without a grab, give a lame answer to the ghost such as "I took it because I was gettin' poor," or simply give up in despair: "I can't remember it!" This uncertainty may be attributable to weak versions of the tale in circulation, or, more likely, to the difficulty that young schoolchildren have with such an artful climax. Since "The Golden Arm" is most popular among younger children, however, it can fall out of a child's active repertoire before the punchline is ever properly mastered.

"The Golden Arm" ends differently from "Bloody Fingers" and the others of that group, but it is still a bona fide funny-scary story. The jump or grab at the end is not as immediately funny as a humorous retort, but it is a splendid releaser of tension. The shout of "You got it!" defuses the suspense generated by the story, and the foolish look on the face of the grabbed victim is the stuff of which comedy is made. The story becomes a spoof rather than a drama, and everyone present can enjoy being part of such a ridiculous situation.

The tale type to which "The Golden Arm" belongs is Aarne–Thompson 366, *The Man from the Gallows*. Its plot structure reflects an ancient and well-entrenched taboo, the ban upon taking parts of a body from a grave. Of course an arm of gold is not an organic part of a body, but in other versions of type 366 the hero or heroine steals one or more real body parts from a grave.

It is interesting that in most versions of "The Stolen Liver," the ghost takes an extremely long time to reach the bed of the hapless grave-robber. Suspense-building is one logical reason for this delay, but another one is the need to establish some distance between the ghost's announcement of his presence and the final pounce. Young storytellers need some preparation for the shout, so that the ghost's arrival doesn't get too frightening. Without this slow build-up, the tale would lose its reliability as a funny-scary story; instead, it would be more like a seriously frightening legend. While some legends appear among the younger schoolchildren, funny-scary stories are much more common and better loved.[3]

UPPER ELEMENTARY SCHOOL: TEN TO TWELVE

There is no clear-cut division between storytelling patterns in the early and later years of elementary school; my inclusion of two stories from ten-year-olds in the previous section makes that fact perfectly clear. Around the age of ten, however, children begin to shift their focus from funny-scary tales to legends that have no happy ending. Their mastery of the simple tales is well established by the fifth grade, as is their ability to cope with fearful sensations in a controlled framework. It is time for them to explore less structured, more down-to-earth stories with variable and often shocking conclusions—in other words, preadolescent legend. I have known nine-year-olds who were already devoted to telling local legends and twelve-year-olds who absolutely refused to hear anything frightening; in fact, some adults of my acquaintance insist that they have *always* avoided scary movies, scary stories, and anything else remotely unsettling within the realm of entertainment. Most children, however, develop an interest in the legend sometime in elementary school. It would be hard for them to keep from being influenced by this genre, as so much legend-telling occurs informally in groups of all sizes.

One very popular legend is "The Fatal Initiation," which is told by many boys—and some girls as well—in the preadolescent or early adolescent years. Its plot concerns a test of endurance that takes place in a graveyard, haunted house, or other dangerous location; the initiate may get away alive, but death and serious wounds are common results. Folklorists have made some good progress in classifying and analyzing this legend (Baughman 1945; Knapp and Knapp 1976, 244). The Knapps' version, collected from a boy, has to do with a boy being dared to stick a knife into a fresh grave; when he does so, he finds that he can't leave because the knife has gone through his own foot. This is a fairly mild consequence compared with the mayhem and madness that occur in numerous other variants.

The idea of going to a scary place for the proof of one's courage and skill seems to strike an especially responsive chord in boys who are beginning to make the transition toward adolescence. Self-proving goes on throughout adolescence and beyond, but it can seem especially perilous at the point when adolescence begins. After all, nobody knows exactly what the outcome of an initiatory test will be, and it is frightening to imagine the worst possible results. Boys who feel great pressure to achieve may find particular significance in this kind of legendry.

Other legends frequently told by boys at camp include the numerous stories of ghosts, monsters, and maniacs. Girls tell these stories, too, but the boys' versions often show particular delight in the gruesome, bloody torture of innocent victims. I am not sure why this difference exists, but a number of girls have assured me that boys tell the *really* horrible camp stories. This discrepancy should lessen in time, as women's liberation encourages girls to express their less "ladylike" feelings. I have certainly collected some real shockers from young female narrators, and I expect that girls' camp stories will grow increasingly lurid as sex-role differences even out.

Jay Mechling shows in a chapter in this volume that camp is one of the most favorable settings for children's folklore. Far from the familiar comforts of home, campers (especially first-timers) are likely to feel nervous and alert to the hazards of being marooned in the woods. Every snapping twig or flashing light may seem sinister at first—and counselors or older campers may fan the flames of this anxiety by telling ghost or monster legends. Usually the story makes some direct reference to the camp and its location; in other words, it is "told for true" and meant to be taken seriously by everyone but seasoned campers and counselors.

One such legend cycle described by James P. Leary (1973) concerns the Boondocks Monster of Camp Wapehani in southern Indiana. This fearsome creature, also known as Boondoggle or the Swamp Monster, is a big-footed outer-space visitor that stays in the swamp and avoids dry areas. Boy Scouts who wander away from the grounds may get caught by the monster, according to the counselors—so the legend serves as a warning to obey the rules and stay put. As Linda Dégh and Andrew Vázsonyi point out in "The Dialectics of the Legend" (1976), social control is a very important function of this kind of story. Children who believe that a monster lurks nearby are much more likely to accept their counselors' restrictions, unless, on occasion, they join in an expedition to catch a glimpse of the monster in its lair. Deliberate sensation-seeking is one of the special pleasures of camping in the woods. If the counselor or camper in charge of the expedition is really enterprising, she or he can produce enough spooky lights, strange noises, or sudden apparitions to send the more timorous campers scampering back to their cabins.

Another memorable frightening figure is the Cropsey maniac of upstate New York. Year after year, my children's folklore students at SUNY–Binghamton have given graphic accounts of their exposure to this legend cycle as young campers. Their spellings of the maniac's name range from Cropsey to Kropsee, Kroppsy and even Crapsy; folk names that exist mainly in oral tradition have infinitely variable spelling. Lee Haring and Mark Breslerman have created a useful classificatory framework for the welter of Cropsey variants (1977). Reduced to its basic components, the story tells of an older, respected member of the community (a judge, businessman, or guard at the camp) who loses one or more members of his family in an accident (fire, fall, or drowning) and swears to avenge himself by taking the lives of nearby campers. Sometimes the camp has been negligent enough to have had something to do with the family members' death, but often there is no good reason for the oath of vengeance.

One especially vivid legend describes Cropsey as "a man with chalk-white hair, red, bloodshot eyes, and swinging a long, bloody ax" (Haring and Breslerman 1977, 15). In another variant, the body of a missing camper is found with the name "Cropsey" burned into her arm (page 19). As with the Boondocks Monster, it is clear that social control is an issue here; but beyond fulfilling this function, the Cropsey legend leaves a lasting impression in the minds of those who hear it. This story of a father who goes berserk and murders innocent children is especially horrifying because it reverses the usual expectation that a parent will take care of his own and other children. Campers who learn of his exploits are not likely to forget him.

Another frightening camp story is the subject of Bill Ellis's study "'Ralph and Rudy': The Audience's Role in Re-creating a Camp Legend" (1982). In this legend the central character, Ralph, becomes a wild man after cutting Rudy's head off and being splattered with his blood. Questioning whether this is folklore or "fakelore," Ellis concludes that the legend is indeed folklore even though it was fabricated by counselors and perpetuated by one teller. The key factor here is audience participation, which exerts a significant control over the development of the story. Ellis widens the usual interpretation of "traditionality" of children's folklore by adding the audience's control of the performer to the criteria of history and content (page 173).

While camp stories are told by both boys and girls, certain other legends tend to be for female listeners. One of these is "The Babysitter," a supposedly true story that exists in several forms. Young girls who are beginning to earn some extra money by babysitting tell stories of such disastrous situations as this one, described by ten-year-old Jennifer in Johnson City, New York: "There's one about this, like lady—she was babysittin' for these, um, these twins and she kept gettin' obscene phone calls and the guy was upstairs givin' her the phone calls and, um, every time she talked he would throw one of the twins out the window. That was in New York City or Long Island, I'm not sure."[4] Compared with some other versions of "The Babysitter," Jennifer's story is quite brief and minimally developed—but that is one of the characteristic forms that the legend takes. This text gets the point across just as well as a longer version with phone call dialogue, screams, and gory mutilations. The point, of course, is that terrible things can happen while a girl is babysitting; a man can get into the house, go after the children, and threaten the sitter's life as well.

The intense feeling of vulnerability that this legend conveys is an exaggerated form of the insecurity many girls feel on their first babysitting engagements. Being alone in a house with young children is a little like being off in the woods, with the important difference that the sitter is the one *in charge* here. She has been entrusted with the welfare of the children under her care, and anything that goes terribly wrong may be seen as her fault. It is interesting that the "Babysitter" legends stress harm to the children, rather than the sitter herself; the message is that responsibility for others is what matters. In this way, girls learn that taking good care of young children is one of their primary duties (boys' stories seldom deliver this message). In some variants, the intruder says to the girl over the phone, "I've got one of your kids and I'm going to get the other." Even though they are not really *her* kids, the babysitter is learning to accept the role of mother-in-training that society is offering to her.

Another kind of legend popular among girls in this age group is the account of a horrible accident or near-accident that happens in the company of a young man. "The Boyfriend's Death" is one shocking legend cycle (Dégh 1968a; Tucker 1976, 367–70). It tells of a boy and girl, or perhaps a man and wife, who drive down a deserted road and run out of gas. The boy or man goes off to get gas, and the girl or woman stays in the car. In ten-year-old Betsy's version, collected in southern Indiana, the horror begins while the woman is waiting: ". . . she heard a—something like "HREECH!" and a drip and something, a THUMP. She looked out the window and started screaming, 'cause her husband was hanging by the tree, and that "CLICK" sound was his throat being cut, the "Drip-drop" was the blood falling on the ground, and the THUMP was him banging against the car." In Betsy's story we see a clear demarcation of sex roles: The man ventures out to get gas, and the woman sits passively and safely in the car. While the woman herself escapes from harm, she has the terrible shock of discovering her husband hanging from a tree, dead and bleeding profusely. The emotional content of this legend varies somewhat according to the main characters; if they are a boy and girl, the fear of being alone with a boy in a deserted place may be predominant. But in this case, where a husband and wife are the characters, the strongest feeling seems to be survivor guilt: The woman has stayed safe and let her husband do the dirty work, and now she has to live with the shock of his horrible death. In either case, there is an emphasis on human relationships and responsibilities—not very far in this respect from the focus of "The Babysitter."

It would not be fair to discuss Betsy's story without giving her credit for her wonderful sound effects, the "HREECH" and "Drip-drop" and the "THUMP." All of these effects add a great deal to the dramatic impact of the story; it is much easier to visualize the scene with the sounds included. Betsy was very proud of her ability to tell good scary stories, and she seemed to work out elaborations in her sound effects as she went from tale to tale. A serious and hard-working girl, Betsy enjoyed a position of leadership among her friends and got special recognition from them for her storytelling abilities.

Telling frightening legends sometimes provides a kind of therapy for children who are very ill. In her article "At a Children's Hospital: A Folklore Survey," Roberta Krell (1980) explores how storytelling helps children to come to terms with their illnesses. One story Krell includes concerns a child who, forced to clean an attic floor as punishment, dies of loneliness or asthma (page 229). Krell points out that "a child who faces his own death every day because of illness may find it easier to handle that fact by telling stories of other children who have died" (page 231). This area of research offers considerable scope for understanding and helping older children who suffer from serious illness.

The last legend that I want to discuss is "The Hook," a perennially popular story told often by girls in upper elementary and junior high or middle school. "The Hook" has been well scrutinized by folklorists (Dégh 1968b) and has been collected from all over the United States. Its plot is simple and fairly consistent: a girl goes out parking with a boy to the local Lovers' Lane, and a bulletin comes to them from the car radio: A dangerous man with a hook-hand has escaped from the insane asylum. Although the boy wants to stay in Lovers' Lane, his girlfriend insists that he drive her home. When he gets out to open the car door on her side, he sees a dreadful indication of what could have happened if they had stayed in Lovers' Lane: a hook hanging from the door handle.

Alan Dundes has analyzed "The Hook" with emphasis upon its psychosexual content, principally from the girl's point of view (1971). He states that girls who go out parking with their boyfriends are afraid that the boys will be "all hands"; they have to resist being overwhelmed by sexual advances, and calling a halt to the adventure is the easiest way to alleviate their anxieties. The hook itself is a phallic symbol, a reminder of what the parking excursion was really all about (page 30). While Dundes's points are well taken, there are other observations that can be made. The girl in this legend is timorous and safety-minded, like the girl or woman in "The Boyfriend's Death"; she does not want to take the chance of doing something that might be life-threatening. The boy, on the other hand, is full of confidence and sexual assertiveness. He leaves only at the girl's urging, often with resentful grumblings. We see the male figure as a self-assured and somewhat reckless but ultimately protective person, while the female figure is more anxious, careful, and protective of both herself and her boyfriend. The female sense of responsibility has a good effect here, but we certainly get the impression that taking risks and being reckless is more of a male prerogative. "The Fatal Initiation" comes to mind again as a paradigm of young men's adventurous risk-taking.

Legends, as well as the funny-scary tales, reworked folk tales, and fantasies of earlier childhood, offer a fascinating set of opportunities to the folklorist. Much work remains to be done in collecting, classifying, and analyzing these stories; it will be very interesting to see how social changes, especially alterations in sex roles, affect children's stories of the future.

1. Collected by Patricia J. Dailey in Binghamton, New York, on 1 May 1982.

2. Collected by Ann Dowling in Rochester, New York, 31 March 1978.

3. For a more thorough discussion of young children's need to protect themselves from serious fright, see Tucker 1981a.

4. Collected by Gail Cohen in Johnson City, New York, on 21 April 1979. Unless otherwise indicated, all other sample stories in this chapter come from my dissertation. I want to thank my student collectors, who have done such a fine job in their work with child informants.

10 TEASES AND PRANKS

Marilyn Jorgensen

INTRODUCTION

Writing about pranks and teases is an especially attractive task, possibly because the study of these two particular forms of expressive activity bring the researcher in such close contact with the child's delight in playful interaction and immense enthusiasm for living life to its fullest.

In the case of pranks (which I prefer to think of as tricks with little degree of harm or mischief intended), the perpetrators have fun at the expense of the hurt or embarrassed victims, and the perpetrators of the pranks are likely to have positive recollections of the deceptive behaviors in which they have engaged. The victims of such pranks, however, might reasonably be expected to try to forget as soon as possible because the victims of taunts may be hurt and embarrassed.

The motivations for children's tricking and teasing victimizations can be either benevolent (as in verbal abuse, or in tricks that may also involve actions and objects) or of a harmful nature (as in verbal taunting, or in pranks in which mischief is intended). But regardless of intentions or perceptions involved in pranks, tricks, taunts, or teases, it is evident that these traditional, prepackaged, and ready-made formulas for playful verbal and kinesic interactions have been integral aspects of children's folklore for generations of children, a means of more fully experiencing and defining the people in their lives and the world in which they live.

In this paper I will discuss taunts, teases, pranks, and tricks as forms of victimization. Verbal teasing, as well as the more serious taunting of individuals, are behaviors that children are likely to experience at almost any time and in any place. These activities occur most often at school in the classroom, at the lunch table, or on the playground—and during play with friends or siblings at home. Taunting (especially if socially unacceptable words or taboos are involved) is usually not done in the presence of adult authorities, but otherwise it is a fairly everyday type of occurrence. On the other hand, tricks and pranks are distinguished from taunts and teases by the fact that although they can and do occur in everyday situations, they also occur on special, set-aside days when such forms of deception and victimization are socially sanctioned and probably even expected .

In the sparse body of literature that does exist on children's trickery, teasing, and related behaviors, there is no consensus with regard to terminology, and terms like "teasing" and "tricking" are often used interchangeably. In addition, attempts such as that by Richard S. Tallman (1974, 269–70) to differentiate between the goals of the practical joker (to fool the opponent) and those of the trickster (to get something for nothing) seem too limited in scope to be applicable to the many kinds of deceptive victimizations that exist in children's lore. Table 1 is designed as a beginning for the identification of the kinds of behaviors and goals present in the four categories I will be discussing:

TABLE 1. Definitional Factors

	Victimization	Deception	Benevolent	Malicious
Taunt	x			
Tease	x		x	
Prank	x	x		x
Trick	x	x	x	

PRANKS AND TRICKS

The pranks and tricks favored by children are examples of what Erving Goffman (1974) in his work on Frame Analysis has termed fabrications: "The intentional effort of one or more individuals to manage activity so that a party of one or more others will be induced to have a false belief about what is going on" (page 83). The deceptive quality of the interactional behavior defined by Goffman as a fabrication is probably what makes pranks and tricks so much fun—especially the thrill and excitement involved in an adventure in which the success or failure of its outcome is at least partially determined by one's own ability to perform. In addition, fabrications like pranks and tricks are forms of children's lore that often are not entirely abandoned by youngsters as they progress through adolescence into adulthood (Welsch 1974). Other forms of children's lore, such as nursery rhymes, jump-rope rhymes, and rhymed taunts, are regularly discarded at crucial ages when they come to be considered appropriate only for younger children. Pranks and tricks continue to be popular through adolescence and even into adult-hood. Thus, the kinds of pranks and tricks attempted and carried out may change as one's age group changes, but not the enjoyment of engaging in playful deceptions of different, possibly more sophisticated, kinds.

A review of the literature on the subject of pranks and tricks reveals that very little attention has been devoted to the subject by folklorists, and even less when only children's trickery is discussed separately from adult behavior. In 1974, however, *Southern Folklore Quarterly* devoted an entire issue to practical jokes in which Richard S. Tallman contributed an article on the classification of practical jokes in terms of the actors and the actions (in terms of nature, intent, and result) involved in the event, as well as the dynamics of the related storytelling activities that sometimes occur afterward as reminiscences. This same issue on practical jokes also contains a valuable article by I. Sheldon Posen (1974a) on the traditional summer camp pranks and practical jokes that children commonly engage in. In his analysis, Posen focused on recurring themes found in the joking behavior he observed.

The following works also discuss schoolchildren's pranks and tricks: The functions of tricking behavior for the schoolchild in the United States are briefly explored by Mary and Herbert Knapp in *One Potato, Two Potato* (1976, 91–100). The most popular pranks of British schoolchildren are discussed in the last chapter of Iona and Peter Opie's *Lore and Language of Schoolchildren* (1959). Finnish schoolchildren's participation in the "deflat-ing tradition" (or tricks at the expense of the unwitting) is discussed by Leea Virtanen in chapter four of "Children's Lore" (1978, 51–58). Pranks (such as raiding orchards and lighting fires) and named tricks (such as "Tick Tack," "Dummy Parcel," and "Ooh, My Toe") engaged in by children in school and on the journey to and from school in different historical periods in New Zealand are presented in Brian Sutton-Smith's comprehensive work *A History of Children's Play: The New Zealand Playground, 1840–50* (1981a, 90–91). The aspects of dissemination and regional variation of terminology in the preadolescent boys' prank the "wedge" are briefly discussed by Gary Alan Fine in the *Center for Southern Folklore Magazine* in its special issue on children's folklore (1980d, 9).

Very little analytical work on the forms and functions of children's pranks and tricks has been done, but Leea Virtanen (1978) has made ob-servations with regard to various factors common to the "deflating tradi-tion," such as the utilization of linguistic ambiguity in the construction of verbal tricks and the social-interactional dynamics involved in "getting the victim to fall into a trap of his own making" (page 53), in which the result of the verbal deception is making a fool of oneself. Virtanen gives several examples of such verbal deception, such as "Spot and Spit were fighting, who won? If the other says 'Spit,' you spit on him" (page 53). The observations made by Virtanen with regard to the use of verbal ambiguity and getting the victim to fall into a trap of which he himself has participated in the making, are common to many forms of children's lore, such as catch routines, knock-knock jokes, riddles, and phone tricks.

Phone tricks, for example, all seem to share a common denominator: They are all fabrications that rely on ambiguity. This ambiguity exists at several levels (Jorgensen 1984, 104–16). Perhaps the most apparent use of ambiguity is with reference to speech play, or the ambiguity of words (puns, homonyms, and so forth) that allows for the possibility of everyday speech to be manipulated for fun and humor. A second level of ambiguity is a kind of social-interactional ambiguity whereby the identity of the caller may not be known to the victim. The use of the phone almost guarantees that the identities of the individuals remain unknown. This ambiguity of identity makes it quite easy for youngsters to engage in phone tricks and to do the exasperating things that they would be highly unlikely to do in other, less safe circumstances. The use of the telephone affords them an anonymity that allows for a certain license to participate in this kind of trickery, relatively free from the fear of the retribution or embarrassment that might occur in face-to-face settings (Jorgensen 1984). The last kind of ambiguity exists at the level of social structure and is related to the position of the teenager in the hierarchy of the social order. The adolescent in our society is in an ambiguous period in his life, being neither child nor adult.

These phone tricks may be viewed as occurring at an ambiguous time in the life of the caller, taking place in an ambiguous social-interactional setting (because of the use of the phone), and sometimes utilizing the ambiguous quality of words in order to play with everyday speech, to demonstrate communicative competence, and to gain a sense of personal power (especially within the peer group). Phone tricks are just one example of the pranks common to children's folklore.

Some of these behaviors are reserved for "special occasions." In the United States the two main times of the year historically set aside for the playing of pranks and tricks are Halloween and April Fools' Day. The same two days are set aside in the British Isles, with the addition of Mischief Night on November 4 (the eve of Guy Fawkes Day), which is considered by Iona and Peter Opie (1959) to be a postponed celebration of Halloween. Mischievous or impolite and disrespectful behavior by children on special days of the year may be viewed as a reversal of everyday norms of polite behavior and it is allowed to some extent or perhaps even anticipated. As long as the tricksters and pranksters don't go too far—as long as their actions do not injure anyone or cause great damage to property or life—the mischief is usually excused. On some other day of the year it might not be. On Halloween, as well as on Mischief Night in England, the behavioral reversals tend to involve children and teenagers as initiators of unsociable acts aimed either at peers, adults, or other authority figures, but on April Fools' Day adults tend to join the children as the initiators of pranks and tricks. Many of the traditional April Fools' tricks, such as the "fool's errand," involve face-to-face interaction between the trickster and the victim, but most of the Halloween pranks (which are often directed against personal property) occur under the cover of darkness: The pranksters are usually unseen and unknown.

The unknown identity of the Halloween prankster is, of course, a safeguard against retribution by the irate victim. The prankster's unsociable and harmful behavior, however, is also reminiscent of the traditional behavior associated with ancestors, ghosts, or other spirit powers, who are given free rein to return to earth and cause trouble or play tricks on the living once a year. Such practices are known in many widely separated cultures throughout the world—from the Druidic celebration of Samhuin on the eve of 1 November to the Day of the Dead in Mexico, and even the Milamala harvest celebration reported by Malinowski in the Trobriand Islands (1954). Some very creative and innovative pranks perpetrated by teenagers in New York in the early 1970s are reported in an article published by Catherine Harris Ainsworth entitled "Hallowe'en," which appeared in September of 1973 in the *New York Folklore Quarterly*. The following excerpts are from essays on the topic of the celebration of Halloween, perceived and experienced by 18- and 19-year-olds, and they illustrate some important points about the social interactions and reversals of everyday polite behavior that are associated with October 31 in our culture. Most of the teenagers who chose to include reports of pranks they had played in their essays were boys, although one young lady did mention briefly that she enjoyed tipping over mailboxes and causing trouble by scaring people. Interestingly, one of the best accounts (in terms of the most detailed recording of socially unacceptable behavior) was signed "anonymous," which is of course symbolic of the social-interactional significance of this special night with regard to the prankish behavior perpetrated by "unseen spirits of the night":

> To start the night rolling we would soap a few windows and rap on them when the people would be watching television. Next we found a tree limb that grew over the road. A couple of us would climb up

and tie a dummy on a rope. As soon as a car was almost under the tree, they swung the dummy right down in front of it. They would either stop and get out and start cussing or just slow down and keep going. (pages 180–81)

I remember Hallowe'en because that's the night the fire company was called out to quench a blaze that measured a few inches in width but stretched over two miles down the center of our local main road. It was also the night the police received several complaints from irate motorists who'd been shocked out of their pants when someone dropped a very life-like looking dummy in front of their car. But as the years passed, we became more mature, which is another way of saying our plans became more devious, more daring, and more imaginative. Ours was the first town with a psychedelic cop car. It was also the first with a stop and go light that turned green in all four directions at the same time. (pages 183–84)

Halloween is a night of mischief for all, not only for young children, but also for the older teenagers. On the way to my friend's house I paid a visit to a few of my neighbors. After receiving dirty looks from them all year I thought it was an appropriate time to harass them. So I broke a few of their pumpkins. I picked up my friends and we headed out toward Main Street. . . . We stood outside of Carrol's Hamburger Place, freezing, for about an hour. We were trying to think of something special to do. Then one kid came up with a great idea. We decided to buy some eggs and plaster the cars of the other guys that were hanging around Carrol's. Within a half hour every car at Carrol's was dripping with egg yolk. The cold weather made the eggs freeze almost instantly. We decided it was time to get home before we either got ran over or shot. (page 186)

These essays show that much effort and ingenuity were involved in the planning and executing of these Halloween pranks, many of which ultimately involved adult authority figures. The two-mile long fire is a good example of such creativity and ingenuity. Although this prank was attention getting it remained relatively harmless.

There is also evidence to support the claim that "once a prankster, always a prankster." Although the types of pranks tend to change with age, pranks remain part of the adult's repertoire. The young man quoted above, says, "But as the years passed, we became more mature, which is another way of saying our plans became more devious, more daring, and more imaginative." It might also be noted that the young man who broke his neighbor's pumpkins explained that he was taking the opportunity to do so on this night of socially licensed misbehavior to retaliate for the dirty looks he had been receiving from them all year long. One could say that this is the way pent-up or repressed hostile emotions are expressed. The most common examples of traditional Halloween pranks in the United States—such as removing gates or barn doors, putting rockers in trees, putting wagons on roofs, turning over outhouses, soaping windows—all involve either the partial destruction of property or its removal from its proper place. These pranks tend to be indirect assaults on persons through their property, rather than confrontation. Conversely, on April Fools' Day, the object is not to damage someone else's property but to cause embarrassment by casting the victim as socially incompetent or foolish through various forms of trickery.

The practice of playing tricks on April Fools' Day is one that seems to be particularly popular with school-aged children. The attraction of such socially sanctioned trickery for young schoolchildren is evident in the words of a twelve-year-old Scottish girl from Edinburgh who was interviewed by Iona and Peter Opie in connection with their research on "Huntigowk Day," the Scottish equivalent to April Fools' Day. The young girl told them: "Huntigowk is a day I love. I like to put a basin of water at the side of my sister's bed and hear her let out a yell when she puts her feet into it. I also put an empty eggshell in an eggcup so that when she opens it she finds that there is nothing inside it" (Opie and Opie 1959, 245). The playful delight in teasing, trickery, and possibly even some undertones of sibling rivalry are all noticeable in this child's testimony. Thus, April 1 might be characterized as a socially sanctioned day on which behavior involving playful trickery can be given free expression by those who find a special pleasure in such activity. It is important to add that the setting aside of this one day for such licensed trickery allows for control of its duration (only a twenty-four-hour period in the United States and only until noon in the British and Canadian traditions) and of the traditional nature of the trickery and deceit (usually only prescribed kinds of tricks are engaged in).

One way to look at April Fools' behavior is to see it as an inversion of everyday politeness or face-saving behavior. This interpretation is based on the assumption that in naturally occurring, everyday talk a certain seriousness is assumed to exist. Normally, speakers and listeners engaging in conversation seek a common understanding of what is being discussed (Mehan and Wood 1975, 124–25). In other words, attempts are normally made to communicate within a common frame of reference. During April Fools' trickery, however, these assumptions of polite seriousness and a common frame of reference are abrogated. A deception is attempted, based on a lack of serious intent, and the potential victim is unaware that the usual seriousness does not apply to the situation at hand. The importance of the victim's being unaware is well illustrated by the fact that it is easiest to accomplish successful deceptions *early* on the day of April 1 before potential victims have had tricks played on them by other tricksters and have thus been alerted to the fact that it is a day on which tricks and jokes are likely to occur.

The purpose of these tricks is to make the victim look foolish. The victim is made into the fool as a result of his or her own actions, as is also the case in children's catch routines, riddling, and knock-knock jokes. Conversely, in teases and taunts victimization does not usually depend on the victim's actions. In most taunts, the body, language, or other characteristics of the person are attacked simply and directly, and no specific social situation is necessary. Although the element of fabrication is largely missing, the embarrassment and discomfort of the victim are still the major element.

TEASES

As will be recalled from the table in the introduction, I prefer to discriminate between taunts and teases on the basis of the degree of harm in the victimization. I consider teases to be relatively mild, possibly even benevolent and playful forms of social interaction of children and sometimes adults.

Valuable studies based on interviews with schoolchildren regarding both taunting and the less disturbing kinds of teasing have been carried out by Scandinavian folklorists Leea Virtanen in Finland (1978) and Erik Kaas Nielsen in Denmark (1976). Each of these children's folklorists, working separately, has identified forms of teasing (both verbal and nonverbal) that can be interpreted as a sign of affection.

Virtanen makes some important observations concerning the interpretation of aggressive teasing behavior in chapter five, "The Teasing Tradition," of "Children's Lore" (1978). She says, "Actions which to an outsider seem aggressive are the socially acceptable manner of showing positive feelings" (page 61), and that girls are capable of regarding "heavy handed treatment" by boys as evidence of positive feelings. This last observation is illustrated by the following excerpt from an interview with a young schoolgirl: "The biggest sign of love was when he hit me on the head with the atlas. It hurt, but it was lovely" (page 61). It is not known, of course, if the boys who engage in this type of teasing would interpret their behavior as a sign of love toward the girls! Virtanen cites other examples of nonverbal teases used by Finnish girls to demonstrate love for a particular boy, such as lifting him by the hair and kicking him, or throwing things like snowballs, pebbles, or lumps of clay at him. Teases like these, which basically involve chasing or attacking, have probably always been prevalent among children. I recall kicking, slapping, and hair pulling as being favorite means of gaining attention from the opposite sex when I was growing up in the mid-1950s in southern California. Retaliation, such as washing the girl's face "with a leather glove till she is as red as fire" (page 61) would follow if the bid for attention was successful. (Ignoring such a claim to attention might be considered to be an insult to the girl seeking such a response!) Virtanen believes that teases, which may also include verbal forms such as name calling or the composing of witty jibes, are a means of establishing contact between the sexes, and that each sex has its favorite procedures for doing so. Virtanen's interpretation is supported by Nielsen's research (1976) into the psychological motivations and sociological functions involved in teasing by Danish schoolchildren (pages 53–54). In a personal communication (September 20, 1981) Nielsen expanded on the idea that the words, gestures, and acts used in teasing are expressive forms of communication, codes that must be decoded: "After all, teasing is a kind of code which you may/must interpret according to your mood and relations to the teaser." Nielsen's interviews revealed that most pupils considered teasing to have both positive and negative aspects and that they understood that "in certain cases teasing is only an attempt to create contact, especially in relation to the opposite sex" (1976, 53), findings very similar to those of Virtanen with regard to using teasing as a means of reducing social distance between individuals. Four of the twelve reasons noted by Nielsen for Danish schoolchildren's teasing are positive: love (the parent's love for the child), friendship, and sympathy; love (emotions for the other sex), flirtations, courting; playfulness, high spirits, need for fun; isolation, solitude, teasing as a means of contact.

The excellent research done by these two Scandinavian children's folklorists concerning the benevolent forms of teasing is supported by Richard W. Howell in his work *Language in Behavior* (1976). Howell advances the idea that playful teasing is an attempt to deny social distance and that it is therefore symbolic of a wished-for closeness between the people involved (page 4) rather than a form of hostility or violence. This analysis of teasing as symbolic of a potential closeness that does not quite exist seems applicable to the boy-girl teasing reported by Virtanen and Nielsen. Play grouping according to sex reflects the social distance between the sexes, especially in the school context, and thus playful teasing (such as boys and girls chasing each other or throwing snowballs or erasers at each other) could be viewed as an attempt to seek contact in a relatively safe, nonserious manner.

If teases can be viewed as contact-seeking devices, then taunts can be distinguished as verbal strategies that attempt the opposite—to increase the social distance between people. While teases are characterized here as being mainly positive, taunts are usually motivated by more malicious intentions and negative emotions (such as hatred, envy, displeasure, revenge, the wish to dominate, or a desire to compensate for one's own weaknesses).

Children's taunts can be examined as reversals of everyday, or normally expected, behavior, as can most other tricks, pranks, and teases. The norms of politeness in society are based on the assumption that it is to the interest of all to attempt to maintain each other's sense of "face" (that is, self-concept, or feelings of self-worth). Brown and Levinson (1978) have labeled acts that threaten this mutual support of face as FTAs, "face-threatening acts" (page 65). They have identified several kinds of FTAs, the two main ones being "off the record" (more ambiguous, or "safe") and "on the record" (no ambiguity, less "safe") (page 74).

Children's use of traditional taunts and retorts at the elementary-school level places these strategies of verbal aggression into the "bald on record" subdivision (page 65) in which there is no attempt at redressive action (or "softening the blow") on the part of the speaker. Applying Brown and Levinson's research on politeness behavior to the subject of children's taunting strategies, it follows that this kind of verbal aggression is "the most direct, clear, unambiguous and concise way possible" (page 74) to carry out an FTA and thus attempt to bring about a loss of face or sense of personal esteem to the victim.

The directness gained by using taunts as "bald on record" FTAs is somewhat offset by the fact that such strategies are less safe than the "off record" ones, which are more open to question or interpretation because of their ambiguity. The use of "bald on record" FTAs is quite likely to upset the victim and cause him or her to seek revenge when exposed to this direct, clear, and unmistakably intentional form of verbal abuse. This element of risk tends to support the idea that those who are not worried about the risks are confident that their own power (verbal or physical) is superior to that of their victims.

The reaction of the victim of such verbal abuse is important. Most verbal assaults are said face-to-face to the intended victim, probably with the purpose of observing his or her reaction, which it is hoped will be one of embarrassment or hurt feelings. It is usually intended that the words chosen for the verbal attack will wound the child in his area of greatest sensitivity and cause him to be visibly upset. Crying is often the proof that this goal has been achieved, as illustrated by the traditional chant "I made you sigh, I made you sigh; And pretty soon I'll make you cry" (Millard 1945, 31). It is always possible, however, that through verbal agility (such as the use of a clever retort, for example) or some other means, the quick-witted child may be able to retaliate and thus reverse the potentially painful situation, making the aggressor the victim instead. In Virtanen's previously cited research on children's verbal aggression, it has been observed that the children who are the most defenseless and seem not to be able to fight back are the ones who are most often chosen as victims, irrespective of the "undesirable" personal traits or other social "shortcomings" that might make them appear to be logical candidates for such abuse (Virtanen 1978, 60).

As with the other traditional pranks, tricks, and teases discussed, it should also be emphasized with regard to taunts that the context of their use is crucial to their meaning. It is possible that the most vicious taunt could be used in such a way that no real harm is intended or experienced by the individuals involved. As an example of one of the many possible uses of verbal aggression, Brown and Levinson discuss the use of seemingly threatening "bald on record" insults and jokes as communicative strategies for asserting that a certain degree of intimacy exists between the people involved. Thus there is minimal danger of "face" being threatened. Conventionalized insults can thus solidify friendship (page 234). In addition, many adults I have questioned in the last few years on the subject of traditional taunts and retorts claim that some of their favorite rhymes as children were valued for their humor rather than their malice. They recalled using taunts such as "Fatty and Skinny were laying in bed; Fatty rolled over and Skinny was dead" in a joking manner, more for the fun of chanting it than for hurting another child's feelings. It should be remembered that children use taunts for a variety of purposes, and that fact should be kept in mind in the attempt to understand the use of taunts and retorts.

Those who wish to pursue this genre of children's folklore will find samples of children's taunts and retorts in various collections of children's lore. Examples of such collections in the English-language tradition include the work of P.H. Evans, Knapp and Knapp, Withers, Northall, Yoffie, and Winslow. In addition, *The Lore and Language of Schoolchildren* (1959) by Iona and Peter Opie is a comprehensive and well-documented collection of various genres, including traditional taunts and retorts from the British Isles. The significance of the material and its analysis, however, is not adequately dealt with (Bernstein 1960).

Journal articles dealing exclusively with the subject of children's jeers are fairly rare. In 1945 an article by Anna K. Stimson dealing with taunts used in New York City at the turn of the century appeared in the *Journal of American Folklore*, and, also in 1945, a similar study of "chaffing formulas" by Eugenia Millard appeared in the *New York Folklore Quarterly*. Millard's article contained a rudimentary attempt at classification on the twofold basis of ethical standards and pseudo-prejudices, but her main interest was in establishing the antiquity of the rhymes within the English tradition. In a more recent work, Winslow (1969) constructed a classification scheme based on derogatory epithets, one that he believed could be applied to the traditional rhymed formulas used by children. His four categories included play on a child's name and comments on physical peculiarities, mental traits, and social relationships.

Martha Wolfenstein's analysis of the thematic content and functions of joking behavior in *Children's Humor* (1954) is a study of the meaning of children's attempts to use language to solve emotional problems. Although mainly concerned with joking and riddling, her analysis of underlying motives and her discussion of the use of rhyme and proper names give important clues to similar processes that might also apply to the jeers used during the child's latency period (six to twelve years), which also make extensive use of rhymed taunts.

In general, the literature contains many collections in which taunts and retorts are studied. A few attempts at classification have been made, but interest in the genre seems to have stopped short of an in-depth analysis of the many possible meanings and functions of taunts, with the exception of the research reported in 1975 by Keith T. Kernan and Claudia Mitchell-Kernan. These scholars compared children's insults in the United States and Samoa. They analyzed insult behavior with the intention of studying the process of enculturation, because of the tendency for such speech acts to carry statements of cultural values. Their research findings indicated that the person insulted is depicted as deviating from culturally defined values. In both cultures, the children's estimations of the extent to which cultural values are implicit in the insults were close to those of the adults. What is still needed in the study of children's taunts and other forms of aggressive verbal behavior is an in-depth study of the use of taunts within the fuller context of children's speech.

OVERVIEW

SETTINGS AND ACTIVITIES

Brian Sutton-Smith

There is a striking contrast between the male-centered interest of the following three chapters by Mergen, Bronner, and Mechling, and the focus on females in the work of Zumwalt, Beresin, and Hughes. The latter chapters were microscaled and highly focused; the former are relatively diffuse and wide-ranging, and that difference might not be accidental. In the following three chapters there is a noticeable absence of girls on the streets, playing with material culture and being captured in total institutions. Here gender difference and same-gender sensitivity combine in an uncertain and perhaps stereotypic amalgam. Fortunately, the combination of the two sections may provide the needed balance.

Within this section we move from a largely historical account of the impact of playgrounds and street play on the behavior of children, "urbanizations and its discontents" as Mergen calls it, to a more arcadian account of the multiple ways in which children themselves transform objects or their environments, "a traditional creative encounter with physical things," as Bronner puts it. Finally, Mechling gives us a sample of those more captive environments, such as summer camps, boarding schools, hospital wards, and orphanages, where "the vibrant resisting folk culture" is carried on, though he seeks to attenuate the suggestion that these are special environments by suggesting that in modern society we are all prisoners. Our point throughout has been that, in part, children's folklore is an outcome of the children as "prisoners" of a larger, normative society. Or at least their condition is partly "prisonerlike," to give it a metaphoric rather than an existential flavor. Mechling's analysis, based on Goffman, of the various cultural performances of the caretakers and the inmates, and of the interactions between the two, probably contributes the most in this *Sourcebook* to our understanding of children's interstitial status and therefore interstitial culture. If we think of his staff as our parents and our children as his inmates, then their rituals, legends, pranks, and games, together with their ceremonies, parties, journals, and assemblies, all make a reasonable model for everyday children's folklore though the latter would, of course, be more multicentered and less focused than the examples that he gives.

Roger Abrahams has suggested that it is at the borders between two societies where tensions occur—here, adult and child—that there emerges those various framed events that we choose to call jokes and games, which are themselves a dramatizing of the differences between the two groups (Abrahams 1981, 304). Out of this dynamic, the cloth of children's folklore is woven. Some of the events have, of course, to do with the tensions among the children themselves, and some between children and adults, at which borders emerges *subversive folklore,* discussed by McMahon and Sutton-Smith in the concluding chapter.

What is missing in this section on settings is probably two extremes. At one end, we need more material on earlier pioneering conditions and rural play and, at the other, we need more on family play. Between these two are needed accounts of urban, ethnic, suburban and future play. In the catalogue *Children's Play, Past, Present and Future* the Please Touch Museum of Philadelphia sought to remedy this deficiency (Sutton-Smith 1985). We know that behavior is closely related to settings and environments, and that, therefore, it is reasonable to expect that forms of folklife in smaller and less public spaces will be different from those associated with larger groups. Only recently, however, has there been an emphasis on folklife in private spaces like the home. For example, it was only in 1974 that the first family folklore tent was erected at the Festival of American Folklife on the National Mall. We discover in the work of Zeitlin, Kotkin, and Baker, *A Celebration of American Family Folklore* (1982), many forms of family folklore.

Recent interest in the family, although minimal, is hardly too soon, given that it is generally true that children begin their expressive and symbolic activities—their play, chants, rhymes, and tales—close to their parents in and near their homes, irrespective of social status (Mergen 1982). Further, the trend toward the embourgeoisement of our society in the past several hundred years has meant that more and more children have spent more time in the family rather than in public groups. The liberation of children from the duties and discipline of preindustrial life and their involvement in schools, recreation programs, and, increasingly, with the television screen in their own rooms has wrought immense changes in children's lives. Such changes have in many ways transformed for children the folklore that once dominated and still engages those who remain in the streets and in the rural areas of the world. Typical modern play involves a child toying with a television-advertised object while solitarily watching a television program. The array of handmade objects and equipment that was once a central part of the child's play world, and which is described by Bronner in a subsequent chapter, has been largely replaced by the multimillion-dollar toy industry and the manufacture of mass-produced toys, board games, and video games. The "Kiddie City" and "Toys R Us" emporia, are, for example, embodiments of this change.

The story of this change even in the past hundred years waits to be told, although we have a general picture of the shift in Sutton-Smith's *History of Children's Play: The New Zealand Playground, 1840–1950* (1981a), Mergen's *Play and Playthings: A Reference Guide* (1982), and, most recently, Karin Calvert's *Children in the House: The Material Culture of Early Childhood, 1600–1900* (1992). One senses from such work that in the last century, although the children were encouraged to be outdoors more than they are today, there was nevertheless much home play. Available accounts of such play in homes suggest that the relatively private, even free spaces such as bedrooms, attics, and basements in the home, and the higher chance of uninterrupted activity there made the home a rich and attractive place for many middle-class children's expressive and symbolic activities (see Mergen 1982 for details from play autobiographies). Further, Dorothy Howard, in her folklore autobiography of the 1902–10 period, *Dorothy's World: Childhood in Sabine Bottom, 1902–1910* (1977), suggests that at least the rural home of the last century was, to a great extent, a base for constructing original playthings and "play pritties," as she calls them. The knife was the central play object then, just as the ball was to be popular between the world wars and as the board game has since become. With the knife, the boys in their yards carved and whittled, made pea shooters, catapults, whistles, slings, bows, popguns, kites, whips, sledges, tree huts, and forts. Although girls were seldom so free with pocketknives, they, for their part, engaged in yard play with flowers, beads, berries, grass, plants, fruit, coins, buttons, matches, eggs, shells, pets, and string figures. By the turn of the century, with the encroachment of commercial materials for childhood, there were scrapbooks of pictures, transfers, and fairy gardens, in contrast to the "play pritties" of Dorothy Howard's world. In the homes of upper-class parents, there were often parties or parlor games involving musical chairs, charades, pretend tea parties, blindman's bluff, and much more (Sutton-Smith 1981a). In today's urban and suburban apartment worlds, many children who have virtually retired from the streets have, in many cases, shifted from dominantly motor, physical and manual concerns to verbal and symbolic ones. Of course, this is not to deny that hopscotch, jump rope and jacks, which have been central to girls' games for over fifty years, continue to be played in the backyard, as do various chasing and hide-and-seek games, as well as Mother may I, old witch, redlight, statues, ball-bouncing, and hand-clapping games. Girls still play these games, both at home and school, although only at home if there are enough playmates present. Likewise, boys' concern with sports continues—although it is confined to yards at home. They catch ball, shoot baskets, trap soccer balls and hit pucks, but these games really require the street or the playground. Adaptations to the backyard can be made but may be dangerous to shrubs, lawns, and flower gardens. Although today the home and yard are still the places where children prepare and practice for the outside world, the world being prepared for is rather different from the world of yesteryear.

11 CHILDREN'S LORE IN SCHOOL AND PLAYGROUNDS

Bernard Mergen

Schools and playgrounds are virtually synonymous with childhood in contemporary America, but their importance to children's folklore is of relatively recent origin. Only after the middle of the nineteenth century did the majority of children attend school, and those that did rarely went for more than a few years. Planned parks and playgrounds are even more recent. Nevertheless, the years of childhood are brief, and many generations of children have passed through schools and playgrounds in the past century. The interaction between children and the physical environment of schools and playgrounds is the focus of this chapter. The fact that less is known about the actual behavior of children in these settings than about the settings themselves is a major limitation, but the growing literature on play, children's folklore, the history of childhood, and the cultural meanings of space makes clear that the scene of a child's play helps to shape the content.

Interest in the relationships between children's lore and their environment, what Gary Fine has called the "ecotypic" approach to folklore, need not exclude other approaches (Fine 1980d, 180). Indeed, as the literature illustrates, we must be ready to ask a broad range of questions about children's cognitive and physiological development, about their concepts of space and place, about the influence of adults and peers, about the games and traditions children bring to the school and playground, and about the uses they make of their physical environment. Yi-Fu Tuan, drawing on the insights of Piaget and others, speculates that "place, to the child, is a large and somewhat immobile type of object" (1977, 29). Later, as their geographical horizons expand, children interact with objects and places with imagination, transforming physical reality through fantasy, active play, or simply by ignoring it.

This ability to transform, or even transcend, physical space is probably functional in the child's development. As Gaston Bachelard argues in his stimulating reflections on the phenomenology of space, imagination separates a person from the past, as well as from reality, causing him to face the future (1964, xxx). A child's ability to imagine, to create, to anticipate the future is clearly part of the learning process. In part, the child uses his imagination in an attempt to control the scene in which he finds himself. In school and schoolyard the struggle is between children and adults as well as among children themselves, while in streets, parks, and playgrounds the interaction is largely among peers. Melvin Williams, describing a black, inner-city junior high school in Pittsburgh in the 1970s, concludes:

> I have never seen students more adept and skillful at manipulating the behavioral dynamics of their classrooms. . . . Each one attempted to outperform the others in acts that denied, defiled, and defied the classroom setting. The student audience encouraged the behavior and reinforced it whenever possible. In such frenzies, chairs were thrown across the classroom, ostensibly to strike another student but not intended to make contact. Boys participated in animated wrestling, lifting one another and pretending to slam each other to the floor with a ferociousness that equalled a staged television fight. Other boys threw one another against walls, making sounds that gave impressions of crushing one's opponent. . . . Most of the students realized that this was a staged drama, but they acted as if it was actually occurring. (1981, 101)

On the unsupervised playground, evidence suggests that children negotiate their own uses of space (Opie and Opie 1969; Hayward, Rothenberg, and Beasley 1974; Sutton-Smith 1981a; L. Hughes 1983; and Beresin 1993).

School, playground, even the streets may be scenes of contention, but this is not always the case. Moreover, for children, play space is a continuum. The journey from home and yard to school and playground is made by way of steps, trees, curbs, alleys, shops, lots, and dozens of other places useful for play (Ward 1978). Roger Hart's pioneering study *Children's Experience of Place* (1979) established a number of useful working hypotheses. For example, he found that parentally defined "free range" for children increased in three steps. Children in the first and second grade in the small New England town where he conducted his research were not permitted to go beyond seeing and calling distance. In grades 3 and 4 the increased frequency of group play allowed the children to go as far as three hundred yards from home. Fifth and sixth graders, particularly boys who had acquired bicycles, were given a wide range, "with permission," or the distance was defined by the time it took to get there. In the upper grades the differences between boys and girls increased, since boys were permitted greater freedom. Moreover, Hart found that children used and valued various places differently at different times. Places were valued because of what could be done there (ball fields, hills, trees, brooks), because of a person who lived or worked there (homes, stores, streets), because of what could be bought there (supermarket, service stations), because of how the place looked or felt (traffic lights, library grounds), and by the lure of danger (streets, quarries, abandoned buildings, graveyards). Although limited in many ways, Hart's study establishes a model for approaching the scenes of children's lore. What is the scene? Who are the characters? What is the play?

CHILDREN'S ENVIRONMENTS IN THE PAST

Our evidence for children's lore before compulsory public education and the playground movement comes chiefly from autobiographies and reminiscences, sometimes touched with a note of nostalgia. Linda Pollock's exhaustive study of 496 published diaries and autobiographies (144 of them American), covering the years 1500 to 1900, asserts that play "does not appear very often in the texts" and goes on to quote from several, including those of Cotton Mather and Henry Wadsworth Longfellow (1983, 236). When Edward Everett Hale describes Boston Common in the 1830s as "a playground for children . . . ours to work our own sweet will upon," we get a glimpse of the play spaces of a less organized era (Hale 1883, 65–66). Hale played marbles, flew kites, rolled hoops, and played an elaborate game involving the delivery and hiding of imaginary mail. A large stone on the Common gave rise to the superstition that if a person went around it backward nine times saying the Lord's Prayer backward, his wish would come true. Hale's playmates also believed that law did not extend onto the mud flats beyond the high water mark, so it was there that they played props (a game in which the tops of small sea shells are cut off and the shells filled with red sealing wax, the player betting that he can throw odd or even numbers of red spots) and other gambling games. The boys of Hale's generation had already adapted to new urban institutions like the volunteer fire department: "Of course we boys supposed that ours was the best in the world," Hale writes. "Each boy in Boston supposed that the engine nearest his house was the best engine in the world, and that, on occasion, it could throw water higher than any other engine" (page 133).

Hale's contemporaries, Lucy Larcom, Henry Adams, William Dean Howells, and William Gordon, report a variety of similar children's lore in their autobiographical writing. Larcom turned a rock quarry near her home in Beverly, Massachusetts, into a play house, while Howells roamed the riverbanks and fields near Hamilton, Ohio. Gordon, growing up in the 1840s in the Georgetown section of the District of Columbia, met his friends in tanneries, bakeries, and carpentry shops, and hung around taverns, stage stops, and steamboat landings to watch people. For boys, the predominant ritual was fighting. Gangs of different ethnic groups and from different neighborhoods fought regularly in Boston and Washington. Adams's depiction of a snowball and rock fight between boys from the Boston Latin School and the poorer boys from the South End is bloody and violent, though acknowledging honor on both sides (1918, 41–42). New boys had to fight for acceptance into a group. Howells describes several cruel tricks, such as blowing pencil dust in someone's eyes, or getting an "unsuspecting child to close the end of an elderwood tube with his thumb, and look hard at you, while you showed him Germany. You did this by pulling a string below the tube, and running a needle into his thumb" (Howells 1890, 71).

Children's lives were shaped by their environments, especially in cities and towns where the places for work and play were differentiated. Elliott West's study of children in Rocky Mountain mining camps suggests that boys and girls as young as eight created a juvenile replica of frontier lawlessness. "Ragged urchins" roamed the streets of Western towns, drinking, gambling, destroying property and harassing adults, particularly ethnic minorities. "Several New Mexican boys showered their town with rocks shot from an old cannon barrel, and on another occasion they set off a keg of black powder under the wagon of a man who had thrown them out of his skating rink" (West 1983, 152). Similar conditions existed in the oil boom towns of Oklahoma after World War I, according to Woody Guthrie (Guthrie 1943). Even when children are successful in playing in public spaces, they also create private, secret spaces. Guthrie recalls his gang's clubhouse in loving detail, and Valerie Quinney has collected information on children's lives in the mill village of Carrboro, North Carolina, in the years 1905–20 that reveals a comparable pattern of public violence and private retreat. "Older boys found a secret cave and fixed it up as a club house where they could play poker. They had to crawl through a barrel to get in. To protect the spot further from preachers and parents, they disguised the barrel opening by putting timber and trash in front of it" (Quinney 1982, 169).

The establishment of schools and playgrounds did not, of course, mean the end of country, vacant lot, and street play. Rural children like Dorothy Howard established special places for play near home, while those living in small towns, like William Allen White in Eldorado, Kansas, and William Carlos Williams in Rutherford, New Jersey, played in surrounding areas (Howard 1977; White 1946; W.C. Williams 1951). Williams, describing a game of hares and hounds, recalls running all Saturday morning through the cedar swamps and hills outside of town, the landscape giving fresh dimensions to the game. The interrelation of place and play was recognized by T.R. Croswell in his 1899 study of "Amusements of Worcester School Children." "One reason why shinney is three times as popular in Worcester as in Brooklyn, and that running games of all kinds appear to be more popular, is undoubtedly the exceptional inducements offered by the physical conditions of the former city; the many small ponds suitable for shinney are a constant invitation to the small boy with a pair of skates, and the innumerable vacant lots, covered with grass—not yet the dirty dumping places so common in large cities—have furnished Worcester, free of charge, an excellent system of small parks for playgrounds" (Croswell 1899, 343). Playing ball topped the list of favorite amusements of the boys of both Brooklyn and Worcester in Croswell's surveys, but the greater urbanization of Brooklyn had already led to modifications in children's folklore.

Stewart Culin, anthropologist and museum curator, discovered boys on the streets of Brooklyn in 1890 playing various kinds of tag adapted to the high stoops and fences of neighborhood buildings, hit the stick and ball games utilizing street corners, and a variation on penny pitching involving picture cards from cigarette packs (Culin 1891). Shinney had become a street hockey game. Stickball was evolving many forms (Silverstein 1965). The many recreation surveys conducted in major cities between 1910 and 1920 show the same result: The majority of children seen out of doors were on the street, not in yards, playgrounds, or even vacant lots (Mergen 1982, 71). The catalog of what these children were doing on the streets is revealing. Some were playing ball, tag, dolls, and jacks, but more were loitering, stealing, breaking things, writing on walls, fighting, drinking, gambling, and watching prostitutes. Clearly children were holding their own on the streets. Even those who played quietly recall an element of contest: "All these games were, of course, extremely inconvenient to pedestrians who had to walk around skelly games, or to automobiles (there weren't very many in those days, remember) that had to drive slowly through punchball games while enduring catcalls. . . . I have never been able to work up much sympathy for those who mourn the plight of the city children crowded into their nasty streets. When I think back on the children of my childhood, all I can remember is that those nasty streets belonged to us and that the boisterous competition and the noisy excitement were the very breath of life to us" (Asimov 1979, 57–58).

Children had institutionalized the streets as playgrounds despite the opposition of police and recreation reformers. A survey in Buffalo in 1925 listed five objections to street play: (1) the danger of automobiles; (2) noise and destruction of property; (3) the unsanitary conditions; (4) the unsuitability of streets for highly organized play; and (5) the moral danger to children who are unsupervised (Buffalo Recreation Survey 1925, 60). An opposite position is taken by Thomas Yukic who was growing up in Buffalo in the same years. For Yukic and his brothers, Allen Avenue and the waterfront offered unlimited possibilities for swimming, collecting junk, and boat building. The dangers of the street and lake merely heightened the enjoyment (Yukic 1975). In the 1930s in Washington, D.C., boys played highly organized games of football and baseball in the street and any open space, such as in the Ellipse behind the White House and on the triangle of grass in front of Union Station. The availability of ball-bearing roller skates further increased the number of children in the streets (Sylvia Shugrue [interview] 1983; Nick Graziano [interview] 1983). Broken skates were reused on homemade scooters. A study of a neighborhood at the northern tip of Manhattan Island, based in part on interviews with people who had grown up there between 1915 and 1970, concluded that children's freedom of access to both supervised and unsupervised play sites declined during that period, although the variety of professionally supervised activities increased, from a single summer sports program in the 1920s to more than twenty teams, clubs, and recreational programs in the 1970s (Gastner 1991). Folklorists and historians should attempt to document changes in street, playground, and school play at the neighborhood and community level in order to better understand the effects of demographic changes, urban renewal, and organized recreation (Gastner 1992).

As early as 1909, authorities in New York City recognized that there were not enough parks and that they could not keep children off the streets, so they closed off some streets for play. A generation later, play streets were a recognized alternative to unsupervised play. In Newark, New Jersey, streets were divided into four areas: circle games for children aged six to nine; red rover, bull-in-the-ring, and whip tag for ten- to twelve-year-olds; relay races and circle ball for those thirteen to fifteen; and volley ball, boxing, hand tennis, and baseball for those over sixteen (Norton 1937, 11). Dozens of tag, ball, and capture games were adapted for the play streets. Yet the organized and supervised play streets remained the exception. As Colin Ward has shown in England, the city is too rich in spaces for children's play to be confined to a few streets. In the United States too, the streets remain a "hearth of play" and the scene of a vast array of children's activities, including many traditional games (Ferretti 1975; Milberg 1976; M. Williams 1981; Zerner 1977; Lukashok and Lynch 1956; Lynch 1978).

The impact of compulsory education was not widely felt in the United States until after the middle of the nineteenth century, but from their first appearance, in Colonial times, schools have provided an environment for the development of special kinds of children's lore. Schools segregate children from adults, subject them to temporary confinement and discipline, and reduce their free time. The school's influence on play is twofold. On the one hand it brings together a larger number of children of various ages than might otherwise play together, thus promoting the diffusion of games. On the other hand, not all kinds of play are compatible with the educational and disciplinary goals of the teachers. Attempts to prohibit and control certain kinds of children's activities are inevitable. An English book published in 1812 and reprinted in Philadelphia in 1821 describes two dozen games played at school. One, hockey, was forbidden because it was deemed too dangerous, and others were restricted to one sex or the other (*Book of Games*, 1821).

Isaac Mickle, a fifteen-year-old schoolboy in 1838, recorded in his diary: "I went to school. Some of the boys who 'could not get the hang of the new school house,' like the boy in the anecdote, 'got the bang of it' under the law which enacts that 'no young gentlemen shall play during the hours allotted for study.' A large rod of correction, alias hickory, alias gad, made its appearance this morning under Domine's desk, indicating that the 'rules were to be exacted to the uttermost farthing' as he says in his advertisement . . ." (Mackey 1977, 22). Mickle goes on to describe a fight between two of his classmates that resulted in a flogging for both by the teacher. In Boston, Mickle's contemporary Edward Everett Hale recalled a gentler but no less restricting experience at an earlier age:

> At my own imprudent request, not to say urgency, I was sent to school with two sisters and a brother, older than I, when I was reckoned as about two years old. . . . The floor was sanded with clean sand every Thursday and Saturday afternoon. This was a matter of practical importance to us, because with the sand, using our feet as tools, we made sand pies. You gather the sand with the inside edge of either shoe for a greater or less distance, as the size of the pie requires. As you gain skill, the heap which you make is more and more round. When it is well rounded you flatten it by a careful pressure of one foot from above. . . . I dwell on this detail at length because it is one instance as good as a hundred of the way in which we adapted ourselves to the conditions of our times. (page 9)

Hale's assertion of autonomy in the classroom was not unique. Nor was sand play the only form of self-expression. In another passage he describes his ability to hide behind the hinged top of his desk. "No schoolboy who has ever had the felicity of such a desk, needs to be told what various orgies we could carry on under such shelter of protection" (page 25). But the custom of Boston school boys in Hale's day that most bespeaks the existence of a folklore of childhood was that of kicking the class water pail to pieces at the end of the term. The pails were bought by class subscriptions to provide water on hot days, and the boys destroyed them in an annual ritual rather than leave them for the next class (page 31). Hale describes other school scenes, including the customary conflict between teacher and students that ultimately created a sense of community and lifelong friendships.

Some historians feel that the feminization of the schools in the late nineteenth century ended this sense of community, by replacing the school master with the school marm, toward whom the elder boys showed more respect. Physical contests with the male teacher and the ritual "barring-out" of teachers appear to decline after 1850 (Fitts 1979, 152). There is evidence to suggest that such rituals survived into the twentieth century in rural areas. Many features of the one-room school encouraged traditional forms of education and play. As one woman who recalled her years in a country school in Waukesha County, Wisconsin, put it: "There was the thrill of competition and the joy of achievement, the hilarity of playtime antics, the embarrassment of classroom error, the tenseness of intrigue, the intimacy and the awakening of youthful romance" (Fuller 1982, 2).

The small number of children of mixed ages, the educational emphasis on memorization and recitation, the standardized simplicity of the school building itself, made the transition from home to school easier in the country than in the city. Books of schoolhouse plans and designs were published as early as 1858, prescribing the locations of windows, doors, and the stove. The building was small enough to permit children to play Andy-over (Anty over, Haley over, etc.: Gulliford 1984, 1992), and many of the sources cited in Wayne Fuller's *Old Country School* recall playing it and crack-the-whip, hide-and-seek, and, in the snow, fox-and-geese. In short, the children's traditions of school grounds, especially the rural school, closely resemble those of New Zealand in the nineteenth century as described by Brian Sutton-Smith (1981a). As educational theories changed and consolidation took place, children found themselves in a much different setting. Larger schools meant longer journeys to and from school for some, often by bus or car. School playgrounds became larger and more fully equipped. Segregated by age, children were less able to learn from each other. Still, some traditions were maintained and children continue to mold their environment within the school and without (Yoffie 1947; Knapp and Knapp 1973; R. Moore 1974; Parrott 1976; M. Williams 1981; Mergen 1982).

A recent study of elementary-school students in an urban area in the eastern United States argues that there are at least two "hidden" curricula in the classroom, in addition to academic subjects. One is gender-role socialization, the other self-taught sex education (Best 1983). The author, a reading specialist who spent four years with one class trying to find out why boys had a higher rate of reading disability, believes that the boys absorbed a "macho" code from the media, textbooks, and adult models that made them reject reading and academic excellence. Since most of the teachers were women, the boys used the lavatory to escape and to defy the teachers. Boys and girls challenged adult authority by playing sex games and by talking obscenely about their sexual activities. In the space of six years, the boys of one school went from chasing and hitting girls to kissing and playing "look and see." Also, by the sixth grade the nightly telephone call to a friend had become a ritual. In contemporary children's culture, traditional lore may be preserved in nontraditional ways.

The work of Ann Richman Beresin (1993), Linda Hughes (1983, 1989) and Christine von Glascoe (1980) suggests that schools are an excellent place to study play. Contrary to earlier belief, children manage to initiate and play their own games apart from adult intrusion. Von Glascoe, and in this *Source book* Beresin and Hughes, show that children spend a great deal of their play time negotiating rules and that playing is a dynamic and complex process in which verbal skills are as important as physical. Girls seem to adjust to the rougher play of boys in the game of foursquare by playing their own game within the framework of the boys' game and by keeping up a continuous oral review of the rules. Thus the real game is played in approximation of the ideal game, and players derive satisfaction from their performance in both the real and the imaginary games (Hughes 1983). Stuart Reifel's study of an elementary-school cafeteria in Texas demonstrates that a wide range of verbal and pretend play goes on unobserved by adults. Jokes and pranks predominate, but some children manage to engage in elaborate fantasy play, using bananas as telephones, imitating other children, and pretending to be animals. Food was used in novel ways. For example, graham crackers were nibbled into the shape of guns and used in mock battles (Reifel 1986). Playing at school must be studied in a variety of specific settings, such as the schoolyard, classroom, cafeteria, lavatory, and hall. Transitions from one scene to another may be important too. Field trips by bus have always provided opportunities for playing in defiance of teachers and chaperons. Many studies of the use of school spaces need to be done.

PLAYGROUNDS

The children's playground movement is generally acknowledged to have begun in Boston in 1885, with sand gardens modeled on ones seen in Berlin by Dr. Marie Zakrewska (Rainwater 1922, 22–43). Before the end of the century, dozens of American cities had playgrounds with sand boxes, seesaws, and swings. Some of these playgrounds were established and maintained by private philanthropy, some by municipal funds, some by both. Settlement houses and settlement-house workers were in the forefront of the movement to establish playgrounds in Boston, New York City, Philadelphia, Chicago, Washington, D.C., and other cities. The playground movement was related to, but distinct from, the park reform efforts of the same time. In both cases, the reformers were concerned with overcrowding in immigrant neighborhoods and sought to provide an organized alternative to informal street life and recreation. Galen Cranz, in her study of park design, identifies four stages in the history of urban parks, in contrast to Clarence Rainwater, whose 1922 review of the play movement was divided into seven stages.

Cranz (1982) labels the first urban parks, such as Central Park in New York City, as "pleasure grounds," intended for aesthetic effect and renewal. The "reform park" of the period 1900 to 1930 was the second stage. Reform parks and playgrounds were intended to teach good citizenship and useful habits. Where the ideal of the pleasure parks was freedom of choice within industrial order, the ideal of the reform-park advocates was orderly socialization within the chaotic city. That is essentially the distinction drawn by the superintendent of playgrounds in the District of Columbia in 1907:

> There are two prevalent ideals of a playground: one, the park ideal, which regards the playground as primarily a "place to play"; it seeks to provide amusement for children and adults; the other is the school ideal which regards the play leader as the most essential element in the playground, and the playgrounds as a means to a fuller and higher education. The park playground ideal has developed naturally from the idea of the park. The park is primarily a place for recreation. All parks are playgrounds, but the old time park was the playground of the leisured and well-to-do citizen of middle or old age who was blessed with a carriage and artistic appreciation. Play is recreation for adults, but for children, as everyone knows, play is not recreation,

and is ofttimes the most serious thing which the child does. (Curtis 1907, 27)

As Curtis makes clear, the reform playground ideal was based firmly on an emerging theory of child development that emphasized play. Belief in the seriousness of play for children also came from Prussia. In the 1870s Froebel-inspired kindergartens were introduced in several Eastern and Midwestern states, and in the 1880s the German-educated psychologist G. Stanley Hall began publishing his research on the behavior of children. Hall trained the first generation of playground leaders at Clark University, where he taught that children recapitulate the stages of human evolution as they mature and that play serves to teach them physical and mental skills and to develop moral character.

Rainwater's summary of the growth of the play movement reflects Hall's influence: The years 1885 to 1895 were the sand garden stage, focusing on the needs of young children; 1895–1900 saw the development of the playground with swings and other equipment for older children; 1900–05 were the years of the small park, with an emphasis on landscaping; 1905–12 was marked by recreation centers, with buildings for indoor activities; the years 1912–15 saw an added concern for civic art, music festivals, theater, and pageants, and children's play was organized on the playgrounds; in 1915–18, neighborhood organization encouraged residents to participate in the management of the centers; and, finally, in 1918–22 a recreation profession emerged that coordinated community services such as schools and philanthropies (Rainwater 1922). A decade later this phase was still characteristic of playgrounds, as defined by the *Encyclopedia of the Social Sciences:* "The playground movement is a broader term and refers not so much to the allotment of space or the acquisition of land as to the organization of community resources for recreation or leisure time activities" (Nash 1934, 161). Cranz's third stage of park design follows this pattern, and what she calls the "recreation facility" lasts from 1930 to 1965. In this period parks become an expected feature of the environment although no one expects them to have much effect on their users. The residents of the neighborhoods served by parks and playgrounds changed rapidly in this period, creating new problems and possibilities during the last and current period. She calls park design since about 1965 "the open space system," which seeks to create vitality in the context of urban decay by encouraging community participation, street fairs, and diversity (Cranz 1982).

Since neither Rainwater nor Cranz is concerned with how children reacted to these changes in theory and design, it is difficult to gauge the effect of the parks on traditional behavior. Gary Goodman and Dominick Cavallo have attempted critical assessments of the playground movement. Both are rich in detail, but neither deals with the perspective of the child. Goodman argues that Jewish immigrant streetlife declined as a result of the success of the middle-class reformers in organizing leisure activities on the Lower East Side in New York City (C. Goodman 1979). Playground organizers, Goodman feels, taught respect for property, the discipline appropriate to factory work, and obedience. "Through the establishment of playgrounds where trained directors formalized play, institutionalized hierarchy, legitimized external control and rewards, and mandated repressed sexuality, the elite was able to 'Americanize' immigrants and teach them such attitudes as would be beneficial toward maintaining the status quo. The shtetl and Lower East Side games of low organization and minimum role differentiation, which were sometimes coed and within which action had not become reified into positions but was rather a part of style form and skill— these games gave way to playground games which were to be vehicles for and symbols of the American Way of Life" (Goodman 1979, 165).

Cavallo too believes that playground training was intended to subvert the authority of immigrant parents and Americanize their children, but he is more aware of the complexities and contradictions in the playground movement than Goodman. The principal intellectual problem of the playground reformers was to reconcile a number of polarities in nineteenth-century American values: "individualism versus social cooperation, private versus public, selfishness versus loyalty, masculine versus feminine, guilt versus shame" (Cavallo 1981, 147). Their solution was to use team games to limit individualism and encourage cooperation and to substitute public approbation for private satisfactions. "Team games symbolized the key goals of modern liberalism: harmony between classes, orderly competition between interest groups, and individual achievement within frameworks of group and social progress" (p. 155). The extent to which the reformers were successful is difficult if not impossible to measure, of course, and neither Goodman nor Cavallo can do more than point to a general similarity between the ideals of the playground reformers and twentieth-century corporate liberalism. Perhaps a closer study by folklorists of what children actually played and what effect that play has had on their values and behavior might illuminate this point.

Clearly, the playground movement did not succeed in getting all children off the street, nor in eliminating traditional forms of play. Various evidence suggests that even as late as the 1930s, a majority of children spent little time on organized playgrounds (Wojtowicz 1975; Asimov 1979;

Borchert 1980; Yukic 1975). What the playgrounds did provide was an alternative to the worst features of street life and the expense of commercial amusements. Jacob Riis's description of the Poverty Gap playground on West Twenty-eighth Street between Tenth and Eleventh avenues in New York City notes simply that the murder rate had decreased and that children now played in sand boxes instead of pelting strangers with mud (Riis 1892, 185). At the founding meeting of the Playground Association of America in 1906, Jane Addams called upon the delegates to find ways of linking the "play" inherent in traditional drama with the transient amusements of youth. "We might illustrate by the 'wild west show' in which the onlooking boy imagines himself an active participant. The scouts, the Indians, the bucking ponies are his real, intimate companions and occupy his entire mind. In contrast with this we have the omnipresent game of tag, which is, doubtless, also founded upon the chase. It gives the boy exercise and momentary echoes of the old excitement, but it is barren of suggestion and quickly degenerates into lawless horse-play" (Addams 1907, 23). As an alternative to the wild west show, the movies, and the commercial amusement parks, the playgrounds simply provided space and equipment. Even the frequent surveys of "What Cities Played Last Year and How," published in the *Playground* from its inception in 1907, implied that there were too few play leaders to supervise the growing number of playgrounds. The best the reformers could hope for was to plant ideas of discipline and cooperation that would be carried over into streets and amusement parks (Curtis 1907, 28).

Playground Design

As a substitute for constant supervision and to compete with amusement-park rides, most playgrounds relied on equipment. When playgrounds were established in Washington, D.C., in 1902, they contained see-saws, slides, and traveling rings. Within two years, the Public Playgrounds Committee owned "73 swings, 18 see-saws, 7 chutes, 10 sand boxes, 5 awnings for sand boxes, 2 sets of parallel bars, 8 sets of traveling rings, 3 sets of flying rings, 2 trapezes, 2 climbing poles, 5 horizontal ladders, 6 incline ladders, 13 sliding poles, 6 sets of basketball goals and posts, 4 sets of volley-ball posts and nets, 2 jumping pits, 5 sets of quoits, 4 giant strides, 2 baseball sets, 8 Indian clubs, 1 storage box and ground tools, 5 horizontal bars, 2 striking bags and frames, and apparatus frames for playground development" (Martin 1912, 10). The purposes of playground equipment were succinctly stated by an early advocate, Everett Mero. Believing that individual gang members are usually well behaved by themselves, Mero proposed scattering equipment in different parts of the playground so "that the gang is put to inconvenience to maintain its organization. . . ." A second purpose of equipment was to save space. "Eighteen boys can be kept busy on a single lot 18 by 20 feet if it is equipped with the proper apparatus and an instructor is at hand." Finally, the climbing apparatus fulfills a biological urge to do "stunts," a belief echoed twenty-four years later by the manufacturers of Junglegym who advertised their structures as meeting "a deepseated instinct for climbing" (Mero 1909, 57–59; Playground Equipment Company 1933, 11).

Playground equipment manufacturers were quick to advertise their products in terms that appealed to purchasing committees. The Fred Medart Manufacturing Company of St. Louis, for example, advertised in the May 1914 issue of *Playground* that a "public playground is intended to cultivate correct physical and moral development, and supervision and the right kind of equipment are equally important. Apparatus well-planned economizes in space and affords the best way to provide for a large number of children." In the same year, the Narragansett Machine Company of Providence published a catalog that emphasized the strength, durability, simplicity, safety, and compactness of its playground gymnastic equipment. Recognizing that many cities fell short of the ideal of providing each playground with a full-time supervisor, the Narragansett catalog noted that "each device should suggest its own use, even to a child" (Narragansett 1914). The Spaulding catalog of 1919 contained complete plans for playgrounds of seven to ten acres divided into areas for boys and girls, children and young adults (Spaulding 1919).

The increasing size of playgrounds and the use of fences to segregate the area reflected two other theories of the early play movement. Henry Curtis advocated fences for schoolyards and playgrounds to keep out rowdies and to make discipline easier. "The fence also makes of the school yard an institution and helps to create loyalties." Within the playground, fences should be placed between the boys' and girls' play areas. "The reasons for it are obvious and sufficient, there are often loose girls and always loose boys coming to the playgrounds, and it is better not to have them together, or where they can corrupt other children" (Curtis 1913, 16). In 1928 and again in 1938, this view was expounded by the Playground and Recreation Association:

> It is almost universally agreed that a children's playground should be fenced. . . . Perhaps the most important reason for fencing the playground is the safety which the fence provides. It prevents the child from running needlessly into the street after a batted ball and also prevents injury to passerby caused by batted balls, for example. Pro-

tection of property is another factor, and the fence not only protects the playground from vandalism but also prevents trespassing upon neighboring property. By putting the playground under complete control and keeping out mischief makers, the fence greatly simplifies the problem of maintenance. The fence often provides the solution of the problem of beautifying the playground. . . . Not the least of the reasons for fencing the playground is that the fence adds to it a degree of individuality. (Playground and Recreation Association of America 1938, 12–13)

Enlargement of playgrounds came in response to increased use by older children and adults. The definition of play was changing from children's games to community leisure, from creation to recreation. As the definition of play changed, the fence became a symbol of the old order. An article in the August 19, 1925, *Evening Star* of Washington, D.C., reported that gangs were terrorizing playground directors and destroying property. Significantly, the chief object of their vandalism seems to have been the playground fences. More than fifty years later, a study of enclosed playgrounds concluded that enclosed play areas increased the imaginative play of preschool children (Barnett and Kruidenier 1981, 323–36).

A general reevaluation of the efficacy of playground equipment was presented in M.W. Johnson's *Child Development* (1935). Reporting an experiment to determine the effects on behavior of variation in the amount of play equipment in groups of three-, four-, and five-year-olds at the University of Michigan Elementary School playground, Johnson concluded, "The more extensively equipped playground for each group is characterized by a greater combined amount of bodily exercise and play with materials and fewer social contacts in games and undesirable behavior [teasing, crying, quarreling, hitting]. The less extensively equipped playground for each group is characterized by a lesser combined amount of bodily exercise and play with materials and a greater number of social conflicts" (Johnson 1935, 66). These rather obvious conclusions are important, however, since they raise the question of whether too much equipment might interfere with social development. To encourage social interaction, Johnson suggested the use of gardens and toy trucks and a return to the use of sand box play. A generation later, research was being published to show that playground equipment of specific kinds—wooden pilings, horizontal bars, and geodesic domes— produced different kinds of movement and spatial awareness in kindergarten children, but the larger questions of the influence of playground apparatus on children's lives and lore have gone unanswered.

From personal memory, the apparatus that combined swings, slides, see-saws, rings, horizontal bars, and a sliding pole, in the public park of a small Western city in the late 1940s, was a focal point for fourth- through eighth-grade boys' after-school activities. Games of chase, tag, and follow-the-leader were played on every part of the apparatus including the top supporting bar. The games involved group fantasies, individual heroics, and occasional injury, all of which stimulated interest and encouraged continued use of the equipment. Outside laboratory observations, play on playground apparatus takes on a different and often unsanctioned character. Moreover, traditional playground equipment is very durable, thus allowing several generations of children to establish and maintain a tradition of use.

In the 1960s and 1970s, manufacturers of playground equipment began to redesign their products, partly in response to a shift in the market and partly because new plastics and other synthetic materials made the manufacture of new kinds of apparatus more profitable. The shift away from public playgrounds to private backyard playgrounds followed the population shift from city to suburb that accelerated after World War II. Although many real-estate developers made the addition of a community playground part of their sales promotion, more and more parents bought small replicas of playground equipment for home use. Both home and public playgrounds had to compete with movies, television, and commercial theme parks for the attention and affection of children. The manufacturers responded with molded plastic animals for riding, pipe outlined rockets, stagecoaches, fire engines, and "storybook villages" (American Playground Device Company 1974; Miracle Playground Equipment Company 1975). One fascinating example of the transformation of a folk playground device to a piece of public playground equipment to a backyard apparatus is the revolving see-saw.

In 1938, Lizzie Davis of Marion, South Carolina, recalled her childhood as a slave for a Federal Writer's Project interviewer: one of her strongest memories was of cutting a small pine tree to make a "flying mare." Boring a hole in the middle of the pine pole and fitting it on a peg fixed on the stump created a revolving see-saw (Rawick 1972, 2:294). John Champlin and Arthur Bostwick illustrate what they call "an ancient french see-saw, called *Bascule Double*," in their 1890 collection of games and sports. This device is two see-saws that cross over a pivot, allowing both up and down and revolving motion (p. 618). A similar ride was illustrated in the July 1913 issue of *Popular Mechanics;* this version was constructed of steel tubing and installed on municipal playgrounds. Forty years later, *Popular Mechanics* again featured the "seesaw [that] doubles as a merry-go-round," this time built of scrap steel and auto parts by the home craftsman (*Popular Mechan-*

ics, July 1913, 116 and March 1953, 173). In 1957 a company in Birmingham, Alabama, advertised a portable "Merri-Go-Whirler" for use indoors and outdoors (Playthings 1957, 180). A generation later, *Mother Earth News,* the *Popular Mechanics* of the counterculture, told its readers how to build "an up'n'down merry-go-round (*Mother Earth News* 1982, 126–27). Such a history strongly suggests that the folk origins of other playground equipment need to be investigated.

Beginning in the 1960s, playground designers began to rethink the uses and form of play areas. Under the influence of Erik Erikson and Jean Piaget rather than G. Stanley Hall and Joseph Lee, landscape architects defined play as freedom from the requirements of work, as a manifestation of choice, and as an exercise in imagination (Dattner 1974; 7–15). The designers were also influenced by Scandinavian and British reformers who advocated "adventure playgrounds" where children could build their own structures using borrowed tools and scrap material (Allen 1969; Bengtsson 1974). A play leader became a combination maintenance man, mediator, and anthropologist (Prince 1972). He was no longer expected to keep order or lead games. American designers began writing about "loose parts," "ambiguity," "flexibility," "diversity," "change," and "open endedness" (Aaron 1965; Friedberg 1970; Nicholson 1971; Dattner 1974; Hogan 1974; R.C. Moore 1974; Frost and Klein 1979). Concern with safety, variety, physical development, and opportunity characterizes playground theory at present.

Drawing on fifty years of research and experience, Lance Wuellner lists forty guidelines for playground design (Wuellner 1979). In listing the theoretical and practical implications of each research conclusion, he reveals many of the assumptions about children currently held by planners and recreation professionals. Some of the assumptions are contradictory, such as the need to promote both solitary and group play, but there is open acknowledgment of these oxymora. There is general recognition that children need to be challenged as they grow and that all children want to be "where the action is." Traditional climbing structures on enclosed playgrounds are being replaced or supplemented by stone pyramids, log pilings, and concrete shells. These objects are often meant to be street sculpture, outdoor art that can be enjoyed aesthetically by adults and kinesthetically by children. The contemporary playground is sometimes a sculpture garden, sometimes an architectural parody. Europeans and Japanese seem to lavish more attention on design, creating futuristic climbing structures and encouraging children to "exercise their sense of discovery, individually and communally" (Rouard and Simon 1977, 13). There is even some evidence that traditional games are played more frequently on playgrounds of contemporary design than on playgrounds equipped with the familiar swings, slides, and climbing apparatus (Hayward, Rothenberg, and Beasley 1974, 150).

USE OF PLAYGROUNDS

Folklorists can help to discover the effect of playground design, location, and size on traditional games. Carol Wojtowicz offers a model in her study of changes in play over three generations in Philadelphia (Wojtowicz 1975). Based on her interviews with persons who grew up in the city before World War I, during the 1920s and 1930s, and a third group from the 1950s and 1960s, she finds that many games survived from generation to generation, but many others were abandoned. In the pre–World War I group, there was no mention of organized playgrounds, despite the fact that the playground association was active at the time. Children played in the street and on vacant lots. The most popular games were tag, dodge ball, volleyball, shadows (in which the pursuer tried to step on the shadow of the pursued), jump rope, jacks, and marbles. For children of the 1920s and 1930s an elaborate playground with a model village provided a change for a few hours a week, but many played varieties of stickball and tip cat. Buck-buck, in which boys pile on each other until the boys on the bottom guess a number, or until the bottom man collapses, was mentioned in all three groups. The same game is called Buck T Buck by black boys in Pittsburgh (M. Williams 1981), indicating its migration westward and across racial lines. Wojtowicz's generation of the 1960s played tag and chase and capture games in playgrounds that were being revitalized by the city recreation department. Some games of the earlier periods, such as Peggy (tip cat) and mumblety peg seem to have vanished.

The discrepancy between what a person remembers playing after thirty or forty years and the range of games that were available to him in his childhood also needs to be studied. Playground supervisors in Washington, D.C., in 1916 encouraged such games as prisoner's base, fox and chickens, and I spy, but none of the three persons I have interviewed recalled these games spontaneously. One person mentioned baby-in-the-hat, a ball and capture game listed by the Department of Playgrounds.[1] The same individual recalled two dozen other activities of his childhood in the 1920s and 1930s, all independent of the playground system. Highly organized games of football were played on any available field. Apparently, the distinctions children make between playing on the sidewalk and street and playing in a municipal playground are based on their folk definition of play. The characteristics of play seem to include the declaration of identity of "player," the elaboration of that identity by behavior that makes use of mutually acceptable actions, and the achievement of a feeling that the identity and behavior are pleasant and fun. Other kinds of activities, including solitary amusement, may be labeled play on further reflection, but, like playground activities, they seem defined by other factors, such as equipment or the absence of other children.

The power of the physical environment to influence and define play is clearly seen in Hayward, Rothenberg, and Beasley's survey of three types of playgrounds (1974). Traditional, contemporary, and adventure playgrounds were used in significantly different ways by quite different populations. Traditional playgrounds had a population composed of 29.48 percent preschool children; 20.84 percent ages six to thirteen; 9.8 percent teenagers; and 39.78 percent adults (nursemaids, parents, and play leaders). Contemporary playgrounds had 35.23 percent preschoolers; 22.21 percent ages six to thirteen; 6.85 percent teenagers; and 35.71 percent adults. Adventure playgrounds had only 1.74 percent preschoolers, but 44.58 percent ages six to thirteen; 32.16 percent teenagers; and 21.52 percent adults. The figures indicate, I think, that traditional and contemporary playgrounds lose their appeal as children grow older and that play in these areas is conducted within sight of adults. According to Hayward and his associates, the most frequent activities in traditional playgrounds are swinging, water play, monkey bars (jungle gym), see-sawing, and what they call "connective," that is going from one activity to another. Passive activities, eating and drinking, and solitary play occupied about 10 percent of the time of the observations. "Games" were observed only three times, for a total of eighteen minutes, out of 1,288 minutes of study.

The most frequently observed activities in contemporary playgrounds were equipment play, water play, sitting, dressing, and sand play. Games were observed eight times for a total of 111 minutes. The differences between the traditional and contemporary seem to be based largely on the kinds of equipment. Given the less differentiated apparatus in contemporary playgrounds, the children seem to turn to games more readily. In contrast, the most frequently observed activities on adventure playgrounds were "clubhouse," building, talking, and "passive activities." Games are unreported and there are many more activities like gardening, singing, arguing, play fighting, and playing with rocks, which were observed only once or twice. How many of these activities would be labeled play by the children themselves is unknown. The skills and concerns of the sociologist, anthropologist, psychologist, historian, and folklorist need to be combined to answer this question.

The importance of time as well as place is implied in three studies of playground language. The Opies have focused on the games used to start games, some of which take several minutes (1969). Counting out rhymes, self-appointment, and argument are all used to begin play activities and should be studied to see if they correlate with particular places and times. The Knapps' study of the terms used to declare a truce or pause during a game also suggests that external environmental factors shape the content of children's lore. The decline of the term "Kings X" and the rise of "Time" or "Times" appears to be due to the growing influence of timed sports (Knapp and Knapp 1973). A report on the use of the term "Olley, Olley Oxen Free" by children when they decide to end a game of hide and seek argues that this variant of "All Outs in Free" is uniquely American both in form and function, since the shift from a single-person hunt to a contest of physical skill allows greater participation by all the players (French 1975).

CONCLUSIONS

The implications of the foregoing for folklorists and others are that playgrounds are defined by both physical characteristics and by use. The site of play may be supervised or unsupervised, occasional or regular, intended or unintended, in playgrounds, backyards, schools or streets (Mason 1982). Each of these factors requires a creative response from children, and each contributes to children's folklore. Psychologists have long been aware of the importance of place and peer group on children's behavior (Gump 1975; Campbell 1964). What was once called "the gang" has been studied for a century. Most of the students of children's gangs sought to eliminate or to change them. A few might agree with Jane Addams that "in these social folkmores, so to speak, the young citizen learns to act upon his own determination," but most rejected the possibility of a worthwhile connection between childhood and adulthood (Campbell 1964, 292). Yet, as James Bennett (1981) has recently shown, there lies buried in past studies of delinquency a rich body of material on children's folklore. "I liked the new game of stealing I had learned, and it really was a game and I played it with much zest and relish," says a boy in one of Shaw's case studies. The reports of Shaw, Frederic Thrasher, and others remind us that much of children's lore is antisocial and that the child and the discipline of urban life have a long history of conflict.

The playground and to a certain extent the school are the products of urbanization and its discontents (R.C. Moore 1986). We need to know much more about the ways in which our culture deals with the contradictions between freedom and constraint, individualism and conformity. We can look for answers in the ways children treat each other and the ways adults have treated children. When the International Playground Association changed its name to the International Association for the Child's Right to Play, it signaled that those rights may need protecting. When we see "No Playing" signs on streets and dumpsters, when we are urged to remove doors from old refrigerators and to fill old wells, are we saving children's lives or merely acknowledging that life is full of hazards? The lure of forbidden play is a strong element in children's lore. Does it help the adult come to terms with his own world? How many battles of life are won on the playing fields of childhood?

These and other questions spring to mind in considering the folklore of children's play spaces. The schools and traditional playgrounds were largely successful in confining children and making them perform the tricks of muscle and mind that adult society demanded, but they failed to suppress the flow of children's lore that entered and left each day with the boys and girls. The playground was a kind of zoo in which the keepers were as caged as the kept (Sutton-Smith 1980b, 4–8). Fences and walls created a false sense that play was controlled, children safe. On the rare occasions when they looked closely, adults were bemused to find that children were physically confined but mentally free. Play on the playground resembled play in the street. Adventure playgrounds, comprehensive playgrounds, and anarchy zones are responses to the discovery of children's lore. Whether they will be any more successful than traditional playgrounds remains to be seen. The struggle for the control of space between adults and children will continue. Space and place are important. The study of children's folklore can help to clarify the nature of the struggle and locate it in place and time.

Note: The author gratefully acknowledges the useful suggestions of the late Frederick Gutheim.

NOTE TO CHAPTER ELEVEN

1. Interviews on their play history were held by the author with the following persons: Nick Graziano, 1983, Tom Kelly, 1983, and Sylvia Shugrue, 1983.

12 MATERIAL FOLK CULTURE OF CHILDREN

Simon J. Bronner

"One of my favorite toys when I was four years old was a piece of stiff wire roughly twelve inches long, bent into the shape of a double letter C. It must have been the piece that holds a thermos bottle firmly in the lid of a metal lunch box. I found it on the beach in southern California and named it 'gropper,' because, I think, the lower part of the C looked to me like the legs of a grasshopper. The upper part looked something like the bill of a duck. In the ensuing months I worked with my mother and grandmother to make a large wardrobe of bright colored socks to pull over the ends of the wire legs and a variety of wool, silk, and cotton tubes to slip over the bill and cover its body. For several years, Gropper held an honored place among my other toys—cars, Teddy Bear, blocks, and soldiers—but at some point I became self-conscious and a bit embarrassed about my fantasy and discarded Gropper, bag and baggage. If I had kept Gropper and donated him, together with the rest of my playthings, to the Smithsonian, what would a curator do with such a bizarre object?" (Mergen 1982, 121–22).

Children, when left to their own devices, can create elaborate things—objects, indeed environments, suited to the spirit and imagination of youth. Yet often such creativity eludes the watchful eye of the parent, no less the curator or ethnographer. The child commonly keeps the creation private. Why? Children may feel embarrassed about making playthings themselves when toys supplied by Mom and Dad sit idly by, or they may be discouraged from strange (by adult standards, anyway) flights of fancy. Many parents take the attitude that the child's world springs from adult hands and tastes. Many folk toys, songs, and games for children, in fact, are really crafted by adults. But children do think for themselves, and thought sparks creativity—a small world of their own making.

This chapter offers a guide to basic issues, approaches, and sources associated with the study of the many material worlds of children. First, I offer a historical background to the study itself, and I follow with a survey of some approaches used today. I make a case for the special study of folk or traditional objects and processes as a special category of research into material culture. In doing so, I realize that some distinctions between mass and folk culture are necessary, although the two cannot easily be separated. Because an important point of this survey is the way that the traditional expressions of children vary, not only by regional or ethnic culture, but also by their very maturation process, I particularly explore developmental approaches. I suggest ways to combine comparison of texts or objects with contexts or processes across the life course, and I examine how ethnicity, gender, region, and class have been especially evident in research on the material folk culture of children.

I begin by offering an example of an object that is both a text and a context and suggests the process by which small worlds are created. The treehouse is an enclosed space that relies greatly on the child's imagination. Usually built by children's hands, the rough exterior and makeshift furniture inside become transformed. The height and cover of the tree offers children, especially, it seems, boys, a certain independence. Engaging in the process of gathering materials, construction, and occupation allows for participation in culture. It responds to, and also establishes, traditions. Children are discovering their technical capabilities and something about aesthetics and design. In the American setting, this design emphasizes a square or rectangular shape and social separation. Thomas Yukic, for example, recalled his 1930s childhood in Niagara Falls for *New York Folklore*. A memory that stood out was of the things his "gang" built: "Tommy Leshak built a complete hut near the elm tree on the island, bringing every scrap of material by boat to construct a small eight foot square building. It was a great place for rainy days and card games. The hut was of corrugated tin roofing and wood planks; Tom poured a cement floor from the left-over cement drippings which were washed off daily by Empire Builders Supply Company trucks near Sandocks" (Yukic 1975, 225).

Down in New York City, Fred Ferretti reported returning to the neighborhood where he grew up, only to find that not as much had changed as he thought. "The empty lot where we built huts out of wood scraps and discarded refrigerator cartons, where we roasted 'Mickies'—the right way to roast them was to dig a shallow hole in the dirt, line it with bricks, fill it with wood, start a fire, and drop the raw potatoes into the flames; they were cooked when their skins were reduced to jet-black powder. To my surprise, the basketball backboard we built and nailed to the telephone pole a couple of houses away from mine was still attached, although there was no hoop"

(Ferretti 1975, 13). He realized upon reflection that adults often believe that their childhood labors were unique. But he found strong continuities between the items made in his childhood and what he found when he returned. He sensed traditions at work.

Manipulating resources and structures to shape things is an everyday experience for youth (Adler 1981, 8–10; Bronner 1986b). Think back to your childhood. I know that in mine play typically involved making things. Stickball bats were made from broom handles, go-carts from skates and boards, slingshots from clothes hangers. Wadded paper became ammunition for jerry-built "spit-shooters" loaded with green pellets taken from wild cherry trees. We made boats out of scrap wood to try out in the park pond. Children on my block hunted down and altered all manner of smooth surfaces for sledding during the winter. We even had a hideout in an isolated lot where we constructed makeshift shelters and tables. You probably also recall long hours altering and using the box the Christmas present came in, long after the gift's attraction passed.

Material folk culture is the term commonly used to describe such traditional, creative encounters with physical things. It is not simply the existence of individual items that is significant but their interconnection of concept and design as well as their association with a social system. As to the *folk* in material folk culture of children, when recording the traditional behavior of children, I look for informal ways children interact and learn. True, they might consult a book or ask a teacher, but I find that informal, or folk, learning through word of mouth, demonstration or imitation, and customary example are still the predominant means by which children acquire knowledge of technique and form. Out on the beach, children begin digging; later they consult one another or imitate models elsewhere in their view. As they build their sand forts, they go through a folk process. To be sure, forms exist that folklorists call folk because they stand up to the usual test of tradition—whether they repeat and vary over time and space. String figures like the cat's cradle, carved wooden chains, and, more recently, the "cootie catcher" made of paper are examples (Boas 1938; Bronner 1981a; Samuelson 1980). Still, my study of "folk" is meant to shed light on the thought and behavior of people; the lore is only a partial representation of the behavior involved in creativity (Bronner 1986a). Especially when dealing with children, I observe the processes of learning, communicating, and making—the active and cognitive parts of traditional expression.

The *material* of material folk culture includes both construction and decoration. In the study of children's material culture, primary attention has been given to toys and other objects used in play (Schlereth 1990). Second is art and craft (often also discussed as part of play), and occasionally body ornamentation commonly applied to hair, nails, and face. Other subjects are neglected, yet could easily be part of the study of children's folk culture. Foodways, clothing, and ephemeral architecture (treehouses, for example), indeed the connection between children's labor and play, still await studies in depth. As material, the objects and environments under study provide tangible evidence that especially suggests considerations of form and creative process (see Bronner 1986a, 1986b). As evidence of shared tradition, the material suggests social interaction and culture in process. Here I am concerned with the ways that the tradition works at a given age, keeping in mind that influencing factors of gender, ethnicity, and region, to name a few variables, have a bearing on cultural expression. In the following discussion, my use of material culture centers on things made or altered *by* children *for* their use.

A primary task taken up in some of the first studies of the material folk culture of children was to describe through American history the variety of skills and crafts children have engaged in. In 1898, Alice Morse Earle wrote a chronicle of Colonial everyday life that covered the rounds of children's life. Looking through diaries and travelers' accounts she found that demands were put on boys and girls to be "useful." A young girl from Colchester, Connecticut, wrote in her diary in 1775: "Fix'd two gowns for Welsh's girls,—Carded two,-Spun linen,—Worked on Cheesebasket,—Hatchel'd flax with Hannah, we did 51 lbs. apiece,—Pleated and ironed,—Read a Sermon of Dodridge's,—Spooled apiece,—Milked the cows,—Spun linen, did 50 knots,—Made a Broom of Guinea wheat straw,—Spun thread to whiten,—Set a Red dye,—Had two Scholars from Mrs. Taylor's,—I carded two pounds of whole wool and felt Nationly,—Spun harness twine,—Scoured the pewter" (Earle 1898, 253). Beyond the chores of the house and farm, girls were expected to indulge in decorative crafts such as embroidery, paper cutting, and lace making. Many of these activities were taught to children by adults. The private world that children made is often harder to uncover. Earle implied, however, that the association of children's material culture almost totally with play is a modern one. She spotlighted material culture as an important part of American social history of family and community life.

The use of a historical outline to describe children's culture persists to the present. Bernard Mergen's survey of play, for example, included a chapter on the artifacts of play (see also Heininger 1984; Graff 1987; West and Petrik 1992). His outline showed a movement from handmade toys taken from nature to games and toys increasingly mass-produced. To categorize the early period, he quoted Dorothy Howard's turn-of-the-century reminiscence: "A 'plaything'—a stick, for example—was not a stick but (metaphorically) a horse to ride, a thermometer for playing doctor, a writing or drawing tool for marking on the ground, a log for building log cabins, a boat to float down a rivulet from a spring shower, play candy, a shotgun for hunting, or another person." "To the bounty of nature," Mergen wrote, "the Industrial Revolution added a vast toy store of play objects: washers, tires, clothespins, coat hangers, tin cans, ball point pens, paper plates, bottle tops, rubber bands, and paper clips" (Mergen 1982, 104). Modern toys, he claimed, are dominated by the mass culture; factory-made toys by this reasoning have overshadowed folk toys in the twentieth century. His linear model harks back to the notion that progress inevitably marches forward and eliminates folk culture. It is problematic to assume that folk culture does not adapt to changing surroundings, or that modernization necessarily means that industry replaces the influence of the handmade object. To be sure, more interaction takes place between folk processes and mass-produced products today, but then again there has always been an interaction between folk and popular culture. Modern toys have also attracted more attention since maintaining childhood as a separate generation of leisure through specialized products has been a recent commercial preoccupation of adults.

Research of artifacts greatly informs the social history of childhood, but the prevailing scholarship tends to overrepresent popular toys and furnishings associated with middle- and upper-class living because they have remained in the historical record (Schlereth 1990; Carson 1989). An additional problem is the tendency to structure history in an exclusively linear and progressive direction. Folk culture scholarship often portrays simultaneous trends toward tradition and change, and examines local worlds for differences. For the subject of playthings through time, the child's hidden folk technics and their interaction with popular culture demand a closer look. A social-historical study by Miriam Formanek-Brunell, for instance, claims that contemporary popular culture has obscured the traditions of doll play in America enacted by both boys and girls during the nineteenth century, before the toy industry commercialized doll play, and, in the author's view, girlhood. A similar argument emerges from Karin Calvert's study of children's furnishings and clothing from 1600 to 1900. Her book brings out the material ways that a nurtured childhood as a separate stage of life developed. As a context for children's creativity, the creation of the child's room, the differentiation of rooms and furnishings by gender, and the dressing of children to encourage special kinds of activities provide critical contexts for ways that children make things and view their surroundings.

The resources of art history have promised to provide some fresh historical perspectives on childhood. Recent studies by Anita Schorsch, and Sandra Brant and Elissa Cullman, outline attitudes of adults toward children by analyzing images of children and their surroundings in painting and sculpture—by some folk, but mostly nonfolk artists. Children's attitudes were more difficult to interpret, since scant evidence remains of children's wares. To their credit, Brant and Cullman include more of this evidence—samplers, drawings, and even hair wreaths made by children—in *Small Folk* than Schorsch did in *Images of Childhood*. But Brant and Cullman stressed the unusual aesthetic quality of the objects, rather than, as would have been called for by folklorists, the typical folk objects of social and psychological significance.

Many museums have aided historians and folklorists by preserving children's folk artifacts and publishing catalogs and essays based on their collections (Mergen 1980, 173–77; Hewitt and Roomet 1979). Some, like the Children's Museum in Indianapolis and the Children's Museum of the Brooklyn Museum, emphasize children's culture and collect folk toys and artifacts. Others are general-history museums that include children's material, although the folk artifacts are commonly not clearly identified. Included in this category are the Smithsonian Institution in Washington, D.C., the Henry Ford Museum in Dearborn, Michigan, and the Shelburne Museum in Burlington, Vermont. America also boasts folk museums that collect historic artifacts of childlife. Especially strong are the Farmer's Museum and Fenimore House in Cooperstown, New York, Old Sturbridge Village in Sturbridge, Massachusetts, and Conner Prairie Pioneer Settlement in Noblesville, Indiana. Generally, such museums are concerned with describing children's toys and playthings as part of children's social life in the distant past (see Carson 1989; Heininger 1984).

Another historical approach, oral history, documents the more recent past by recording childhood memories of the elderly. Among the most informative and compassionate is folklorist Roger E. Mitchell's biography of his Maine father, "I'm a Man That Works." The childhood he describes in Maine, as elsewhere, separated tasks appropriate to either boys or girls. Girls worked inside, especially with fabric and food. Boys worked with wood; they were outdoors. Mitchell recounts making sleds on the model of the bigger bobsleds (Mitchell 1978, 27). Similarly, Thomas Yukic recalls boys building boats in Niagara Falls, New York (Yukic 1975, 211–28). This is what boys did, after all, he says. But with modern social changes in sexual roles, questions now arise about the actual persistence and variation of such patterns. The memory that people recount becomes itself a kind of object to be manipulated to fulfill an image of present selves. Material folk culture of childhood is often remembered as an index of attitudes toward and ideals of sexual roles and symbols.

Having compiled the objects of childhood, many researchers opt to compare their textual and formal qualities, much in the manner of literary critics. In a groundbreaking folkloristic report on American children's material culture, Fanny Bergen in 1895 published reports of children making paints from plants. Pigweed gave a green liquid; bloodroot produced orange; keel yielded red. She wanted to know the circulation of such customs. Play fights with violets, for instance, she found in the United States, Canada, and Japan. She saw some significance in the similarity among customs of societies around the world, and used the distribution of children's customs to illustrate variation within the unity of culture.

In her valuable inventory of childhood practices, Bergen also mentioned children who produced the figure of a baby or an old lady out of an ox-eye daisy, made trombones of the prickly leaf-stalks of pumpkins, strung horse-chestnuts on dogwood berries, and created boats out of peapods (Bergen 1895c). To many, these practices reflect children's fascination with the shape and life of the plant world. Often parents report that their children notice details of the vegetation around them that the parents took for granted. Bergen reported the practices as curiosities; to her, however, they were surprising customs showing a combination of social tradition and primitive creativity. Even today, a patronizing attitude sometimes shows in treating children's things. But since those things train the youngster to consider manipulating the environment, solving problems, and building symbols, more than inventorying objects is necessary.

Many folklorists of the period encouraged comparing the types of the objects after inventorying them. But collecting comparative data on objects for the ultimate purpose of interpretation had pitfalls. Analyzing often ignored the object's setting and cultural context. Looking back, folklorists now realize that they should have been sure that sufficient background information existed on the objects, so that mere conjectures on relations among objects were avoided. The maker, locale, and setting of the objects needed to be taken into account. After categories are drawn, researchers today check more carefully whether objects assigned to the category are indeed comparable.

Stewart Culin, a comparative folklorist of the period, looking closely at material culture, claimed that similarities between American Indian games and sacred rites were so close as to suggest an origin of children's gaming objects in religious ceremonies (Culin 1898). One type was related to the common practice of drawing lots—making or notching sticks to be pulled from the hand. Culin reported, "The Pima employ three twigs with a finger loop at one end, and among some of the tribes of Arizona and southern California, where the game receives the Spanish name of peon, the lots are attached to the wrist with a cord fastened to the middle. This is done to prevent the players from changing them. The four bones, two male and two female, like the sticks in the four-stick game, probably represent the bows of the twin War Gods" (Culin 1907, 267). The critic today would ask if Culin was too quick to assume cultural similarities among different tribal cultures. Are the categories of play and religion comparable in these societies? Can the conclusion really be extended to Western society because of some kind of cultural evolution?

Although open to criticism, comparativists like Bergen and Culin were successful in pointing out the importance of the object in affecting the behavior of people and reflecting their mores and values. Today, researchers still compare objects in their studies, especially for archival collections, but the claims for such analysis are more modest. Comparative study today serves to highlight the continuity and vitality of local traditions (see Abernethy 1989; Page and Smith 1993). Jan Harold Brunvand's recent guide for Utah folklore collectors illustrates the use of textual collection among children. He included as prominent examples of material folk culture two reports of children's folk creations. The first is recounted from the memory of an elderly woman, a doll made from hollyhocks, clothespins, and thread. The second is from a college woman who remembered making gum-wrapper chains in junior high school. She recalled that a girl added to the chain until it was the height of the boy she liked. Then if she set fire to one end and it burned all the way up without going out "it meant that he liked you too!" (Brunvand 1971, 102–3). Brunvand emphasized the need for documenting the background and custom attached to folk technics as well as noting the maker, locale, and setting of the object. The researcher outside Utah can consult this material to confirm the circulation of the custom, and to note differences and similarities in form and practice.

The attention to the local setting and people as a defining characteristic of a unique culture is informed by many anthropologists who have examined differences in the childhood of aboriginal groups and "bounded" societies as a result of cultural nurturing even more than biological nature. The differences, and often the apparent exoticism, of customs are the result of the different functions that such customs serve. The stories, rhymes, and objects may serve the society by instilling values in children that will be important to them as adults and will help solidify the society as a bound community. Sister M. Inez Hilger, for example, studied Chippewa child life on reservations in the upper Midwest of the United States during the 1930s. When she observed children playing house, she noted that girls tended not to emphasize possessiveness. "One-room 'houses' with walls of 1-inch-deep ridges of soil were marked off on well-scraped ground in the yard," she wrote. She continued, "These houses were equipped with household furniture, such as is found in their own meagerly furnished homes, made of most perfectly modeled clay forms—the gumbo soil in the area (western section) being well adapted to modeling. Although models were only 2 or 3 inches in length, tables had grooved legs and rounded corners; chairs had curved or straight backs; rockers had runners; and sideboards, designs on doors! None of the furnishings were considered precious enough to be saved for the next day's house playing; new ones were made three successive days" (Hilger 1951, 110).

The application of this functional attention to behavior and context can frequently be found as well in the so-called "open" or "complex" industrialized settings of Europe, Australia, and America. Mary and Herbert Knapp's book *One Potato, Two Potato* is comparative to an extent, but they divided their collections primarily by what function the lore served. Does it give prestige and power to the teller? Does it primarily serve to teach a skill or value? Does it help organize and structure children's social interaction? Two categories in the Knapps' book that feature material culture are "Coping with the Here and Now" and "Coping with the Unknown." In the first category are reactions to the troubling present that express hostility or allow a creative escape. The Knapps report on reflections of the violent times in which we live, such as soda-straw blowguns for spitballs and elaborate rubber band and bobby-pin slingshots. Rapid technological change becomes evident now in children's making of rockets from the silver paper around sticks of gum (Knapp and Knapp 1976, 225–31). Citing functions of lore, however, does not explain origin or emergence, although finding the conscious and unconscious uses to which folklore is put sheds light on its persistence, appeal, or transformation (Bronner 1979, 1988; Factor 1988).

"Coping with the Unknown" refers to the lore that predicts the future, or present events out of view. The lore thus helps to alleviate fear or give a sense of control lost by the unpredictable. The widespread gum-wrapper chain is an example of predicting a boyfriend's emotions. Another is a fortune-telling device called by the Knapps a "wiggle-waggle," although I have heard of it too as a type of "cootie catcher." Paper is folded to allow one to unveil predictions for the future. After a certain number or color is read aloud to the beat of folding and unfolding movements, a flap is lifted to reveal a crystal-gazing message. As a cootie catcher, the device can be used to remove dreaded cooties—imaginary insects, disease, or ritual dirt making some person or trait undesirable—from your body. Indeed, the obsession of post–World War II children with cooties has spawned a host of material folk preventatives and cures (Samuelson 1980).

The functional approach of the Knapps tends to lump together a variety of settings under the rubric of "American." Some critics have argued that folk traditions respond more immediately to the physical environment of the neighborhood, urban or rural. Further, they point out that many of the traditions created in response to this environment are emergent and spontaneous, such as Bernard Mergen's fanciful "Gropper," which opened this chapter. An enlightening survey of such response in New York City is found in *City Play* by Amanda Dargan and Steven Zeitlin. "Play can happen on a stoop, a box on the sidewalk, a small part of one block, on one street, in one neighborhood, in one borough, in one city, at one point in history. Yet, it is in this highly localized activity that our experience of the city is shaped," they write (Dargan and Zeitlin 1990, 2; see also Nasaw 1985). They explain children's use of paper hats, go-carts, and makeshift clubhouses as a need to create identities and skills for themselves from the resources in their environment. The results are varied and often individualized; the emergence of tradition anew is emphasized rather than the lineage of texts.

In many past studies of material folk culture, a tendency existed to celebrate the old in childlore. Items and informants need not be old to be folk, but researchers often sought to find lore they could trace back in history, instead of noting the emergent culture. Much of today's material culture research calls for getting in there with children to see and illuminate processes as well as grasp objects. Keen eyes and a quick hand are necessary to note and preserve creative events. More so than the tape recorder so precious to the scholar of oral traditions, the camera and notepad become primary aids. Of course, the words and gestures must be recorded as well.

Research on the material folk culture of children lags behind work done on children's language, belief, and narrative. This dearth of research stems historically from the largely verbal orientation of folklorists and historians in their studies of adults and children alike. In addition, things made by children for their own use are commonly private and ephemeral; they are regularly discarded, forgotten, or hidden. Further, adults are generally easier for the adult researcher to talk to. Indeed, much of our knowledge of childlore comes from the memories of the elderly. When children are approached, they are commonly "interviewed" rather than observed. The researchers didn't know what to ask about material culture, because they typically were not aware of it.

Revisionist approaches to the material folk culture of childhood are based on the uses and perceptions, rather than the mere appearances, of objects. Objects are considered part of human thought and behavior. Newer folkloristic approaches offer an interdisciplinary mix of cultural perspectives drawn from anthropology, social psychological methods and ideas, and the legacy of analyzing traditions informed by the history of folklore studies. Whether the object is traditional is of less concern than whether the use is informally shared by others. Although varied situations are observed, so that a comparative method might be suggested, usually it is the differences, rather than similarities, of style and behavior observed in natural contexts that are stressed.

Let's begin with the developing child. As the child develops, he or she can do more; on the other hand, adults often can't do what they could as children. By looking at creative behavior with objects across the lifespan, one can organize study developmentally. Such behavior can reveal cultural beliefs about aging. Many may "analytically" assume that the organization of development proceeds according to age, but Hilger, in her study of Chippewa child life, found that "culturally" children's growth was not counted in years. Childhood among the Chippewa began with birth and ended with puberty, and it was divided into two periods. She writes, "Before it reached the dawn of reason, it might be described as having been 'just old enough to remember,' or 'before it had any sense.' Children between the age of reason and puberty were designated as having been 'so high'—a gesture of the hand indicating the height" (Hilger 1951, ix).

An "analytical" rather than "cultural" approach to organizing development has often been borrowed from the observations of Jean Piaget, who made the argument that at the outset of life, the child's awareness is of a singular, central object—the child's own body. This argument moves away from the common assumption of children's society as a unified culture and suggests instead that childhood exists as part of a changing system of relations. A decentering process gradually occurs whereby the child becomes aware of other objects and spatiotemporal relations. The development of that awareness and a sense of tradition become related. In the early stage of life, children's own actions dominate their perception. Within eighteen months, children learn of actions outside their own, and of causal relations between other actions, such as a bottle being brought and their own feeding. Touch is important in the early going, as the child cognitively grasps the three dimensionality of the environment and seeks the comfort and meaning of physical and social contact (Bronner 1982, 1986b). Children's objects invite movement and stress texture.

Two behavioral scientists, Mihaly Csikszentmihalyi and Eugene Rochberg-Halton have pointed out that children's objects require some physical manipulation to release their meaning, whereas adult things like art and books stress contemplation (1981, 96–97). They added, "The importance of objects of action in the early years is a reminder of the powerful need children have to internalize actions and to define the limits of their selves through direct kinetic control" (p. 100). As cultural critics, they are concerned with objects, because the "most basic information about ourselves as human beings—the fact that we *are* human—has been traditionally conveyed to us by the use of artifacts" (page 92).

The infant learns to recognize people as a category separate from things. The child indeed then notices differences in the form and feeling of individuals and their surroundings. From this springboard comes the idea that a personal environment can be shaped. You can have "your" things and have the space be consequentially "yours." You can even manipulate the things to control the space, to form an identity. A couple with a one-year-old recently reported to me that their baby would no longer just find a place on the floor to play. The infant's sense of place and surroundings emerged—in the crib. There he would experiment with different arrangements of objects in relation to his own position. When unhappy, he called for his own space and things. The child made meanings take shape.

The shape of the space is in many ways a social aesthetic that the child inherits. The early spaces in the Western child's experience are rectangular—the crib, the room, the house. Straight lines and sharp angles become standards of balance, proportion, and order (Toelken 1979, 227–28). Indeed, some argue, the plan of the child's surroundings largely mirrors the shape of the body, with its paired and symmetrical design (Bronner 1983; Glassie 1972). Later the child develops an identity based on the space he or she knows or alters. Play space, for example, can be formally defined by playgrounds and parks, but is mentally drawn, too, in public streets, buildings, parts of the house, and lots, according to the perception of what is appropriate and aesthetically pleasing to the play group (R. Hart 1979; Mergen 1982, 85–90).

Around the child's second year, Piaget claimed, the child shows behaviors that imply creativity—the formation of, or reference to, objects and events not already present. Aware of a social aesthetic, the child nonetheless develops more personal designs by altering and rearranging physical materials. The loss of control from decentering is being compensated for by a technical control over operative things. The child takes something apart to see what is inside or how it works, and the child rearranges the line and color. Often, children create things for the thrill of creating itself (like the sand mound on the beach); they delight in the power to change shapes and to build anew. The achievement of a product offers its own reward. Mothers like to tell me, for instance, of the amazing things children do with their food—mashed potato mountains and string bean designs. This is not to say that children's creations are not purposeful. With concept in mind, the child rigs together an object for his personal world: the wooden boat, the stickball bat, or the clover chain. Jonah is a boy I know, for example, who shaped a boat out of clay. It didn't fit into any pattern his mother could recognize, but Jonah worked and reworked the boat according to a blueprint he had in his head. His sisters shared the excitement he felt over the creation, and gave advice. Playing along the nearby river days later, they piled variously shaped rocks to make elaborate sculptures jutting out of the shallow water. Each child worked on an individual design, yet they carefully consulted one another on the form and function of the sculptures and ultimately the sculptures resembled one another. The children used the creations to express their ideas in material form.

Beyond the interaction between the child's unique mind and his creation are the influences of region, ethnicity, and class. Differences also exist between the experiences of rural, suburban, and urban children. How much, for example, can be inferred from folklorist Henry Glassie's observation: "Of the flotsam of the streets and back alleys, Philadelphia boys construct a variety of traditional weapons: bows and arrows, 'top shooters,' bolas, slingshots with subtypes for bobby pins or rocks, spears, whips, slings, and—when they are a little older—zip guns. A coat hanger after a little bending becomes a 'key' with which simple locks can be jimmied" (Glassie 1968, 217–18). Befitting the intellectual image of cities as ugly, decadent places, material culture research has overstated the importance of objects representing the seedier side of urban life. In contrast, Americans are accustomed to romanticized accounts of harmless whittling and dollmaking among rural children. An honest inventory of childhood's objects—both innocent and unchaste, delicate and crude, sacred and profane, is warranted.

Although folk processes will continue to hold sway in children's lives because of the basic needs and demands of human development, commercial influences add a powerful variable in the modern world. Through various media, companies specializing in children's toys try to persuade the parent and child of what a particular age should have, rather than answering the question of what they might need. To be sure, the borders between folk and commercial culture are fuzzy at best, but some distinctions are possible. Commericial or mass culture stresses consumption and novelty; folk culture values construction and reuse. Mass culture's products tend toward uniformity and faddism, folk culture toward variation and tradition. In the mass culture you can be told what the fashion is. Companies therefore consciously attempt to control the material culture of children and discourage the supposedly jerry-built folk culture. Often, folk products like the stickball bat, go-cart, and wooden puzzle are usurped and repackaged. Companies depend too on the exploitation of media heroes and fads. The very persistence of creative self-exploration and traditional play among children outside of commercial intervention attests to the developmental entrenchment of folk practice.

One reaction to mass culture is to alter the factory-made product to suit one's tastes. A deck of cards became to my childhood friends a marvelous thing with which to show off the patience and prowess needed to build a house or create a design. They took Erector sets and communally figured out ways to use the steel rods and bolts from the sets in their homemade carts and boats. Such experiences emphasized their control, their personalizing of things around them. By allowing them to conceive, control, create, or alter things informally, their things helped them identify more with the object, and ultimately externalize their identity better.

The relation of object and action underlies what Brian Sutton-Smith called "a developmental psychology of play and the arts." His idea was to "ask not whether play and art are serious or nonserious, real or unreal, but to ask rather what sort of cultural adaptation they are" (Sutton-Smith 1971b, 8). Folk arts emerge as communication systems for various segments of society. Using dramaturgical terminology, Sutton-Smith describes the sequence of structures in play and art. The props used in performance become symbolic; the dramatic patterns become expressive structures. In some cases, like puppetry, the theatrical metaphor directly reveals "an existing understanding of being on stage, having imaginary characters, changing affects, anticipations and dramatic properties" (Sutton-Smith 1971, 13). But also, in other expressive encounters of creative play, the child enacts roles, conceptualizes form, overlays meanings to representation, and unfolds situations (M. Jones 1980; Sutton-Smith 1979a). At around two years old, objects become symbols; at three, toys become properties; from four to seven, such properties are used freely in dramatic play. Children's folk play and art are not trivial, therefore, but the central spine of learning and development.

Beyond the questions posed about specific situations and the conditions for creativity are queries about humanistic continuities of children's art. The word "childlike," used to describe pictures, triggers among most adults similar ideas about relations of line, proportion, and color. Intuitively, at least, a shared idea exists about the basic structures of children's expressions of form. This problem has primarily sparked psychological discussion rather than study of art history for most art historians generally see the artworld as an adult concern. Yet the precedents in children's work demand attention for what they say about consistencies in artistic traditions. Rhoda Kellogg ambitiously reduced the children's art of several societies to basic pictorial motifs. She then suggested that distinct similarities of line and shape found among children throughout the world lend support to the existence of a limited number of designs. Compare all those children's drawings on refrigerator doors, for instance, and you would come up with more of an organized set of repeated forms than you think, she implied. Does the combination of competence at a certain age and social contact thus produce universal and culture-specific sets of folk forms upon which all art is based?

The debate over such a provocative question revolves around how one conceives that structural concepts of folk forms are inherited. Do they spring from a common response to growing up, or rather to the culturally diverse situations of social interaction? Some Freudian advocates claim that childlike forms emerge from anxiety-producing conflicts—especially sexual ones (Kris 1962). Anton Ehrenzweig, for example, claimed that at age five, "libidinous scribblings" surface just when Oedipal conflict typically occurs in childhood (Ehrenzweig 1965, 169). Although tensions and conflicts commonly spark artistic expression, the production of children's art is more commonly explained as a development of creativity and identity through expression (Rank 1945, 276; Bronner 1981b, 65–83).

And what about children's consistent choice of bright or clashing colors? The child generally feels less restricted by adult standards of conformity (which usually stress duller and darker shades) and is allowed more freedom to combine clashing colors. As American children grow, for example, so usually do their conformity to more conservative ideas of color coordination and reliance on linear form. When I wear something particularly bright or outrageous, I am disparagingly accused of acting like a kid (and couldn't that be another reason we often find ourselves denying or forgetting the material culture of our childhood?). Besides psychological demands, then, persistent structural and aesthetic models present in the environment and patterned socializing that takes place in childhood probably lie at the foundation of children's consistent pictorial creations.

Yet with the rush to identify the collective child, we are in danger of neglecting the individual who, in shape and vision, tells of a personal side to creativity. Material is too often collected from a youth and ascribed to a faceless category of "children," rather than to a real name and personality. Why, after all, is the lore—that learning that includes technical skills and creations—in the possession of that particular child? What happens to the lore later in life? We are anxious to record Granddad before his memories die with him, but we can also turn to the critical task of documenting our children before early experiences fade from view.

The core of any approach is to arrive at meaning. Why do children do what they do? Why does their world look the way it does? Why do they become who they are, and will be? Objects provide tangible expressions of ideas and feelings, and thus give a telling symbol of meaning dramatized in three dimensions. In my work on chain carving, for instance, I observed elderly men making chains out of a single block of wood (Bronner 1984). They were men who grew up on farms but who now lived in Indiana factory towns. As children they learned to use a pocketknife from a father, uncle, or grandfather. To show their prowess and creativity, they made a chain—a visual riddle—to impress other boys, even elders. They learned to use tools, work with wood, and operate outside the home—all masculine values. They adjusted to adulthood partly aided by the tension-relieving objects of folk creativity. In adulthood they left the farm to work in nearby factories. Most dropped their chain carving; yet upon retirement or a wife's death, they once again took to carving. Carving once more helped them in a time of adjustment. It enabled them to display their productivity and skill in a society that celebrated youth. It reminded the men of their idyllic (in their minds, anyway) boyhoods. The stroking and touching of wood alleviated tensions and anxieties common to their situation. The objects they wanted to make anew told of unspoken hopes, goals, experiences, and frustrations they shared.

Childhood can set patterns for later life, indeed for the society. Those objects we made and used as children can carry great import for us later. The skills we know, the aesthetics we develop, and the values we learn find manifestation in the technics practiced as children and in the creations that result. Turning to observations of children playing with wood, I found continuities over time.[1] Despite changing societal attitudes toward proper sexual roles, traditional masculine and feminine technical roles were still being enacted in rural boys' play. Finding the meanings of such activity at that moment of enactment and later in life for those particular boys and girls requires the kind of folkloristic study still being awaited (Petersen 1972).

Analyzing creative processes and objects that represent the skills, goals, tensions, values, and ideas of children and the society around them leads to revelations about human expression. Indeed, children often cannot articulate their hidden feelings in speech or gesture, but they do express them-selves through things. Psychologists have used this idea to help abused chil-dren. Children who cannot talk about their experience create paintings and sculpture to dramatize their feelings. Working within certain traditional con-ventions of form, line, and color, the child can project conflicts onto an ex-ternal, nonthreatening outlet. This situation allows for inventiveness while it also maintains a conservative attitude toward tradition and experience.[2]

Once the range of objects made by and for children has been better identified, it should be possible to build classifications based on an aware-ness of "process" that help organize collecting and suggest interpretations. Such classifications may help researchers get beyond the simple division of "toys and games" and help add the constructions often left out of surveys of children's objects (see Bronner 1988). For instance, I have found that children's folk objects commonly fall into categories I call *transformational, synthetic (and syndetic), imitative, and inventive or manipulative.*

Transformational objects are commercial or adult things altered to suit children's needs and images. Philadelphia's "half-ball," used for alley stickball, is made by slicing a whole "pimple ball" bought from the corner store. Openings cut into playground fences, according to children's prefer-ences rather than the architect's design, are another example. In my child-hood neighborhood, many transformational objects were made from bottlecaps. Children weighted them down with a coin to make a Scully puck or they used them for body decoration. Transformational objects usually take away, relocate, or change the utility of factory-produced objects to arrive at a new folk object, an object overlaid with one's handiwork and control.

Synthetic objects result from accretion. Things are combined or built up from existing objects. At Halloween an effigy is commonly put on the front porch by putting together stuffed sheets, pans, sticks, and old clothes into the shape of a scary figure. Children enjoy piling rocks, dirt, or cans to see larger shapes emerge from the small. Loose rubber bands are wrapped together to form a ball that grows over time; the snowball packs a smaller object from the larger environment. The most persistent example of children's folk sculpture, the snowman, is a synthetic object that brings form from the inviting blanket of snow. Children delight in feeling the figure grow, harden, and take shape. Related to this feeling is what anthropologist Robert Plant Armstrong calls "syndesis." The object is put together, but not developed; it grows from repetition of similar units. The ordinary spot in the woods converted to a child's shrine and one's fingers used to make a steeple (whose reverse is the people) take on a special, sometimes artistic or sacred quality that is commonly attached to syndesis. The processes of synthesis and syndesis learned in childhood constitute basic "modes in which the human consciousness apprehends and enacts the world and the self" (R. Armstrong 1981, 13).

Imitative objects resemble larger artifacts in real world. A model hydroplane, for instance, abstractly made from clip-type clothespins and included in the Knapps' collection (1976, 225) signified some Seattle boys' preoccupation with the excitement and power of modern boats. Jonah's clay boat, which I mentioned earlier, is also imitative. Children have several versions of jet planes and helicopters made by folding paper. The treehouse made from boards in a natural environment could be the ultimate imitative object. Although a new and apparently original form, the knowledge of making these structures was passed among the youthful creators informally. It is a prime example of folk process causing emergent designs. The process of imitation blends fantasy and reality to create a personal world that belongs to the child. Objects in the imitative category represent youth's aping of, and through that interpretation of, adult materialism and technology.

The inventive or manipulative object is made from natural resources into a new, more technical shape (Boas 1938). Sand sculpture on the beach stands out as an example, but think too of string figures, carved chains, and paints made from rock and plants. Then there is Brian Sutton-Smith's example of his daughters' fashioning leaves and grass into clothes for their doll (Sutton-Smith 1979d). Much of the fascination for children of objects in this category comes from their ability to handle and control substances and create apparently original shapes and lines. Clay remains popular, for instance, because it is so easily manipulated and it lends itself quickly to working out inventive ideas within traditional forms and formulas. Manipulation heightens the senses and lifts the ego. Handling string figures delights the eye and hand because line and form become manipulable and complex by learned movements.

This classificatory scheme is a limited excursion into the types of objects encountered in childhood. These are to them what constitutes attention-keeping activities. The inventive or manipulative objects are related to the child's curiosity about details of nature. Yet the imitative object speaks loudly about the modern child's fascination with glittering machinery. Moreover, the imitative object has usually been favored by boys. I have seen boys attach shirt buttons to clay in imitation of knobs, and create imaginary gadgets. Nonetheless, the imitative object that glorifies technology has not eliminated the inventive or transformational object. Indeed, the transformational object often mocks and abuses technological design. In the synthetic object is found a basic metaphor for the accumulation of experience and property, for the child celebrates growth by increments. Children may prefer different technical activities, but rarely to the exclusion of others. We often find children delighting in miniaturizing some figures or exaggerating and enlarging others. As children who are developing concepts of self in relation to the society, they are testing the limits of appropriateness socially and personally by using design. They often gravitate toward the very big or the incredibly small, or they experiment with the inner intricacy of realistic scale. They are exploring the built and natural world by themselves, working at different times with peers and parents, friends and neighbors. Play and creativity, commonly informal, are their frequent modes of discovery, release, and testing of the many worlds they encounter.

Such classifications raise questions about the social implications of the creative processes children learn in life. For example, with synthetic objects can researchers validate whether in a sample population, boys prefer the hefty and rough textures of stones and boards and girls choose the softer textures of fabric and vegetation? Variables which might suggest correspondences could be activities stressing rhythm and repetition or strength and cooperation. Whether correlated by style, age, sex, place, ethnicity, or class, hypotheses based on statistical analysis need elaboration. Mihaly Csikszentmihalyi and Eugene Rochberg-Halton, for example, asked children, parents, and grandparents to identify objects with special meanings within their homes (1981, 99). They created classes of meaning for the objects: memories, associations, experiences, self, past, and present-future. Children scored much higher on objects with meanings for self, for experiences, and for present and future. Parents and grandparents rated higher than children on objects with meanings for memories, for associations, and for the past. Folk objects which are made, or objects used according to folk processes, constitute another important body of data to evaluate. Folk objects are only a slice of all children's objects, but they can be extremely useful because they represent informal learning and communication. Researchers can, and should, ask what folk objects and activities can tell of children's preferences. In addition how do social changes affect the traditional toys, labors, and environments of children? Indeed, how do changes in children's material folk culture effect social change? What skills are especially prevalent in children's material culture of different areas and backgrounds? Answering these questions involves far more than mere "child's play."

Still lingering is the sticky problem of weighing the interplay between folk and popular culture in children's creativity. Separating the two is often difficult or misleading, since they commonly appear inexorably entwined.

Popular culture is more visible, but nonetheless suggests relations with the private, often hidden realms of children. Children's magazines like *Boy's Life,* for example, regularly suggest projects taken from folk crafts. Are they invigorating the tradition or removing the craft from tradition? Popular culture can reinforce or standardize folk culture, but more often it intertwines with folklife. When I interviewed chain carvers, many reported learning from both popular mechanical magazines and other boys. Some had extra incentive to try their hand at carving, since in the 1930s radio hero Jack Armstrong offered pocketknives to children on every show! Recently, I had another example of the interrelationship of popular and folk culture when a student in my class convincingly argued that the Boy Scout manual had influenced the formation of boys' material folk culture. Among other artifacts and environments, Boy Scouts prepare small cars made from wood to run in a miniature derby. Over the years the boys have developed informal rules and tastes for building and decorating the cars. Especially aware of folkloristic approaches, Jay Mechling has extensively reported in several articles on objects and environments fabricated by and for the Boy Scouts (Mechling 1984b, 1987, 1989).

Look closely at those objects children like to make. They are often related to prevalent folk ideas and practices, or can reveal much about the making of tradition. Take note of the behaviors surrounding the conception and completion of forms for the thoughts they express.

William Golding touched the hearts of readers when he wrote such behaviors into his bitter allegory *Lord of the Flies* (1954). Children were alone on an island after the adults had been killed in a plane crash. The children created their own model of society with "littluns" and "biguns." The littluns "had built castles in the sand at the bar of the little river. These castles were about one foot high and were decorated with shells, withered flowers, and interesting stones. Round the castles was a complex of marks, tracks, walls, railway lines, that were of significance only if inspected with the eye at beach level. The littluns played here, if not happily, at least with absorbed attention; and often as many as three of them would play the same game together" (Golding 1954, 67). The biguns destroyed the castles, "kicking them over, burying the flowers, scattering the chosen stones." Yet they could not discern or destroy "the particular marks" in which the littluns were absorbed. Our adult eyes need to be put at beach level, to discern the particular marks and their deep meanings for the children and for the society. Much work in material folk culture still lies ahead, so that we can indeed know the child's world, which is in fact our world.

1. These are covered in Bronner 1984. Since that study I also observed children's play in Harrisburg, Pennsylvania, which is discussed in Bronner 1988 and 1990. I give grateful acknowledgment to my students in American Folklore: Culture and Aging, at Penn State Harrisburg for additional data and thought-provoking discussion. Students in American Folklore at the University of California at Davis, whom I taught as visiting distinguished professor in 1990, also contributed to the data presented here. I appreciate comments provided to me by colleagues Jay Mechling, David Wilson, Patricia Turner, and Sue Samuelson.

2. The feature of childlore most prevalent in the literature is that children's expressions are somehow simultaneously liberal and conservative toward cultural change in traditions. Gary Alan Fine has called this feature "Newell's Paradox" after nineteenth-century folklorist William Wells Newell, who studied the feature in children's games. In Fine's important essay "Children and Their Culture: Exploring Newell's Paradox," he explains the existence of this apparent paradox between inventiveness and stability in childlore by examining the features of inventiveness in the components of folklore itself: text, context, and performance. Although concerned mostly with oral and customary lore, Fine's postulation of a stable text, changing context, and both imaginative and conservative performance also applies to material culture.

Jay Mechling

Even when they are not literally so, young people in American culture some-times feel like prisoners in the institutions controlled by adults. Their pri-mary institutional experience during the course of a day is one of being in "the custody of" adults, from parents to teachers to athletic coaches to Scout leaders and beyond. To be sure, there are islands of autonomous children's culture that offer refuge from adult supervision, islands located behind the locked door of the child's bedroom, within the dark hideout of the school bathroom, or in the open space of the vacant lot, fields, or woods. But, gen-erally, our children are an underclass perpetually in the one-down power position (Mechling 1986).

Nowhere is this more true than in the residential institutions estab-lished for children. The home and family certainly are residential institutions that can be the setting for the emergence of the expressive culture of chil-dren, both as part of the family folk culture and possibly as a semiautono-mous "sibling culture" interactive with the family culture. But this *Source-book* chapter examines residential institutions other than the traditional family, institutions that sometimes replace the family but more often are a temporary residence away from the family. They include summer camps, boarding schools, children's hospitals, and a range of custodial institutions that make the young person a "ward" of the adult caretakers, either to pro-tect the ward (as in the case of orphanages), to correct the ward's behavior (as in juvenile detention facilities and group homes), or to protect society from the ward's behavior (juvenile prisons, no matter what the euphemism).

Erving Goffman named "total institutions" those places of residence and work "where a large number of like-situated individuals, cut off from the wider society for an appreciable period of time, together lead an enclosed, formally administered round of life" (Goffman 1961a, xiii). A central ele-ment present in total institutions is the breakdown of the barriers normally separating the realms of sleep, work, and play in everyday life. Although Goffman distinguishes five rough groupings of total institutions in American society, they all seem to share most, if not all, of the following attributes:

First, all aspects of life are conducted in the same place and under the same single authority. Second, each phase of the member's daily activity is carried on in the immediate company of a large number of others, all of whom are treated alike and required to do the same things together. Third, all phases of the day's activities are tightly scheduled, with one activity leading at a prearranged time to the next, the whole sequence of activities being imposed from above by a system of explicit formal rulings and a body of officials. Finally, the various enforced activities are brought together into a single rational plan purportedly designed to fulfill the official aims of the institution (Goffman 1961a, 6).

Goffman's analytic description of total institutions came out of his fieldwork in a mental hospital, so his definition tends to emphasize the more tightly controlled sort of total institution. The children's residential institutions examined here vary considerably, representing something of a continuum of voluntariness, control, length of residence, degree of privacy, degree to which the residents can help set the institution's agenda, and so on. Yet, despite the stark contrast in our minds between a summer camp or exclusive prep school and a juvenile prison, we ought not miss the point that even the most benign of these settings shares some of the basic characteristics of a total institution.

Residential institutions have a binary character, which is to say that there really are two worlds where there seems to be only one. The basic division is between the residents (the campers, the students, the patients, the "inmates" of Goffman's total institutions) and the staff. The staff have an advantage over the resident children and adolescents to the extent that the staff may participate in the institution only during, say, an eight-hour shift, and even summer-camp counselors have "staff night out." So for staff members, their participation in the culture of a residential institution may be only one among many experiences.

It might be better to speak of the "tertiary character" of the residential institution, because my view is that there really are three distinct realms of cultural production the folklorist finds in these settings. Two of the realms are those folk cultures created by the staff among themselves and by the residents among themselves. The cultural productions, performances, and genres in these two realms are likely parallel, possibly even mirror images of one another. At least they are complementary.

The third realm of cultural production is one Goffman recognizes but most people working in this area overlook. This is the culture at "the border," the realm of interaction between the staff's world and the residents' world. Goffman, for example, focuses upon the "institutional ceremonies" through which staff and inmates come together, and it is not surprising that Goffman acknowledges in a footnote (1961a, 7) that it was Bateson who first alerted him to the staff/inmate dialectic. Indeed, Bateson's notion of "schismogenesis," the creation of meaning out of the confrontation of difference, is precisely what happens when the staff and residents interact, and it would have been interesting to have seen Goffman pursue Bateson's lead by using the latter's concepts of complementary and reciprocal schismogenesis to explore the staff/inmate dialectic (Bateson 1958 [1936]; Mechling 1983).

The folklorist must understand this perspective on the three cultures of a total institution. Whereas "normative" social science adopts the viewpoint of the dominant group, seeing socialization as the making of complete persons (that is, adults) out of incomplete persons (that is, children), "interpretive" social science "restores the interaction between adults and children based on interpretive competences as the phenomenon of study" (Mackay 1974, 183). Normative social science tends to favor the center of a cultural system, while interpretive social science looks to the fringes, the borders where differences meet and where people engage in creative actions as they interpret the other and interpret themselves for others (MacCannell 1979).

As we shall see, a serious problem with most of the scholarship on residential institutions for children and adolescents is that it takes the perspective of normative, rather than interpretive, social science. Much of the literature is by, about, and for the adult managers, helpers, and "child savers" (Platt 1969) who run the residential institutions. A chief goal of this chapter is to reverse this trend, to redirect scholarship on residential institutions toward the interpretive approach.

This chapter has four main sections. The first is a discussion of the cultural productions of the residents' world and of the staff world. This is a discussion of genres of "cultural performances" (Geertz 1973) prominent in the two worlds and does not substitute for more extensive treatments of genres in other chapters of this *Source Book* and in other standard folklore textbooks, such as Dorson's (1972, 1983) or Brunvand's (1978).The second section examines those "institutional ceremonies" through which the staff and residents come together to make the public, interactive culture of the institution. I discuss there Goffman's seven ceremonies and add some more I think are relevant. The third section surveys existing literature on the special features of each of the four categories of residential institutions for children and adolescents. The final section identifies special issues or problems that ought to concern folklorists as they embark on the research this chapter outlines.

CULTURAL PERFORMANCES AMONG RESIDENTS AND STAFF

I am adopting here Geertz's term (1973, 113) "cultural performances" to denominate that large class of cultural productions that interest the folklorist. "Ritual" and "play" are two of the most important sorts of cultural performance, and some of the best work available to folklorists comes to deal, one way or another, with these two and the relation between them. Rituals tend to be the traditionalizing productions meant to confer legitimation and order upon cultural ideas (Moore and Myerhoff 1977). Rituals serve to fix public meanings, the objects and other symbols in the ritual aiding in the process of making "visible and stable the categories of culture" (Douglas and Isherwood 1979). Ritual and its symbolic adjuncts are both "models of" and "models for" larger cultural patterns (Geertz 1973, 93).

Play, and all the cultural performances that are playful, are also especially framed realities, but in the case of play the function of the frame is as often as not to cast doubt upon everyday life. Where ritual confirms, play doubts (Handelman 1977, 1980). Play, Sutton-Smith reminds us, tends to be antithetical, and play frames permit "transformations" of status, experiment with otherwise terrifying objects or ideas, and a safe territory for trying out alternative solutions to everyday problems (Schwartzman 1978). Our goal is to be able to describe not only the structures and functions of these framed experiences but to capture something of the "style" these children and adolescents bring to their cultural performances (Hebdige 1979).

Having said this much about ritual and play as two possible frames for cultural performances, we might identify some genres of performance we would expect to find in the residents' culture. Many of these will be what Goffman calls "secondary adjustments," that is to say, "practices that do not directly challenge staff but allow inmates to obtain forbidden satisfactions or to obtain permitted ones by forbidden means" (Goffman 1961a, 54). Put differently, many of the cultural performances we find among the residential children are strategies of resistance, folk offensives in the political struggle over "whose institution is this, anyway?"

We expect, for example, that the residents of one of these institutions will develop a range of *folk speech,* an "institutional lingo" including nicknames, special words for places, a special folk speech referring to the institutional food, and so on (Jackson 1965, 326–27). Lambert and Millham's

1968 study of boys' and coeducational boarding schools in England and Wales is full of the specialized folk speech of those institutions, and the great virtue of their collection is that they used the diaries and other writings of nearly seventeen hundred pupils. The authors found that these children created their own private languages either by translating ordinary vocabulary into a private one (for example, by adding "-mble" to all possible words, so "grim" becomes "grimble" and "yes" becomes "yemble") or by bestowing upon an existing word "a special meaning which, by and large, only the underworld fully comprehends and savours." Giallombardo (1974) found that each of the three institutions for juvenile delinquents had complex sets of "campus names," nicknames that were sometimes personal, sometimes linked the young woman to one of the fictitious campus families that constituted the prison social system, and sometimes distinguished those occupying male and female roles. A whole complex of prison folk speech sustains the social system of these incarcerated adolescent females, including use of the masculine pronouns to refer to those assuming a male identity. Thus, in a Midwestern prison the inmates' typology is of "studs, pimps and foxes" (where a "popcorn" is an inmate who switches roles), and in a western prison the typologies contrast "fems and butches," "finks and snitchers," "squares and straights." A young woman in the western institution also may have a number of nicknames, "chick terms" (Giallombardo 1974, 212–22).

Total institutions sometimes attempt to control communications between the adolescent inmates, so there arise genres of folk speech both to refer to illicit communications and to communicate illicitly. Again, prisons seem to have the most developed versions of these codes. In the East Coast institution Giallombardo studies, inmates communicated by letter (an "issue") and developed an elaborate set of abbreviations and numbers to be used in the margins, at the end of an "issue," or on the corner of the envelope. TDDUP, for example, meant "Til Death Do Us Part," and H.n.W.A. meant "Husband and Wife Always." The numerical code "110" (pronounced one-ten) meant "I Love You," and Giallombardo found that the inmates sometimes increased the sentiment by doubling (220), tripling (330), and so on. The number "225" meant a relationship as being terminated, "333" meant a kiss, "711" a marriage, and "117" a divorce (Giallombardo 1974, 154–67).

Other genres of oral performance, including insults, jokes, toasts, and similar shorter narratives, help create solidarity and hierarchy among the residents. Polsky (1962) found ritual insults, "ranking," to be an important form of communication in his study of a residential program for delinquent boys, and I certainly found considerable "ranking" and joking among the

Boy Scouts I studied at their summer encampments (Mechling 1980a, 1981).

Residents are likely to have longer *narratives* as well, stories about legendary happenings, colorful characters, and the like. Some may be personal history narratives, some cautionary tales. Single-sex camps have their stories about the camper who "made it" to the other side of the lake to "make it" with opposite-sex campers, and custodial institutions have rich traditions of stories about escapes and captures. Jackson found in his prison research a clear code among the inmates: "Don't inform, don't meddle, don't bring heat—says the code. . . . A Folklore repertory accompanies the Code—stories illustrating it in action or the dire retributions visited upon violators" (Jackson 1965, 320). A sociologist employed by the California Youth Authority tells me that supervisors have found handwritten lists of rules laying out just such a code.

Residential institutions are also likely to have *legends and ghost stories,* two genres that depend the most upon children and adolescents for their survival and diffusion. Leary (1973) traces the history of one legend through three decades in one Boy Scout troop and across several groups, making the point that "Swamp Man" legends allow the adult leaders to exercise indirect control over campers' behavior. Ellis (1981b, 1982) makes the same point in his analysis of the contextual uses of legends by the staff members of a camp serving potentially unruly, "underprivileged" children from urban Cleveland. Bronner (1988, 152–54; 315–16) discusses camp legends (see his discursive footnotes in the fully annotated edition of his volume) and Wells (1988) recounts the uses of the Girl Scout camp legend, "Red Eyes." Residential institutions may also have "humorous anti-legends" (Vlach 1971; Bronner 1988, 154–59).

Ghost stories constitute a special case of legends at residential institutions. Hawes's 1968 collection and analysis of "La Llorona" stories told among the female inmates of a California correctional institution for girls shows us how we may relate the symbolic content of the story texts to the concerns of these girls, ages fourteen to sixteen, who were at Las Palmas for sexual offenses or for habitual truancy. Hawes concludes that "this multifaceted, loving, hating ghost-mother seems the explicit embodiment of the emotional conflicts of the adolescent delinquent girl" (Hawes 1968, 165). Similarly, Krell (1980, 227–30) gives us a long text of a ghost story told among thirteen- and fourteen-year-olds at a children's hospital in Denver.

Young residents in the less restrictive insitutions are prone to pranks and practical joking. Beds and food are two favorite targets, with water, urine, excrement, and animals serving as favorite substances for pranks. Krell's informants (1980, 230) put toothpaste on toilet seats, Saran Wrap over toilet bowls, and one hapless boy "got into his bed to find a tampax covered with jelly." Posen (1974a) surveys a broad array of pranks and practical jokes he found at a summer camp, including the "apparent transsubstantiation of supernatural figures from ghost stories told by the staff." Posen mentions such classic practical jokes as the "Snipe Hunt" and notes how campers maintain a "practical joke etiquette" at camp (see also Bronner 1988, 170–71).

Sometimes pranks expand into something closer to a riot. At camp these larger performances may take the form of panty raids and similar raids by one group (such as a cabin group) upon another. At boarding schools there may be institutionalized riots, as there are at some universities (for example, the University of Pennsylvania "rowbottoms"). At juvenile detention institutions the true riot might be a cultural performance, and folklorists might want to examine the symbolic details of riots to see if there is not in them a large element of play (albeit tragic). The residents' capturing of the staff is far more important as a symbolic inversion of ordinary roles than it is a strategic move for getting away from the institution.

Residents are likely to play traditional games and invent new ones. I refer here to the group's true folk games, in contrast to the sports and games that the staff may make them play (although the folk can also subvert those compulsory games and turn them to their own uses). I have seen Boy Scouts improvise a game of "king of the donut" (a ringlike raft) during an unstructured "free swim" at camp, and this is only one of dozens of occasions on which boys created a game. Gump, Sutton-Smith, and Redl (1955) observed fire play among the campers they studied, and it is often the case that campers will turn into a game their play with the three substances—fire, water, and the woods—that are the most alien to their urban or suburban everyday lives. Burch's comments (1965) on "the meaning of different forms of forest play" and his notion of "symbolic labor" among campers might be relevant in analyzing children's play at camp.

Another sort of cultural performance highlights one of the methodological difficulties facing folklorists who would study residential culture. These are the *forbidden rituals,* such as one finds in the collective use of intoxicating substances. The caretakers call this "substance abuse" and the residents mights call it "recreational drug use," but in any guise it is the use of alcohol, marijuana, inhalants, hard drugs, and even tobacco as part of the expressive culture of the group. Other illicit activities may include the smuggling of contraband or gambling (Lambert and Millham 1968). Tattooing, body piercing, and scarification are forbidden rituals of special interest now that folklorists and others in cultural studies have drawn our attention to "the body as social text." The adult folklorist will have great difficulty penetrating the residents' folk culture enough to be witness to forbidden rituals, except in those cases where the residents use the ritual to test or initiate the folklorist. In any case, this raises perplexing ethical questions for the folklorist (Fine and Glassner 1979).

Of course, sexual behavior ranks with substance abuse as one of the two most serious illicit activities from the caretaker's point of view. The topics of heterosexuality and homosexuality pervade the folk cultures of children and adolescents in residential institutions. Several of the genres already mentioned (folk speech, jokes, pranks, insults, narratives) may include matters sexual. Raphael's informants (1988, 76–77) reported a summer camp contest featuring a "Beat the Meat" recording the number of times each boy in the cabin masturbated. And there also may be a complex body of customary lore surrounding sex in the institution, such as the elaborate customs Giallombardo (1974) found regarding courtship, marriage, and divorce in the adolescent women's prisons she studied. Sexual meanings may also underlie folk performances not explicitly sexual (Dundes 1971). To whatever extent folklore responds to deeply felt needs and anxieties, it is likely that the 1 million American adolescents who live in total institutions (Shore and Gochros 1981) will generate a considerable repertoire of expressive culture relating somehow to their sexuality.

Finally, the residents' world has a *material culture* of its own. Jackson (1965, 328–29) and Cohen and Eilertsen (1985) describe some artifacts of the prison world, including the use of tattoos and special ways of tying shoelaces as signals of identity and affiliation. Giallombardo (1974) describes in detail the ways the female adolescent inmates use makeup, clothing, and hair styles to communicate their primary gender identity and power relationships. Contraband in residential institutions can range from forbidden food at summer camps (especially diet camps, see Rashap 1982) to the more serious contraband of children's prisons—knives, zip guns, and the like. In these artifacts we see the "bricolage" of American folk crafts, as the inmates piece together from objects intended for other uses the artifacts of self-defense and attack. We can include even such things as cabin "totems" at camp, the wearing of special folk costume, the use of animal bones and skins, and so on (Mechling 1987).

When we turn our attention to the folk culture of the staff, we do not have to generate a new list of likely settings and genres. The staff world, it turns out, is at most times not much different from that of the residents. It is for them a work setting, so the burgeoning literature on the folklore of occupations and organizations is relevant to our understanding of the staff world. We would expect to find nicknames, folk speech, jokes, insults, oral narratives, cautionary tales, personal memorates, pranks, games, material artifacts, and even the recreational use of drugs among staff. In some cases, such as summer-camp counselors, the staff may even have among them former residents, creating a further interpenetration of the two cultures. The staff creates and sustains these cultural performances for many of the same reasons the residents do, to make visible the categories of their world view and to fix the public meanings of beliefs and values.

INSTITUTIONAL CEREMONIES

The interpretive approach to the cultures of a residential institution suggests to the folklorist that in addition to the subcultures of residents and staff there is a creative, expressive realm of cultural production at the border where the two subcultures meet. Goffman calls the cultural performances in this realm "institutional ceremonies," a set of practices that "express unity, solidarity, and joint commitment to the institution rather than differences between the two levels" (Goffman 1961a, 94).

Goffman lists seven of these institutional ceremonies. The first is the house organ, the institution's newspaper. The folklorist may very well find in a house organ written by residents or staff items of humor, public ritual, pranks, and institutional narratives. Related to this form would be the xerography lore that might circulate among the two subcultures and appear in the house organ.

Goffman refers to forms of self-government and "group therapy" as the second class of residential institutional ceremonies. Summer camps and boarding schools are more likely to have some form of self-government than therapy groups, while hospitals and custodial institutions may well have both.

The third institutional ceremony in which staff and inmates come together is the annual (or seasonal) party. On these occasions the members of the institution mix for eating, playing, and possibly dancing. Seasonal holidays such as Christmas or the Fourth of July are likely occasions for institutional parties, during which time normal boundaries may be suspended and caste lines crossed. The legitimation of symbolic inversions for Halloween may create some interesting situations in a total institution (Santino 1983).

Institutional theatricals are the fourth institutional ceremony, and Goffman notes that, while the inmates typically are players and the staff are in charge of production, there are sometimes "mixed" casts. Theatricals are common in residential camps, even at adult encampments like the famous

Bohemian Club (Domhoff 1974). The handbooks and novels connected with Boy Scout, Girl Scout, Campfire Girl, and Y camps describe skits, plays, and pageants. In my own fieldwork with a troop of Boy Scouts I endured a number of patrol skits, many of which contained in their story line and symbolic details clues to the concerns of the boys (Mechling 1980a, 1981; also Brandes 1980, on skits). Songs are often part of these theatricals, from the campfire songs of Boy Scouts to those of summer camps (Mechling 1980a, Posen 1974b). The two "tribes" into which the girls at one summer camp were divided were each responsible for an evening's theatrical (Chandler 1981).

Ellis's perceptive analysis of the "mock ordeal" at a summer camp demonstrates how an institutional theatrical of a very different sort requires camper and staff member alike to participate in the construction of the play frame (Ellis 1981a). Camp legends and their performance (Leary 1973; Ellis 1981b, 1982) are also institutional theatricals, as are the "proto-dramas" described by T. Green (1978).

The fifth institutional ceremony common at residential institutions is the open house. An open house is an institutional display for the public, and as such it has that quality of fabrication that Goffman's frame analysis dissects so nicely (Goffman 1974). During the open house, staff and residents cooperate in creating a public symbolic drama about the nature of the institution. In this sort of cooperative institutional display, as in the others, the folklorist might want to pursue the activities that "break" the fragile construction of an institution's image.

Intramural sports are the sixth sort of institutional display the folklorist finds in a residential institution for youths. Staff and campers, for example, might square off for a softball game. Included in this category, too, would be sport events between rival institutions. The theatrical film *Meatballs* (1979) builds much of its plot around the sports rivalries between adjacent summer camps, and it is a common feature of boarding schools for interschool rivalries to give rise to a variety of folklore expressions. The Boy Scout camp I studied had several organized games in which staff and campers played together, and it was in the details of those games of "poison," "capture the flag," and "treasure hunt" that I discovered much about the relations between the staff and camper cultures (Mechling 1980b, 1981, 1984b, 1985).

Sunday services and Sunday amusements are Goffman's seventh and last category of institutional ceremonies. Religious ceremonies are the obvious ritual occasions of interest to the folklorist, but we should not overlook a score of other Sunday amusements. Summer camps frequently run in weekly cycles, so weekends turn out to be the setting for rituals of transition—campers leaving and campers arriving. Sundays may be the days of the rituals of incorporation and separation, discussed below.

To Goffman's seven institutional ceremonies I want to add four more. Goffman underestimates the role of *meals* as institutional ceremonies. There is considerable foodways research for the folklorist to draw upon here, including some on the reactions of young people to institutional food. Summer-camp and boarding-school populations always seem to have a rich vocabulary to describe the food (for example, the persistence of "bug juice" for Kool-Aid). Lambert and Millham (1968, 108–50) pay considerable attention to their informants' folk speech about food. Ashley (1968, 256–71) provides a splendid catalog of the words British children use to describe foods, including in his "scoff lore" some items drawn from the Opies (1959; see also Farmer 1968 and Marples 1940). Especially likely in these settings are folk beliefs about foreign matter in the food, beliefs ranging from those studied by Domowitz (1979) and Fine (1980c) to the persistent male worry about saltpeter (Rich and Jacobs 1973). I found at a Boy Scout camp a strong tendency to link food and feces in the speech play of the boys, and I am certain this pattern reflects both social concerns about pollution (M. Douglas 1966) and psychological concerns about being male in American society (Mechling 1984a).

Cookouts are another summer camp setting for expressive behavior regarding both the food and the fire. Even food fights in residential institutions may be folk performances. Finally, the folklorist should note that sociologists like Polsky (1962) learn a great deal about residential institutions by attending to seating arrangements in the dining hall and to the dozens of small dramas that get played out during a meal.

Assemblies are still another institutional ceremony of great importance in camps and boarding schools. Flag ceremonies are common in those settings, especially military schools. Assemblies can be occasions for just about anything in a residential institution, from talks by visiting dignitaries to "town meeting" affairs. Once more, the folklorist's interest in the assembly is how the staff and residents may discover ways to "break frame" and assault the fragile collective construction. One is reminded, for example, of the closing scenes in Lindsay Anderson's film *If* (1968).

Rituals of incorporation and rituals of separation are the last two institutional ceremonies I would commend to the folklorist's attention. Both sorts of ritual are dramatizations of a change in status. They occur at the borders of the residential institutions themselves and at interior borders. Turner (1974a) reminds us to follow Van Gennep's lead (1960) in looking at the threshold situations in cultural processes. A residential institution usually has an official orientation session, sometimes including artifacts that are symbolic adjuncts to the ritual (Fortes 1968). Thus, campers may receive a distinctive item of clothing and prisoners may get haircuts and be stripped naked before donning the institutional uniform. Once past this initial threshold, the child or adolescent may face unofficial forms of initiation into the folk culture of the group. The "mock ordeal" described by Ellis (1981a) is one such initiation ritual, as are a "snipe hunt" and assorted other forms of hazing. The folk group tests the neophyte, through verbal assault, exploitative games, and dares (R. Johnson 1978).

The rituals of separation come at the other threshold, the border the child crosses to rejoin everyday society. Awards ceremonies often cap the residential period and camps and schools may have true "graduation" ceremonies. We have no studies of these folk rituals, but Myerhoff's insightful analysis (1978) of a concocted graduation ceremony at a senior citizen center provides good folkloristic questions to pose in the case of graduation ceremonies for youngsters.

Having added four ceremonial occasions—meals, assemblies, rituals of incorporation, and rituals of separation—to Goffman's list, we now have at least eleven sorts of performance occasions in which to look for the emergence of children's folklore. So far this discussion has taken genre and performance context as primary categories, treating as roughly interchangeable the four sorts of residential institutions. To offset the impression that these performance contexts across the four institutions are really the same, I shall turn now to each sort of institution to comment briefly upon its unique characteristics and the extant scholarship.

SPECIAL FEATURES OF EACH INSTITUTION

Summer camps certainly are the most benign of the total institutions for children and adolescents, fitting closest the adult's romantic notion of what the child's folk culture should be. The folklorist should note, however, that there are many kinds of camps, from the general recreational, to the ones connected with youth groups (Boy Scouts, Girl Scouts, YMCA, etc.), to camps featuring single activities (sports, art, cheerleading, computer), to camps for special populations (handicapped, ill, disadvantaged, delinquent). The day-camper's experience will overlap with that of residential campers, so it is good to ask what features of the campers' folk culture we can attribute to the long-term stay.

Unfortunately, we do not yet have much in the way of folkloristic study of camps. Chandler's 1981 essay on a Girl Scout camp, Wells's 1988 study of a Girl Scout camp, Rashap's 1982 work on a camp for overweight teenagers, Ellis's (1981a, 1981b, 1982) several essays on a camp for under-privileged urban children, Savin-Williams's work on summer camps (1980a, 1980b), Tillery's 1992 ongoing work on a YMCA camp, and my own work on a Boy Scout camp are the only sustained studies of camp experiences from a point of view valuable to folklorists. Most other studies of camps feature an interventionist frame of mind coming out of normative social science's view of socialization. The investigation of camp experiences created to serve some other goal, such as better racial relations (Eaton and Clore 1975) or the treatment of emotionally disturbed children (Behar and Stephens 1978), rarely includes evidence of the campers' folk culture.

The scholarship on boarding schools is more plentiful than that for camps, thanks largely to research on the British public school. McLachlan's 1970 history of the boarding school in America provides good background for understanding whose children go to boarding schools and why (see also Levine 1980). For work taking the children's point of view, however, it is still hard to surpass the work done by the British. Lambert and Millham (1968) and Ashley (1968) I've already praised for their collection of the ac-tual lore of children. On American schools we have less data, but Gillespie (1970) is a good example. More recently, noted feminist psychologist Carol Gilligan and her coworkers (1990) have been working at a private girls' school in upstate New York as part of a larger "Harvard Project on the Psy-chology of Women and Development of Girls."

The study of the folklore of children and adolescents in hospitals suf-fers somewhat the same interventionist fate as the study of camps. Krell's 1980 survey is folkloristic, but the folklorist might also get something out of the work of the interventionists who are interested in using play as an adjunct to medical treatments (M. Adams 1976; D. Hall 1977; Miura 1981). Bluebond-Langner's work (1978, 1981) with dying children also contains some insight into the ways the children and parents construct reality, though one wishes the author had paid more attention to the ways in which dying children cre-ate expressive support groups among themselves. Bergmann's 1965 case his-tories of children in a hospital in Cleveland, Ohio, include incisive observa-tions on the denials, regressions, defensive devices and "constructive resources the children use to battle fears." But, again, the folklorist wishes Bergmann more often stepped aside from her etic, psychoanalytic perspective (Anna Freud was a collaborator) and presented a more emic account of the children's ex-pressive culture in the face of disease, amputation, and death. Beuf's 1979 study of the lives of children in hospitals is our most complete ethnographic study, and that contains much of use to the folklorist.

It is an odd paradox that the children's residential institutions for which we have some of the best folklore data are the residential correctional facilities, the institutions in which it would be the most difficult for the outside folklorist to penetrate the folk group. This paradox ought to warn us that the plentiful data has some hidden contextual conditions. Most of the studies of group homes, residential treatment centers, and prisons clearly espouse an adult, interventionist point of view, and we easily may dismiss these studies (for example, Balbernie 1966; Tizard, Sinclair, and Clarke 1975) as unlikely to provide much of use to the folklorist.

But there is a whole middle range of studies done by sociologists and psychologists who are interventionist in their goals while, at the same time, displaying an ethnographic respect for the small-group culture of the children and adolescents in these institutions. These fieldworkers practice something closer to the "interpretive" rather than the "normative" approach to socialization. As is the case in the study of children's lore in boarding schools, some of the best work on the folk cultures of children in residential correctional institutions comes out of England, where studies on the "Borstal boys" already constitute a long research tradition. Walter's 1977 critique of research in British "approved schools" is a good introduction to this literature, especially in light of Walter's view that the best work is done by those who attempt to present the boys' or girls' perspective. Walter admires the work of Gill (1974) in this regard.

Turning to American institutions for juvenile offenders, the folklorist would do well to begin with Polsky's classic Cottage Six study (1962). A young postdoctoral fellow at the time, Polsky entered Hollymeade residential treatment center as a participant-observer. He discovered in this coeducational institution what we now recognize as the folk culture of the 195 inmates (boys aged eight to eighteen, girls twelve to eighteen). In the words of Leonard Cottrell, Jr., from the introduction to Polsky's book, "Dr. Polsky demonstrates beyond cavil that it is possible for at least a significant segment of the resident population of even a first-rate institution like Hollymeade to create, maintain, and transmit a separate deviant subculture that supports values and a social system that are counter to the institution itself and in substantial part negate even the most intensive and skillful individual therapeutic efforts" (Polsky 1962, 6–7).

Polsky had found, in short, the folk culture of the cottage, of the residential group, that persisted beyond members' coming and going and that was the cultural context for sustaining deviant behavior. Polsky's book is full of ethnographic detail that will delight the folklorist, including a close reading of a dining-hall incident in which one group's control over access to certain foods becomes a symbolic performance of power. Polsky's typology of deviant interactive modes—namely aggression, deviant skills and activities, threat gestures, ranking, and scapegoating—translate into familiar folk genres. Especially enlightening is Polsky's candid, confessional chapter on the "Participant Observer in a Deviant Subculture," wherein he recounts how the boys tested him by making him smoke (against the rules), by "ranking" him with their ritual insults, and occasionally by physically attacking him.

In many ways Polsky's accomplishment in the Cottage Six study has not been duplicated. Even Polsky's later study of another residential treatment center (Polsky and Claster 1968) is too preoccupied with applying a Bales/Parsons scheme and quantifying the results, failing to match the rich ethnographic detail of the Cottage Six work. Empey and Lubeck (1971) similarly fail to describe in detail the delinquent subculture the authors know exists at such residential facilities. The surveys by Street, Vinter, and Perrow (1969), by Cole (1972), and Feld (1981) hint at the subcultures of the inmates of a broad range of residential institutions for juvenile offenders, but ultimately they fail to deliver the details the folklorist wants.

Fortunately, there are a few ethnographic studies by folklorists who were able to penetrate to some extent the cultures of children in custodial institutions. R. Roberts's 1965 study of an industrial school for boys is an early example. Cohen and Eilertsen (1985) discovered through interviews a broad range of folklore at a New Jersey correctional institution for boys, but they were unable to do the follow-up fieldwork that would have located these folk genres in their natural contexts (see Bennett 1981 for a history and overview of the uses of the delinquent's life history). The research by Horan while he worked as a staff member at a New Jersey boys' home holds the most promise, and in his study of play fighting (1988) and of patterns of sharing and withholding possessions (1984) Horan displays deft control of the folklorist's inquiry.

We still do not have the data we would need to determine, for example, if the folk cultures of the inmates differ significantly across kinds of institutions (private/public, large/small, open/closed, religious/secular, rural/urban). Clearly, we need to replicate Hawes's (1968) sort of study for all these institutional variations. Giallombardo's (1974) very fine work on imprisoned girls is a good model in this vein. There is still much to do.

SPECIAL ISSUES AND PROSPECTS

The discussion so far has been something of a survey of the existing literature on the folklore of children and adolescents in residential institutions, organized in the first section by genres in performance settings, in the second by types of institutional ceremonies, and in the third by type of institution. In this final section I want to address more what needs to be done by folklorists, alerting the reader to certain problems and certain possibilities that seem to me unique and exciting.

Regarding the special problems of fieldwork in residential institutions for children, there is not much more to be added to the warnings and advice offered by Fine and Glassner (1979), Fine (1987, 222–44), and Foley (1990, 206–31). Obviously, the fieldworker will have more and more trouble establishing a trusting relationship with the informants the closer the institution gets to being a "total institution." Nonetheless, Giallombardo's success (1974) is encouraging. Most folklorists will probably enter these institutions through the staff world, so the great task is to establish a relationship of trust with the residents. I would recommend Polsky's chapter seven (1962) as a reminder to fieldworkers what they might have in store for them in the process of building that trust.

Folklorists working in these settings might try some special fieldwork techniques. Sol Worth's film projects, teaching first Philadelphia black gang members, then Navajo gang members, how to use 8-mm cameras to make films of their worlds (Worth and Adair 1972), seem to me a promising model for work in residential institutions, where the folklorist could provide the children with low-cost video equipment. Of course, the children would have to be assured that their own narratives would not be "used against them" by the adult authorities, and the folklorist should keep that promise. Csikszentmihalyi, Larson, and Prescott's technique (1977) of using beepers to signal adolescents to enter into diaries what they are doing is another idea that could be used in residential settings. Caughey (1982) seems to get good results asking students to use introspective reports as data, and these techniques could be added to the institutional repertoire of interviews and projective tests.

As may be evident in some of my examples above, I also believe that the folklorist will find in some unlikely places examples of the folklore of children and adolescents in residential institutions. In literature, for example, John Knowles's novel *A Separate Peace* (1959), James Kirkwood's novel *Good Times, Bad Times* (1968), and Robert Morasco's play *Child's Play* (1970) are all set in boarding schools and contain examples of the lore of the schools. Autobiographies are another literary genre that may contain a participant's comments on the folk cultures of residential institutions. Walter (1977) discusses autobiographies and memoirs by men who attended British approved schools.

Commercial feature films, such as *Meatballs* (1979) and *Little Darlings* (1980), are set in summer camps, as are the several *Friday the Thir-*

teenth films that dramatically render adolescent legends wherein the penalty for teenage sex is mutilation by a crazed monster. Lindsay Anderson's cult film *If* (1968) is set in a British boarding school, and *Bad Boys* (1983) is filled with ethnographic detail of an Illinois prison for adolescent males.

In addition to the commercial films are a few folklore or ethnographic films set in residential facilities for youthful offenders. Broomfield and Churchill's *Tattooed Tears* (1978) is a powerful film about a California youth detention center and training school. A dramatized version of this sort of scene is *Juvie* (1976). The CBS News special report *What Are We Doing to Our Children?—Locked Up, Locked Out* (1973) follows a ten-year-old delinquent boy through the legal system and into the threatening world of a modern "children's treatment center." These are merely examples; folklorists should be on the lookout for similar films on residential settings.

I mentioned above, in my discussion of the literature on residential institutions for youthful offenders, that we lack enough rich ethnographies of the folk cultures of several sorts of institutions to be able to determine if there are significant variations across settings. The comparative approach is essential to the study of folklore. Eventually, we would like to know how folk performance texts vary across contexts. What difference, for example, does gender make in the folklore of children's residential institutions? I have found the little work there is on Girl Scout camps (such as Chandler 1981 and Wells 1988) to be immensely helpful in my understanding of a Boy Scout camp. Giallombardo (1974) makes much of the influence of gender upon the expressive culture she found in women's prisons. She noted significant differences between the adolescent women's inmate culture and that of adolescent males. Why the difference? To be sure, admits Giallombardo, "the adult male and female inmate cultures *are* a response to the deprivations of prison life, but the *nature* of the response in both prison communities is influenced by the differential participation of males and females in the external culture. . . . The family group in female prisons is singularly suited to meet the inmates' internalized cultural expectations of the female role" (1974, 3). Hawes's 1968 interpretation of the meaning of "La Llorona" similarly rests upon the fact that this is a legend told among female adolescents. Barrie Thorne's (1993) book on the ways children construct and deconstruct gender in their play on school grounds provides several hypotheses which folklorists might test for residential insitutions.

Folklorists will want to attend, as well, to the confounding effects of other variables in addition to setting and gender. Do ethnicity or social class matter? What of religion? One of my Boy Scout informants had worked as a staff member in both a Boy Scout camp and a YMCA camp, and he was sure there were differences in style and values attributable to the explicit religious orientation of a Y camp (see also Tillery 1992). The comparative approach also must include cross-cultural perspectives. We have the British/American comparison on boarding schools and residential treatment centers, but what of camps and hospitals?

Finally, I want to comment briefly on what I see as the implications of study in this area for what is known as "applied folklore." First, for the sake of getting folklorists into these institutional settings, we ought to train staff members to be folklorists. A folklore education for continuing students with jobs in residential institutions will simultaneously yield an increasing body of ethnographic descriptions of the folk cultures of these institutions and, in the bargain, make these staff members better caretakers. I mean "better" in the sense that they will have a new cognitive respect for the expressive culture of their wards; and better, too, in the sense that the very act of collecting the lore becomes a mode of communication between caretaker and ward. Savin-Williams (1980a) gathered his information thanks to his role as program director for two groups of counselors-in-training, and there is no reason that we cannot have an army of folklore fieldworkers living and working in residential institutions and bringing their studies back to the classroom. I see Outward Bound programs and special camps (public and private) for "troubled teens," for example, as two fieldwork settings desperately in need of the folklorist's perspectives.

There is also something the folklorist has to offer the adult caretaker, even if that caretaker does not wish to "join up" and become a participant-observer. On one level, the folklorist can offer his or her services as a paid consultant, to come into a residential institution, study the folk cultures of both staff and inmates, and make recommendations to the administrators of the institution. Folklorists are doing this already for businesses and not-for-profit organizations, so I see no reason why we cannot offer our expertise to the organizations that have as their wards millions of American children.

There are seductions to beware of here, and I want to be realistic about this. Some folklorists will be ineffective because they will maintain too romantic a notion that folkloristics can ameliorate the sometimes awful conditions in these institutions. And some folklorists, no doubt, will be coopted early and find themselves serving the manipulative, interventionist goals of the bureaucratic managers. But I am counting on the good sense and good sensibilities of the greater number of folklorists who apply their expertise to these "practical" settings with a proper sense of what folkloristics can and cannot do.

I began this chapter by saying that American children sometimes feel like prisoners in the institutions controlled by adults. I declared that I prefer the interpretive to the normative approach to socialization, and everything I wrote thereafter betrays (no doubt) that my sympathies lie more with the vibrant, resisting folk culture of the residents and inmates than with the adult staff. But the staff often feel like prisoners, too, and this may be the final truth of this chapter—that the nature of modern civilization is such that we all feel like prisoners. I am not sure if it is uniquely folkloristic to side with the oppressed, any more than I am certain this is a uniquely American trait, but I do know that a large part of the exhilaration I get from studying the expressive folk cultures of children in residential institutions is to see how resilient are human beings in controlled settings. No matter how deeply we folklorists probe into the most awful and alienating human situations, we usually find those humans able to make an artistic performance out of the little left to them. Children are neither the innocents nor the enemy within. They are just human beings, like us, a fact we sometimes forget.

The Past in the Present

Theoretical Directions for Children's Folklore

Felicia R. McMahon and Brian Sutton-Smith

We believe that with this collection of articles the groundwork has been laid for future studies of children's folklore. The articles themselves vary between older or newer approaches to the discipline—in that respect they are fairly representative of the field as it currently stands—and they also indicate the areas in which more work needs to be done. In an attempt to advance the field, we begin this final chapter by analyzing past scholarship before preceding with suggestions for future directions. Mechling, for example, is confident that the "interpretive" trend will become the major force in children's folklore; that we will have more studies like those of Beresin and Hughes of specific children in specific places and in consequence a more multifarious set of children's subcultures—and less children's folklore composed simply of collections or only of an historical kind. The authors in this *Sourcebook* are split about evenly among traditional, ethnographic, performance, and interpretive kinds of approach.

The Older Tradition

The field of folklore began with an interest in origins, with survivals, and with history, and this interest will probably continue; many of the problems of historical origins and historical change have not been solved. Iona and Peter Opie, for example, present us with an interesting test case. They are undoubtedly the world's most famous children's folklorists, and over the past forty years they have turned out classic after classic on children's lore (rhymes, poems, tales, sayings and games). Their latest book, *The Singing Game* (1985), is a product of anecdotal collections from many informants and historical sources using meticulous literary scholarship. In this work they largely eschew theory and interpretation and provide instead a grand colligation of items organized in an encyclopedic manner. Insofar as there is a main theme, it is that human nature is constant and continuous and gives forth in different eras similar expressions in play, game, and song. They support this theme by offering sporadic evidence of ancient games or songs persisting into modern times. In their present collection of 133 games, however, of which eighty-two are singing games—the others being clapping, chanting, or dramatic games—no more than half of those listed have persisted beyond World War II, and only a handful of those that have persisted exhibit much vigor in modern play. The exceptions appear to be Big ship sails (a modern and reduced version of the ancient Thread the needle), Oranges and lemons, A duke a riding, Rosey apple, Sally water, wallflowers, old Roger, Jenny Jones, Romans and English, Nuts in May, the Mulberry bush and Dusty bluebells.

Despite their interest in origins, what the Opies actually give us is a picture of historical change as much as a picture of historical continuity. In general, modern children, being younger players at these games than their forebears, prefer games of simpler organization: circles with central persons, chain games rather than couple games, or contest games and processional games, which were once played so frequently by what we would now call teenagers. Most striking in their work, and not commented on by the Opies, is the remarkable upsurge in post-television years of games of buffoonery, impersonation, dance routines, and clapping. These are by and large the simplest unison games with all players acting in concert, singing either nonsense or topical songs, and with players taking turns in the center. While there are historical forerunners to many of these games, what most strikes our attention is their fadlike character and their ephemerality. Children's folklore appears in many games to have taken on the character of modern mass-media culture, with its cycles of fashion and popularity. Dance routines, in particular, come and go as quickly as the topical songs that stimulate them. There is, in addition, a more explicit vulgarity and sexuality in many of these than was the case in the singing games of the prior century (Sutton-Smith 1987, 239–40).

But the most interesting picture of change in these fascinating pages of *The Singing Game* is that which takes place from the lusty Middle Ages to the bowdlerized late nineteenth century. These singing games were originally for couples with marital interests (at the advanced ages of twelve to fifteen), who, through wild and bawdy actions, could try out their choices. But in the 1800s, after centuries of church and civil suppression, they came finally to be the games of unsophisticated girls who could make their choices among other girls largely without the presence of boys at all. The games became an enacted fantasy of marriage without the prospect that one might in fact find one's real partner in the course of the play. But then the same kind of domestication occurred during the nineteenth century to nursery rhymes, children's literature, and dangerous outdoor games. Children were put into schools, and their recreation was increasingly organized and supervised to remove from it remnants of mediaeval excess. Although the Opies' work on "survivals" is itself something of a theoretical survival in modern folklore, the beauty of their work *The Singing Game,* with its songs and games, reminds us that authentic description and systematic scholarship within a field are often the greater gift. One can, for example, review Lady A.B. Gomme's collections from the 1890s of the traditional games of the British Isles, which are not in any way modern surveys, and still respond with wonder at the unique accounts to be found therein.

It may well be as Susan Stewart has asserted in an insightful and provocative analysis that these written accounts of folkgames and children's folklore in general are examples of what she terms "crimes of writing" (1991a). Stewart convincingly argues that the recording of these folk materials helped to establish an academic orthodoxy about the way in which these games should be perceived, and that that perception had very little to do with the original conditions of their play, deceiving us about their folk originality. The forces for the organization of children's play, including the veneration of a few selected game and folk traditions, also had its source, however, in many other Enlightenment-derived pressures for the education of the nineteenth-century child. We need to concede that these collected game records (whatever their biases) are better than most other things collected about the play of children in prior centuries. If this is indeed a crime of writing in the Foucaultian sense, it seems from our present distance to have been better than no writing at all.

THE MODERN CONDITION

All of which is to argue that although we agree with Jay Mechling about the current trend in children's folklore scholarship, the work of the Opies and Gomme is an illustration both of an earlier viewpoint and of the necessity of continuing scholarship on the nature of both origins and historical change. Their work is also a commentary on the view that childhood as we know it is disappearing. What we have just noted is the way in which much of children's folklore has taken on the velocity of the fads and fashions of the modern entertainment world. If modern mass entertainments are, as Raymond Williams (1979) has opined, the spectator "culture" that goes with modern industrial society, then children's imitation of these fads indicates that their folklore is also shifting rather than disappearing. Given that modern work life is largely nonmanual and schooling is universal, we would also expect much of children's folklore now to be increasingly more verbal or symbolic rather than physical. We suspect that the emphasis on rhymes, riddles, humor, tales, and verbal tricks in the chapters by McDowell, Roemer, Sullivan and Tucker, is not just an outcome of their own sociolinguistic training but a response also to the greater importance of these kinds of materials in modern childhood. One can't help but note that when one compares the Opies' *Lore and Language of Schoolchildren* (1959) with their *Children's Games in Street and Playground* (1969) and their *Singing Game* (1985), the earlier collections consist of more traditional material than the later, which have less to say about origins and more to say about current practices. Similarly, the American equivalent, *One Potato, Two Potato* by Mary and Herbert Knapp (1976), is about two-thirds given over to verbal play. More than one half of the more recent book *American Children's Folklore* by Simon Bronner (1988) is about speech play. This contrasts with the earlier books by Newell (1883) and Gomme (1894), in which there is relatively little mention of verbal play.

So childhood is not disappearing; it has perhaps become more verbal and harder to locate in concrete behavioral space. That is always supposing that this change between the books of earlier days and the books of today does in fact correspond to a real change in children's behavior. In *A History of Children's Play* (Sutton-Smith 1981a) based on comparing the reminiscences of the elderly with the play of the young, such change certainly seems to have occurred. Perhaps current childhood does indeed occupy more verbal crevices and less obvious physical space than used to be the case. Playgrounds were initially events in the cultural taming of rural childhood and urban vagabonds, as Mergen makes clear. The idea of "the playground" persists, however, in part as a romantic fantasy among adult playground advocates who talk about the child's rights to play, while confining it in their own select forms of physical space. We have tried to move in a contrary and less domesticating direction by talking about the playground as a festival (Sutton-Smith 1990b). The reality is, however, that in some places playgrounds have been abandoned because of their imagined or real dangers and have been replaced by physical-education lessons. It is possible that playing verbally in the cracks of so much powerful adult organization is often the only alternative left for some children. Which is to say, the shift from physical to verbal play may reflect not only the general cultural changes in the world of adult work, from manual to symbolic, but also changes in the actual freedom that children have to carry on their older traditions of play.

In the meantime, today's more symbolically mobile children are sometimes more likely to be found in their own bedrooms or in front of a television set or at a home computer than in the streets or the playgrounds. But they are also more directly exploitable by the marketplace, which has steadily developed them as a consumer resource over the past two decades. Much of the disquiet of modern parents has to do with this increasing and direct availability of their children to the marketplace through television. Three hundred years of the bourgeoisie's sloughing off the parochial folk controls over children through the culture of traditional neighborhood games has been called into question by this sudden susceptibility of modern children to commercial infringement.

But children's sharing of this vicarious media world with their parents doesn't mean that they are no longer children. Most parents deny that they simply bow to what television suggests for their children (Sutton-Smith 1986), and those other special arrangements for children's domestication (schools, books, toys, and recreation programs) continue apace. Whatever may be happening to their parents in the occupational world, it is still the fate of children to be put in their own separate zoos run by adult educators and other supervisors of children. This fundamental segregation is not altered because there is this new development of shared symbolic television space. Nor is there much indication of any modification on the American scene of the desire by most educated parents to shelter real children from real violence, grossness, vulgarity, or sex, no matter what may be happening on the television screen or in dysfunctional families. In short, childhood continues but we often have so little adequate descriptive research about it that we cannot tell how it is different or how it is the same as in times past.

The Disjunction of Child and Adult

The basic underlying condition of modern childhood seems to be its disjunction from adulthood. Modern enculturation is founded on this discontinuity. In folklore terms this means that as long as the two groups, adult and child, differ in power and life space, then the interaction between them will lead to the kinds of tensions from which the lore of each group about the other will usually arise. The more unique their separate needs and their opposition, the greater the folklore and the development of group lore calculated to respond to them. On the one hand, there are the parents, the teachers, and the psychological experts banding together for the preservation of their own values about childhood; on the other, there are dyads, cliques, and gangs of children developing their own business of life and often using traditional materials to do so.

Mechling asks whether there can be a theory that makes all the material of this work hang together, that unites the irrational with the rational, the spirit of childlore with the socialization of adults. Perhaps to expect the two to be brought together is a "rational" kind of view, "an enlightenment view" that is simply not what children's folklore is about and presumably not what folklore scholars should be about (Spariosu 1989). The very danger of this sourcebook is that it provides more means for some adults to supervise children more carefully in order to get rid of their folklore. What Tatar aptly writes about adult revisions of fairytales for children stands for their approach to children's play in general: There is "the idea that a literature targeted for them must stand in the service of pragmatic instrumentality rather than foster an unproductive form of playful pleasure" (1992, xxv). Bauman, the erstwhile director of the largest funded project on children's folklore and education, expresses concern that researchers themselves continue to place too much emphasis on the didactic uses of children's folklore and neglect in consequence the study of "the aggressive, obscene, scatological, antiauthoritarian, and inversive elements . . . that any student of childen's folklore knows well to be a central part of the expressive culture of childhood" (1982, 173). Here Bauman is referring to children's folklore that very few folklorists have cared to publish, such as the article "High Kybo Floater: Food and Feces in the Speech Play at a Boy Scout Camp" (Mechling 1984b). Perhaps some of the adults reading this book will acknowledge the memories of childhood being evoked here that they have hitherto refused to acknowledge; in consequence, they may make more provision for this rueful joyfulness to take place in childhood. After all, a conclusion about play, by all those who work in play therapy at least, is that a major meaning of play in childhood is that it is a pretense of society and self of a vigorous and life-restoring kind (Erikson 1950). Play's promise may lie in human optimism and commitment to life, rather than those other incidental correlates of problem solving, creativity, and imagination that have taken on a vogue in recent psychology and education.

THEORY FOR CHILDREN'S FOLKLORE

Perhaps there is something we can do for Mechling's theoretical call without falling into the usual rationalistic traps. If we begin by not accepting the usual romantic disjunction of childhood and adulthood but instead apply to children the same kind of theories we apply to adults in distinctive cultural groups, we might make some progress. It is, for example, the promise of children's folklore that it can bring a sense of the same cultural relativity to our view of childhood that we generally apply to other groups. Thus, although the "savages" and the "women" may have escaped from the unilinear theory of cultural evolution (of which Zumwalt speaks), the children are still not free. By and large in official academic and educational quarters their life is thought of as a series of steps and stages to higher forms of adult maturity. Whereas just as cultural relativity implies that each human group fashions its own forms of human adaptation and expression and that each has its wonder and beauty (as well as disasters), so with childhood there is an aesthetic for each age, which may be celebrated (or cursed) by adults, rather than simply glossed as an inevitably inferior step on the way to the "wonders" of adults' civilization, reason, and morality.

Importantly, because children are members of the most politically powerless group, their folklore is usually favored for purposes that are not especially those of the children. It is seldom possible to be rationally in favor of children without interfering with much that they do that is not very rational. For this reason, we see the study of children's folklore as a very special territory in which groundbreaking research can still be accomplished, that is, if we pay it the tribute of considering it in terms of various contemporary cultural theories that are taken very seriously on the adult level but seldom applied to children. Thus we may argue that the whole field of children's folklore can take new directions by incorporating the recent cultural ideas about power as expressed among heteronomous groups of scholars like James C. Scott, Roger M. Keesing, Joan N. Radner, and Susan S. Lanser. Our first step is to recognize that their theories allow us to look beneath the superficially placid surface of children's play to understand how important are the power-related aspects of children's folklore and its formation. It would not be false to argue that although there are multiple interpretations of children's folklore in the foregoing pages, the dominant theme throughout is that of the power the children exercise over each other, and the power they seek in their relationship to adults, mythical or real. There is also throughout these chapters a diffuse and seldom fully explicated rhetorics of progress at work. When one considers that 99 percent of the books about or for children have progress as their explicit or hidden agenda, the child-power-oriented contents of this book constitutes a massive denial of the validity of those adultcentric orientations.

PERFORMANCE STUDIES IN CHILDREN'S FOLKLORE

Before we proceed further with the power analysis, however, we need also mention what might be regarded as an equally valid contemporary concern in current adult folklore with tradition as a series of cultural performances. This focus manifests itself in a concern with the microanalytics of the ways in which the children themselves maintain and present their own traditional folk culture to each other in behavior, speech, gestures, rules, codes, and secrets (Sutton-Smith 1989a). We need not spend time on demonstrating what this means in this conclusion, because it is very well shown by a number of the articles in this *Sourcebook,* particularly those by Beresin and the authors in Section III. This approach, which privileges aesthetic performance issues, is refreshingly alive compared with the older concern with collecting texts only or making formal accounts children's activities. Still, along with the rhetoric of progress, the rhetoric of fancy, of which performance theory is a manifestation, leads to an idealization of childhood life, and pleasant and nostalgic as that is for us elders, it can be called into question (Sutton-Smith, in press). Power theorists, for example, tend to downplay performance theory's implicit avoidance or perpetuation of the inequalities of race, gender, social class, sexuality, and nationality, which are present in the world of folklore (Briggs 1993). In defense of performance, however, we could argue that these performance-oriented studies nicely demonstrate that despite the importance of the power context of the folklore which we are about to discuss, the lore itself, whatever its rhetorical usage, is sustained primarily by the very universal interest of players in the enjoyment they get through their own activation of these playforms. There is an inherent and probably built-in neurological logic to play that is the first cause of all of these phenomena, no matter what other important causes may also come to be served within the larger culture. There is nothing that will allow us to say that the children's own drive for aesthetic enjoyment is not as important as their drive for empowerment. What we can say is that both of these rhetorics so well evidenced in this work contrast mightily with all other books about and for childhood in which the rhetoric of progress is dominant. This book is a powerful manifesto against what has been taken for granted throughout the culture throughout the past two hundred years, that the business of childhood is to grow up and shut up.

CHILDREN'S FOLKLORE AS A MANIFESTATION OF POWER RELATIONSHIPS

The material of children's folklore permits us to look at it as a power phenomenon in a number of ways:

1. An earlier way was to describe the various transformations of power that are mirrored by the play structures themselves (Sutton-Smith 1954). Thus, if games are ordered in terms of their increasing complexity with age, one can sketch out the sequence of power transformations that playing children participate in with age. Structurally, using the writings of either Propp or Lévi-Strauss, one can generate the binary character and order of power relationships as thus mirrored in child development. Younger children deal in central person power relationships ("it" games) and these

are transformed with age so that the power originally centered on the central person is increasingly shared with or shifted to the hands of the group of others (sports). The games very neatly model the crucial nature of power achieved or lost in the interaction between opposing characters or groups. The games constitute a simple grammar of the nature of political power in which all children participate insofar as they play games of any sort. The research of Roberts and Sutton-Smith (Sutton-Smith 1972a) also established on an anthropological (and not just psychological) level that cross-culturally the triad of games of chance, strategy, and physical skill mirrored parallel processes in the larger societies of which they were a part. Both of these kinds of research on types and levels of power had their heyday in the intellectual climate of "structuralism."

2. With the increasing vogue for ethnographic and performance studies in folklore, it became clear that when particular groups playing particular games were studied in their own context many complications were observed that greatly modified the picture of power relationships sketched in the above fairly abstract ways. The chapter by Hughes in the present volume is a groundbreaking example of such research. It turns out that quite apart from the larger abstract structural account of power relationships described above, there are many other power manipulations also taking place on a more covert level. The rules of the games state one power relationship; the actual gaming of those rules reveals differences in the various ways in which every group attempts to manipulate those rules in their own favor.

3. In addition, however, to the machinations of the players within their own games or folklore from which various power relationships and systems can be inferred, what Scott et al. make clear is that folklore also contains echoes of the way in which the players are also relating to the adult culture of which they are a part when these games are played. Traditionally, play has been seen as largely a mimetic phenomenon, an interpretation which privileges the adult world as the model. What is apparent, however, is that much of play is a mockery of that adult world at the same time as it is a mimicry. So what we wish to sketch in the rest of this conclusion is not only the way in which play models and manifests power relationships, but also the way in which play expresses power and powerlessness by being subversive of the normative culture of which it is a part. But it is important to stress here that the play is generally both dialectically normative and subversive at the same time in varying degrees (Sutton-Smith 1978a). By subversive we mean all those multifaceted expressions of the child groups that undermine the authority of the dominant culture, well illustrated in this volume in the chapters by Jorgensen, McDowell, Mechling, Sullivan, and

Zumwalt. It is at the privileged site of clandestine folklore that the subversive thrives. Scott (1990) has argued that a partly sanitized, ambiguous and coded version of this subversive "hidden transcript" is always present somewhere in the public discourse of subordinate groups, and further: "The dialectic of disguise and surveillance that pervades relations between the weak and the strong will help us, I think, to understand the cultural patterns of domination and subordination. The theatrical imperatives that normally prevail in situations of domination produce a public transcript in close conformity with how the dominant group would work to have things appear. The dominant never control the stage absolutely, but their wishes normally prevail. In the short run, it is in the interest of the subordinate to produce a more or less credible performance" (1990, 40).

Most of the research to this point has been done on the way in which subordinate colonial, racial, ethnic, or gender groups use their own folklore. McMahon has shown, for example, the daring ways that women undermine their more powerful spouses while in their very presence using coded and apparently joking statements that the women know will be incorrectly perceived by their husbands. These "flaunted" hidden transcripts are clandestinely and gleefully understood by the other women present (McMahon 1993). Likewise, as children compose the most powerless subaltern group, we should expect them to have multiple and complex ways of subverting authority—behaviors that must be taken into account by researchers.

Sutton-Smith (1990a) has presented a typology for identifying the strategic ways that children create the folklore that subverts adults and empowers children. His provisional schemata consists of disorder, failure, and antithesis. We can rephrase these categories and further develop them in terms of the literature in the adult field of resistance as follows: Disorder and failure are similar to Radner's and Lanser's "appropriation" and "incompetence," which are categories in their typology for the identification of women's strategic codes (1993). The latter, Sutton-Smith's antithesis, is like the logic of opposition in Keesing's discussion of "contestation" (1992) because it is a way that empowers and subverts under the noses of those who wield power. To illustrate the material for a further analysis of children's folklore as a documentation of power relationships, consider the following details:

Disorder. Here we deal with the delight that children have in creating disorder out of order. On the child level this is reflected in unisons of shoutings and noise-making, knocking down blocks and sand castles, laughing hysterically at deviations in adult behavior (as in cartoons, Charlie Chaplin, Three Stooges, Batley) rolling about on the ground, falling down on purpose, phonological and repetitive babble, telling stories full of mixed disasters such as being lost, stolen, angry, dead, stepped on, hurt, burned, killed, crashed, and so forth (Sutton-Smith 1981b). Remembering that adults also take joy in carnivals, festivals, roller coasters, clowns, rock concerts, and contact sports, where disorder is also a central characteristic, it is possible to argue that this impulse for disorderly play is a universal characteristic, perhaps itself not unrelated to such human disorderly fatefulness as war, catastrophe, hurricanes, death, and riots. Bakhtin's emphasis upon laughter as the basic and universal human reaction against fate through its disordering impact, further suggests a certain universality in the phenomenon. We remember his accounts of the orgiastic peasant festivals described by Rabelais as such a deep and universal reaction to endless suppression. As a character in Paul Willis's more modern *Learning to Labour* says about the battle that some adolescent British boys put up against their schooling, "I think that fuckin laffing is the most important thing in fuckin everything. Nothing ever stops me laffing. . . . I don't know why I want to laff, I dunno why it's so fuckin important. It just is. . . . I think it's just a good gift, that's all, because you can get out of any situation. If you can laff, if you can make yourself laff, I mean really convincingly, it can get you out of millions of things. . . . You'd go fuckin berserk if you didn't have a laff occasionally" (Willis 1977, 29). What this and some of the earlier examples show is that no matter what dimensions of universality laughter and disorder may have, much of this apparently irrational playfulness is in childhood directed against adult suppression and interference and order. Other examples in this volume are the pranks examined by Mechling and Jorgensen as well as Fine's mention of his data on children's fartlore. What we have in this material on closer view is a demystification of the structure of the dominant adult culture that demonstrates its ephemeral control. Sluckin, for example, discusses what is called a "taxi" ritual by some British schoolboys in which when one denies to the teacher that he has passed wind, then the whole class passes wind (1981, 32). Many a schoolteacher has been unraveled simply by being laughed at by the whole class either openly or surreptitiously. Such behavior is so common that "taunting the teacher" may actually constitute a genre in its own right (Oxrieder 1976). As it has been explained elsewhere, however, much of the disorder of children's play is an assertion of control within that play itself, rather than being directed at the adult culture (Sutton-Smith 1977). Apparently life as well as adults generate this response in us all.

Failure. Modern children grow up in an achievement society where they are graded endlessly on their accomplishments. A kind of disorder, therefore, which they especially seem to cherish is the disorder of failure, though unlike many of the earlier physical disorders this one apparently doesn't make its appearance until school days. Perhaps the most spectacular examples are the moron jokes, where stupidity is most celebrated. But folly and stupidity is revered also in riddles (You go to the bathroom American. You come out of the bathroom American. What are you in the bathroom? European). There are Mary Jane jokes (Mary Jane went to the doctor and he told her she was going to have twins. She laughed and laughed because she knew she hadn't done it twice), cruel mummy jokes, elephant jokes, dead baby jokes, Helen Keller jokes, Dolly Parton jokes, Christa McCauliffe jokes, grosser than gross jokes, and so forth. In many of these there is fictionalized failure at the expense of some conventional attitude or authority or nicety or decency. The teller achieves a magical distance in telling the tale of the failures of life—not in some way unlike the adult gambler whose mastery is in choosing how and where to lose, or a golf player whose mastery is much of the time in choosing to play badly for the rest of his or her life, but at least to keep playing. It is not hard to see much of the folklore of childhood, or adulthood for that matter, as a lore of empowerment, of fictional mastery over the presented fates.

The general undercurrent of an interest in playful disorder or failures becomes public on those occasions when it is suddenly used directly against authority, as when a class clown is applauded by his or her peers for sabotaging a teacher's efforts in the classroom with his or her nonsense or "traditional" inappropriate answers. These particular occasions justify us in saying that much of children's folklore exists in an interstitial world between fantasy and reality. This is like most of the subcultures that Scott discusses, where there are multiple traditions of antagonism but these are muted and indirect and fantasied until a moment when particular hostilities bring them to the surface. But they do nevertheless exist as an ongoing culture of self-regard and group confirmation. This is as true of the adult underclass as it is of the child underclass.

Antithesis. Disorder is at base a fairly undirected primordial chaos. Failure directs the blame at the persons who are stupid or without power. The implication that more powerful persons are responsible is not directly drawn. But with antithesis the fictional attack upon the mighty is rendered more clearly. Antithesis is an expressive behavior that presupposes an oppositional tension and demystifies the dominant culture through parody, mirroring, or inversion. Sullivan cites the work of the Knapps, who recorded the following song parody: "My Bonnie lies over the ocean; my Bonnie lies over the sea. My daddy lies over my mommy, and that's how they got little me (Knapp and Knapp 1976, 172, 185). So, too, Bronner recorded several song parodies such as "Row, row row your boat; gently down the stream.

Throw your teacher overboard, and listen to her scream" (1988, 101).

Other kinds of antithesis suggested by the writings of Radner and Lanser include such concepts as that of trivialization, in which subversive expressions play off dominant culture expectations about what is trivial. When Butler (1989, 94) asked a young Dutch girl to recite her favorite jump-rope rhyme, the child responded with this verse (which rhymes in Dutch): "A dog made a poopoo/Under a tree/A Frenchman came along/And ate it." Although the child's mother and grandmother were present, there was little that could be said about the child responding to a request to recite a "mere" jump-rope rhyme. Then there is indirection, which Radner and Lanser (1993) define as hedging or leaving out key words that members of the group know are also part of the text. Reinterpreting their category for women's strategy coding, we include here what Dundes (1967) terms the "evasive answer," which is one of his thirteen genres of children's folklore. Indirection can also occur with tongue twisters that are disguised so as to appear innocent: "I slit a sheet, a sheet I slit. Upon this slitted sheet I sit" (Dundes 1967; Galvin 1990, 168). Also, adults may be familiar with only one version of a text, such as: "Jeff and Mary sitting in a tree, K-I-S-S-I-N-G. First comes love, then comes marriage. Then comes Jeff in the baby-carriage."Children, however, may actually know another version of the text in which "F-U-C-K-I-N-G" replaces "kissing." In the presence of disapproving adults, the words are just whispered or, as Zumwalt has illustrated in this *Sourcebook,* just abbreviated: "Oh , you M-F, T-S, T-B-B!" Or there is Radner's and Lanser's distraction, which is similar to indirection but involves drowning out of a message, such as children's humming the tune of "Jack and Jill" instead of reciting a version known to the group, such as "Jack and Jill/Went up the hill/To get a pail of water/Jill came down with a five dollar bill/Do you really think she went up for water?" And most adults would choose to ignore a version of Jingle Bells, sung by a twelve-year-old boy in Harrisburg, Pennsylvania: "Jingle bells, shotgun shells; Santa Claus is dead. Someone stole my .30-.30 and shot him in the head" (Bronner 1988, 108).

Such examples demonstrate how challenging and socially relevant the study of children's subversive folklore is, but beyond this what is the value of developing such a typology? The broad goal is presumably to identify forms of folklore that are hidden in order to understand the relation of children's folklore to various forms of domination. Other related critical questions to be explored include discovering under which conditions children's folklore becomes subversive and by what processes children as well as other oppressed groups create subversive folklore. How do the forms of children's folklore relate to different forms of domination and dominant cultural values?

In setting out these examples of various kinds of subversion, however, it is necessary to emphasize the methodological point that researchers need to avoid the trap of "reading into" children's folklore what simply isn't there. Subversion is more than a text; it is an event that must be systematically accounted for before determining whether a particular act is subversive. A child could repeat some of these rhymes above with no sense whatsoever of such implication. This is the point implied by Winslow in an early work on children's derogatory epithets. As Winslow demonstrated, there are levels of meaning and contexts that exist in the ethnography of speaking. Researchers must be careful before assuming that the expression is always used in the same manner. For example, "A child may good-naturedly accept his nickname in the course of normal social interaction, but the same name may be used derogatorily in other contexts, especially if it is repeated enough" (1969, 256). This means close examination of the context—both historical and situational. Determinations can never simply be made by reading textual surfaces in abstraction from the specific event. For example, in Butler's *Skipping Around the World: The Ritual Nature of Folk Rhymes* (1989) and Lurie's *Don't Tell the Grown-ups: Subversive Children's Literature* (1990), each scholar has provided the reader with examples of children's folklore that are only *potentially* subversive, with little contextual information to support the researchers' interpretations. Therefore, we suggest proceeding cautiously in making such power interpretations, first recording or noting the situation which is external to the folklore itself and then actually identifying the taboos and values imposed on children.

Yet it is not our intent either to romanticize subversive aspects of children's folklore as "playful" nor to divert attention from darker aspects by ignoring instances of victimization of children by children. Some children's advocates fall into the trap of not only celebrating children's folklore purely for its didactic uses or viewing it as innocent diversion, but assuming the "unity" or "inclusiveness" of children as a group. Diversity exists everywhere and, as a result, uneven power relations also exist among children. Children as well have multiple identities related to gender, class, religion, and race. Works by scholars such as Fischer (1986) on ethnicity have even shown that although some differences often deny inclusiveness, they can be fundamental in identity formation for the group itself. As Roemer in this volume notes, researchers have generally ignored differences in, for example, children's riddling styles resulting from varying ages as well as ethnic heritages. This diversity is most apparent, for example, in studies like that of Stoeltje (1978), who noted subtle but important differences in hand-clapping games of Anglo and African American girls.

Obviously, the ideal is neither to reject nor to romanticize whatever there is in the children's world of powerlessness nor to make value judgments about what is appropriate to record. In exploring the ingenious ways that children create, regardless of their ethical flavor, we come to understand the simultaneous processes of their accommodation to adult values and their expressions of subversiveness. At times children's lore is an expression of defiance, challenging controlling forces in a symbolic power struggle, but sometimes this folklore is cruel, directed at members of the child's own group, such as when tag becomes "cooties tag" because the targeted child is said to have "cooties" because of race, religion, gender, or class. Such examples include what Sullivan terms "rhymes of prejudice" and provide us with very clear examples of children's folklore that adults have consistently avoided including in scholarly folklore collections. Children quite naturally replicate adult hierarchies in their own play and are as likely to generate cruel, dark, or mean folklore as they are to generate kindlier forms. Modern idealization of children's play as a part of childhood "innocence" often makes it difficult to recognize or accept these phenomena.

Finally, these investigations of folklore as power show that there is a real need to seriously reassess our fieldwork in relation to the voice and authority we exercise, which is an ethical concern well articulated by Fine and Mechling in this *Source Book*. For whether the author collects texts, or studies performance, or looks at power relationships in ethnographic ways, or romanticizes play, or contrastingly emphasizes its cruelty; whether appreciating or depreciating the children's own power struggles; whether rationalizing childhood or glorying in its irrationality—all of these are as much a commentary on the stance or rhetorics of the authority as on the condition of childhood. Children's folklore and that of adults was once much used to confer authenticity on the nationality or the ethnicity of the folk being studied, and also to claim authenticity for the discoveries of the scholar so involved. The activity of the Brothers Grimm is perhaps the most famous case in point (Briggs 1993). Postulating the authenticity of children's endeavors has, however, hardly been a prestigious activity in our post-Enlightenment culture, where adults are generally more interested in children's progress than in their past. But there has always been a small minority of scholars, from Newall to the Opies, who have hung in at their child-oriented posts and attempted to make us realize there was something there in children's folklore worth preserving or recording—whether they called it tradition, "natural" childhood, or folk subculture.

We pay a tribute to these scholars, as well as to the contributors to this *Source Book,* for their research of whatever kind and for the scholarly merit they derive from the authenticity of their own research endeavors. It is a scholarly "game" to engage one's fellows with a more adequate approach to the scholarly subject matter than existed hitherto, as if there is only our own new way of being authentic. But our editorial gamesmanship requires that we suggest, on the contrary, that there are multiple ways of being authentic about the authenticity of those we study. It is not a zero sum game. We live, rather, in a world of multiple childhoods and multiple ways in which these can be studied, to the credit of all parties. We say this despite our own persistent rhetoric about child empowerment. We choose to finish, therefore, selectively by asking the question how is it that our adult culture so typically suppresses the power-related aspects of children's lives so clearly represented in this present document? Is the "triviality barrier" (Sutton-Smith 1970a) in children's folklore only an adult reaction formation against the dangers of recognizing that the world would be very different if we attended to the neotony of children's struggles for power?

Glossary

This list of terms was created by *Source Book* contributors, who listed and defined those words that they considered basic for readers' understanding of their respective chapters. It is hoped that this glossary will be useful for those who are new to the field of folklore and for students in the classroom.

analytical category: form of classification generated by analyst for the purposes of comparison (see **cultural category**).

antithesis: a category in McMahon and Sutton-Smith's typology for children's subversive folklore that represents expressive behaviors that presuppose an oppositional tension and demystify the dominant culture through parody, mirroring, or inversion.

block element: one or more features of a riddle proposition that interferes with the proposition's facile solution.

bounded (or closed) society: homogeneous social group marked by isolation from other groups; members rely on one another for subsistence and social functions. Usually used to describe aboriginal and peasant communities (see **open society**).

catch riddle: a type of riddle in which the surprise or victimization of the respondent is a necessary element in the proposition.

childhood underground: a term used to describe the subculture of children that exists apart from the culture dominated and controlled by adults. In their book *One Potato, Two Potato: The Secret Education of American Children* (1976), Mary and Herbert Knapp explain this concept in detail.

childlore: children's folklore.

children's folklore: shared expressive behaviors of children; more specifically, according to Bauman, ". . . the traditional formalized play activities of children, including forms of speech play and verbal art, that are engaged in and maintained by the children themselves, within the peer group.

Familiar genres of children's folklore include riddles, games, jokes, taunts, retorts, hand-claps, counting-out rhymes, catches, ring plays, and jump-rope rhymes . . . distinguished on the one hand from nursery rhymes. . . . It is likewise distinguished from, though it may share items and genres and have other continuities with, adult folklore" (1982, 172).

contentious riddling: a type of riddling interaction during which participants are verbally aggressive, take liberties with one another, and test each other's social competence. See McDowell 1979, 122.

context: according to Duranti and Goodwin, the "notion of context . . . involves a fundamental juxtaposition of two entries: 1) a focal event; and 2) a field of action within which that event is embedded" (1992, 3). The relationship between focal event and context is "much like that between 'organism' and 'environment.'. . . 4) Contextual attributes most often attended to in folkloristic and anthropological scholarship include: a) setting ("i.e., the social and spatial framework within which encounters are situated"); b) behavorial environment ("i.e., the way that participants use their bodies and behavior as a resource for framing and organizing their talk"); c) language as context (the "way in which talk itself both invokes context and provides context for other talk"); and d) extrasituational context (that is, the participants' "background knowledge") (pages 6–8).

cultural category: form of classification generated by members of a cultural group to describe themselves (see **analytical category**).

descriptive routine: a madeup (that is, nontraditional) riddlelike routine depending solely or primarily on the technique of description. For an alternate definition, see McDowell 1979.

dialogue riddle: a type of riddle in which the proposition contains a quotation from characters in a fictitious interactional encounter. The riddle answer identifies the speakers. See Abrahams and Dundes 1972, 135. For an example, see riddle no. 14 in Roemer's chapter in this volume.

disorder and anarchy: a category in McMahon and Sutton-Smith's typology for children's subversive folklore that represents expressive behaviors as types of appropriation that demystify the structure of the dominant culture by demonstrating its ephemeral nature.

distraction: a category in Radner and Lanser's typology for women's strategic coding, adapted by McMahon and Sutton-Smith to indicate the forms of children's folklore that subvert authority by drowning out a message.

double dutch: a style of children's jump rope utilizing two ropes or one long rope doubled, turned egg beater fashion. Typically, two people turn, one at each end, with a jumper performing specific rhythmic motions in the middle while stepping over the cascading ropes.

emergence: the process whereby expressive forms take shape in the crucible of social interaction.

ethnomethodology: a research perspective that studies the organization and achievement of everyday life, including that of everyday talk. See Sudnow 1972 and R. Turner 1974.

experiment: a research method for investigating cause and effect under controlled conditions.

failure: a category in McMahon and Sutton-Smith's typology for subversive forms of staged incompetent behaviors that resist dominant group expectations.

folktale: a form of folk narrative told primarily for entertainment, with an emphasis on action and adventure within a fictional framework. While the folktale as delineated in Aarne and Thompson's *Types of the Folktale* (1961) has both simple and complex forms, the folktales discussed in Tucker's chapter in this volume are all Märchen, or fairytales in which a single hero encounters supernatural influences and tries to succeed at a quest. Generally, in magic tales, the hero and other deserving characters live "happily ever after" while villains are severely punished.

function: that which folklore "does" for the people who employ it.

funny-scary story: a folktale with a "catch" or humorous ending. Children use this term to indicate that, while a story of this kind may seem frightening, its climax has no truly fearful elements.

gesunkenes Kulturgut: the theory that folklore is directed downward in social hierarchies.

imitative objects: things made by children that resemble larger artifacts in the adult world. An example is a model hydroplane abstractly made from clip-type clothespins.

in-depth interview: a series of questions administered personally by a researcher to respondents, allowing the respondent to reply in detail.

indirection: a category from Radner's and Lanser's typology for women's strategic coding used to indicate expressive behaviors such as hedging or leaving out key words; similar to the genre of children's folklore that Dundes identified as the "evasive answer" (1967). Indirection is another category adapted by McMahon and Sutton-Smith in their refashioned typology for children's subversive folklore.

induced performances: folklore performances set up and encouraged by a researcher in a not fully natural situation.

informed consent: describing to a research subject the nature and goals of the research in which she or he is involved.

interreference: the dynamic process that operates between two or more cultures: central to the idea of "ethnicity," which Fischer (1986) views as "a deeply rooted component of identity."

interrogative ludic routine: small-scale verbal exchanges making playful use of the interrogative system in a language.

intraconversational narrative: a narrative embedded in the natural flow of conversation. Folklorists usually give careful consideration to the entire conversation when considering the meanings of this kind of narrative.

inventive or manipulative object: things made from natural resources into a new, more technical shape. An example is sand sculpture made by children on a beach.

joking riddle: a type of riddle in which the proposition serves primarily as a setup for the punch-line answer. For examples, see Roemer's riddle examples nos. 36–37 in this volume.

kinesics: the study of body movement and human communication, as pioneered by Ray L. Birdwhistell.

legend: less formally structured than the folktale, the legend features realistic characters and may be told as a true story. Two popular subtypes of this genre are the supernatural legend or "ghost story" and the horror legend in which monsters, maniacs, and other nonsupernatural forces predominate.

Märchen: the traditional European tale of wonder and magic; synonymous with "fairy tale" and "conte des fées."

material folk culture: interconnection of mental concept and traditional design shared within a social group. Includes objects and environments that characterize traditions of the group made by its members.

media narraform: a term coined by Sylvia Grider to classify the children's stories based on movies or TV shows (see Grider 1981). These stories, often diffuse and imprecise, may be told collaboratively in an effort to create the best possible synopsis of the original show.

move: sociologist Erving Goffman has written of "the move": "Now when an individual is engaged in talk, some of his utterances and nonlinguistic behavior will be taken to have a special temporal relevance, being directed to others present as something he wants assessed, appreciated, understood, *now*. I have spoken here of a move. Now it seems that sometimes the speaker and his hearers will understand this move to be primarily a comment on what has just been said, in that degree allowing us to speak of a response; at other times the move will be primarily seen as something to which a response is called for, in which degree it can be called a statement" (1981, 71–71).

mutation: an expressive item that has been altered through performance.

narrative: prose utterances with a sequential plot that may be fictional or nonfictional. Folktales, legends, and media narraforms are among the most popular narrative told by children.

oicotypification: the adaptation of an expressive item to fit a specific social and cultural environment.

open (or complex) society: heterogeneous social group marked by high degree of individuation. Usually associated with urban, industrialized nations.

parodic riddle: a type of joking riddle that extends the humor of the answer to the realm of the fantastic or the absurd. What the riddle as a whole proposes is nonsensical, given a conventional understanding of the "real" world. See examples in this volume by Roemer, nos. 38–44.

participant observation: a method in which researchers systematically observe people while participating in their routine activities.

psychoanalytic method: analysis of folk narratives that relies upon the precepts of Sigmund Freud, Carl Jung, Joseph Campbell, and others. Sexual symbolism that comes from the unconscious is a major focus in this school of interpretation.

riddle act: a unit of social interaction that consists of all the interactional moves involved in posing and responding to a single riddle proposition. The riddle act is the basic interactional unit of riddling. See Burns 1976, 142.

riddle session: a unit of social interaction during which a series of riddle acts is produced. The riddles may be interspersed with other performance material or with conversation. See Burns 1976, 142.

routine: a set of sequentially produced discourse acts (utterances, gestures, strategic use of silence) that is organized beyond the level of the individual sentence. A riddle act is a routine that is characteristically produced by more than one participant. See Hymes 1971.

semantic field: in discourse study, a domain of content or meaning.

solicitation: a type of speech act whose function is to elicit a verbal or physical response. See Bauman 1977b, 24.

story: synonym for **narrative,** defined above.

structuralism: analysis of the sequence of plot elements, called "functions" in Propp's *Morphology of the Folktale* (1958). Propp attempted to explain the structure of all Russian folktales, while Dundes further developed Propp's approach using the term "motifeme" in lieu of "function" in his *Morphology of North American Indian Folktales* (1964a).

subversive folklore: mulifaceted expressions of a group that undermine the authority of the dominant culture; also, any folklore involving victimization of others in the same group—such as children by more powerful children—which in effect also subverts adult authority because it involves taboo behavior.

survey research: a research method in which subjects respond to a series of questions in a questionnaire or structured interview.

syndesis: term used by anthropologist Robert Plant Armstrong to describe an object that grows from repetition of smaller units. Two examples are an ordinary spot in the woods converted to a child's shrine and one's fingers used to make a steeple (whose reverse is the people).

synthetic objects: things that are combined or built up from existing objects. An example is a Halloween effigy.

taunt: a malicious verbal expressive activity involving a victim.

tease: a verbal expressive activity involving a minimal degree of victimization, usually with "fun" rather than hurt as the motivation.

tenor: in a metaphoric construction, the subject word to which a metaphoric word (that is, the vehicle) is applied (M. Abrams 1957, 61).

transcription: the act of writing down verbatim actual interaction or dialogue, usually recorded first on audio or videotape; can refer to the text, conversation, or nonverbal communication or the written record of such translation.

transformational objects: commercial or adult things altered to suit children's needs and images. An example is a "half-ball" used for alley stickball and made by slicing a whole rubber ball.

triangulation: a methodology for collecting folklore that does not rely on any single method but instead is a combination of several techniques.

trick: a deceptive expressive activity with minimal victimization or harm intended, with "fun" as the motivating force.

trivialization: a category in Radner's and Lanser's typology for women's strategic coding, adapted here to indicate children's subversive expressions that play off dominant culture expectations about what is trivial.

true riddle: a type of riddle that involves "a comparison between the unstated answer and something else that is described in the question" (Brunvand 1986, 90). The answer to a true riddle can be reasoned out based on information supplied in the riddle proposition and the respondent's adequate experience with and recall of tropes, symbols, and other relevant conventions shared within the particular culture. See Taylor 1951 and examples by Roemer in this volume (riddle nos. 1, 2, 4–8, 32–35).

vehicle: in a metaphoric construction, the metaphoric word itself. In the sentence "John, the pawnshop owner is a shark," the word *shark* functions as the metaphoric vehicle.

video ethnography: the use of video in ethnographic or qualitative research, where the examination of video records serves as the main documentation for a specific social phenomenon.

visual descriptive riddle: a type of riddle in which the proposition consists of a sketch and some version of the question "What is it?" The answer consists of a sketch in representational terms, for example "a popcorn lid seen from the inside." For examples in this volume, see nos. 28–31 by Roemer.

Wellerism: a type of proverb "in the form of a quotation followed by a phrase ascribing the quotation to someone who has done something humorous and appropriate" (Brunvand 1986, 77).

word charade: a type of riddle in which the proposition divides the answer word into syllables and provides a description of each. The riddle answer supplies a referent word (or morpheme) for each of the descriptions in the proposition in the order in which those descriptions were given. The resulting series of referent words forms the answer word. See Abrahams and Dundes 1972, 135. In this volume, see Roemer's example, riddle no. 5.

Bibliography of Children's Folklore

Thomas W. Johnson

(supplemental entries by Felicia R. McMahon)

A comprehensive bibliography of works on folklore *of* and *for* children has yet to be compiled. It would certainly consist of a book far thicker than this entire *Source Book*. What follows here is a combined bibliography for all of the articles in this volume, plus a number of important additional works on children's folklore that did not happen to be cited by any of the authors included here. For these additional items, I have tried to select those I deemed to be most important to the field and likely to be readily available in any medium-size college library or through interlibrary loan. Each citation lists the most recent reprint I could find, rather than a possibly obscure first printing. Recent scholarship has been emphasized, and early works are listed only when they are especially significant or are excellent examples of a type of approach. There is also an emphasis on the folklore of American children, although a few works on children's folklore from other regions are included where there were especially good collections. The emphasis, as in this entire work, is on the folklore *of* children, rather than folklore *for* children, although a few significant works *for* children have also been included.

In addition to the somewhat limited listing which follows, there are a number of other sources that should be pursued by the dedicated scholar. Several bibliographies of children's folklore appear in this listing, all of them as well as a large number of additional sources that could not be added here for reasons of space. The reader is referred especially to Grider (1980b), whose excellent bibliography has been so thoroughly incorporated into my personal listing that it is impossible for me to separate it from items I discovered through other sources. It forms a significant part of the base of all that follows, although it also contains many items that were omitted here. Halpert (1982) has provided a supplement to Grider that is especially useful for European materials. Kirshenblatt-Gimblett (1976a), Mergen (1982), and Schwartzman (1976 and 1978) have compiled excellent bibliographies on children's toys, games, play, and speech play. Dundes (1976b) provides access to the many M.A. theses and Ph.D. dissertations on children's folklore. Though generally difficult to access, these are an important and an often neglected resource in the field.

The *Journal of American Folklore* and *Western Folklore* seem to devote the greatest space to children's folklore of any of the many journals in the field, although other journals in folklore and in many related disciplines (such as anthropology, education, psychology, and sociology) frequently publish interesting articles as well. The *Newsletter of the Children's Folklore Section of the American Folklore Society* (which is the organizational sponsor of this volume) carries news of recent developments, as well as some brief articles and commentary. This has become the *Children's Folklore Review* since 1990, under the editorship of C.W. Sullivan III. The *Australian Children's Folklore Newsletter* and the *Newsletter of the Association for the Anthropological Study of Play* (TAASP) are also excellent resources, containing useful articles as well as news of the associations. TASP (formerly TAASP) has also produced a series of volumes of papers presented at their annual meetings (beginning in 1975), many of the articles being about children's play (see Lancy and Tindall 1976; Stevens 1977; Salter 1978; Schwartzman 1978; Cheska 1981; Loy 1982; Manning 1983; Sutton-Smith and Kelly-Byrne 1984; Blanchard 1986; Mergen 1986; and Fine 1987.) Thereafter the articles of this society appeared in the journal *Play and Culture,* 1988–92; and in the journal *Play Theory and Research,* 1993. Volumes on the folklore of a *place* often contain a chapter on children's folklore and are another resource to be checked. Welsch (1966b) is included in this bibliography, not only because it has significant data on children's folklore but also to serve as an excellent example of this type of work and a reminder of its importance.

In the listing that follows, I have placed an asterisk (*) before items I consider not only the most interesting but the most basic to the study of children's folklore. This is a purely idiosyncratic listing, and one that I am certain each of the authors in this volume would dispute. It is included to provide a starting point for beginners in the field. The square brackets [ ] enclose brief annotations of some of the works, providing some indication of their content and significance beyond what their titles convey.

This bibliography, like any, should be viewed as a work in progress. While I was on sabbatical leave in Japan in 1993–95, Felicia McMahon continued to keep the bibliography up to date. In spite of our efforts, it is hopelessly incomplete, although a good beginning for research in a fascinating but understudied field.

Aarne, Antti, and Stith Thompson
    1961   *The Types of the Folktale: A Classification and Bibliography*. Helsinki, Finland: F.F. Communications #184, Scientific Finnish Academy.

Aaron, David
    1965   *Child's Play: A Creative Appeal to Play Spaces for Today's Children*. New York: Harper and Row.

Abernethy, Francis Edward (ed.)
    1989   *Texas Toys and Games*. Publications of the Texas Folklore Society, no. 48. Dallas: Southern Methodist University Press.

Abrahams, Roger D.
    1963   "Some Jump-Rope Rimes from South Philadelphia." *Journal of American Folklore* 8 (January): 3–5.
    1969   *Jump-Rope Rhymes: A Dictionary*. Austin: University of Texas Press.
    1980   *Counting-Out Rhymes: A Dictionary*. Austin: University of Texas Press.
    1981   "Shouting Match at the Border: The Folklore of Display Events." In *And Other Neighborly Names*, edited by R. Bauman and R. Abrahams, 303–21. Austin: University of Texas Press.

Abrahams, Roger D., and Alan Dundes
    1972   "Riddles." In Richard Dorson (ed.), *Folklore and Folklife: An Introduction*. Chicago: University of Chicago Press.

Abrahams, Roger D., and Lois Rankin
    1980   *Counting Out Rhymes: A Dictionary*. Austin: University of Texas Press.

Abrams, David M., and Brian Sutton-Smith
    1977   "The Development of the Trickster in Children's Narratives." *Journal of American Folklore* 90:29–47.

Abrams, M.H.
    1957   *A Glossary of Literary Terms*. 3d ed. New York: Holt, Rinehart and Winston.

Adams, G.B.
    1965   "Counting Rhymes and Systems of Numerations." *Ulster Folklife* 2:87–97.

Adams, Henry
    1918   *The Education of Henry Adams*. Boston: Massachusetts Historical Society.

Adams, M.A.
    1976   "Hospital Play Programs: Helping Children with Serious Illness." *American Journal of Orthopsychiatry* 46:416–24.

Addams, Jane
    1907   "Public Recreation and Social Morality." *Charities and the Commons*. August 22–24.

Adler, Elizabeth Mosby
    1981   "Creative Eating: The Oreo Syndrome." *Western Folklore* 40:4–10.

Ager, Lynn P.
    1975   "Storyknifing: An Alaskan Eskimo Girl's Game." *Journal of the Folklore Institute* 11:187–98.

Ainsworth, Catherine Harris
    1961   "Jump Rope Verses Around the United States." *Western Folklore* 20:179–99. [Results of a mail questionnaire to seventh-grade teachers; 152 verses from nine schools in as many states.]
    1962   "Black and White and Said All Over." *Southern Folklore Quarterly* 26:263–95. [Collection of 535 riddles from ninth-grade students in six states.]
    1973   "Hallowe'en." *New York Folklore Quarterly* 29:163–93.

Alcott, Louisa May
    1963   *Little Men*. New York: Macmillan.

Allen, Patricia R. Boyd
    1969   *An Annotated Bibliography of Play Environments: Planning, Design and Evaluation*. Chicago: Council of Planning Librarians, Exchange.

Bibliography no. 1184.

Altman, Terry
  1978   "Folklore and Education: A Selected Annotated Bibliography of Periodical Literature." *Keystone Folklore Quarterly* 22:53–85.
American Playground Device Company
  1974   Catalog. Anderson, Indiana.
Ames, Kenneth L.
  1980   "Folk Art: The Challenge and the Promise." In *Perspectives on American Folk Art*, edited by I.M.G. Quimby and S.T. Swank, 293–324. New York: W.W. Norton.
Ames, Louise B.
  1966   "Children's Stories." *Genetic Psychological Monographs* 73:337–96.
Anderson, Walter
  1951   *Ein Volkskundliches Experiment*. Folklore Fellows Communication. Helsinki: Scientific Finnish Academy.
Anderson, Wanni Wibulswasdi
  1980   *Children's Play and Games in Rural Thailand: A Study in Enculturation and Socialization*. Bangkok: Chulalongkorn University Social Research Institute. [Results of a field study of a single village of 160 people. Originally her 1973 Ph.D. dissertation at the University of Pennsylvania.]
Appleton, Lilla Estelle
  1910   *A Comparative Study of Play Activities of Adult Savages and Civilized Children: An Investigation of the Scientific Basis of Education*. Reprinted 1976. New York: Arno.
Apte, Mahadev L.
  1985   *Humor and Laughter, an Anthropological Approach*. Ithaca, New York: Cornell University Press.
Ariès, Philippe
  1962   *Centuries of Childhood: A Social History of Family Life*. New York: Alfred A. Knopf. [Original French edition, 1960. Immediately became a classic with its description of changes in adult European attitudes toward children and their play. For other views, see the work of De Mause (1974) and Wilson (1980)].
Armstrong, Robert Plant
  1981   *The Powers of Presence: Consciousness, Myth, and Affecting Presence*. Philadelphia: University of Pennsylvania Press.
Armstrong, William Howard
  1969   *Sounder*. New York: Harper and Row.
Ashley, Leonard R.N.
  1968   "Scoff Lore: An Introduction to British Words for Food and Drink." *Names* 6:238–72.
Asimov, Isaac
  1979   *In Memory Yet Green: The Autobiography of Isaac Asimov, 1920–1954*. Garden City, N.Y.: Doubleday.
Association for the Anthropological Study of Play
  1974   *TAASP Newsletter*. Middle Tennessee State University, Murfreesboro.
Atkinson, Robert M.
  1967   "Songs Little Girls Sing: An Orderly Invitation to Violence." *Northwest Folklore* 2:2–8. [A field collection.]
Aufenanger, Heinrich
  1958   "Children's Games and Entertainments among the Kumngo Tribe in Central New Guinea." *Anthropos* 53:575–84. [Field collection of materials with a brief description of their functions from an area little studied by folklorists. Reprinted in Sutton-Smith 1976c.]
Austin, John Langshaw
  1962   *How to Do Things with Words*. Oxford: Clarendon.

1970   *Philosophical Papers*. Oxford: Clarendon.
Australian Children's Folklore Newsletter
    1981– Kew, Victoria: Institute of Early Childhood Education.
Avedon, Elliott M.
    1971   "The Structural Elements of Games." In *The Study of Games*, edited by E.
            Avedon and B. Sutton-Smith, 419–26. New York: John Wiley.
Avedon, Elliott M. and Brian Sutton-Smith
    *1971   *The Study of Games*. New York: John Wiley. [A collection of twenty-three
            important articles plus extensive bibliographies on all aspects of games.]
Axline, Virginia Mae
    1964   *Dibs in Search of Self*. New York: Ballantine.
Ayoub, Millicent, and Stephen A. Barnett
    1965   "Ritualized Verbal Insult in White High School Culture." *Journal of Ameri-
            can Folklore* 78:337–44.
Babcock, W.H.
    1886a   "Song Games and Myth Dramas at Washington." *Lippincott's Monthly
            Magazine* 37:239–57. [A field collection with comments on possible origins
            of the materials.]
    1886b   "Carols and Child-lore at the Capitol." *Lippincott's Monthly Magazine*
            38:320–42. [A field collection.]
    1888   "Games of Washington Children." *American Anthropologist* 1:243–84.
            [Field collection reprinted in Sutton-Smith 1976c.]
Bachelard, Gaston
    1964   *The Poetics of Space*. New York: Orion.
Balbernie, Richard
    1966   *Residential Work with Children*. London: Human Context.
Bar-Adon, Aaron, and Werner F. Leopold (eds.)
    1971   *Child Language: A Book of Readings*. Englewood Cliffs, N.J.: Prentice-Hall.
Baring-Gould, Sabine
    1895   *The Book of Nursery Songs and Rhymes*. Reprint. Detroit: Singing Tree,
            1969.
Barker, Roger G., and Herbert F. Wright
    1951   *One Boy's Day: A Specimen Record of Behavior*. New York: Harper and
            Row.
Barker, T. Steven
    1973   "Games Our Parents Hated." *North Carolina Folklore Journal* 21:37–39.
Barnes, Douglas
    1976   *From Communication to Curriculum*. Harmondsworth, Middlesex, En-
            gland: Penguin.
Barnet, Judith
    1978   "Folk Wit and Wisdom." *Intercom* 90–91:14–16.
Barnett, L.A., and P. Kruidenier
    1981   "Effects of Encapsulation on Preschool Children's Imaginative Play." *Jour-
            nal of Leisure Research* 13:323–36.
Barrick, Mac E.
    1963   "Riddles from Cumberland County." *Keystone Folklore Quarterly* 8:59–
            74.
    1964   "The Shaggy Elephant Riddle." *Southern Folklore Quarterly* 28:266–90.
            [Collection of 245 with brief analysis.]
    1966   "Games from the Little Red School House." In *Two Penny Ballads and Four
            Dollar Whiskey*, edited by K.S. Goldstein and R.H. Byington, 95–120.
            Hatboro, Pa.: Folklore Associates.
    1974   "The 'Newspaper' Riddle Joke." *Journal of American Folklore* 87:253–57.
Bartlett, Frederick C.
    1932   *Remembering*. Cambridge: Cambridge University Press.

Bartlett, Steve
    1971   "Interaction Patterns of Adolescents in a Folklore Performance." *Folklore Forum* 4:39–67.

Barton, F.R.
    1908   "Children's Games in British New Guinea." *Journal of the Royal Anthropological Institute* 38:259–79.

Bascom, William R.
    1949   "Literary Style in Yoruba Riddles." *Journal of American Folklore* 62:1–16.
    1954   "Four Functions of Folklore." *Journal of American Folklore* 67:333–49.

Basgoz, Ilhan
    1965   "Functions of Turkish Riddles." *Journal of the Folklore Institute* 2:132–47.

Bateson, Gregory
    1936   *Naven.* 2d ed. 1958. Stanford, Calif.: Stanford University Press.
    1972   *Steps to an Ecology of Mind: Collected Essays in Anthropology.* New York: Ballantine.

Baughman, Ernest
    1945   "The Fatal Initiation." *Hoosier Folklore Bulletin* 4:30–32.

Bauman, Richard
    1977a   *Verbal Art as Performance.* Reprinted 1984. Prospect Heights, Ill.: Waveland.
    1977b   "Linguistics, Anthropology, and Verbal Art: Toward a Unified Perspective with a Special Discussion of Children's Folklore, Linguistics and Anthropology." *Report of the Twenty-Eighth Annual Georgetown University Round Table on Language and Linguistics,* edited by M. Saville-Troike, 13–36. Washington, D.C.: Georgetown University Press.
    1982   "Ethnography of Children's Folklore." *Children in and Out of School: Ethnography and Education.* edited by P. Gilmore and A.A. Glatthorn, 172–86. Washington, D.C.: Center for Applied Linguistics.

Bauman, R., Rosalind Eckhardt, and Margaret K. Brady
    1975   *Black Girls at Play.* Austin, Tex.: Southwestern Educational Development Laboratory.

Bauman, Richard, and Joel Sherzer (eds.)
    1974   *Explorations in the Ethnography of Speaking.* New York: Cambridge University Press.

Beaglehole, Ernest
    1946   *Some Modern Maoris.* Wellington, New Zealand: New Zealand Council of Educational Research.

Beaujour, M.
    1984   "Delayed Replay: The Renaissance as "Mimicry" and Representation." Paper presented at Conference on the Forms of Play in the Early Modern Period. University of Maryland, March 1984.

Beckwith, Jay
    1980   "State of the Playground Industry." *Association for the Anthropological Study of Play Newsletter* 7:12–13.

Behar, L., and D. Stephens
    1978   "Wilderness Camping: An Evaluation of a Residential Treatment Program for Emotionally Disturbed Children." *American Journal of Orthopsychiatry* 48:644–53.

Ben-Amos, Dan
    1971   *Folklore Genres.* Austin: University of Texas Press.

Bender, Lauretta, and Paul Schilder
    1936   "Form as a Principle in the Play of Children." *Journal of Genetic Psychology* 49:254–61.

Bengtsson, Arvid
    1974   *The Child's Right to Play.* Sheffield, England: International Playground Association.

Bennett, James
  1981 *Oral History and Delinquency: The Rhetoric of Criminology*. Chicago: University of Chicago Press.
Beresin, Ann Richman
  1993 "The Play of Peer Cultures in a City School Yard: 'Reeling,' 'Writhing,' and 'A Rhythmic Kick.'" Ph.D. dissertation, University of Pennsylvania.
Bergen, Fanny
  1895a "Pigments Used by Children in Their Play." *Journal of American Folklore* 8:151.
  1895b "Violet Fights." *Journal of American Folklore* 8:151–52.
  1895c "Poppy Shows." *Journal of American Folklore* 8:152–53.
Bergmann, Thesi, with Anna Freud
  1965 *Children in the Hospital*. New York: International Universities Press.
Berkovits, Rochele
  *1970 "Secret Languages of Schoolchildren." *New York Folklore Quarterly* 26:127–52. [An excellent field collection, including parts of the actual interviews, showing field methods.]
Berlyne, D.E.
  1960 *Conflict, Arousal and Curiosity*. New York: McGraw-Hill.
Berne, Eric
  1964 *Games People Play: The Psychology of Human Relationships*. New York: Grove.
Bernstein, Basil
  1960 "A Review of the Lore and Language of Schoolchildren by Iona and Peter Opie." *British Journal of Sociology* 11:178–81.
  1964 "Elaborated and Restricted Codes: Their Social Origins and Some Consequences." *American Anthropologist* 66:55–69.
Best, Raphaela
  1983 *We've All Got Scars: What Boys and Girls Learn in Elementary School*. Bloomington: Indiana University Press.
Bett, Henry
  1924 *Nursery Rhymes and Tales: Their Origin and History*. Reprinted 1969. Folcroft, Pa.: Folcroft Press.
  1929 *The Games of Children: Their Origin and History*. London: Methuen.
Bettelheim, Bruno
  1976 *The Uses of Enchantment: The Meaning and Importance of Fairy Tales*. New York: Alfred A. Knopf.
Beuf, Ann
  1979 *Biting the Bracelet*. Philadelphia: University of Pennsylvania Press.
Bhagwat, Durga
  1965 *The Riddle in Indian Life, Lore, and Literature*. Bombay: Popular Prakashan.
Bick, M.
  1980 "The Rights of Passage: Rituals and Team Sports in American Society Reexamined." *Association for the Anthropological Study of Play Newsletter* 6:3–24.
Birdwhistell, Ray L.
  1970 *Kinesics and Context: Essays on Body Motion Communication*. Philadelphia: University of Pennsylvania Press.
Birksted, I.K.
  1976 "School Performance Viewed from the Boys." *Sociological Review* 24:63–78.
Blacking, John
  1961 "The Social Value of Venda Riddles." *African Studies* 20:1–32.
  1967 *Venda Children's Songs: A Study in Ethnomusicological Analysis*.

Johannesburg: Witwatersrand University Press. [An excellent ethnographic study of the role of folklore in society.]

Blackowski, S.
1937   "The Magical Behavior of Children in Relation to School." *American Journal of Psychology* 50:347–61.

Blanchard, Kendall
1986   *The Many Faces of Play.* Champaign, Ill.: Human Kinetics Publishers.

Blount, Ben G.
1975   "Review Article—Studies in Child Language: An Anthropological View." *American Anthropologist* 77:580–600.

Bluebond-Langner, Myra
1978   *The Private Worlds of Dying Children.* Princeton: Princeton University Press.
1981   "Knowing, Concealing, and Revealing: Communication in Terminally Ill Children." In *Children and Their Organizations: Investigations in American Culture*, edited by R.T. Sieber and A.J. Gordon, 218–33. Boston: G.K. Hall.

Boas, Franz
1938   "Invention." In *General Anthropology*, edited by F. Boas, 238–81. Boston: D. C. Heath.

Boaz, Peggy B.
1973   "Take It Off; Knock It Off; Or Let the Crows Pick It Off." *Tennessee Folklore Society Bulletin* 39:77–78. [Description of a game with variants.]

Bock, Kenneth
1956   *The Acceptance of Histories.* Berkeley: University of California Press.

Bodding, P.O.
1940   *Santal Riddles.* Oslo: A.W. Brøggers.

Bogdan, Robert, and Steven J. Taylor
1975   *Introduction to Qualitative Research Methods: A Phenomenological Approach to the Social Sciences.* New York: Wiley-Interscience.

Bolton, Henry Carrington
1888   *The Counting-Out Rhymes of Children: Antiquity, Origin, and Wide Distribution.* Reprinted 1969. Detroit: Singing Tree. [Done in classic nineteenth-century style.]
1897   "More Counting-Out Rhymes." *Journal of American Folklore* 10:313–21. [Collection of items mailed to him from all over the world as a result of his above publication.]

Bonte, Eleanor P., and Mary Musgrove
1943   "Influences of War as Evidenced in Children's Play." *Child Development* 14:179–200.

Book of Games; or a History of Juvenile Sports Practiced at the Kingston Academy
1821   Philadelphia: Benjamin Warner. [Originally published, London 1812.]

Borchert, James
1980   *Alley Life in Washington: Family, Community, Religion, and Folklife in the City, 1850–1970.* Urbana: University of Illinois Press.

Borman, K.M., and N.T. Lippincott
1982   "Cognition and Culture: Two Perspectives on 'Free Play.'" In *The Social Life of Children in a Changing Society*, edited by K.M. Borman, 123–42. Norwood, N.J.:Ablex.

Borneman, Ernest
*1973   *Unsere Kinder im Spiegel ihrer Lieder, Reime, Verse und Ratsel. Studiem zur Befreiung des Kindes, Band I.* Berlin: Olten und Freiburg.
*1974   *Die Umwelt des Kindes im Spiegel seiner "verbotenen" Lieder, Reime, Verse und Ratsel. Studien zur Befreiung des Kindes, Band II.* Berlin: Olten und Freiburg.

Botvin, Gilbert J.
1976   "The Development of Narrative Competence: A Syntagmatic Analysis of

Children's Fantasy Narratives." Ph.D. dissertation, Columbia University.

Brady, Margaret K.

1974 "Gonna Shimmy Shimmy 'Til the Sun Goes Down: Aspects of Verbal and Nonverbal Socialization in the Play of Black Girls." *Folklore Annual* 6: 1–16.

1975 "This Little Lady's Gonna Boogaloo: Elements of Socialization in the Play of Black Girls." In *Black Girls at Play: Perspectives on Child Development,* 1–56. Austin: Southwest Educational Development Laboratory.

1984 "Some Kind of Power": Navajo Children's Skinwalker Narratives." Salt Lake City: University of Utah Press. [Revised version of her 1978 Ph.D. dissertation at the University of Texas.]

Brandes, Stanley

1980 *Metaphors of Masculinity: Sex and Status in Andalusian Folklore.* Philadelphia: University of Pennsylvania Press.

Brant, Sandra, and Elissa Cullman

1980 *Small Folk: A Celebration of Childhood in America.* New York: E.P. Dutton.

Brenner, M.

1982 "Actors' Powers." In *The Analysis of Action,* edited by M. von Cranach and R. Harre, 213–29. Cambridge: Cambridge University Press.

Brewster, Paul G.

1939 "Rope-Skipping, Counting-Out, and Other Rhymes of Children." *Southern Folklore Quarterly* 3:173–85. [Collection from Indiana and Missouri.]

1942 "Some Notes on the Guessing Game, How Many Horns Has the Buck?" Reprinted in *The Study of Folklore* , edited by A. Dundes, 338–68. Englewood Cliffs, N.J.: Prentice-Hall, 1965.

1945 "Some Unusual Forms of 'Hopscotch.'" *Southern Folklore Quarterly* 9:229–31. [Brief description of five forms with diagrams. Reprinted in Sutton-Smith 1976c].

*1952 "Children's Games and Rhymes." In *The Frank C. Brown Collection of North Carolina Folklore.* Vol. 1, 29–219. Durham, N.C.: Duke University Press. [Also reprinted as a separate volume in 1976 by the Arno Press, New York].

*1953 *American Non-Singing Games.* Norman: University of Oklahoma Press. [A large collection with annotations and brief comments. Excellent bibliography.]

1959 "Three Russian Games and Their Western (and Other) Parallels." *Southern Folklore Quarterly* 23:126–31.

Briggs, Charles L.

1988 *Competence in Performance: The Creativity of Tradition in Mexicano Verbal Art.* Philadelphia: University of Pennsylvania Press.

1993 "Metadiscursive Practices and Scholarly Authority in Folkloristics." *Journal of American Folklore* 106:422:387–434.

Britton, James

1970 *Language and Learning.* Harmondsworth, Middlesex, England: Penguin.

Bronner, Simon J.

1977 "Concrete Folklore: Sidewalk Box Games." *Western Folklore* 36:171–73.

1978a "A Re-examination of Dozens Among White Adolescents." *Western Folklore* 37:118–27.

1978b "'Who Says?' A Further Investigation of Ritual Insults Among White Adolescents." *Midwestern Journal of Language and Folklore* 4:53–69.

1979 "Concepts in the Study of Material Aspects of American Folk Culture." *Folklore Forum* 12:133–72.

1981a "The Folk Technics of Chain Carving." *Studies in Traditional American Crafts* 4:3–19.

1981b "Investigating Identity and Expression in Folk Art." *Winterthur Portfolio* 19:65–83.

1982   "The Haptic Experience of Culture." *Anthropos* 77:351–62.

1983   "Manner Books and Suburban Houses: The Structure of Tradition and Aesthetics." *Winterthur Portfolio* 18:61–68.

1984   *Chain Carvers.* Lexington: University Press of Kentucky.

1985   "'What's Grosser Than Gross?' New Sick Joke Cycles." *Midwestern Journal of Language and Folklore* 11:39–49.

1986a   "Folk Objects." In *Folk Groups and Folklore Genres: An Introduction*, edited by Elliott Oring, 199–224. Logan: Utah State University Press.

1986b   *Grasping Things: Folk Material Culture and Mass Society in America.* Lexington: Kentucky University Press.

1988   *American Children's Folklore.* Little Rock: August House.

1990   "'Left to Their Own Devices': Interpreting American Children's Folklore as an Adaptation to Aging." *Southern Folklore* 47:101–15.

Brooks, Ken

1981   "High Jinks on the Party Line." *Modern Maturity* (August–September):81–82.

Brown, Penelope, and Stephen Levinson

1978   *Universals in Language Use: Politeness Phenomena.* In *Questions and Politeness*, edited by E.N. Goody, 56–289. Cambridge: Cambridge University Press.

Brown, Waln K.

1973   "Cognitive Ambiguity and the 'Pretended Obscene Riddle'." *Keystone Folklore* 18:89–101.

1974   "Cultural Learning Through Game Structure: A Study of Pennsylvania German Children's Games." *Pennsylvania Folklife* 22:2–11.

Browne, Ray B.

1954   "Children's Taunts, Teases, and Disrespectful Sayings from Southern California." *Western Folklore* 13:190–98. [Sixty-one items with variants.]

1955   "Southern California Jump-Rope Rhymes: A Study in Variants." *Western Folklore* 14:3–22.

Brukman, Jan C.

1973   "Language and Socialization: Child Culture and the Ethnographer's Task." In *Learning and Culture*, edited by S.T. Kimball and J.H. Burnett, 43–58. Seattle: University of Washington Press.

Bruner, Jerome, A. Jolly, and K. Sylvan

1976   *Play.* New York: Basic Books.

Brunvand, Jan Harold

1971   *A Guide for Collectors of Folklore in Utah.* Salt Lake City: University of Utah Press.

1978   *The Study of American Folklore: An Introduction.* 2d ed. New York: W.W. Norton.

1981   *The Vanishing Hitchhiker: American Urban Legends and Their Meaning.* New York: Norton.

1986   *The Study of American Folklore.* New York: W.W. Norton.

Buchanan, Kerry

1984   "Hip Hop to Be Bop." *And* 2:75–80.

Buffalo Recreation Survey

1925   Buffalo, N.Y.: Buffalo City Planning Association.

Bullard, M. Kenyon

1975   "Marbles: An Investigation of the Relationship Between Marble Games and Other Aspects of Life in Belize." *Journal of American Folklore* 88:393–400.

Burack, Lynda (ed.)

1978   "Folklore and Education: Special Issue." *Keystone Folklore* 22 (nos. 1 and 2):13–102. [About half of this special issue is devoted to an annotated bibliography.]

Burch, William R., Jr.
  1965 "The Playworld of Camping: Research into the Social Meaning of Outdoor Recreation." *American Journal of Sociology* 70:604–12.
Burke, Kenneth
  1941 *The Philosophy of Literary Form: Studies in Symbolic Action.* Baton Rouge: Louisiana State University.
  1945 *A Grammar of Motives.* Reprinted. Berkeley: University of California Press, 1969.
  1966 *Language as Symbolic Action.* Berkeley: University of California Press.
Burling, Robbins
  1966 "The Metrics of Children's Verse: A Cross-Linguistic Study." *American Anthropologist* 68:1418–41.
Burnett, Jacquetta Hill
  1969a "Ceremony, Rites and Economy in the Student System of an American High School." *Human Organization* 28:1–10.
  1969b *Pattern and Process in Student Life: A Study of Custom and Social Relationships Among the Students of an American High School.* New York: Teachers College Press.
Burnett, Frances Hodgson
  1962 *The Secret Garden.* Philadelphia: J.B. Lippincott.
Burns, Thomas A.
  1976 "Riddling: Occasion to Act." *Journal of American Folklore* 89:139–65.
Butler, Francelia
  1989 *Skipping Around the World: The Ritual Nature of Folk Rhymes.* Hamden, Conn.: Library Professional Publications.
Butler, George D. (ed.)
  1938a *The New Play Areas: Their Design and Equipment.* New York: A.S. Barnes.
  1938b *Playgrounds: Their Administration and Operation.* New York: A.S. Barnes.
Caillois, R.
  1961 *Man, Play and Games.* Glencoe, Ill.: Free Press.
Calvert, Karin
  1992 *Children in the House: The Material Culture of Early Childhood, 1600–1900.* Boston: Northeastern University Press.
Campbell, John D.
  1964 "Peer Relations in Childhood." In *Review of Child Development Research,* vol. I, edited by M.L. Hoffman and L.W. Hoffman, 289–322. New York: Russell Sage Foundation.
Cansler, Loman D.
  1968 "Midwestern and British Children's Lore Compare." *Western Folklore* 27:1–18.
Cardozo-Freeman, Inez
  1975 "Games Mexican Girls Play." *Journal of American Folklore* 88:12–24.
Carlson, Ruth Kearney
  1972 "World Understanding Through the Folktale." In *Folklore and Folktales Around the World,* edited by R.K. Carlson. *Perspectives in Reading* Series No. 15. Newark, Del.: International Reading Association.
Carroll, Lewis
  1865 *Alice in Wonderland.* Reprint, edited by D.L. Gray. New York: W.W. Norton, 1971.
Carson, Jane
  1989 *Colonial Virginians at Play.* Williamsburg: Colonial Williamsburg Foundation.
Cassidy, Frederick G.
  1984 "Regionalism in Children's Games." *North American Culture* 1:55–64. [Descriptions and maps from the *Dictionary of American Regional English.*]

Castiglione, B.

1968   *The Book of the Courtier*. London: Penguin.

Castleman, Craig

1982   *Getting Up: Subway Graffiti in New York*. Cambridge: MIT Press.

Caughey, John

1982   "Ethnography, Introspection, and Reflexive Culture Studies." In *Prospects: An Annual of American Cultural Studies*, vol. 7, edited by J. Salzman, 115–39. New York: Burt Franklin.

Cavallo, Dominick

1981   *Muscles and Morals: Organized Playgrounds and Urban Reform, 1880–1920*. Philadelphia: University of Pennsylvania Press.

Cazden, Courtney

1982   "Four Comments." In *Children In and Out of School: Ethnography and Education*, edited by P. Gilmore and A.A. Glatthorn, 209–26. Washington, D.C.: Center for Applied Linguistics.

Cervantes, M.

1605   *Don Quixote*. New York: Heritage, 1938.

Chamberlain, Alexander Francis

1896   *The Child and Childhood in Folk-Thought*. New York: Macmillan. [Subtitled *The Child in Primitive Culture*. Excellent example of nineteenth-century anthropology.]

Chambers, R. (ed.)

1864   *The Book of Days*. Vol. 1. London: W. and R. Chambers.

Champlin, John D., and Arthur E. Bostwick.

1890   *The Young Folks' Cyclopedia of Games and Sports*. New York: Holt.

Chandler, Joan

1981   "Camping for Life: Transmission of Values at a Girls' Summer Camp." *Children and Their Organizations: Investigations in American Culture*, edited by R.T. Sieber and A.J. Gordon, 122–37. Boston: G.K. Hall.

Cheska, Alyce Taylor (ed.)

1981   *Play as Context*. West Point, N.Y.: Leisure. [Proceedings of the 1979 annual meeting of the Association for the Anthropological Study of Play.]

Children's Aid Society

1978   *New York Street Kids*. New York: Dover.

Children's Folklore Newsletter

1978   Greenville, N.C.: East Carolina University.

Chomsky, Noam

1965   *Aspects of a Theory of Syntax*. Cambridge: MIT Press.

Chukovsky, Kornei

1963   *From Two to Five*. Berkeley: University of California Press.

Clar, Mimi

1959   "Songs of My California Childhood." *Western Folklore* 18:245–50. [Words, music, and commentary.]

Clarke, D.D.

1982   "The Sequential Analysis of Action Structure." In *The Analysis of Action*, edited by M. von Cranach and R. Harre, 191–212. Cambridge: Cambridge University Press.

Clarke, Kenneth

1964   "Folklore of Negro Children in Greater Louisville Reflecting Attitudes toward Race." *Kentucky Folklore Record* 10:1–11. [Describes the role of children's folklore in socialization of attitudes.]

Clemens, Samuel Langhorne

1884   *Adventures of Huckleberry Finn*. 2d ed. New York: W.W. Norton, 1977.

1897   *How to Tell a Story and Other Essays*. New York: Harper's.

Clore, G.L. et al.

1978 "Interracial Attitudes and Behavior at a Summer Camp." *Journal of Personality and Social Psychology* 36:107–16.

Cohen, David Steven, and John Eilertsen
1985 "Folklore and Folklife in a Juvenile Corrections Institution." *Western Folklore* 44:1–22.

Cole, Larry
1972 *Our Children's Keepers: Inside America's Kid Prisons*. New York: Grossman.

Coleman, James S.
1961 *The Adolescent Society*. New York: Free Press.

Collett, P.
1977 "The Rules of Conduct." In *Social Rules and Social Behavior*, edited by P. Collett, 1–27. Oxford: Basil Blackwell.

Collins, Camilla
1975 "Bibliography of Urban Folklore." *Folklore Forum* 8, (nos. 2 and 3) 57–125. [See 116–19 for section on children's folklore.]

Conger, John Janeway
1977 *Adolescence and Youth: Psychological Development in a Changing World*. 2d ed. New York: Harper and Row.

Conn, J.H.
1951 "Children's Awareness of Sex Differences: Play Attitudes and Game Preferences." *Journal of Child Psychiatry* 2:82–99.

Cott, Jonathan
1983 "Profiles: Finding Out Is Better." *New Yorker*, April 4, 47–91. [Discussion of the lives and work of Peter and Iona Opie.]

Cottle, Thomas R.
1973a "The Life Study: On Mutual Recognition and the Subjective Inquiry." *Urban Life and Culture* 2:344–60.
1973b "Memories of Half a Life Ago." *Journal of Youth and Adolescence* 2:201–11.

Covenay, P.
1957 *The Image of Childhood*. Baltimore, Md.: Penguin.

Cox, John Harrington
1942 "Singing Games." *Southern Folklore Quarterly* 6:183–261. [An excellent collection of forty games with words and music. Includes references to variants and a description of the games. Collected in West Virginia.]

Crane, T. F.
1917–18 "The External History of the Brothers Grimm." *Modern Philology* 14:129–62; and 15:99–127.

Cranz, Galen
1982 *The Politics of Park Design: A History of Urban Parks in America*. Cambridge: MIT Press.

Cray, Ed
1970 "Jump-Rope Rhymes from Los Angeles." *Western Folklore* 29:119–27.

Cray, Ed and Marilyn E. Herzog
1967 "The Absurd Elephant: A Recent Riddle Fad." *Western Folklore* 26:27–36.

Croswell, T. R.
1899 "Amusements of Worcester School Children." *Pedagogical Seminary* 6:314–71.

Csikszentmihalyi, Mihaly
1975 *Beyond Boredom and Anxiety*. San Francisco: Jossey-Bass.

Csikszentmihalyi, Mihaly, Reed Larson, and Suzanne Prescott
1977 "The Ecology of Adolescent Activity and Experience." *Journal of Youth and Adolescence* 6:281–94.

Csikszentmihalyi, Mihaly and Eugene Rochberg-Halton
1981 *The Meaning of Things: Domestic Symbols and the Self*. Cambridge:

Cambridge University Press.

Culin, Stewart
> 1891 "Street Games of Boys in Brooklyn, N.Y." *Journal of American Folklore* 4:221–37. [Describes 36 games collected from a single 10-year-old boy. Reprinted in Sutton-Smith 1976c.]
> *1895 *Korean Games: With Notes on the Corresponding Games of China and Japan.* Reprinted as *Games of the Orient: Korea, China and Japan.* Tokyo: Charles E. Tuttle, 1958.
> 1898 "American Indian Games." *Bulletin of the Free Museum of Science and Art of the University of Pennsylvania* 3:99–116.
> 1907 *Games of the North American Indians.* Reprint. New York: Dover Publications, 1975.

Curtis, Henry S.
> 1907 "Playground Progress and Tendencies of the Year." *Charities and the Commons* 8:25–29.
> 1913 *The Reorganized School Playground.* Washington, D.C.: Government Printing Office.

Danielson, Larry
> 1976 "The Uses of Folk Literature in the English Classroom." *Illinois English Bulletin* 46:2–14.

Dargan, Amanda and Steven Zeitlin.
> 1990 *City Play.* New Brunswick, N.J.: Rutgers University Press.

Darwin, Charles
> 1852 *Journal of Researches into the Natural History and Geology of the Countries Visited During the Voyage of H.M.S.* Beagle *Round the World.* London: Murray, Albemarle.
> 1859 *On the Origin of Species by Means of Natural Selection or the Preservation of Favored Races in the Struggle for Life.* 2 vols. Reprint. New York: Appleton and Co., 1897.
> 1871 *The Descent of Man and Selection in Relation to Sex.* 2 vols. London: Murray, Albemarle.

Dattner, Richard
> 1974 *Design for Play.* Cambridge: MIT Press.

Davis, B.
> 1982 *Life in the Classroom and Playground.* London: Routledge and Kegan Paul.

Davis, Janet
> 1972 "Teachers, Kids, and Conflict: Ethnography of a Junior High School." In *The Cultural Experience: Ethnography in a Complex Society,* edited by J.P. Spradley and D.W. McCurdy, 114–55. Chicago: SRA.

Decker, H. Max
> 1972 "Local Folklore: An Untapped Resource." *School and Community* 58:23.

Dégh, Linda
> 1968a "The Boyfriend's Death." *Indiana Folklore* 1:101–06.
> 1968b "The Hook." *Indiana Folklore* 1:92–100.

Dégh, Linda, and Andrew Vázsonyi
> 1971 "The Hypothesis of Multi-Conduit Transmission in Folklore." In *Folklore Communication and Performance,* edited by D. Ben-Amos and K. Goldstein, 201–52. The Hague: Mouton.
> 1976 "The Dialectics of the Legend." *Folklore Preprint Series* 1, no. 6 (December): 12–14.

De Koven, Bernard
> 1978 *The Well Played Game.* New York: Anchor.

Delamar, Gloris T.
> 1983 *Children's Counting-Out Rhymes, Fingerplays, Jump-Rope and Bounce-Ball*

Chants and Other Rhymes. Jefferson, N.C.: McFarland.

De Mause, Lloyd

1974   *The History of Childhood.* New York: Psychohistory Press.

Denzin, N.K.

1977   *Childhood Socialization.* San Francisco: Jossey-Bass.

Desmonde, William H.

1951   "Jack and the Beanstalk." *American Imago* 8:287–88. Reprinted in *The Study of Folklore,* edited by A. Dundes, 107–09. Englewood Cliffs, N.J.: Prentice-Hall, 1965.

Dickens, Charles

1965   *Great Expectations.* New York: Macmillan.

Diegner, Edward, and Rick Crandall

1978   *Ethics in Social and Behavioral Research.* Chicago: University of Chicago Press.

Dirks, Martha

1963   "Teen-Age Folklore from Kansas." *Western Folklore* 22:89–102.

Doke, Clement M.

1927   "Lambda Folklore." In *Memoirs of the American Folklore Society, Volume 20.* New York: G.E. Stechert.

Domhoff, G. William

1974   *The Bohemian Grove and Other Retreats: A Study in Ruling-Class Cohesiveness.* New York: Harper and Row.

Domowitz, Susan

1979   "Foreign Matter in Food: A Legend Type." *Indiana Folklore* 12:86–95.

Donzelot, J.

1979   *The Policing of Families.* New York: Pantheon.

Dorson, Richard

1955   "The Eclipse of Solar Mythology." *Journal of American Folklore* 68:393–416.

1968   *The British Folklorists: A History.* Chicago: University of Chicago Press.

1973a   "The Lesson of 'Foxfire.'" *North Carolina Folklore Journal* 21:157–59.

1973b   "Folklore of the Youth Culture." In *America in Legend: Folklore from the Colonial Period to the Present,* 257–59. New York: Pantheon.

Dorson, Richard (ed.)

1972   *Folklore and Folklife.* Chicago: University of Chicago Press.

1983   *Handbook of American Folklore.* Bloomington: Indiana University Press.

Dorson, Richard, and Inta Gale Carpenter

1978   "Can Folklorists and Educators Work Together?" *North Carolina Folklore Journal* 26:3–13.

Douglas, Mary

1966   *Purity and Danger: An Analysis of Concepts of Pollution and Taboo.* London: Routledge and Kegan Paul.

Douglas, Mary, and Baron Isherwood

1979   *The World of Goods: Towards an Anthropology of Consumption.* New York: Norton.

Douglas, Norman

1916   *London Street Games.* Reprint. Detroit: Singing Tree Press, 1968.

Dresser, Norine

1973   "Telephone Pranks." *New York Folklore Quarterly* 29:121–30. [Analysis of functions with examples.]

Dudycha, George J., and Martha M. Dudycha

1941   "Childhood Memories: A Review of the Literature." *Psychological Bulletin* 38:668–82.

Duncan, Margaret Carlisle

1988   "Play Discourse and the Rhetorical Turn: A Semiological Analysis of Homo Ludens." *Play and Culture* 1:28–42.

Dundes, Alan

1962   "Some Examples of Infrequently Reported Autograph Verse." *Southern Folklore Quarterly* 26:127–30.

1964a   *Morphology of North American Indian Folktales.* Folklore Fellows Communications. Helsinki: Suomalainen Tiedeaktemia.

1964b   "On Game Morphology: A Study of the Structure of Non-Verbal Folklore." *New York Folklore Quarterly* 20:276–88.

1965   *The Study of Folklore.* Englewood Cliffs, N.J.: Prentice-Hall. [Brings together several articles that are otherwise difficult to find.]

*1967   "Some Minor Genres of American Folklore." *Southern Folklore Quarterly* 31:20–36. [Brief descriptions with examples of thirteen genres found among children and adolescents, such as "tongue twisters," "evasive answers," and "feigned apologies."]

1969a   "The Devolutionary Premise in Folklore Theory." *Journal of the Folklore Institute* 6:5–19.

1969b   "Folklore as a Mirror of Culture." *Elementary English* 46:471–82.

1971   "On the Psychology of Legend." In *American Folk Legend: A Symposium,* edited by W.D. Hand, 21–36. Berkeley: University of California Press.

1976a   "Projection in Folklore: A Plea for Psychoanalytic Semiotics." Reprinted In *Interpreting Folklore,* edited by A. Dundes, 33–61. Bloomington: Indiana University Press, 1980.

1976b   *Folklore Theses and Dissertations in the United States.* Austin: University of Texas Press.

1978   Foreword to *Children's Humor* by M. Wolfenstein, 6–10. Bloomington: Indiana University Press.

1979   "The Dead Baby Joke Cycle." *Western Folklore* 38:145–57.

1980   *Interpreting Folklore.* Bloomington: Indiana University Press.

1987   *Cracking Jokes: Studies of Sick Humor Cycles and Stereotypes.* Berkeley: Ten Speed Press.

1991   "Bruno Bettelheim's Uses of Enchantment and Misuses of Scholarship." *Journal of American Folklore* 104:74–83.

Dundes, Alan, Jerry W. Leach, and Bora Ozkok

*1970   "The Strategy of Turkish Boys' Verbal Dueling Rhymes." *Journal of American Folklore* 83:325–49.

Duranti, Alessandro, and Charles Goodwin

1992   "Rethinking Context: an Introduction." In *Rethinking Context: Language as an Interactive Phenomenon.,* edited by Duranti and Goodwin, 1–42. Cambridge: Cambridge University Press.

Earle, Alice Morse

1898   *Home Life in Colonial Days.* Reprint. Stockbridge, Mass.: Berkshire Traveler Press, 1974.

Eaton, W.O., and G.L. Clore

1975   "Interracial Imitation at a Summer Camp." *Journal of Personality and Social Psychology* 32:1099–1105.

Eckhardt, Rosalind

1975   "From Handclap to Line Play." In *Black Girls At Play: Perspectives on Child Development,* 57–101. Austin, Tex.: Southwestern Educational Development Laboratory.

Eder, D., and S. Sanford

1986   "The Development and Maintenance of Interactional Norms Among Early Adolescents." *Sociological Studies of Child Development* 1:283–300.

Ehrenzweig, Anton

1965   *The Psychoanalysis of Artistic Vision and Hearing.* New York: Braziller.

Eifermann, Rivka R.

1971   "Social Play in Childhood." In *Child's Play,* edited by E. Herron and Brian

Sutton-Smith, 270–309. New York: Wiley.

1979   "It's Child's Play." In *Games in Education and Development*, edited by L.M. Shears and E.M. Bower 75–102. Springfield, Ill.: Human Kinetics.

Eisenberg, E.M.

1984   "Ambiguity as Strategy in Organizational Communication." *Communication Monographs* 51:227–42.

Eisenstadt, Shmuel Noah

1956   *From Generation to Generation: Age Groups and Social Structure.* Glencoe, Ill.: Free Press.

Elder, Jacob D.

1965   *Song Games from Trinidad and Tobago.* Austin: University of Texas Press.

Eliot, Alexander

1971   "Games Children Play." *Sports Illustrated* 34 (January 11): 46–51, and 55–56.

Elkin, Frederick A., and William A. Westley

1955   "The Myth of Adolescent Culture." *American Sociological Review* 20:680–84.

Ellis, Bill

1981a   "The Camp Mock-Ordeal: Theatre as Life." *Journal of American Folklore* 94:486–505.

1981b   "Majaska: Mythmaking in Greater Cleveland." *Kentucky Folklore Record* 27:76–96.

1982   "'Ralph and Rudy': The Audience's Role in Re-creating a Camp Legend." *Western Folklore* 41:169–91.

Ellis, John

1983   *One Fairy Story Too Many.* Chicago: University of Chicago Press.

Eltgroth, M.B.

1988   "Explore-a-Story: A Brand New View." *Home Office Computing* 6:106.

1989   "KidWriter Golden Edition." *Home Office Computing* 7:85.

Empey, LaMar T., and Steven G. Lubeck

1971   *The Silverlake Experiment: Testing Delinquency Theory and Community Intervention.* Chicago: Aldine.

Emrich, Duncan

1970   *The Nonsense Book of Riddles, Rhymes, Tongue-Twisters, Puzzles and Jokes from American Folklore.* New York: Four Winds.

Emrich, Marion Vallat, and George Korson

*1947   *The Child's Book of Folklore.* New York: Dial. [In contrast to most books for children, this is one of real folklore from and by children.]

Erasmus, Desiderius

1536   *In Praise of Folly.* Princeton, N.J.: Princeton University Press, 1969.

Erikson, Erik H.

1950   *Childhood and Society.* New York: W.W. Norton.

Erickson, Frederick

1990   "Qualitative Methods." In *Quantitative Methods and Qualitative Methods,* edited by Robert L. Linn and Frederick Erickson. Research in Teaching and Learning, vol. 2, American Educational Research University, Institute for Research on Teaching.

Erickson, F., and J. Shultz

1981   "When Is a Context? Some Issues and Methods in the Analysis of Social Competence." In *Ethnography in Educational Settings,* edited by J. Green and C. Wallat, 147–60. Norwood, N.J.: Ablex.

Erickson, F., and J. Wilson

1982   *Sights and Sounds of Life in Schools: A Research Guide to Film and Videotape for Research and Education.* Research Series No. 125. East Lansing: Michigan State University.

Espinosa, Aurelio M.
   1916   "New-Mexican Spanish Folk-Lore. X. Children's Games. XI. Nursery Rhymes and Children's Songs." *Journal of American Folklore* 29:505–35.
Evans, David
   1976   "Riddling and the Structure of Context." *Journal of American Folklore* 89:166–88.
Evans, J.
   1986   "In Search of the Meaning of Play." *New Zealand Journal of Health, Physical Education and Recreation* 19:19.
Evans, Patricia H.
   1961   *Rimbles: A Book of Children's Classic Games, Rhymes, Songs and Sayings*. Garden City, N.Y.: Doubleday. [A collection of jump-rope rhymes, hopscotch variations, counting-out rhymes, and jacks games for parents and children.]
Evening Star
   1925   *City Playgrounds' Benefits Marred by Hoodlum Boys*. Washington, D.C.: August 19, 4–5.
Factor, June
   1980   *Captain Cook Chased a Chook: Children's Folklore in Australia*. Ringwood, Australia: Penguin.
   1988   "A Forgotten Pioneer: Dorothy Howard, American Student of Australian Children's Folklore." *Victorian Educational Magazine,* Australia.
Factor, June, and Gwenda Davey
   1983   "Remembering a Pioneer [Dorothy Howard]." *Australian Children's Folklore Newsletter* 5:1.
Fagen, Robert
   1980   *Animal Play Behavior*. New York: Oxford University Press.
Fait, H. F.
   1964   *Physical Education for the Elementary School Child*. Philadelphia: W.B. Saunders.
Farb, Peter
   1974   *Word Play: What Happens When People Talk*. New York: Alfred Knopf.
Farina, Albert M., Sol H. Furth, and Joseph M. Smith
   1959   *Growth Through Play*. Englewood Cliffs, N.J.: Prentice-Hall.
Farjeon, Eleanor
   1937   *Martin Pippin in the Daisy Field*. Philadelphia: J.B. Lippincott.
Farmer, John
   1968   *The Public-School Word-Book*. Detroit: Gale.
Faulkner, William
   1966   *The Wishing Tree*. New York: Random House.
Feld, B. C.
   1981   "Comparative Analysis of Organizational Structure and Inmate Subcultures in Institutions for Juvenile Offenders." *Crime and Delinquency* 27:336–63.
Ferretti, Fred
   1973   *The Great American Marble Book*. New York: Workman.
   *1975   *The Great American Book of Sidewalk, Stoop, Dirt, Curb, and Alley Games*. New York: Workman.
Fine, Gary Alan
   *1979a   "Folklore Diffusion Through Interactive Social Networks: Conduits in a Preadolescent Community." *New York Folklore* 5:87–126. [Excellent study of the spread of a single legend within a single group of children.]
   1979b   "Small Groups and Culture Creation: The Idioculture of Little League Baseball Teams." *American Sociological Review* 44:733–45.
   1980a   "Cracking Diamonds: Observer Role in Little League Baseball Settings and the Acquisition of Social Competence." In *Fieldwork Experience: Qualitative*

Approaches to Social Research, edited by W.B. Shaffir et al., 117–32. New York: St. Martin's.

*1980b "Children and Their Culture: Exploring Newell's Paradox." *Western Folklore* 39:170–83.

1980c "The Kentucky Fried Rat: Legends and Modern Society." *Journal of the Folklore Institute* 17:222–43.

1980d "Children's Folklore: How It Spreads." *Center for Southern Folklore Magazine* 3:9.

1980e "Childlore, Friendship and Performance." *Southwest Folklore* 4:87–92.

1980f "Preadolescent Slang: Local, Regional and National Speech Patterns Among American Children." *Midwestern Journal of Language and Folklore* 6:5–16.

1981 "Rude Words: Insults and Narration in Preadolescent Obscene Talk." *Maledicta* 5:51–68.

1983 *Shared Fantasy: Role-Playing Games as Social Worlds.* Chicago: University of Chicago Press.

1987 *With the Boys: Little League Baseball and Preadolescent Culture.* Chicago: University of Chicago Press.

1988 "Good Children and Dirty Play." *Play and Culture* 1:43–56.

Fine, Gary Alan, and Barry Glassner

1979 "Participant Observation with Children: Promise and Problems." *Urban Life* 8:153–74.

Fine, Gary Alan, and Bruce Noel Johnson

1980 "The Promiscuous Cheerleader: An Adolescent Male Belief Legend." *Western Folklore* 39:120–29.

Fine, Gary Alan, and Kent L. Sandstrom

1988 *Knowing Children: Participant Observation With Minors.* Newbury Park, Calif.: Sage.

Finnegan, Ruth

1970 *Oral Literature in Africa.* Oxford: Clarendon.

1977 *Oral Poetry: Its Nature, Significance, and Social Context.* Cambridge: Cambridge University Press.

Firth, Raymond

1930 "A Dart Game in Tikopia." *Oceana* 1:64–96.

1967 *Tikopia Ritual and Belief.* Boston: Beacon.

Fischer, Michael M.J.

1986 "Ethnicity and the Post-Modern Arts of Memory." In *Writing Culture: The Poetics and Politics of Ethnography,* edited by James Clifford and George E. Marcus, 194–233. Berkeley: University of California Press.

Fish, Lydia

1972 "The Old Wife in the Dormitory—Sexual Folklore and Magical Practices from State University College." *New York Folklore Quarterly* 28:30–36.

Fitts, Deborah

1979 "Una and the Lion: The Feminization of District School Teaching and its Effects on the Roles of Students and Teachers in Nineteenth-Century Massachusetts." In *Regulated Children/Liberated Children: Education in Psychohistorical Perspective,* edited by B. Finkelstein, 140–57. New York: Psychohistory Press.

Fluegelman, Andrew (ed.)

1976 *The New Games Book.* New York: Dolphin.

Foley, Douglas E.

1990 *Learning Capitalist Culture: Deep in the Heart of Texas.* Philadelphia: University of Pennsylvania Press.

Formanek-Brunell, Miriam

1993 *Made to Play House: Dolls and the Commercialization of American Girl-*

hood. New Haven: Yale University Press.

Fortes, Meyer
- 1967 "Tallensi Riddles." In *To Honor Roman Jakobson: Essays on the Occasion of His Seventieth Birthday*, vol. 1, 678–87. The Hague: Mouton.
- 1968 "On Installation Ceremonies." *Proceedings of the Royal Anthropological Institute*: 5–20.

Foucault, Michel
- 1973 *Madness and Civilization*. New York: Vintage.
- 1987 *Mental Illness and Psychology*. Berkeley: University of California Press.

Fowke, Edith
- 1969 *Sally Go Round the Sun: 300 Songs, Rhymes and Games of Canadian Children*. Toronto: McClelland and Stewart.

Fraser, Amy Stewart
- 1975 *Dae Ye Min' Langsyne? A Pot-pourri of Games, Rhymes, and Ploys of Scottish Childhood*. London: Routledge and Kegan Paul.

French, Florence Healy
- 1975 "Olley, Olley Oxen Free: America's Contribution to Hide and Seek." *New York Folklore* 1:161–68.

Friedberg, M. Paul
- 1970 *Play and Interplay: A Manifesto for New Design in Urban Recreational Environment*. New York: Macmillan.

Friedenberg, Edgar Z.
- 1963 *Coming of Age in America: Growth and Acquiesence*. New York: Vintage.

Friedl, John
- 1981 *The Human Portrait: Introduction to Cultural Anthropology*. Englewood Cliffs, N.J.: Prentice-Hall.

Frost, Joe L., and Barry L. Klein
- 1979 *Children's Play and Playgrounds*. Boston: Allyn and Bacon.

Frye, Ellen
- 1973 "Children's Rhythm Games from New York City." *Western Folklore* 32:54–56.

Fuller, Wayne E.
- 1982 *The Old Country School: The Story of Rural Education in the Middle West*. Chicago: University of Chicago Press.

Gadamer, H. G.
- 1982 *Truth and Method*. New York: Crossroad.

Gaidoz, Henri
- 1984 "Folklore in the United States." *Folklore Historian* 1:3. Special Supplement: Reprint Series of Classic Articles in the History of Folkloristics, No. 1. Translated by C. Oliver. [First published in French in *Melusine* 2 (1885).]

Gaignebet, Claude
- *1974 *Le Folklore Obscene des Enfants*. Paris: G.-P. Maisonneuve et Larose.

Galvin, Sean
- 1990 "Collecting Children's Folklore." In *The Emergence of Folklore in Everyday Life*, edited by George H. Shoemaker, 165–70. Indiana: Trickster.

Ganim, Mary
- 1970 "A Study of Children's Folklore." *New York Folklore Quarterly* 26:50–63.

Gardner, Emelyn E.
- 1918 "Some Counting Out Rhymes in Michigan." *Journal of American Folklore* 31:521–36.

Gardner, Howard
- 1972 "Style Sensitivity in Children." *Human Development* 15:325–38.
- 1974 "Metaphors and Modalities: How Children Project Polar Adjectives onto Diverse Domains." *Child Development* 45:84–91.

Gardner, Richard A.

1971 *Therapeutic Communication with Children: The Mutual Storytelling Technique*. New York: Science House.

Garfinkel, Harold
1967 *Studies in Ethnomethodology*. Englewood Cliffs, N.J.: Prentice-Hall.

Garrenton, Valerie
1973 "Children's Games." *North Carolina Folklore Journal* 21:27–31. [Field collected from a fourth-grade class.]

Garvey, Catherine
1977 *Play*. Cambridge, Mass.: Harvard University Press.

Gastner, Sanford
1991 "Urban Children's Access to their Neighborhood: Changes Over Three Generations." *Environment and Behavior* 23:70–85.
1992 "Historical Changes in Children's Access to U.S. Cities: A Critical Review." *Children's Environments* 9:23–36.

Geer, Blanche
1970 "Studying a College." In *Pathways to Data*, edited by R.W. Habenstein, 81–98. Chicago: Aldine.

Geertz, Clifford
1973 *The Interpretation of Cultures*. New York: Basic Books.
1983 "Blurred Genres: The Refiguration of Social Thought." In *Local Knowledge: Further Essays in Interpretative Anthropology*, 1–35. New York: Basic Books.

Gelman, Susan
1978 "Toward the Study of Postal Graffiti: Text and Context in an Adolescent Girls' Genre." *Western Folklore* 37:102–18.

Georges, Robert A.
1969 "The Relevance of Models for Analyses of Traditional Play Activities." *Southern Folklore Quarterly* 33:1–23.
1972 "Recreations and Games." In *Folklore and Folklife*, edited by R.M. Dorson, 173–89. Chicago: University of Chicago Press.

Georges, Robert A., and Alan Dundes
1963 "Toward a Structural Definition of the Riddle." *Journal of American Folklore* 76:111–18.

Gergen, Kenneth J.
1982 *Toward Transformation in Social Knowledge*. New York: Springer-Verlag.

Giallombardo, Rose
1974 *The Social World of Imprisoned Girls: A Comparative Study of Institutions for Juvenile Delinquents*. New York: John Wiley and Sons.

Gill, Owen
1974 "Residential Treatment for Young Offenders: The Boys' Perspectives." *British Journal of Criminology* 14:318–35.

Gillespie, Angus K.
1970 "Comments on Teaching and Collecting Folklore." *Keystone Folklore Quarterly* 15:59–73.

Gilligan, Carol
1982 *In a Different Voice: Psychological Theory and Women's Development*. Cambridge: Harvard University Press.

Gilligan, Carol, N.P. Lyons, and T.J. Hanmer (eds.)
1990 *Making Connections: The Relational World of Adolescent Girls at Emma Willard School*. Cambridge: Harvard University Press.

Glass, Bentley (ed.)
1968 *Forerunners of Darwin, 1745–1869*. Baltimore: Johns Hopkins Press.

Glassie, Henry
1968 *Pattern in the Material Folk Culture of the Eastern United States*. Philadelphia: University of Pennsylvania Press.

1972 "Folk Art." In *Folklore and Folklife: An Introduction*, edited by R.M. Dorson, 253–80. Chicago: University of Chicago Press.

1982 *Passing the Time in Ballymenone*. Philadelphia: University of Pennsylvania Press.

Glassner, Barry

1976 "Kid Society." *Urban Education* 11:5–22.

Glazer, Mark (ed.)

1982 *Flour from Another Sack and Other Proverbs, Folk Beliefs, Tales, Riddles and Recipes*. Edinburg, Tex.: Pan American University.

Gluckman, Max

1962 "Les Rites de Passage." In *Essays on the Rituals of Social Relations*, edited by M. Gluckman, 1–52. Manchester: Manchester University Press.

Goffman, Erving

1956 "Embarrassment and Social Organization." *American Journal of Sociology* 62:264–71.

1959 *The Presentation of Self in Everyday Life*. New York: Doubleday.

1961a *Asylums: Essays on the Social Situation of Mental Patients and Other Inmates*. Garden City, N.Y.: Anchor-Doubleday.

1961b *Encounters*. Indianapolis, Ind.: Bobbs-Merrill.

1963 *Behavior in Public Places*. New York: Free Press.

1967 *Interaction Ritual*. Garden City, N.Y.: Doubleday Anchor.

1974 *Frame Analysis*. New York: Harper and Row.

1981 *Forms of Talk*. Philadelphia: University of Pennsylvania Press.

Golding, William

1954 *Lord of the Flies*. Reprint. New York: Coward-McCann, 1962.

Goldstein, Kenneth

1963 "Riddling Traditions in Northeastern Scotland." *Journal of American Folklore* 76:330–35.

1964 *A Guide for Field Workers in Folklore*. Hatboro, Pa.: Folklore Associates.

1967a "Experimental Folklore: Laboratory vs. Field." In *Folklore International*, edited by D.K. Wilgus, 71–82. Hatboro, Pa.: Folklore Associates.

1967b "The Induced Natural Context: An Ethnographic Field Technique." In *Essays in the Verbal and Visual Arts*, edited by J. Helm, 1–6. Seattle: University of Washington Press.

*1971 "Strategy in Counting-Out: An Ethnographic Folklore Field Study." In *The Study of Games*, edited by E. Avedon and B. Sutton-Smith, 167–78. New York: John Wiley.

1975 "The Telling of Non-Traditional Tales to Children: An Ethnographic Report from a Northwest Philadelphia Neighborhood." *Keystone Folklore* 20 (no. 3): 5–17.

Gomme, Alice B.

*1894–98 *The Traditional Games of England, Scotland, and Ireland*. 2 vols. Reprint. New York: Dover Spectacular Victorian Scholarship, 1964. [Description and comparisons of games from throughout the British Isles. Emphasis on singing games.]

1900 *Old English Singing Games*. London: David Nutt.

Gomme, Alice B., and Cecil J. Sharp (eds.)

1909–12 *Children's Singing Games*. Reprint. New York: Arno, 1976. [Words, music and detailed descriptions of thirty traditional games for use by educators.]

Gomme, Laurence, and Alice B. Gomme

1916 *British Folklore, Folk-Songs, and Singing Games*. London: David Nutt.

Goodman, Gary

1979 *Choosing Sides: Playground and Street Life on the Lower East Side*. New York: Schocken.

Goodman, Mary Ellen

1970   *The Culture of Childhood: Child's Eye-View of Society and Culture.* New York: Columbia University Press.

Goodwin, Marjorie H.
1985   "The Serious Side of Jump Rope: Conversational Practices and Social Organization in the Frame of Play." *Journal of American Folklore* 98: 315–30.
1990   *He-said-she-said: Talk as Social Organization among Black Children.* Bloomington: Indiana University Press.

Goodwin, M. H., and C. Goodwin
1983   "Children's Arguing." Paper presented to Conference on Sex Differences in Language, Tucson, Ariz., January.

Gordon, William A.
1917   "Recollections of a Boyhood in Georgetown." *Records of the Columbia Historical Society of Washington, D.C.* 20:121–40.

Gossen, Gary
1974   *Chamulas in the World of the Sun: Time and Space in a Maya Oral Tradition.* Cambridge: Harvard University Press.

Graff, Harvey J. (ed.)
1987   *Growing Up in America: Historical Experiences.* Detroit: Wayne State University Press.

Grahame, Kenneth
1895   *The Golden Age.* New York: Dodd, Mead and Co., 1925.
1908   *The Wind in the Willows.* Golden Anniversary Edition. New York: Charles Scribner's Sons, 1961.

Graves, Donald
1983   *Writing: Teachers and Children at Work.* Exeter, N.H.: Heinemann.

Green, Thomas A.
1978   "Toward a Definition of Folk Drama." *Journal of American Folklore* 91:843–50.

Green, Thomas A., and W. J. Pepicello
1978   *Wit in Riddling: A Linguistic Perspective. Genre* 11:1–13.
1979   "The Folk Riddle: A Redefinition of Terms." *Western Folklore* 38:3–20.
1980   "Sight and Spelling Riddles." *Journal of American Folklore* 93: 23–24.

Greenaway, Kate
1889   *Kate Greenaway's Book of Games.* New York: Viking, 1976.

Greenberg, Andrea
1973   "Drugged and Seduced: A Contemporary Legend." *New York Folklore Quarterly* 29:121–58.

Greene, T. M.
1984   "Ceremonial Play and Parody in Renaissance Literature." Paper presented at conference on the Forms of Play in the Early Modern Period, University of Maryland.

Gregor, Walter
1891   *Counting-Out Rhymes of Children.* Reprint. Darby, Pa.: Norwood Editions, 1973.

Grider, Sylvia Ann
1973   "Dormitory Legend-Telling In-Progress: Fall, 1971–Winter, 1973." *Indiana Folklore* 6:1–31.
1975   "Con Safos: Mexican-Americans, Names and Graffiti." *Journal of American Folklore* 88:132–42.
1976   "The Supernatural Narratives of Children." Ph.D. dissertation, Indiana University.
1980a   "The Study of Children's Folklore." *Western Folklore* 39:159–69.
1980b   "A Select Bibliography of Childlore." *Western Folklore* 39:248–65. [Survey of the English-language literature. Includes many obscure items. Halpert

1982 is a supplement for European materials.]

1981   "The Media Narraform: Symbiosis of Mass Media and Oral Tradition." *Arv: Scandinavian Yearbook of Folklore* 37:125–31.

Grider, Sylvia Ann (ed.)

*1980   "Children's Folklore." *Western Folklore* 39:159–265. [A special issue including several excellent articles.]

Grimshaw, A.

1980   "Mishearings, Misunderstandings, and Other Non-successes In Talk: A Plea for Redress of Speaker-oriented Bias." *Sociological Inquiry* 50:31–74.

Gruneau, R.S.

1980   "Freedom and Constraint: The Paradoxes of Play, Games and Sports." *Journal of Sport History* 7:68–85.

1983   *Class, Sports, and Social Development*. Amherst: University of Massachusetts Press.

Gulliford, Andrew

1984   *America's Country Schools*. Washington, D.C.: The Preservation.

1992   "Fox and Geese in the School Yard: Play and America's Country Schools, 1840-1940." In *Hard at Play: Leisure in America, 1840-1940*, edited by Kathryn Grover, 188-209. Amherst: The University of Massachusetts Press.

Gump, Paul V.

1975   "Ecological Psychology and Children." In *Review of Child Development Research*, vol. 5, edited by E.M. Hetherington, 75–126. Chicago: University of Chicago Press.

Gump, Paul V., and Brian Sutton-Smith

*1955   "The 'It' Role in Children's Games." [Reprinted in Avedon and Sutton-Smith 1979, 390–97 and in Sutton-Smith 1972a, 433–41.]

Gump, Paul V., Brian Sutton-Smith, and Fritz Redl

1955   *Influence of Camp Activities Upon Camper Behavior*. Detroit: Wayne State University.

Gumperz, John J., and Dell Hymes (eds.)

1972   *Directions in Sociolinguistics: The Ethnography of Communication*. New York: Holt, Rinehart and Winston.

Guthrie, Woody

1943   *Bound for Glory*. New York: Dutton.

Hagstrom, W.O.

1966   "What Is the Meaning of Santa Claus?" *American Sociologist* 1:248–52.

Hale, Edward Everett

1883   *A New England Boyhood*. Boston: Cassell.

Haley, Gail E.

1970   *A Story, A Story: An African Tale*. New York: Atheneum.

Hall, David J.

1977   *Social Relations and Innovation: Changing the State of Play In Hospitals*. London: Routledge and Kegan Paul.

Hall, Edward T.

1977   *Beyond Culture*. Garden City, N.Y.: Doubleday.

Hall, Gary

1973   "The Big Tunnel: Legends and Legend-Telling." *Indiana Folklore* 6:139–73.

Halliwell, James

1842   *The Nursery Rhymes of England*. London: Percy Society.

Halpert, Herbert

*1982   "Childlore Bibliography: A Supplement." *Western Folklore* 41:205–28. [Expands Grider 1980 with excellent annotations as well. Covers Europe well, with some references to the rest of the world.]

Handelman, Don

1977   "Play and Ritual: Complementary Frames of Meta-Communication." In *It's*

a Funny Thing, Humour, edited by A.J. Chapman and H.C. Foot, 185–92. Oxford: Pergamon.
1980   "Re-thinking Naven: Play and Identity." In *Play and Culture,* edited by H.B. Schwartzman, 58–70. West Point, N.Y.: Leisure.
Hannerz, Ulf
1969   *Soulside.* New York: Columbia University Press.
Hansen, Marian
1948   "Children's Rhymes Accompanied by Gestures." *Western Folklore* 7:50–53.
Harder, Kelsie
1957   "The Preacher's Seat." *Tennessee Folklore Society Bulletin* 23:381–39. [Description of a prank from the 1930s.]
Haring, Lee.
1985   "Malagasy Riddling." *Journal of American Folklore* 98:163–90.
Haring, Lee, and Mark Breslerman
1977   "The Cropsey Maniac." *New York Folklore* 3:15–28.
Harre, Romano
1977   *Rules In the Explanation of Social Behavior.* Totowa, N.J.: Littlefield, Adams.
Harre, Romano, and Paul F. Secord
1972   *The Explanation of Social Behavior.* Totowa, N.J.: Littlefield, Adams.
Harries, Lyndon
1971   "The Riddle In Africa." *Journal of American Folklore* 84:377–93.
Harris, Trudier
1978   "Telephone Pranks: A Thriving Pastime." *Journal of Popular Culture* 12:138–45.
Hart, Craig H.
1993   "Toward a Further Understanding of Children on Playgrounds." In *Children on Playgrounds: Research Perspectives and Applications,* edited by Craig H. Hart, 1–28. Albany N.Y.: SUNY Press.
Hart, Donn V.
1964   *Riddles In Filipino Folklore: An Anthropological Analysis.* Syracuse, N.Y.: Syracuse University Press.
Hart, Roger
1979   *Children's Experience of Place.* New York: Irvington.
Haut, Judith
1992   "I Want to Call It 'Cactus Arachnophobia': One Young Child's Use and Understanding of Narrating." *Children's Folklore Review* 15:1:33–45.
Hawes, Bess Lomax
1968   "'La Llorona' In Juvenile Hall." *Western Folklore* 27:153–69.
1974   "Folksongs and Functions: Some Thoughts on the American Lullaby." *Journal of American Folklore* 87:140–48.
Hawkins, Roberta
1971   "Nursery Rhymes: Mirrors of Culture." *Elementary English* 48:617–21.
Hawthorne, Ruth
1966   "Classifying Jump-Rope Games." *Keystone Folklore Quarterly* 11:113–26. [Types of games and a sampling of the rhymes that go with them.]
Hayward, D. Geoffrey, Marilyn Rothenberg, and Robert R. Beasley
1974   "Children's Play and Urban Playground Environments: A Comparison of Traditional, Contemporary, and Adventure Playground Types." *Environment and Behavior* 6:131–68.
Hearne, Betsy
1989   *"Beauty and the Beast": Visions and Revisions of an Old Tale.* Chicago: University of Chicago Press.
Hebdige, Dick
1979   *Subculture: The Meaning of Style.* London: Methuen.

Heck, Jean Olive

*1927　"Folk Poetry and Folk Criticism: as Illustrated by Cincinnati Children in their Singing Games and in Their Thoughts about These Games." *Journal of American Folklore* 40:1–77. [Magnificent early work on children's attitudes toward their folklore. One hundred and three field-collected items with an analysis of children's comments about them.]

Heininger, Mary Lynn Stevens (ed.)

1984　*A Century of Childhood, 1820–1920.* Rochester, N.Y.: Margaret Woodbury Strong Museum.

Hellendorn, Joop, Rimmert van der Kooij, and Brian Sutton-Smith

1994　*Play and Intervention.* Albany, N.Y.: State University of New York Press.

Herron, Robert E., and Brian Sutton-Smith (eds.)

1971　*Child's Play: Collected Readings on the Biology, Ecology, Psychology and Sociology of Play.* New York: John Wiley.

Hewitt, Karen, and Louise Roomet (eds.)

1979　*Educational Toys In America: 1800 to the Present.* Burlington, Vt.: Robert Hall Fleming Museum, University of Vermont.

Hickerson, Joseph, and Alan Dundes

1962　"Mother Goose Vice Verse." *Journal of American Folklore* 75:249–59.

Hilger, Sister M. Inez

1951　*Chippewa Child Life and Its Cultural Background.* Washington, D.C.: Smithsonian Institution, Bureau of American Ethnology, Bulletin 146.

1966　*Field Guide to the Ethnological Study of Child Life. Behavior Science Field Guides,* vol. l. New Haven, Conn.: Human Relations Area Files.

Hiner, N. Ray

1978　"The Child In American Historiography: Accomplishments and Prospects." *Psychohistory Review* 7:13–23.

Hirschberg, L.R.

1913　"Dog Latin and Sparrow Languages Used by Baltimore Children." *Pedagogical Seminary* 20:257–58.

Hobsbawm, Eric, and Terence Ranger (eds.)

1983　*The Invention of Tradition.* Cambridge: Cambridge University Press.

Hodgen, Margaret

1936　*The Doctrine of Survivals.* London: Allenson and Co.

Hoffman, Dan G.

1950　"Lemonade: A Children's Game from New York City." *New York Folklore Quarterly* 6:2:95–97. [On a tag/charade game in a tenement area.]

Hogan, Paul

1974　*Playgrounds for Free.* Cambridge: Massachusetts Institute of Technology.

Holbrook, David

1957　*Children's Games.* London: Gordon, Frazer.

Hollingshead, August B.

1975　*Elmtown's Youth and Elmtown Revisited.* New York: Wiley.

Hollis, A.C.

1909　*The Nandi: Their Language and Folklore.* Oxford: Clarendon.

Horan, Robert

1984　"'Giving and Giving It Up': the Social and Emotional Economics of Male Adolescents at Boys' Home." Unpublished paper read at the meeting of the American Folklore Society in San Diego, Calif.

1988　"The Semiotics of Play Fighting at a Residential Treatment Center." In *Adolescent Psychiatry,* vol.15, edited by Sherman C. Feinstein, 367–84.

Howard, Dorothy Mills

1937　"Onward and Upward with the Arts: Songs of Innocence." *New Yorker,* November, 37.

1938　"Folk Jingles of American Children: A Collection of Rhymes Used by Children Today." Ed.D. dissertation, New York University.

1949　"The Rhythms of Ball-Bouncing and Ball-Bouncing Rhymes." *Journal of American Folklore* 62:166–72.

1950　"Folklore in the Schools." *New York Folklore Quarterly* 6:99–107.

1958　"Australian 'Hoppy' (Hopscotch)." *Western Folklore* 17:163–75. [Field collection of many variants with diagrams of twenty-five.]

1959　"Ball Bouncing Customs and Rhymes In Australia." *Midwest Folklore* 9:77–87. [Field collection. Reprinted in Sutton-Smith 1976c.]

1960　"Marble Games of Australian Children." *Folklore* 71:165–79. [Reprinted in Avedon and Sutton-Smith 1971 and in Sutton-Smith 1976c.]

1964　Introduction to *The Traditional Games of England, Scotland, and Ireland*, by Alice Bertha Gomme. Reprinted, New York, Dover Publications.

1965　Folklore of Australian Children. *Keystone Folklore Quarterly* 10:99–115.

*1977　*Dorothy's World: Childhood in Sabine Bottom, 1902–1910*. Englewood Cliffs, N.J.: Prentice-Hall. [Autobiography of the childhood of one of the prominent children's folklorists.]

Howard, Dorothy Mills (consultant)

1968　*Folklore In the Elementary Schools*. Lincoln: University of Nebraska/Tri-University Project In Elementary Education.

Howell, Richard

1976　*Language in Behavior*. New York: Human Sciences Press, 1985.

Howells, William Dean

1890　*A Boy's Town*. New York: Harper and Brothers.

Hufford, David J.

1970a　Editor's preface in Hufford 1970b, 55–58.

1970b　"Teaching and Collecting Folklore at a Boys' Prep School: Field Work Examples from 'The Academy'—Pennsylvania." *Keystone Folklore Quarterly* 15:55–113. [A special issue with six articles on fieldwork studying boys at a single private schoool. Covers such topics as fieldwork methods, nicknames for teachers, and dirty jokes. Compare with Johnson 1884 for early work in a similar institution.]

Hughes, Gladys F.

1951　"Rhymes Sung by Japanese Children." *Western Folklore* 10:34–54.

Hughes, Linda A.

1983　"Beyond the Rules of the Game: Girls' Gaming at a Friends' School." Ph.D. dissertation, University of Pennsylvania.

1988　"But That's Not *Really* Mean": Competing in a Cooperative Mode. *Sex Roles* 9:669–87.

1989　"Foursquare: A Glossary and 'Native' Taxonomy of Game Rules." *Play and Culture* 2:102–36.

1991　"A Conceptual Framework for the Study of Children's Gaming." *Play and Culture* 4:3:284–301.

1993　"'You Have to Do It with Style': Girls' Games and Girls' Gaming." In *Feminist Theory and the Study of Folklore*, edited by T. Hollis, L. Pershing, and M.J. Young, 130–48. Urbana: University of Illinois Press.

Huizinga, Johann

1950　*Homo Ludens: A Study of the Play Element In Culture*. Reprint. Boston: Beacon Hill, 1955.

Hullum, Jan

1972–3　"The 'Catch' Riddle: Perspectives from Goffman and Metafolklore." *Folklore Annual* 4–5:52–59.

Humphreys, Humphrey

1948　"Jack and the Beanstalk." Reprinted in *The Study of Folklore*, edited by A. Dundes, 103–6. Englewood Cliffs, N.J.: Prentice-Hall, 1965.

Hurvitz, Nathan

1954   "Jews and Jewishness In the Street Rhymes of American Children." *Jewish Social Studies* 16:135–50.

Hutchinson, Ann.

1977   *Labanotation: A System of Analyzing and Recording Movement.* New York: Theatre Arts.

Hymes, Dell

1969   *Reinventing Anthropology.* New York:Vintage Books.

1971   "On Linguistic Theory, Communicative Competence, and the Education of Disadvantaged Children." In *Anthropological Perspectives on Education,* edited by M.L Wax, S. Diamond, and F.O. Gearing. New York: Basic Books.

1980   Foreword in *Communication Rules: Theory and Research,* edited by S.B. Shimanoff, 9–27. Beverly Hills, Calif.: Sage.

Ingham, Curtis, and Harriet Lyons

1975   "The Sporting Life: Learning the Ropes." *Ms. Magazine,* October, 26–27. [On double dutch and its transformation in tournaments in Harlem.]

Ives, Edward D.

1974   "A Manual for Field Workers." *Northeast Folklore* 15:1–76.

Jablow, Alta, and Carl Withers

1965   "Social Sense and Verbal Nonsense In Urban Children's Folklore." *New York Folklore Quarterly* 21:243–57. [An analysis of materials collected through a questionnaire.]

Jackson, Bruce

1965   "Prison Folklore." *Journal of American Folklore* 78:317–29.

1967   *The Negro and His Folklore In Nineteenth Century Periodicals.* Austin: University of Texas Press.

Jansen, William Hugh

1968   "Riddles: 'Do-It-Yourself Oracles.'" In *Our Living Traditions,* edited by T.P. Coffin, 204–27. New York: Basic Books.

Jayne, Caroline Furness

1906   *String Figures and How to Make Them: A Study of Cat's Cradle In Many Lands.* Reprint. New York: Dover, 1962. [A classic study of the genre with 867 diagrams.]

Jerome, Katie

1975   "Three Generations of Tag." *North Carolina Folklore Journal* 23:101–4. [A first-rate student term paper on tag as played by three generations of her own family.]

Jetté, Father Julius

1913   "Riddles of the Ten'a Indians." *Anthropos* 8:181–201.

Johnson, Guy B.

1930   *Folk Culture on St. Helena Island, South Carolina.* Chapel Hill: University of North Carolina Press.

Johnson, John, Jr.

1884   "Rudimentary Society Among Boys." *Johns Hopkins University Studies In Historical and Political Science* 2 (November): 1–56. [Pioneer work on children's lore in an institutional setting.]

Johnson, Kinchen

1971   "Folksongs and Children Songs from Peiping." *Asian Folklore and Social Life Monographs* Nos. 16 and 17. Taipei: Orient Cultural Service.

Johnson, Marguerite Wilker

1935   "The Effect on Behavior of Variation in the Amount of Playground Equipment." *Child Development* 6:56–68.

Johnson, Robert

1978   "Youth in Crisis: Dimensions of Self-Destructive Conduct Among Adolescent Prisoners." *Adolescence* 13:461–82.

Johnson, Thomas F.
  1973   "Tsonga Children's Folksongs." *Journal of American Folklore* 86:225–40.
Johnson, Thomas W.
  1975   *Shonendan: Adolescent Peer Group Socialization in Rural Japan. Asian Folklore and Social Life Monographs* No. 68. Taipei: Orient Cultural Service. [Strongest on games and nonverbal materials. Bibliography of Japanese-language sources.]
Jones, Bessie, and Bess Lomax Hawes
  1972   *Step It Down: Games, Plays, Songs, and Stories from the Afro-American Heritage.* New York: Harper and Row.
Jones, Michael Owen
  1966   "Chinese Jump Rope." *Southern Folklore Quarterly* 30:256–63. [Excellent description (with diagrams) of game as collected from a fifth-grade class in Wichita, Kansas.]
  1980   "G.I. Joe and the Germs: Conceptualizing Form." Paper presented at California Folklore Society, Berkeley.
Jones, Nicholas G. Blurton (ed.)
  1972   *Ethological Studies of Child Behavior.* Cambridge: Cambridge University Press. [Natural scientists' view of children.]
Jordan, David K.
  1973   "Anti-American Children's Verses from Taiwan." *Western Folklore* 32: 205–09.
Jorgensen, Marilyn
  1978   "A Teacher's Handbook for the Study of Games." *Newsletter of the Association for the Anthropological Study of Play* 5 (February): 9–17.
  1980   "An Analysis of Boy-Girl Relationships Portrayed in Contemporary Jump Rope and Handclapping Rhymes." *Southwest Folklore* 4:63–71.
  1982   "A Comparison of U.S. and British Children's Play Rhymes." *London Lore* 1 (September): 111–14.
 *1984   "A Social-Interactional Analysis of Phone Pranks." *Western Folklore* 43:104–16. [First annual W.W. Newell Prize paper in children's folklore.]
Jusczyk, Peter W.
  1975   "Rhymes and Reasons: The Child's Appreciation of Aspects of Poetic Form." Ph.D. dissertation, University of Pennsylvania.
Juska, Jane
  1985   "Levitation, Jokes and Spin the Bottle: Contemporary Folklore in the Classroom—A Teacher's View." *English Journal* 74:37–38.
Juvie
  1976   A film by Paulist Productions. Color, 16 mm, twenty-seven minutes.
Kane, Alice
  1983   *Songs and Sayings of an Ulster Childhood.*, edited by E. Fowke. Toronto: McClelland and Stewart.
Keesing, Felix M.
  1960   "Recreative Behavior and Culture Change." In *Men and Cultures*, edited by A.F.C. Wallace, 130–33. Philadelphia: University of Pennsylvania Press.
Keesing, Roger M.
  1992   *Custom and Confrontation: The Kwaio Struggle for Cultural Autonomy.* Chicago and London: University of Chicago Press.
Kellogg, Rhoda
  1969   *Analyzing Children's Art.* Palo Alto, Calif.: National Press.
Kelman, Herbert
  1968   *A Time to Speak: On Human Values and Social Research.* San Francisco: Jossey-Bass.
Kelsey, N.G.N.
  1981   "When They Were Young Girls: A Singing Game Through the Century."

Folklore 92:104–9. [Study of a singing game collected by both Gomme and Newell at the end of the nineteenth century to show both its stability and its variation to the present day. Excellent historical survey using field-collected material.]

Kendon, Adam
  1979   "Some Theoretical and Methodological Aspects of the Use of Film in the Study of Social Interaction." In *Emerging Strategies of Social Psychological Research*, edited by G.P. Ginsburg, 67–91. New York: Wiley.
  1981   *Nonverbal Communication, Interaction, and Gesture: Selections from Semiotica*. The Hague: Mouton.
  1990   "Some Context for Context Analysis: A View of the Origins of Structural Studies of Face-to-Face Interaction." In *Conducting Interaction: Patterns of Behavior In Focussed Encounters*, 15–49. Cambridge: Cambridge University Press.

Kenny, Maureen
  1975   *Circle Round the Zero: Play Chants and Singing Games of City Children*. St. Louis, Mo.: Magnamusic-Baton.

Kernan, Keith T., and Claudia Mitchell-Kernan
  1975   "Children's Insults: America and Samoa." In *Sociocultural Dimensions of Language Use*, edited by M. Sanches and B. Blount, 307–15. New York: Academic Press.

Kett, Joseph F.
  1977   *Rites of Passage: Adolescence in America, 1790 to the Present*. New York: Basic Books.

Kirkton, C. M.
  1971   "Once Upon a Time . . . Folk Tales and Storytelling." *Elementary English* 48:1024–32.

Kirkwood, James
  1968   *Good Times, Bad Times*. New York: Simon and Schuster.

Kirschenblatt-Gimblett, Barbara
  1976a   "Bibliographic Survey of the Literature on Speech Play and Related Subjects." In 1976b, 179–284.
  1976b   *Speech Play: Research and Resources for Studying Linguistic Creativity*. Philadelphia: University of Pennsylvania Press.
  1978   "Introduction." *Keystone Folklore Quarterly* 1–2:15–20.
  1983   "The Future of Folklore Studies in America: The Urban Frontier." *Folklore Forum* 16:175–234.

Kittredge, George Lyman, and Helen Sargent (eds.)
  1904   *English and Scottish Popular Ballads*. Boston: Houghton Mifflin.

Klintberg, Bengt af
  1980   "Mexicans and Giraffes: Droodles Among Swedish School Children." In *Folklore on Two Continents: Essays in Honor of Linda Dégh*, edited by N. Burlakoff and C. Lindhal, 187–201. Bloomington, Ind.: Trickster.

Knapp, Mary, and Herbert Knapp
  1973   "Tradition and Change in American Playground Language." *Journal of American Folklore* 86:131–41.
  1975   Childlore: Locking a Game. *Western Folklore* 34:55–57.
  *1976   *One Potato, Two Potato: The Secret Education of American Children*. (The MSO *Folklore of American Children*). New York: W.W. Norton.

Knowles, John
  1959   *A Separate Peace*. New York: Bantam.

Kochman, Thomas
  1972   *Rappin' and Stylin' Out: Communication in Urban Black America*. Urbana: University of Illinois Press.

Kohl, Herbert
  1972   *Golden Boy as Anthony Cool*. New York: Dial.

Kohlberg, Lawrence
1966 "A Cognitive-developmental Analysis of Children's Sex-role Concepts and Attitudes." In *The Development of Sex Differences*, edited by E.E. Maccoby, 82–173. Stanford, Calif.: Stanford University Press.

Konopka, Gisela
1966 *The Adolescent Girl in Conflict*. Englewood Cliffs, N.J.: Prentice-Hall.

Kooij, Rimmert van der, and Roel de Groot
1977 *That's All in the Game: Theory and Research, Practice and Future of Children's Play*. Rheinstetten, Germany: G. Schindele Verlag. [Fine history and summary of the educational view of play in Europe, sponsored by the International Council for Children's Play.]

Korkiakangas, Pirjo
1992 "The Games Children May Not Play: Improper, Prophetic or Dangerous." *Ethnologia Scandinavica: A Journal for Nordic Ethnology* 22:95–104.

Koss, Deborah
1975 "A Collection of Interviews About a Porter County Ghost Hunt." *Indiana Folklore* 8:99–125.

Kotkin, Amy J., and Holly C. Baker
1977 "Family Folklore." *Childhood Education* 53:137–42.

Krell, Roberta
1980 "At a Children's Hospital: A Folklore Survey." *Western Folklore* 39:223–31.

Kris, Ernst
1962 *Psychoanalytic Explorations in Art*. New York: International University Press.

Krohn, Kaarle
1971 *Folklore Methodology*. Translated by R. Welsch. Austin: University of Texas Press. [Originally published in 1926.]

Krueger, John R.
1968 "Parodies in the Folklore of a Third Grader." *Southern Folklore Quarterly* 32:66–68. [Nice collection from a single eight-year-old boy.]

Kurelek, William
1973 *A Prairie Boy's Winter*. Boston: Houghton Mifflin.
1975 *A Prairie Boy's Summer*. Montreal: Tundra.

Kurlansky, Mervyn, John Naar, and Norman Mailer
1974 *The Faith of Graffiti*. New York: Praeger.

Lakoff, George, and Mark Johnson
1980 *Metaphors We Live By*. Chicago: University of Chicago Press.

Lambert, Royston, with Spencer Millham
1968 *The Hothouse Society: An Exploration of Boarding-School Life Through the Boys' and Girls' Own Writings*. Middlesex: Penguin.

Lancy, David F.
1980 "Play In Species Adaptation." *Annual Review of Anthropology* 5:471–95. [Survey of the literature on nonhuman species.]

Lancy, David F., and B. Allan Tindall (eds.)
*1976 *The Anthropological Study of Play: Problems and Prospects*. Cornwall, N.Y.: Leisure. [Proceedings of the 1975 annual meeting of the Association for the Anthropological Study of Play. First in what has become an annual series of excellent volumes.]

Langstaff, John, and Carol Langstaff
1973 *Shimmy Shimmy Coka-Ca Pop: A Collection of City Children's Street Games and Rhymes*. Garden City, N.Y.: Doubleday.

Lanham, Betty B., and Masao Shimura
1967 "Folktales Commonly Told American and Japanese Children." *Journal of American Folklore* 60:33–48.

Larcom, Lucy

1889   *A New England Girlhood.* Boston: Houghton Mifflin.
Laubach, David
    1980   *Introduction to Folklore.* Rochelle Park, N.J.: Hayden.
Leach, Maria (ed.)
    1949   *The Standard Dictionary of Folklore, Mythology and Legend.* New York:
            Funk and Wagnalls.
Leary, James P.
    1973   "The Boondocks Monster of Camp Wapehani." *Indiana Folklore* 6:174–
            90. [Study of change in a legend at a Boy Scout camp from the 1950s to 1973.]
    1977   "White Guys' Stories of the Night Street." *Journal of the Folklore Institute*
            14:59–72.
    1979   "Adolescent Pranks in Bloomington, Indiana." *Indiana Folklore* 12:55–64.
Lee, Hector
    1970   "American Folklore in the Secondary School." *English Journal* 59:994–
            1004.
Leemon, Thomas A.
    1972   *The Rites of Passage in a Student Culture: A Study of the Dynamics of Tra-
            dition.* New York: Teachers College Press.
Leventhal, Nancy, and Ed Cray
  *1963   "Depth Collecting from a Sixth Grade Class." *Western Folklore* 22:l59–63,
            231–57. [Work with thirty-one students resulted in 3,397 versions of 363 items.]
Lever, Janet
    1976   "Sex Differences in the Games Children Play." *Social Problems* 23:478–87.
    1978   "Sex Differences in the Complexity of Children's Play and Games." *Ameri-
            can Sociological Review* 43:471–83.
Levine, S.B.
    1980   "Rise of American Boarding Schools and the Development of a National
            Upper Class." *Social Problems* 28:63–96.
Liben, Meyer
    1984   *New York Street Games.* New York: Schocken.
Licht, M.
    1974   "Some Automotive Play Activities of Suburban Teenagers." *New York Folk-
            lore Quarterly* 30:44–65.
Lindblom, Gerhard
    1935   *Kamba Folklore.Vol. III: Riddles, Proverbs, Songs.* Uppsala: Appelbergs
            Boktryekeri Aktiebolag.
Lindsay, Jack
    1960   *The Writing on the Wall: An Account of Pompeii in Its Last Days.* Lon-
            don: F. Muller.
Lindsay, P. L., and D. Palmer
    1981   *Playground Game Characteristics of Brisbane Primary School Children.*
            Canberra: Australian Government Publishing Service.
Lindsay, R.
    1977   "Rules as a Bridge Between Speech and Action." In *Social Rules and So-
            cial Behavior,* edited by P. Collett, 150–73. Oxford: Basil Blackwell.
Loomis, C. Grant
    1958   "Mary Had a Parody: A Rhyme of Childhood in Folk Tradition." *Western
            Folklore* 17:45–51. [Historical survey of parodies of the nursery rhyme, 1869
            to the present.]
Lord, Albert
    1960   *The Singer of Tales.* Cambridge: Harvard University Press.
Loy, John W. (ed.)
    1982   *The Paradoxes of Play.* West Point, N.Y.: Leisure. [Proceedings of the 1980
            annual meeting of the Association for the Anthropological Study of Play.]
Lukashok, Alvin, and Kevin Lynch

1956   "Some Childhood Memories of the City." *Journal of the American Institute of Planners* 22:142–52.

Lurie, Alison
   1973   "Back to Pooh Corner." *Children's Literature* 2:11–17.
   1990   *Don't Tell the Grown-ups: Subversive Children's Literature.* Boston: Little, Brown.

Luthi, Max
   1970   *Once Upon a Time: On the Nature of Fairy Tales.* Bloomington: Indiana University Press.

Lynch, Kevin
   1978   *Growing Up in Cities: Studies of the Spatial Environment of Adolescence in Cracow, Melbourne, Mexico City, Salta, Toluca, and Warsaw.* Cambridge: MIT Press.

McCall, George J.
   1969   "Data Quality Control in Participant Observation." In *Issues In Participant Observation,* edited by G.J. McCall and J.L. Simmons, 128–41. Reading, Mass.: Addison-Wesley.

McCann, Robert
   1982   "Before Suburbia Collapses: Teaching and Collecting Folklore Among Adolescents." *Keystone Folklore* 1:34–50.

MacCannell, Dean
   1979   "Ethnosemiotics." *Semiotica* 27:149–71.

McCosh, Sandra
   1976   Children's Humour: A Joke for Every Occasion. London: Granada. [Over one thousand field-collected jokes from England and the United States. The forty-three-page introduction on children, folklore, and sex by Gershon Legman adds immensely to an already magnificent book.]
   1977   "Aggression in Children's Jokes." *Maledicta* 1:125–32.

McDowell, John H.
   1974   *Interrogative Routines in Mexican-American Children's Folklore.* Austin,Tex.: Working Papers in Sociolinguistics, No. 20.
   1975   "The Speech Play and Verbal Art of Chicano Children: An Ethnographic and Sociolinguistic Study." Ph.D. dissertation, University of Texas.
   1976   *Riddling and Enculturation: A Glance at the Cerebral Child.* Austin, Tex.: Working Papers In Sociolinguistics, No. 36.
   1979   Children's Riddling. Bloomington: Indiana University Press.
   1980   "Animal Categories in Chicano Children's Spooky Stories and Riddles." In *Folklore on Two Continents: Essays in Honor of Linda Dégh.,* edited by N. Burlakoff and C. Lindhal, 168–74. Bloomington, Ind.: Trickster.
   1982   "Beyond Iconicity: Ostension In Kamsá Mythic Narrative." *Journal of the Folklore Institute* 19:119–39.

McGhee, Paul E.
   1979   *Humor: Its Origin and Development.* San Francisco: W.H. Freeman. [Excellent introduction to the psychological view, using children's humor as the primary data.]

McLachlan, James
   1970   *American Boarding Schools: A Historical Study.* New York: Charles Scribner's Sons.

McMahon, Felicia R.
   1993   "The Worst Piece of 'Tale': Flaunted 'Hidden Transcripts' in Women's Play." *Play Theory and Research* 1 (April):251–58.

McNeil, William K.
   1968   "The Autograph Album Custom: A Tradition and Its Scholary Treatment." *Keystone Folklore Quarterly* 13:29–40.

1969a   "Proverbs Used in New York Autograph Albums, 1820–1900." *Southern Folklore Quarterly* 33:352–59.

1969b   "From Advice to Laments: New York Autograph Album Verse, 1820–1850." *New York Folklore Quarterly* 25:175–94.

1970   "From Advice to Laments: New York Autograph Album Verse, 1850–1900." *New York Folklore Quarterly* 26:163–203.

Maccoby, Michael

1976   *The Gamesman*. New York: Simon and Schuster.

Machiavelli, Niccolo

1513   *The Prince*. New York: Crofts Classics, 1947.

Mackay, Robert W.

1974   "Conception of Children and Models of Socialization." In *Ethnomethodology: Selected Readings*, edited by R. Turner, 180–93. Middlesex: Penguin.

Mackey, Philip (ed.)

1977   *A Gentleman of Much Promise: The Diary of Isaac Mickle*. Philadelphia: University of Pennsylvania Press.

Magoun, Francis P., and Alexander Krappe (eds.)

1960   *The Grimms' German Folk Tales*. Carbondale: Southern Illinois University Press.

Malinowski, Bronislaw

1922   *Argonauts of the Western Pacific*. Reprint. New York: E.P. Dutton, 1961.

1954   *Magic, Science and Religion*. Garden City, N.Y.: Doubleday Anchor.

Maltz, Daniel N., and Ruth A. Borker

1982   "A Cultural Approach to Male-Female Miscommunication." In *Language and Social Identity*, edited by J.J. Gumperz, 196–216. Cambridge: Cambridge University Press.

Manning, Frank E. (ed.)

1983   *The World of Play*. West Point, N.Y.: Leisure. [Proceedings of the 1981 annual meeting of the Association for the Anthropological Study of Play.]

Manuel, E. Arsenio

1962   "Bagobo Riddles." *Asian Folklore Studies* 21:123–85.

Maranda, Elli Köngäs

1976   "Riddles and Riddling: An Introduction." *Journal of American Folklore* 89:127–38.

1978   "Folklore and Culture Change: Lau Riddles of Modernization." In *Folklore in the Modern World*, edited by Richard Dorson, 207–18. The Hague: Mouton.

Maranda, Elli Köngäs, and Pierre Maranda

1970   *Structural Models in Folklore and Transformational Essays*. The Hague: Mouton.

Marples, Morris

1940   *Public School Slang*. London: Constable.

Marsh, P.

1982   "Rules and the Organization of Action: Empirical Studies." In *The Analysis of Action*, edited by M. von Cranach and R. Harre, 231–41. Cambridge: Cambridge University Press.

Martin, Edgar

1912   *The Playground Movement in the District of Columbia*. Washington, D.C.: Government Printing Office.

Maryott, Florence

1937   "Nebraska Counting Out Rhymes." *Southern Folklore Quarterly* 1 (April):39–62. [Collection.]

Mason, John

1982   *The Environment of Play*. West Point, N.Y.: Leisure.

Maynard, D.W.
  1985 "How Children Start Arguments." *Language In Society* 14:1–30.
Mead, George Herbert
  1934 *Mind, Self and Society.* Chicago: University of Chicago Press.
Mead, Margaret
  1928 *Coming of Age In Samoa: A Psychological Study in Primitive Youth for Western Civilization.* New York: Morrow.
Mechling, Jay
  1980a "The Magic of the Boy Scout Campfire." *Journal of American Folklore* 93:35–56.
  *1980b "Sacred and Profane Play in the Boy Scouts of America." In *Play and Culture,* edited by H.B. Schwartzman, 206–13. West Point, N.Y.: Leisure.
  *1981 "Male Gender Display at a Boy Scout Camp." In *Children and Their Organizations: Investigations in American Culture,* edited by R.T. Sieber and A.J. Gordon, 138–60. Boston: G.K. Hall.
  1983 "Mind, Messages, and Madness: Gregory Bateson Makes a Paradigm for American Culture Studies." In *Prospects: An Annual Review of American Cultural Sudies,* vol. 8, edited by Jack Salzman, 11–30. New York: Cambridge University Press.
  1984a "Patois and Paradox in a Boy Scout Treasure Hunt." *Journal of American Folklore* 97:24–42.
  1984b "High Kybo Floater: Food and Feces in the Speech Play at a Boy Scout Camp." *Journal of Psychoanalytic Anthropology* 7:256–68.
  1985 "Male Border Wars as Metaphor in Capture the Flag." In *The Many Faces of Play,* edited by Kendall Blanchard, 218–31. Champaign, Ill.: Human Kinetics.
  1986 "Children's Folklore." In *Folk Groups and Folklore Genres,* edited by Elliot Oring, 91–120. Logan: Utah State University Press.
  1987 "Dress Right, Dress: The Boy Scout Uniform as a Folk Costume." *Semiotica* 64:319–33.
  1989 "The Collecting Self and American Youth Movements." In *Consuming Visions: Accumulation and Display of Goods in America, 1880–1920,* edited by Simon J. Bronner, 255–86. New York: W.W. Norton.
Meckley, Alice
  1994 "The Social Construction of Young Children's Play." Ph.D. dissertation, Philadelphia, University of Pennsylvania.
Mehan, Hugh, and Houston Wood
  1975 *The Reality of Ethnomethodology.* New York: Wiley.
Mehrabian, Albert
  1976 *Public Places and Private Spaces: The Psychology of Work, Play, and Living Environments.* New York: Basic Books.
Mercier, D., et al.
  1974 "Nipsy: The Ethnography of a Traditional Game of Pennsylvania Anthracite Region." *Pennsylvania Folklife* 23:12–21.
Mergen, Bernard
  1975 "The Discovery of Children's Play." *American Quarterly* 27:399–420.
  1980 "Games and Toys." In *Handbook of American Popular Culture,* edited by M.T. Inge, 163–90. Westport, Conn.: Greenwood.
  *1982 *Play and Playthings: A Reference Guide.* Westport, Conn.: Greenwood.
  1986 *Cultural Dimensions of Play, Games, and Sport.* West Point, N.Y.: Leisure.
Mero, Everett B.
  1909 *American Playgrounds: Their Construction, Equipment, Maintenance and Utility.* 2d ed. Boston: Dale Association.
Messenger, John C., Jr.
  1960 "Anang Proverb-Riddles." *Journal of American Folklore* 73:225–35.

Mieder, Wolfgang, and Stewart A. Kingsbury (eds).
1993   *A Dictionary of Wellerisms*. Oxford: Oxford University Press.
Milberg, Alan
1976   *Street Games*. New York: McGraw-Hill. [Large field collection, but by one who seems unaware that there is any literature or academic standard in the field. Excellent diagrams and photographs].
Millard, Eugenia L.
1945   "Sticks and Stones: Children's Teasing Rhymes." *New York Folklore Quarterly* 1:21–32.
1951–52   "Children's Charms and Oracles." *New York Folklore Quarterly* 7:253–68; 8:46–57.
1954   "What Does It Mean? The Lore of Secret Languages." *New York Folklore Quarterly* 10:103–10. [Historical collection.]
1957   "A Sampling of Guessing Games." *New York Folklore Quarterly* 13:135–43.
1959   "Racing, Chasing, and Marching with the Children of the Hudson-Champlain Valleys." *New York Folklore Quarterly* 15:132–50. [Collection.]
Miller, S.
1973   "Ends, Means, and Calumphing: Some Leitmotifs of Play." *American Anthropologist* 75:87–98.
Milne, A.A.
1926   *Winnie-the-Pooh*. New York: E.P. Dutton, 1961.
Mintz, Thomas
1966   "The Psychology of a Nursery Rhyme: One, Two, Buckle My Shoe." *American Imago* 23:22–47.
Miracle, Andrew W., Jr.
1980   "School Spirit as a Ritual By-Product: Views from Applied Anthropology." In *Play and Culture*, edited by H.B. Schwartzman, 98–103. West Point, N.Y.: Leisure.
Miracle Playground Equipment Company
1975   *Catalog*. Grinnell, Iowa.
Mitchell, Carol A.
1969   "The White House." *Indiana Folklore* 2:97–109.
Mitchell, Roger
1978   "'I'm A Man That Works': The Biography of Don Mitchell of Merrill, Maine." *Northeast Folklore* 19:9–129.
Miura, K.
1981   "Interaction of Young Children on a Ward for Physically Handicapped as Demonstrated by the Present Game." *Journal of Clinical Psychology* 37:577–81.
Montiero, G.
1964   "Parodies of Scripture, Prayer, and Hymn." *Journal of American Folklore* 77:46–52.
Moore, Danny W.
1974   "The Deductive Riddle: An Adaptation to Modern Society." *North Carolina Folklore Journal* 22:119–25.
Moore, Robin C.
1974   "Anarchy Zone: Encounters in a Schoolyard." *Landscape Architecture* 64:364–71.
1986   *Childhood's Domain: Play and Place in Child Development*. Dover, N.H.: Croom Helm.
Moore, Sally F., and Barbara G. Myerhoff
1977   "Introduction-Secular Ritual: Forms and Meanings." In *Secular Ritual*, edited by S.F. Moore and B.G. Myerhoff, 3–24. Amsterdam: Van Gocum.
Morasco, Robert
1970   *Child's Play*. New York: Random House.

Morley, Patricia
1977   "The Good Life, Prairie Style: The Art and Artistry of William Kurelek."
       Children's Literature 6:141–49.

Moss, Joy
1982   "Reading and Discussing Fairy Tales: Old and New." *Reading Teacher*
       35:56–60.

Mother Earth News
1982   *An Up'N'Down Merry-Go-Round.* No. 75: 126–27.

Much, N.C., and R.A. Shweder
1987   "Speaking of Rules: The Analysis of Culture in Breach." In *Moral Devel-
       opment,* edited by W. Damon, 19–39. San Francisco: Jossey-Bass.

Mullen, Patrick
1979–81   "Black Consciousness in Afro-American Children's Rhymes: Some Ohio
          Examples from the Early 1970s." *Ohio Folklife* 6:1–20.

Mullen, Patrick, and Linna Funk Place
1978   *Collecting Folklore and Folklife In Ohio.* Washington, D.C.: Office of Edu-
       cation, Ethnic Heritage Studies Branch.

Musick, Ruth Ann, and Vance Randolph
1950   "Children's Rhymes from Missouri." *Journal of American Folklore* 63:425–
       37.

Myerhoff, Barbara
1978   *Number Our Days.* New York: Touchstone/Simon and Schuster.

Nadel, Ira Bruce
1982   "'The Mansion of Bliss' or the Place of Play in Victorian Life and Litera-
       ture." *Children's Literature* 10:18–36.

Narragansett Machine Company
1914   *Catalog H-4 Playground Gymnastic Apparatus.* Providence, R.I.

Nasaw, David
1985   *Children of the City: At Work and Play.* New York: Oxford University Press.

Nash, Jay B.
1934   "Playgrounds." In *Encyclopedia of the Social Sciences* 12:161–63. New
       York: Macmillan.

Newell, William Wells
*1883   *Games and Songs of American Children.* Expanded 1903. Revised ed. Re-
        print. New York: Dover, 1963. [The starting point for modern work on
        children's folklore. Excellent collection. Carl A. Withers's introduction to the
        reprint is a significant contribution in its own right.]

Nicholson, Edward W.B. (ed.)
*1897   *Golspie: Contributions to Its Folklore.* Reprint. Norwood, Pa.: Norwood
        Editions, 1975. [A collection by children with extensive annotations and com-
        ments.]

Nicholson, Simon
1971   "How Not to Cheat Children: The Theory of Loose Parts." *Landscape Ar-
       chitecture,* October, 30–34.

Nielsen, Erik Kaas
1976   "Born Driller [Children are Teasing]." *Folk og Kultur:22–55.*

Northall, G.F.
1892   *English Folk-Rhymes.* London: Kegan Paul, Trench, Trubner.

Norton, Edward
1937   *Play Streets.* New York: A.S. Barnes.

Olmert, Michael
1983   "Points of Origin." *Smithsonian* 14, no. 9 (Dec.) 40, 42.

Opie, Iona, and Peter Opie [The preeminent collectors of British children's folklore.
       Essential reference for any future work.]
1947   *I Saw Esau: Traditional Rhymes of Youth.* London: Williams and Norgate.

1952   *The Oxford Dictionary of Nursery Rhymes.* Oxford: Clarendon.

*1959   *The Lore and Language of Schoolchildren.* Oxford: Clarendon. [Probably the single most important modern work.]

*1969   *Children's Games In Street and Playground: Chasing, Catching, Seeking, Hunting, Racing, Duelling, Exerting, Daring, Guessing, Acting, Pretending.* Oxford: Clarendon. [Collection from the 1960s of twenty-five hundred games. Historical notes. Many variants. The subtitle indicates the range of this important work.]

1973   *The Oxford Book of Children's Verse.* Oxford: Clarendon.

1985   *The Singing Game.* New York: Oxford University Press.

Ord, Priscilla A. (ed.)

1981   "Special Section: Folklore." Reprint. *The First Steps: Best of the Early ChLA Quarterly* 93–109. Purdue University: ChLA Publications, 1984.

Oring, E. (ed.)

1986   *Folk Groups and Folklore Genres.* Logan: Utah State University Press.

Östergren, Ewa

1983   "66 Sätt att Rya en Giraff." ("Sixty-six Ways of Drawing a Giraffe." *Torbaggen* (Newsletter of the Swedish Folklore Society.) 1:6–7.

Oxrieder, Julia W.

1976   "Taunting the Teacher: Rhymes and Songs Collected In the Historic Triangle." *Kentucky Folklore Record* 22:95–99. [Collection of a very common and seldom-studied genre.]

1977   "The Slumber Party: Transition into Adolescence." *Tennessee Folklore Society Bulletin* 43:128–34.

Page, Linda Garland, and Hilton Smith (eds.)

1993   *The Foxfire Book of Appalachian Toys and Games.* Reprint. Chapel Hill: University of North Carolina Press, 1985.

Paley, Vivian Gussin

1984   *Boys and Girls: Superheros in the Doll Corner.* Chicago: University of Chicago Press.

1990   *The Boy Who Would Be a Helicopter.* Cambridge: Harvard University Press.

Parker, Drucilla Pegeeo

1975   "A Dictionary of Adolescent Folk Speech in Oakland [California]." M.A. thesis, University of California, Berkeley.

Parr, Joy (ed.)

1982   *Childhood and Family in Canadian History.* Toronto: McClelland and Stewart.

Parrott, S.

1976   "Games Children Play: Ethnography of a Second-Grade Recess." In *The Cultural Experience: Ethnography in a Complex Society,* edited by J.P. Spradley and D.W. McCurdy, 207–20. Chicago: Science Research Associates. [A very nice undergraduate term paper.]

Pearce, Ann Philippa

1959   *Tom's Midnight Garden.* Philadelphia: J.B. Lippincott.

Pearson, Karl

1897   *Chances of Death.* London: Edward Arnold.

Peck, Thomas

1970   "Dirty Jokes at The Academy and Angela Morrison." *Keystone Folklore Quarterly* 15:93–105.

Pellegrini, Anthony D.

1987   "Children on the Playground: A Review of 'What's out There.'" *Children's Environments Quarterly* 4 (July):1–7.

Pepicello, W.J., and Thomas A. Green

1984   *The Language of Riddles: New Perspectives.* Columbus: Ohio State University Press.

Peretti, Peter O., Richard Carter, and Betty McClinton
1977   "Graffiti and Adolescent Personality." *Adolescence* 12:31–42.

Petersen, Dennis R.
1972   "Summer Activities of Rural Adolescent Boys in the Contemporary Society of Otsego County, New York." M.A. thesis, Cooperstown Graduate Program of the State University of New York.

Petsch, Robert
1899   *Neue Beitrage zür Kenntnis des Volkratsels* (Palaestra 4). Berlin: Mayer and Muller.

Philip, Andrew
1966   "The Street Songs of Glasgow." *Tradition* (London)1:11–17.

Piaget, Jean [Piaget's work in child psychology has greatly affected nearly everyone in the field. The following are representative works of particular interest to folklorists.]
1932   *The Moral Judgment of the Child.* Reprint. New York: Free Press, 1965.
1951   *Play, Dreams, and Imitation in Childhood.* New York: W.W. Norton.
1959   *The Language and Thought of the Child.* New York: Humanities.
1964   *The Construction of Reality in the Child.* New York: Basic Books.
1965   *The Child's Conception of the World.* Totowa, N.J.: Littlefield Adams.
1973   *The Child and Reality: Problems of Genetic Psychology.* New York: Grossman.

Piaget, Jean, and Barbel Inhelder
1969   *The Psychology of the Child.* New York: Basic Books.

Pickard, P.M.
1961   *I Could a Tale Unfold: Violence, Horror, and Sensationalism in Stories for Children.* New York: Humanities.

Pilant, Elizabeth
1953   "Family Folklore." *Elementary English* 30:148–49.

Pitcher, Evelyn G., and Ernst Prelinger
1963   *Children Tell Stories: An Analysis of Fantasy.* New York: International Universities Press.

Platt, Anthony M.
1969   *The Child Savers: The Invention of Delinquency.* Chicago: University of Chicago Press.

Platzner, R.L.
1979   "Child's Play: Games and Fantasy in Carroll, Stevenson, and Grahame." In *Proceedings of the Fifth Annual Conference of the Children's Literature Association,* 78–86.

Play And Recreation
1917   *Bulletin of the Indiana Extension Division,* 2. Bloomington: Indiana University.

Playground, The
1907–1907–1915, New York; published 1916–23, Cooperstown, N.Y.; published 1923–24, Greenwich, Conn.; 1924–29, New York; published as *Playground and Recreation* 1918–30, New York; published as *Recreation* 1931–65, New York; published as *Parks and Recreation* 1966, Arlington, Va.

Playground and Recreation Association of America
1938   *Play Areas: Their Design and Equipment.* New York: A.S. Barnes.

Playground Equipment Company
1933   *Junglegym the Climbing Structure.* n.p.

Playthings
1957   March advertisement for "Merrie-Go": 180.

Polgar, S.K.

1976   "The Social Context of Games, or When Is Play Not Play." *Sociology of Education* 49:265–71.

Pollock, Linda A.
1983   *Forgotten Children: Parent-Child Relationships from 1500 to 1900.* Cambridge: Cambridge University Press.

Polsky, Howard W.
1962   *Cottage Six: The Social System of Delinquent Boys in Residential Treatment.* New York: Wiley.

Polsky, Howard W., and Daniel S. Claster
1968   *The Dynamics of Residential Treatment: A Social System Analysis.* Chapel Hill: University of North Carolina Press.

Popular Mechanics
1913   "Revolving Seesaw for Playgrounds." 20:116.
1953   "Seesaw Doubles as Merry-Go-Round." 99:173.

Porter, Kenneth W.
1958   "Circular Jingles and Repetitious Rhymes." *Western Folklore* 17:107–11.
1965   "Racism in Children's Rhymes and Sayings, Central Kansas, 1910–1918." *Western Folklore* 24:19–96.

Posen, I. Sheldon
1974a   "Pranks and Practical Jokes at Children's Summer Camps." *Southern Folklore Quarterly* 38:299–309.
1974b   "Song and Singing Traditions at Children's Summer Camps." M.A. thesis, Memorial University of Newfoundland.

Postman, Neil
1982   *The Disappearance of Childhood.* New York: Delacorte.

Potter, Charles Francis
1949   "Riddles." In *The Standard Dictionary of Folklore, Mythology and Legend*, edited by M. Leach, 938–44. New York: Funk and Wagnalls.

Preece, A.
1987   "The Range of Narrative Forms Conversationally Produced by Young Children." *Journal of Child Language* 14:353–73.

Prentice, Norman M., and Robert E. Fathman
1975   "Joking Riddles: A Developmental Index of Children's Humor." *Developmental Psychology* 11:210–16.

Preston, Michael J.
1982   "The English Literal Rebus and the Graphic Riddle Tradition." *Western Folklore* 41:104–38.

Prince, Peter
1972   *Play Things.* London: Arrow.

Pritchard, Violet
1967   *English Medieval Graffiti.* Cambridge: Cambridge University Press.

Propp, Vladimir
1958   *Morphology of the Folktale.* Austin: University of Texas Press.

Quinney, Valerie
1982   "Childhood in a Southern Mill Village." *International Journal of Oral History* 3:167–92.

Rabelais, François
1534   *Gargantua and Pantagruel.* London: Penguin, 1955.

Radcliffe-Brown, A.R.
1922   *The Andaman Islanders.* Glencoe, Ill.: Free Press, 1948.

Radner, Joan N., and Susan S. Lanser
1993   "Strategies of Coding in Women's Cultures." In *Feminist Messages*, edited by Joan N. Radner, 1–30. Urbana: University of Illinois.

Raglan, Lord
1936   *The Hero: A Study in Tradition, Myth, and Drama.* London: Watts and

Company.

Rainwater, Clarence
   1922   *The Play Movement in the United States: A Study of Community Recreation*. Chicago: University of Chicago Press.

Ramsey, Eloise
   1952   *Folklore for Children and Young People: A Critical and Descriptive Bibliography for Use in the Elementary and Intermediate School*. Reprint. New York: Kraus Reprint Co., 1970. [While basically for, rather than by children, there are many useful items, well annotated, in this book.]

Randolph, Vance
   1953   "Counting-Out Rhymes in Arkansas." *Southern Folklore Quarterly* 17:244–48. [A short collection with brief comments by informants.]

Randolph, Vance, and Nancy Clemens
   1936   "Ozark Mountain Party-Games." *Journal of American Folklore* 49:199–206.

Randolph, Vance, and Mary K. McCord
   1948   "Autograph Albums in the Ozarks." *Journal of American Folklore* 61:182–93.

Randolph, Vance, and Isabel Spradley
   1934   "Ozark Mountain Riddles." *Journal of American Folklore* 47:81–89.

Rank, Otto
   1945   *Will Therapy, and Truth and Reality*. New York: Alfred A. Knopf.

Raphael, Ray
   1988   *The Men From the Boys: Rites of Passage in Male America*. Lincoln: University of Nebraska Press.

Rashap, Amy
   1982   "An Exploration of the Limits and Boundaries of Control at a Camp for Overweight Individuals." Paper presented to American Folklore Society annual meeting, Minneapolis, Minnesota.

Rawick, George P. (ed.)
   1972, 1977 *The American Slave: A Composite Autobiography*. Series I, nineteen volumes; Series II, twelve volumes. Westport, Conn.: Greenwood.

Read, Allen Walker
   1941   "The Spelling Bee: A Linguistic Institution of the American Folk." *Publications of the Modern Language Association* 56:495–512.

Reifel, Stuart
   1986   "Play in the Elementary School Cafeteria." In *Play, Games, and Sport*, edited by B. Mergen, 29–36. West Point, N.Y.: Leisure.

Rich, George, and David F. Jacobs
   1973   "Saltpeter: A Folkloric Adjustment to Stress." *Western Folklore* 32:164–79.

Riis, Jacob
   1892   *Children of the Poor*. New York: Scribner's.

Ritchie, James T.R.
   1964   *The Singing Street*. Edinburgh: Oliver and Boyd.
   1965   *Golden City*. Edinburgh: Oliver and Boyd. [Two volumes of material collected from schoolchildren in Edinburgh.]

Robe, Stanley L.
   1963   *Hispanic Riddles from Panama*. University of California Folklore Studies, no. 14. Berkeley: University of California Press.

Roberts, John M.
   1987   "Within Culture Variation: A Retrospective Personal View." *American Behavorial Scientist* 31:266–79.

Roberts, John M., M.J. Arth, and R.R. Bush
   1959   "Games in Culture." *American Anthropologist* 61:579–605.

Roberts, John M., and Michael L. Forman
   1971   "Riddles: Expressive Models of Interrogation." *Ethnology* 10:509–33. [Also published in *Directions in Sociolinguistics of Communication*, edited by John

J. Gumperz and Dell Hymes, 180–209. New York: Holt, Rinehart and Winston.]

Roberts, John M., and Brian Sutton-Smith
1962　"Child Training and Game Involvement." Reprinted in Avedon and Sutton-Smith 1971, 465–87. New York: Wiley.

Roberts, Leonard W.
1959　*Up Cutshin and Down Greasy: Folkways of a Kentucky Mountain Family.* Lexington: University of Kentucky Press.

Roberts, Rod
1965　"Folklore in a Southwest Industrial School." Unpublished M.A. thesis, Indiana University.

Roberts, Warren
1949　"Children's Games and Game Rhymes." *Hoosier Folklore* 8:7–34. [Student collections with annotations and references.]

Roemer, Danielle
1972　"Scary Story Legends." M.A. thesis, University of Texas at Austin.
1977　"A Social Interactional Analysis of Anglo Children's Folklore: Catches and Narratives." Ph.D. dissertation, University of Texas at Austin.
1980　"'Deep Down in the Heart of Texas': Interactional Negotiation as a Theme in Children's Jokes." *Southwest Folklore* 4 (March–April): 11–25.
1982a　"In the Eye of the Beholder: A Semiotic Analysis of the Visual Descriptive Riddle." *Journal of American Folklore* 95:173–99.
1982b　"Semantic and Syntactic Parallelism in Children's Storytelling." *Working Papers in Sociolinguistics* 102:1–27.
1983　"Children's Verbal Folklore." *Volta Review* 85 (May): 55–71.

Roheim, Geza
1943　"Children's Games and Rhymes in Duau (Normandy) Island." *American Anthropologist* 45:99–119.

Rosenberg, Bruce G., and Brian Sutton-Smith
1960　"A Revised Conception of Masculine-Feminine Differences in Play Activities." *Journal of Genetic Psychology* 96:165–70.

Rosenberg, Jan
1980　"Piles of Sand to Monkeybars." *The Association for the Anthropological Study of Play Newsletter* 7:8–12.

Rosenzweig, Roy
1979　"Middle-Class Parks and Working-Class Play: The Struggle Over Recreational Space in Worcester, Massachusetts, 1870–1910." *Radical History Review* 21:31–46.

Rouard, Marguerite, and Jacques Simon
1977　*Children's Play Spaces: From Sandbox to Adventure Playground.* Woodstock, N.Y.: Overlook.

Rubin, Kenneth H., Greta G. Fein, and Brian Vandenberg
1983　"Play." In *Handbook of Child Psychology,* vol. 4, edited by E. Mavis Hetherington, 693-774. New York: Wiley.

Rumpf, Marianne
1955　"Ursprung und Entstehung von Warn- und Schreckmarchen." *Folklore Fellows Communication* 160. Helsinki: Suomalainen Tiedeakatemia.

Sabini, John, and Maury Silver
1982　*Moralities of Everyday Life.* New York: Oxford University Press.

Sacks, Harvey
1972　"On the Analyzability of Stories by Children." In *Directions in Sociolinguistics: The Ethnography of Communication,* edited by J.J. Gumperz and D. Hymes, 325–45. New York: Holt, Rinehart, and Winston.

Salamone, Frank
1979　"Children's Games as Mechanisms for Easing Ethnic Interaction in

Ethnically Heterogeneous Communities: A Nigerian Case." *Anthropos* 74:202–10.

Salamone, Frank, and Virginia Salamone
 1991 "Children's Games in Nigeria Redux: A Consideration of the 'Uses' of Play." *Play and Culture* 4 (February): 129–38.

Salter, Michael A. (ed.)
 1978 *Play: Anthropological Perspectives.* West Point, N.Y.: Leisure. [1977 proceedings of the Association for the Anthropological Study of Play.]

Samuelson, Sue
 1979 "The White Witch: An Analysis of an Adolescent Legend." *Indiana Folklore* 12:18–37.
 *1980 "The Cooties Complex." *Western Folklore* 39:198–210. [Fascinating article about an important children's folk belief.]
 1981 "European and American Adolescent Legends." *Arv: The Scandinavian Yearbook of Folklore* 37:133–39.

Sanches, Mary, and Barbara Kirshenblatt-Gimblett
 *1976 "Children's Traditional Speech Play and Child Language." In *Speech Play: Research and Resources for Studying Linguistic Creativity*, edited by B. Kirshenblatt-Gimblett, 65–110. Philadelphia:University of Pennsylvania Press.

Santino, Jack
 1983 "Halloween in America: Contemporary Customs and Performances." *Western Folklore* 42:1–20.

Savin-Williams, R.C.
 1980a "Dominance Hierarchies in Groups of Middle to Late Adolescent Males." *Journal of Youth and Adolescence* 9:75–85.
 1980b "Social Interactions of Adolescent Females in Natural Groups." In *Friendship and Social Relations in Children*, edited by Hugh C. Foot, Anthony J. Chapman, and Jean R. Smith, 343–64. New York: Wiley.

Schapera, I.
 1932 "Kxatla Riddles and Their Significance." *Bantu Studies* 6:215–31.

Schatzman, L., and Anselm Strauss
 1973 *Field Research.* Englewood Cliffs, N.J.: Prentice-Hall.
 1980 "Play and Culture." *1978 Proceedings of the Association for the Anthropological Study of Play.* West Point, N.Y.: Leisure.

Schechner, R.
 1988 "Playing." *Play and Culture* 1:3–19.

Schiller, Friedrich
 1793 *On the Aesthetic Education of Man.* New York: Frederick Unger, 1965.

Schlereth, Thomas J.
 1990 "The Material Culture of Childhood: Research Problems and Possibilities." In *Cultural History and Material Culture: Everyday Life, Landscapes, Museums*, 89–112. Ann Arbor: UMI Research.

Schorsch, Anita
 1979 *Images of Childhood: An Illustrated Social History.* New York: Mayflower.

Schwartz, Gary, and Don Merten
 1967 "The Language of Adolescence: An Anthropological Approach to Youth Culture." *American Journal of Sociology* 72:453–68.

Schwartzman, Helen B.
 1976 "The Anthropological Study of Children's Play." *Annual Review of Anthropology* 5:289–328. [History of the field to date with a bibliography of 298 significant works.]
 *1978 *Transformations: The Anthropology of Children's Play.* New York: Plenum. [Excellent survey of the history of the field to date with important suggestions for the future. Includes a list of films (with sources) and thirty pages of bibliography.]

Scott, James C.

1990   *Domination and the Arts of Resistance: Hidden Transcripts.* New Haven: Yale University Press.

Scriven, Michael

n.d.   "Evaluation of Southwest Education Development Laboratory's Children's Folklore Project: 'Pass It On.'" Berkeley: Educational and Development Group.

Seagoe, May V.

1962   "Children's Play as an Indicator of Cross-Cultural and Intra-Cultural Differences." *Journal of Educational Sociology* 35:278–83.

1970   "An Instrument for the Analysis of Children's Play as an Index of Degree of Socialization." *Journal of School Psychology* 8:139–44.

Shah, D.K.

1981   "The Toughest Whistles." *Newsweek.* January 5:32.

Shaw, Frank

1970   *You Know Me, Anty Nelly? Liverpool Children's Rhymes.* London: Wolfe.

Sherif, Muzafer, and Caroline Sherif

1964   *Reference Groups.* Chicago: Henry Regnery.

Sherrod, Lonnie, and Jerome L. Singer

1979   "The Development of Make-Believe Play." In *Sports, Games, and Play: Social and Psychological Viewpoints,* edited by J.H. Goldstein, 1–28. Hillsdale, N.J.: Lawrence Erlbaum.

Sherzer, Joel

1978   "Oh! That's a Pun and I Didn't Mean It." *Semiotica* 22:335–49.

Shimanoff, Susan B.

1980   *Communication Rules: Theory and Research.* Beverly Hills, Calif.: Sage.

Shiver, S.M.

1941   "Finger Rhymes." *Southern Folklore Quarterly* 5:221–34.

Shore, David A., and Harvey L. Gochros (eds.)

1981   *Sexual Problems of Adolescents in Institutions.* Springfield, Ill.: Charles C. Thomas.

Shultz, Thomas R.

1974   "Development of the Appreciation of Riddles." *Child Development* 45:100–5.

Shultz, Thomas R., and Frances Horibe

1974   "Development of the Appreciation of Verbal Jokes." *Developmental Psychology* 10:13–20.

Shwayder, D.S.

1965   *The Stratification of Behavior.* New York and London: Routledge and Kegan Paul.

Sieber, R. Timothy (ed.)

1981   *Children and Their Organizations: Investigations in American Culture.* Boston: G.K. Hall.

Silverstein, Arthur B.

1965   "Variations on Stickball." *New York Folklore Quarterly* 21:179–83.

Simon, R.L.

1985   *Sports and Social Values.* Englewood Cliffs, N.J.: Prentice-Hall.

Simons, Elizabeth Radin

*1980   "The Slumber Party as Folk Ritual: An Analysis of the Informal Sex Education of Preadolescents." M.A. thesis, University of California, Berkeley.

1984   "The Folklore of Naming: Using Oral Tradition to Teach Writing." *Teachers and Writers* 16:1–4. [A section of the article was not printed in this issue and appears in vol. 17.]

1985   "Levitation, Jokes, and Spin the Bottle: Contemporary Folklore in the Classroom—A Folklorist's View." *English Journal* 74:32–36.

Sinclair, J.McH., and R.M. Coulthard

1975   *Towards an Analysis of Discourse: The English Used by Teachers and Pu-*

pils. London: Oxford University Press.

Singer, Jerome L.
1973   *The Child's World of Make-Believe: Experimental Studies of Imaginative Play*. New York: Academic.

Sitton, Thad, and Jan Jeter
1980   "Discovering Children's Folklore." *Teacher* 97:58–61.

Skolnik, Peter
1974   *Jump Rope*. New York: Workman.

Sliney, Deanna
1974   "Haunted Sites in Indiana: A Preliminary Survey." *Indiana Folklore* 7:27–51.

Sluckin, Andy
1981   *Growing Up in the Playground: The Social Development of Children*. London: Routledge and Kegan Paul.

Smith, Beatrice M.
n.d.   "B. Smith (Biography)." New Orleans, La.: Renaissance Gallery.

Smith, P.K.
1984   *Play in Animals and Humans*. London: Blackwell.

Snow, E.
1983   "'Meaning' in Children's Games: On the Limitations of the Iconographic Approach to Breughel." *Representations* 1 (February): 27–60.

Soileau, Jeanne
1980   "Children's Cheers as Folklore." *Western Folklore* 39:232–47.

Solomon, Jack, and Olivia Solomon
1980   *Zickary Zan: Childhood Folklore*. Birmingham: University of Alabama Press.

Sorensen, Virginia
1955   *Where Nothing Is Long Ago: Memories of a Mormon Childhood*. Reprint. New York: Harcourt Brace and World, 1963.

Spariosu, M.
1989   *Dionysus Reborn: Play and the Aesthetic Dimension in Modern Philosophical and Scientific Discourse*. Ithaca, N.Y.: Cornell University Press.

Spaulding
1919   *Spaulding Efficient Apparatus for the Playground*. Catalog. n.p.

Speier, Matthew
1970   "The Everyday World of the Child." In *Understanding Everyday Life: Toward the Reconstruction of Sociological Knowledge*, edited by J.D. Douglas, 188–217. Chicago: Aldine.
1976   "The Adult Ideological Viewpoint in Studies of Childhood." In *Rethinking Childhood*, edited by A.S. Skolnick, 168–86. Boston: Little, Brown.

Spencer, Herbert
1876   *The Comparative Psychology of Man*. Reprint. Washington: University Publications of America, 1977.

Spiller, Mary Anne
1979   "Some Contrasts in Rhymes Related by Children and Remembered by Adults in the San Gabriel Valley." *Folklore and Mythology Studies* 3:47–64.

Spradley, James P.
1979   *The Ethnographic Interview*. New York: Holt, Rinehart and Winston.

Stansell, Christine
1982   "Women, Children, and the Uses of the Streets: Class and Gender Conflict in New York City, 1850–1860." *Feminist Studies* 8:308–35.

Stephanoff, Alexander
1970   "College Interviews as a Folklore Genre." *Keystone Folklore Quarterly* 15:106–13.

Stevens, Phillips (ed.)
1977   *Studies in the Anthropology of Play: Papers in Memory of B. Allan Tindall*.

West Point: N.Y.: Leisure. [Proceedings of the 1976 annual meeting of the Association for the Anthropological Study of Play.]

Stevenson, Robert Louis

1885   *A Child's Garden of Verses.* New York: Charles Scribner's Sons.

Stewart, Susan

1978   *Nonsense: Aspects of Intertextuality in Folklore and Literature.* Baltimore: Johns Hopkins University Press.

1991a   *Crimes of Writing.* New York: Oxford University Press.

1991b   "Notes on Distressed Genres." *Journal of American Folklore* 104:411:5–31.

Stimson, Anna K.

1945   "Cries of Defiance and Derision and Rhythmic Chants of West Side New York City, 1893–1903." *Journal of American Folklore* 58:124–29. [A collection of thirty items with brief notes.]

Stoeltje, Beverly J.

1978   *Children's Handclaps: Informal Learning in Play.* Austin, Tex.: Southwest Educational Development Laboratory. [Excellent brief survey with music, diagrams, and photographs. Suggestions for school teachers.]

Stone, Kay F.

1985   "The Misuses of Enchantment: Controversies on the Significance of Fairy Tales." In *Women's Folklore, Women's Culture,* edited by Rosan A. Jordan and Susan J. Kalcik, 125–45. Philadelphia: University of Pennsylvania Press.

Stone, Lawrence J.

1977   *The Family, Sex and Marriage in England, 1500–1800.* New York: Harper and Row.

Stone, Lawrence J., and Joseph Church

1957   *Childhood and Adolescence.* New York: Random House.

Street, David, Robert D. Vinter, and Charles Perrow

1969   *Organization for Treatment: A Comparative Study of Institutions for Delinquents.* New York: Free Press.

Strutt, Joseph

1801   *Sports and Pastimes of the People of England.* London: T. Tegg.

Sudnow, David (ed.)

1972   *Studies in Social Interaction.* New York: Free Press.

Sullivan III, C.W.

1980   "Peanuts and Baloney." *Center for Southern Folklore Magazine* 3:9.

Summers, T.A.

1988   "Monsters and Make-Believe and Transportation Transformation." *Home Office Computing* 6:100.

Sutton-Smith, Brian [Certainly the most prolific (and probably the best) researcher and author on children's lore today. Listed are only a few items in his immense bibliography.]

1951   "The Meeting of Maori and European Cultures and Its Effects upon the Unorganized Games of the Maoris." *Journal of the Polynesian Society* 60:93–107.

1952   "New Zealand Variants of the Game Buck Buck." *Folklore* 63:329–33.

1953   "Traditional Games of New Zealand Children." *Folklore* 64:411–23.

1954   "The Historical and Psychological Significance of the Unorganized Games of New Zealand Primary School Children." Ph.D. dissertation, University of New Zealand.

1959a   "The Kissing Games of Adolescents in Ohio." *Midwest Folklore* 9:189–211. [Reprinted in Avedon and Sutton-Smith 1979 and in Sutton-Smith 1972.]

1959b   *The Games of New Zealand Children.* Berkeley: University of California Press. [Reprinted in Sutton-Smith 1972a.]

1959c   "A Formal Analysis of Game Meaning." *Western Folklore* 18:13–24.

1960   "Shut Up and Keep Digging: The Cruel Joke Series." *Midwest Folklore*

10:11–22. [A collection of 155 jokes told by students from fifth grade through college. Unfortunately, there are no notes on the ages of the tellers of specific jokes.]

1966   "Piaget on Play: A Critique." *Psychological Review* 73:104–10.

1967   "The Role of Play in Cognitive Development." *Young Children* 6:361–70.

1968   "The Folk Games of Children." In *Our Living Traditions: An Introduction to American Folklore,* edited by T. P. Coffin, 179–91. New York: Basic Books.

1969   "The Two Cultures of Games." Reprinted in Sutton-Smith 1972a, 295–311.

*1970a "Psychology of Childlore: The Triviality Barrier." *Western Folklore* 29:1–8. [Reprinted in Sutton-Smith 1976c.]

1970b "The Cross Cultural Study of Games." In *A Cross Cultural Analysis of Sports and Games,* edited by Gunther Luschen, 452-478. Champaign, Ill.: Stipes.

1971a "The Expressive Profile." *Journal of American Folklore* 84:80–92. [Reprinted in Sutton-Smith 1972a.]

1971b "A Developmental Psychology of Play and the Arts." *Perspectives on Education.* (Spring): 8–17.

*1972   *The Folk Games of Children.* Austin: University of Texas Press. [Collection of fifteen previously published articles and one book *The Games of New Zealand Children* (1959b) by the acknowledged master of the study of children's games.]

1976a "A Structural Grammar of Games and Sports." *International Review of Sport Sociology* 2:117–37.

1976b "A Developmental Structural Account of Riddles." In *Speech Play: Research and Resources for Studying Linguistic Creativity,* edited by B. Kirshenblatt-Gimblett, 111–19. Philadelphia: University of Pennsylvania Press.

1976c *A Children's Games Anthology: Studies in Folklore and Anthropology.* New York: Arno. [Thirty important articles reprinted from obscure or difficult-to-find sources.]

1977   "Games of Order and Disorder." *Newsletter of the Association for the Anthropological Study of Play* 4:19–26.

1978a *Die Dialektik des Spiels.* Verlag Karl Hoffman, Schorndorf, Germany.

1978b "Listening to Little Stories. Special Section: 'The Child's Mind.'" *Harper's* 256 (April): 53–55.

1979a *Play and Learning.* New York: Gardner.

1979b "Play as Performance." In *Play and Learning,* edited by B. Sutton-Smith, 295–322. New York: Gardner.

1979c "The Play of Girls." In *Women in Context: Becoming Female,* edited by C.B. Kopp and M. Kirkpatrick, 228–57. New York: Plenum.

1979d "Toys for Object and Role Mastery." In *Educational Toys in America: 1800 to the Present,* edited by K. Hewitt and L. Roomet, 11–24. Burlington, Vt.: Robert Hull Fleming Museum, University of Vermont.

1979e "Folkgames." *In American Folklore Series,* edited by H. Cohen. Delanda, Fl.: Cassette Curriculum.

1980a "Children's Play: Some Sources of Play Theorizing." In *Children's Play: New Directions for Child Development,* edited by K. Rubin, 1–19. San Francisco: Jossey Bass.

1980b "The Playground as a Zoo." *Newsletter of the Association for the Anthropological Study of Play* 7:4–8.

1981a *A History of Children's Play: The New Zealand Playground, 1840–1950.* Philadelphia: University of Pennsylvania Press.

1981b *The Folkstories of Children.* Philadelphia: University of Pennsylvania Press. [Analysis of the development of narrative elements by children aged two to ten; large collection of actual stories divided by child, age, and date collected.]

1982   "Play Theory of the Rich and for the Poor." In *Children In and Out of School,* edited by P. Gilmore and A. Glathorn, 187–205. Philadelphia: University of Pennsylvania Press.

1983 "One Hundred Years of Research on Play." *Newsletter of the Association for the Anthropological Study of Play* 9:13–16.

1984 "The Origins of Fiction and the Fictions of Origin." *American Ethnological Society Proceedings, 1983.* Edited by E.M. Bruner. "Text, Play and Story." Washington, D.C.

1985 *Children's Play, Past, Present, & Future.* Philadelphia: Please Touch Museum.

1986 *Toys as Culture.* New York: Gardner.

1987 "Review of *The Singing Game*." *Journal of American Folklore* 99:392:238–40.

1988 "In Search of the Imagination." In *Imagination and Education,* edited by Kieran Egan and Dan Nadaner, 3–29. New York: Teachers College Press.

1989a "Introduction to Play as Performance, Rhetoric and Metaphor." *Play and Culture* 2 (March):189–92.

1989b "Children's Folkgames as Customs." *Western Folklore* 47 (January):33–42.

1989c "Games as Models of Power." In *The Content of Culture Constants and Variants: Studies in Honor of John M. Roberts,* edited by Ralph Bolton. New Haven: Human Relations Area Files.

1990a "Multi- and Mad-Mindedness of Children." Lecture prepared for Growing Up by Design (IDCA).

1990b "School Playground as Festival." *Children's Environments Quarterly* 7 (February): 3–7.

1990c "The Future Agenda of Child Study and the Implications for the Study of Children's Folklore." *Children's Folklore Review* 1 (January):117–21.

1992a "Commentary: At Play in the Public Arena." *Early Education and Development* 3, 4: 390–400.

1992b "Tradition from the Perspective of Children's Games." *Children's Folklore Quarterly* 14(February): 3–16.

1993 "Suggested Rhetorics in Adult Play Theories." *Play Theory and Research* 1 (February): 102–16

1994 "A Memory of Games and Some Games of Memory." In *Life and Story, Autobiographies for a Narrative Psychology,* edited by D. John Lee, 125-142. Westport, Conn.: Praeger.

in press *The Rhetorics of Adult and Child Play Theory.* Cambridge, Mass.: Harvard University Press.

Sutton-Smith, Brian, J. Gerstmyer, and A. Meckley

1988 "Playfighting Folklore Amongst Preschool Children." *Western Folklore* 161–76.

Sutton-Smith, Brian, and Donna Kelly-Byrne

1984 *The Masks of Play.* West Point, N.Y.: Leisure. [Proceedings of the 1982 annual meeting of the Association for the Anthropological Study of Play.]

Sutton-Smith, Brian, and Mary Ann Magee

1989a "Reversible Childhood." *Play and Culture* 2:52–63.

Sutton-Smith, Brian, and Benjamin G. Rosenberg

*1961 "Sixty Years of Historical Change in the Game Preferences of American Children." *Journal of American Folklore* 74:17–46. [Reprinted in Herron and Sutton-Smith 1971 and in Sutton-Smith 1972a.]

1970 *The Sibling.* New York: Holt, Rinehart and Winston.

Tallman, Richard S.

1972 "Folklore in the Schools: Teaching, Collecting, Publishing." *New York Folklore Quarterly* 28:163–86.

1974 "A Generic Approach to the Practical Joke." *Southern Folklore Quarterly* 38:259–74.

Tamony, Peter

1974   "The Teddy Bear: Continuum in a Security Blanket." *Western Folklore* 33:231–38.

Tanzer, Helen
1939   *The Common People of Pompeii: A Study of the Graffiti*. Baltimore, Md.: Johns Hopkins University Press.

Tatar, Maria
1992   *Off With Their Heads! Fairytales and the Culture of Childhood*. Princeton: Princeton University Press.

Tattooed Tears
1978   A film by Nick Broomfield and Joan Churchill. Color, 16 mm, eighty-five minutes.

Taylor, Archer
1943   "The Riddle." *California Folklore Quarterly* 2:129–47.
1949   "Wellerisms." In *The Standard Dictionary of Folklore, Mythology and Legend*, edited by M. Leach, 1169–70. New York: Funk and Wagnalls.
1951   *English Riddles from Oral Tradition*. Berkeley: University of California Press.

Teggart, Frederick J.
1941   *Theory and Processes of History*. Reprint. Berkeley: University of California Press, 1977.

Thigpen, Kenneth A., Jr.
1971   "Adolescent Legends in Brown County: A Survey." *Indiana Folklore* 4:141–215.

Thiselton Dyer, T. F.
1966   *Folk-Lore of Shakespeare*. New York: Dover.

Thompson, Donna
1976   "Space Utilization: Criteria for the Selections of Playground Equipment for Children." *Research Quarterly* 47:472–83.

Thompson, Leslie M.
1978   "The Driver's License: Emblem of a Modern Rite of Passage." In *Paisanos: A Folklore Miscellany*, edited by F.E. Abernethy, 153–56. Publications of the Texas Folklore Society, no. 41. Nacogdoches: Texas Folklore Society.

Thorne, Barrie
1993   *Gender Play: Girls and Boys in School*. New Brunswick, N.J.: Rutgers University Press.

Thorne, B., and Z. Luria
1986   "Sexuality and Gender in Children's Daily Worlds." *Social Problems* 33:176–90.

Thrasher, Frederick
1927   *The Gang*. Chicago: University of Chicago Press.

Tillery, Randall K.
1992   "Touring Atadia: Discursive Simulation and Cultural Struggle at a Children's Summer Camp." *Cultural Anthropology* 7:374–88.

Titiev, Estelle
1969   "Children's Game Songs of Okayama Prefecture." In *Studies in Japanese Culture II*, edited by C.L. French, 67–138. Ann Arbor: University of Michigan Center for Japanese Studies, Occasional Papers, no. 11. [Field collection of fifty songs with music by a musicologist; only a brief description of the game that accompanies each song.]

Tizard, Jack, Ian Sinclair, and R.V.G. Clarke (eds.)
1975   *Varieties of Residential Experience*. London: Routledge and Kegan Paul.

Toelken, Barre
1979   *The Dynamics of Folklore*. Boston: Houghton Mifflin.

Tri-University Project
1968   *Tri-University Project in Elementary Education Curriculum*, Vol. 6: *Folk-*

lore in the Elementary Schools. Lincoln: University of Nebraska Center.

Trout, Lawana

1977 "The Student as Folklorist." *English Journal* 66:83–87.

Tuan, Yi-Fu

1977 *Space and Place: The Perspective of Experience.* Minneapolis: University of Minnesota Press.

Tucker, Elizabeth

1976 Personal communication with Gary Alan Fine.

1977 "Tradition and Creativity in the Storytelling of Pre-Adolescent Girls." Ph.D. dissertation, Indiana University.

1980a "The Dramatization of Children's Narratives." *Western Folklore* 39:184–97.

1980b "Concepts of Space in Children's Narratives." In *Folklore on Two Continents: Essays in Honor of Linda Dégh,* 19–25. Bloomington, Ind.: Trickster.

1981a "Danger and Control in Children's Storytelling." *Arv: The Scandinavian Yearbook of Folklore* 37:141–46.

1981b "The Cruel Mother in Stories Told by Pre-Adolescent Girls." *International Folklore Review* 1:66–70.

1992 "Texts, Lies and Videotape: Can Oral Tales Survive?" *Children's Folklore Review* 15:25–32.

Turner, Ian

1969 *Cinderella Dressed in Yella.* Melbourne: Heinemann.

Turner, Ian, June Factor, and Wendy Lowenstein

*1978 *Cinderella Dressed in Yella.* 2d ed. Richmond, Australia: Heinemann.

Turner, Roy (ed.)

1974 *Ethnomethodology: Selected Readings.* Baltimore, Md.: Penguin.

Turner, Victor

1969 *The Ritual Process: Structure and Anti-Structure.* Ithaca, N.Y.: Cornell University Press.

1974a "Betwixt and Between: The Liminal Period in Rites de Passage." In *New Approaches to the Study of Religion,* edited by J. Helm, 4–20. Seattle: University of Washington Press.

1974b *Dramas, Fields and Metaphors.* Ithaca, N.Y.: Cornell University Press.

1974c *From Ritual to Theatre: The Human Seriousness of Play.* New York: Performing Arts Journal Press.

Tylor, Edward B.

1871 *Primitive Culture.* Reprint. London: John Murray, 1929.

1879 "Remarks on the Geographical Distribution of Games." *Journal of the Royal Anthropological Institute* 9:23–30.

Umiker-Sebeok, D. Jean

1979 "Preschool Children's Intraconversational Narratives." *Journal of Child Language* 6:91–109.

Upadhyaya, Hari S.

1970 "Indian Family Structure and the Bhojpuri Riddles." *Folklore* 81:115–31.

Van Gennep, Arnold

1960 *The Rites of Passage.* Translated by M.B. Vizedom and G.C. Chaffee. Chicago: University of Chicago Press.

Vidich, Arthur

1955 "Participant Observation and the Collection and Interpretation of Data." *American Journal of Sociology* 60:354–60.

Virtanen, Leea

*1978 "Children's Lore." *Studia Fennica* 22. Helsinki: Suomalisen Kirjallisuuden Seura. [Excellent study of the various lore of Finnish children's play groups.]

Vlach, John

*1971 "One Black Eye and Other Horrors: A Case for the Humorous Anti-Legend." *Indiana Folklore* 4:95–140. [Excellent analysis of 144 legends told by fifth graders in a single community.]

Von Cranach, M.
1982 "The Psychological Study of Goal-directed Action: Basic Issues." In *The Analysis of Action*, edited by M. von Cranach and R. Harre, 35–73. Cambridge: Cambridge University Press.

Von Glascoe, C.A.
1980 "The Work of Playing 'Redlight.'" In *Play and Culture*, edited by H.B. Schwartzman, 228–30. West Point, N.Y.: Leisure.

Von Sydow, C.M.
1948 "Folktale Studies and Philology: Some Points of View." Reprinted in *The Study of Folklore*, edited by A. Dundes, 218–42. Englewood Cliffs, N.J.: Prentice-Hall, 1965.
1971 *Selected Papers in Folklore*. New York: Arno Press.

Walter, J.A.
1977 "Critique of Sociological Studies of Approved Schools." *British Journal of Criminology* 17:361–69.

Ward, Colin
1978 *The Child in the City*. New York: Pantheon.

Wardetzsky, Kristin
1990 "The Structure and Interpretation of Fairytales Composed by Children." *Journal of American Folklore* 103:157–76.

Washington Post
1901 "For Work and Play." September 15.

Watson, W.
1953 "Play Among Children in an East Coast Mining Community." *Folklore* 64:397–410. [Good functional analysis of a community in Scotland.]

Wax, Rosalie
1971 *Doing Field Work*. Chicago: University of Chicago Press.

Webster's New Twentieth Century Dictionary
1961 Unabridged, 2d ed. New York: Publishers Guild.

Weiner, Meryl
1970 "The Riddle Repertoire of a Massachusetts Elementary School." *Folklore Forum* 3:7–38.

Weir, Ruth
1962 *Language in the Crib*. The Hague: Mouton.

Wells, Patricia Atkinson
1988 "The Paradox of Functional Dysfunction in a Girl Scout Camp: Implications of Cultural Diversity for Achieving Organizational Goals." In *Inside Organizations: Understanding the Human Dimension*, edited by M.O. Jones, M.D. Moore, and R.C. Snyder, 109–17. Newbury Park, Calif.: Sage.

Welsch, Roger L.
1966a "Nebraska Finger Games." *Western Folklore* 25:173–94. [Collection of fifty-three games, some with diagrams.]
1966b *A Treasury of Nebraska Pioneer Folklore*. Lincoln: University of Nebraska Press. [See "Children's Games, 281–306 (a fine example of the many short sections on children's lore to be found in larger works on the folklore of specific places).]
1974 "A Note on Practical Jokes." *Southern Folklore Quarterly* 38:253–57.

Wesselski, Albert
1931 *Versuch einer Theorie des Marchens*. Reichenberg i.B.

West, Elliott
1983 "Heathens and Angels: Childhood in the Rocky Mountain Mining Towns." *Western Historical Quarterly* 14:145–64.

West, Elliott, and Paula Petrik (eds.)

1992   *Small Worlds: Children and Adolescents in America, 1850–1950.* Lawrence: University Press of Kansas.

What Are We Doing To Our Children? Locked Up, Locked Out
1973   A film by CBS News. Color, 16 mm, thirty minutes.

Wheelock, A.K.
1984   "Games in Dutch Art: Innocent Pleasures or Moral Exemplars." Paper presented at conference on the Forms of Play in the Early Modern Period, University of Maryland.

White, William Allen
1946   *The Autobiography of William Allen White.* New York: Macmillan.

Whitt, J. Kenneth, and Norman M. Prentice
1977   "Cognitive Processes in the Development of Children's Enjoyment and Comprehension of Joking Riddles." *Developmental Psychology* 3:129–36.

Whitten, Norman E., Jr., and John F. Szwed
1982   *Afro-American Anthropology: Contemporary Perspectives.* New York: Free Press.

Whyte, William Foote
1955   *Street Corner Society.* 2d ed. Chicago: University of Chicago Press.

Whyte, William H.
1980   *The Social Life of Small Urban Spaces.* Washington, D.C.: Conservation Foundation.

Widdowson, John D. A.
1971   "The Bogeyman: Some Preliminary Observations on Frightening Figures." *Folklore* 82:99–115.
1972   "Figures Used for Threatening Children, 1: A Newfoundland Example." *Lore and Language* 7:20–24.
1977   *If You Don't Be Good: Verbal Social Control in Newfoundland.* Social and Economic Studies, no. 21. Institute of Social and Economic Research, Memorial University of Newfoundland.

Wigginton, Eliot
1974   "A Reply to 'The Lesson of Foxfire.'" *North Carolina Folklore Journal* 22:35–41.
1980   *Foxfire 6.* Garden City, N.Y.: Doubleday. [Predominantly toys and games from Georgia, as collected and written up by high-school students. Many detailed drawings and photographs.]

Wilder, Laura Ingalls
1932   *Little House in the Big Woods.* New York: Harper and Row, 1971.
1935   *Little House on the Prairie.* New York: Harper and Row, 1971.
1961   *Little Town on the Prairie.* New York: Harper and Row, 1971.

Wilkinson, Paul F. (ed.)
1980   *Innovation in Play Environments.* New York: St. Martin's.

Willard, Nancy
1976   *Simple Pictures Are Best.* New York: Harcourt Brace Jovanovich.

Williams, Melvin D.
1981   *On the Street Where I Lived.* New York: Holt, Rinehart and Winston.

Williams, Raymond
1979   *Politics and Letters.* London: Verso.

Williams, William Carlos
1951   *The Autobiography of William Carlos Williams.* New York: New Directions.
1967   *"Children's Games": Pictures from Brueghel and Other Poems.* New York: New Directions.

Williamson, Billie
1975   "Fun and Games of Mountain Children." *Kentucky Folklore Record* 21 43–55. [Good collection, but no analysis.]

Willis, Paul
1977   *Learning to Labour.* London: Gower.
Wilson, A.
1980   "The Infancy of the History of Childhood: An Appraisal of Philippe Ariès." *History and Theory* 19:132–53.
Wimbush, Erica, and Margaret Talbot (eds.)
1988   *Relative Freedoms: Women and Leisure.* Philadelphia: Open University Press.
Winslow, David J.
1966a   "An Introduction to Oral Tradition Among Children." *Keystone Folklore Quarterly* 11:43–58.
1966b   "The Collecting of Children's Lore." *Keystone Folklore Quarterly* 11:88–98.
1966c   "An Annotated Collection of Children's Lore." *Keystone Folklore Quarterly* 11:151–202. [The three articles above are collectively subtitled "Oral Tradition Among Children in Central New York State" and provide an excellent introduction to the subject.]
1969   "Children's Derogatory Epithets." *Journal of American Folklore* 82:255–63.
Wintemberg, W. J., and Katherine H. Wintemberg
1918   "Folklore from Grey County, Ontario." *Journal of American Folklore* 31:121–22.
Withers, Carl A.
1946   *Counting Out.* New York: Oxford.
*1947a "Current Events in New York City Children's Folklore." *New York Folklore Quarterly* 3:212–22. [Very nice demonstration of the currency of children's lore.]
1947b   *Ready or Not, Here I Come.* New York: Grosset and Dunlap.
1948   *A Rocket in My Pocket: The Rhymes and Chants of Young Americans.* New York: Holt.
1963   Introduction to *Games and Songs of American Children* by W.W. Newell. Reprint. New York: Dover.
1965   *I Saw a Rocket Walk A Mile: Nonsense Tales, Chants, and Songs from Many Lands.* New York: Holt, Rinehart and Winston.
1974   *A Treasury of Games, Riddles, Mystery Stunts, Tricks, Tongue Twisters, Rhymes, Chants, Singing.* New York: Grosset and Dunlap.
Withers, Carl, and Sula Benet
1954   *The American Riddle Book.* New York: Abelard-Schuman.
Wojtowicz, Carol
1975   "Play in Philadelphia." *Pennsylvania Folklife* 24:17–23.
Wolfenstein, Martha
1951   "A Phase in the Development of Children's Sense of Humor." *Psychoanalytic Study of the Child* 6:336–50.
1953   "Children's Understanding of Jokes." *Psychoanalytic Study of the Child* 9:162–73.
*1954   *Children's Humor: A Psychological Analysis.* Reprint. Bloomington: Indiana University Press, 1978. [Classic analysis of how American children reveal their anxieties through their jokes and riddles.]
1955   "Jack and the Beanstalk: An American Version." In *Childhood in Contemporary Cultures,* edited by M. Mead and M. Wolfenstein, 243–45. Chicago: University of Chicago Press.
Worth, Sol, and John Adair
1972   *Through Navajo Eyes: An Exploration in Film Communication and Anthropology.* Bloomington: Indiana University Press.
Wuellner, Lance H.
1979   "Forty Guidelines for Playground Design." *Journal of Leisure Research*

11:4–14.

Yates, Norris
1951   "Children's Folk Plays in Western Oregon." *Western Folklore* 10:55–62.

Yawkey, T.D., and A.D. Pellegrini
1984   *Child's Play: Developmental and Applied.* Hillsdale, N.J.: Lawrence Erlbaum.

Yoffie, Leah R.
1947   "Three Generations of Children's Singing Games in St. Louis." *Journal of American Folklore* 60:1–51. [Interesting survey touching on three periods (1895–1900, 1914, and 1944). Seventy-one items, with presence in each period noted.]

Yohe, Charles
1950   "Observations on an Adolescent Folkway." *Psychoanalytic Review* 37:79–81.

Young, Katherine
1993   *Bodylore. Publication of the American Folklore Society.* Nashville: University of Tennessee Press.

Young, Monique
1981   "Drinking Games: A Survey." M.A. thesis, University of California, Berkeley.

Yukic, Thomas S.
1975   "Niagara River Playground: The Allen Avenue Gang, 1925–1946." *New York Folklore* 1:211–28.

Zerner, Charles J.
1977   "The Street Hearth of Play." *Landscape* 22:19–30.

Zeitlin, Steven J., Amy J. Kotkin, and Holly Cutting Baker
1982   *A Celebration of American Family Folklore.* New York: Pantheon Books.

Zigler, Edward, Jacob Levine, and Laurence Gould
1966   "Cognitive Processes in the Development of Children's Appreciation of Humor." *Child Development* 37:507–18.

Zipes, Jack
1979   *Breaking the Magic Spell: Radical Theories of Folk and Fairy Tales.* Austin: University of Texas Press.
1983   *Fairy Tales and the Art of Subversion: The Classical Genre for Children and the Process of Civilization.* New York: Wildman. London: Heinemann.

Zumwalt, Rosemary Lévy
1972   "On the Lips of Little Girls: A Collection and Analysis of Little Girls' Oral Tradition." Senior thesis in anthropology, University of California at Santa Cruz.
*1976   "Plain and Fancy: A Content Analysis of Children's Jokes Dealing With Adult Sexuality." *Western Folklore* 35:258–67. [A brief article that almost immediately became a classic.]

INDEX